Great Conversations
3

SELECTED AND EDITED BY

Daniel Born

Mike Levine

Donald H. Whitfield

CONTRIBUTORS

Steven Craig

Bryan Gaul

Sophia Krol-Michniak

Judith McCue

Gary Schoepfel

Donald C. Smith

Great Conversations 3

THE GREAT BOOKS FOUNDATION
A nonprofit educational organization

The Great Conversations series receives generous support from Harrison Middleton University, a Great Books distance-learning college.

Published and distributed by

THE GREAT BOOKS FOUNDATION
A nonprofit educational organization

35 E. Wacker Drive, Suite 2300
Chicago, IL 60601-2205
www.greatbooks.org

With generous support from
Harrison Middleton University,
a Great Books distance-learning college
www.chumsci.edu

ISBN 1-880-323-17-6

First printing
9 8 7 6 5 4 3 2 1

Library of Congress Cataloging-in-Publications Data
Great conversations 3 / selected and edited by Daniel Born, Mike Levine, Donald H. Whitfield.
p. cm.
ISBN 1-880323-17-6 (pbk. : alk. paper)
1. Literature--Collections. I. Born, Daniel. II. Levine, Mike. III. Whitfield, Donald. IV. Title: Great conversations three.
PN6012.G76 2007
808.8--dc22

2007003921

Book cover and interior design:
Judy Sickle, Forward Design
Chicago, Illinois

PREFACE

Great Conversations 3 offers another opportunity to grapple with the ideas of some of the world's best writers. Like the two preceding volumes in the Great Conversations series, this new collection extends our awareness that great writers share in a dialogue across place, time, and culture—a dialogue they carry on with one another and with us. Whether we are casual readers or students pursuing a liberal arts education, the great books matter because they hold our deepest values and beliefs up to scrutiny.

The best writers invite us to test our ability to reason and imagine. At the same time, they offer us the opportunity to talk back. Thinking readers will ask not only what the text *means*; they will also inquire whether, and in what sense, the text is *true*. In that spirit, we have appended two kinds of questions to each selection in this book. The first set of questions, designed to assist in close reading and textual interpretation, encourages readers to immerse themselves in the text and consider its possible meanings. The second set of questions ("For Further Reflection") invites readers to weigh the relative merits of the selection in light of their own experiences and other readings. Both kinds of questions matter, but we strongly recommend starting with the interpretive questions before moving to the realm of evaluation and judgment.

Some of these selections will likely elicit strong responses. Many are known to have provoked explosive reactions in their own time and beyond, stimulating not only great conversations but, indeed, great arguments. It is useful to remember that many of the great books have survived generations of readers because they do more than invite gentle applause and polite appreciation; frequently they make conventional wisdom tremble. One misconceived but still popular notion is that the great books offer protection against dangerous ideas, when in fact throughout history the great books have often been the carriers of dangerous ideas. The first three authors featured in this anthology—Geoffrey Chaucer, David Hume, and Percy Shelley—wrote works that at various times have provoked moral disapproval or outright suppression. Luigi Pirandello's unconventional dramatic interrogation of the nature of the self initially set off strong negative reactions among his audience. Many of Rudyard Kipling's stories revolve around troubling questions of imperial activity about which few readers can remain neutral. Simone de Beauvoir's writings shook the foundations of Western philosophy and popular culture.

By the same token, individuals willing to inquire why we think or believe as we do often challenge authority. When Socrates consented to drink the hemlock upon order of the state, his life became testimony to the power—and threat—that the process of questioning implies. We hardly intend that this book will get readers into trouble, but we do advocate Shared Inquiry,™ the Great Books Foundation's method of text-based Socratic discussion, with a strong sense of its transformative potential for communities of serious readers. Shared Inquiry is a method that challenges established opinion—just as the great books themselves so often do. Interpretation becomes the task of all participants, not just the domain of experts. Every statement—both those found in the language of the text and those made by participants gathered around the text—becomes grist for examination and response. Shared Inquiry is not intended as a substitute for a lecture but rather as an active vehicle by which to question and challenge ideas and discover meaning in a text. The selections in this anthology have been chosen for their potential to stimulate such discourse, whether in oral or written form.

Briefly, these are the guidelines for Shared Inquiry discussion that we recommend for users of this book:

1. **Read the selection carefully before participating in the discussion.** This ensures that all participants are equally prepared to talk about the ideas in the work and helps prevent talk that would distract the group from its purpose.

2. **Support your ideas with evidence from the text.** This keeps the discussion focused on understanding the selection and enables the group to weigh textual support for different answers and to choose intelligently among them.

3. **Discuss the ideas in the selection and try to understand them fully before exploring issues that go beyond the selection.** Reflecting on the ideas in the text and the evidence to support them makes the exploration of related issues more productive.

4. **Listen to other participants and respond to them directly.** Shared Inquiry is about the give-and-take of ideas and the willingness to listen to others and talk with them respectfully. Directing your comments and questions to other group members, not always the leader, will make the discussion livelier and more dynamic.

5. **Expect the leader to ask only questions.** Effective leaders help participants develop their own ideas, with everyone gaining a new understanding in the process. When participants hang back and wait for the leader to suggest answers, discussion tends to falter.

The fifteen reading selections, plus the discussion guides for two longer works not included in the anthology itself (Niccolò Machiavelli's *The Prince* and Charlotte Brontë's *Jane Eyre*) make it compatible with semester-long offerings in the humanities, where writing assignments can further develop interpretation. The selections range across sixteen hundred years of history, and include fiction, poetry, drama, and philosophy. Professors or book group leaders who prefer to read the book thematically rather than chronologically can refer to the thematic index at the back of the book. Headnotes are provided for each selection, providing a modest biographical and historical context for authors.

Footnotes by the author are not bracketed; footnotes by the Great Books Foundation, an editor, or a translator are [bracketed].

Spelling and punctuation have been modernized and slightly altered for clarity.

GEOFFREY CHAUCER

Geoffrey Chaucer (c. 1343–1400) is best known for *The Canterbury Tales,* but he earned the title "father of English poetry" (bestowed upon him by John Dryden) not so much for any single work as for the formal innovations that influenced the poets who followed him. He wrote in what we now call Middle English at a time when the language of culture—as opposed to the spoken language—in England was either French or Latin. More important, he brought to English poetry a rhyme scheme and meter then common in French poetry, the heroic couplet: rhyming pairs of lines, with each line containing five stressed syllables.

Chaucer, born in London, was the son of a successful wine merchant. By 1357, he was employed as a page in the household of Elizabeth, Countess of Ulster and daughter-in-law of Edward III. After a stint in the royal army, during which he was captured in battle in France and ransomed, Chaucer began a lifelong career as a diplomat and civil servant. His appointments included Esquire of the Royal Household of Edward III; Controller of the Customs of Wools, Skins, and Hides for the Port of London; and Clerk of the King's Works under Richard II. Around 1366, Chaucer married Philippa Pan, who had also served the Countess of Ulster; their marriage lasted until her death, around 1387. Records suggest that they probably had four children. When Chaucer died, he was buried in Westminster Abbey.

Chaucer's first original work was *The Book of the Duchess,* an elegy for Blanche of Lancaster, written around 1369 in the style of *Roman de la Rose,* a French love poem he had translated. The elegy takes the form of a dream-vision, common in poetry of the time. Even in this early work, Chaucer's ability to create realistic characters and dialogue can be glimpsed. In the 1370s, he produced another dream-vision, the unfinished *House of Fame,* which exhibits more advanced technical skill. During this decade, Chaucer also made two diplomatic visits to Italy that had a profound effect on his development as a poet: he discovered the work of Dante, Petrarch, and Boccaccio. Elements of the work of all three poets made their way into Chaucer's poetry, though it is difficult to know exactly how direct their influence was. In the 1380s, Chaucer wrote *Legend of Good Women*—a relatively unsuccessful poem that stands as a formal precedent to *The Canterbury Tales* in that it employs heroic couplets and is structured as a series of stories. He also wrote *Troilus and Criseyde*, a love story set during the Trojan War that some consider superior to *The Canterbury Tales*.

Chaucer began writing *The Canterbury Tales* around 1387, working on the poem for the remaining thirteen years of his life without completing it. The organizing framework of the poem is that a group of about thirty religious pilgrims have set out from Southwark, near London, for Canterbury and the shrine of St. Thomas à Becket. To pass the time, they engage in a storytelling contest. The surviving manuscript, which includes a general prologue in which the host and each pilgrim is introduced, consists of fragments that have been placed by editors in the order Chaucer appears to have intended. The poem as a whole is remarkable for its complexity on many levels—especially in the relationships between the characters, between the different tales, and between each character and the tale he or she chooses to tell. A rich representation of daily life in medieval England, *The Canterbury Tales* is also extraordinary for its detailed depictions of individuals occupying vastly different positions in English society. "The Pardoner's Prologue" and "The Pardoner's Tale" are typical in that, taken together, they constitute a multifaceted, subtly wrought portrait of one of the pilgrims.

GEOFFREY CHAUCER

The Pardoner's Tale

The Pardoner's Prologue

Gentlemen," said he, "I take pains to preach
In churches with a lofty, resonant voice,
Regular as a bell I ring it out,
For everything I say I have by heart:
My text's the same one as it always was—
Radix malorum est cupiditas.[1]
"To start with, I declare where I've come from,
And then produce my certificates, one by one;
My licence with the seal of our lord bishop
Which I show first—that's to protect myself
So that nobody, whether priest or cleric,
Dares interdict me from Christ's holy work.
It's only after that I say my piece:
Documents, certificates, mandates, bulls
From popes, patriarchs, bishops, cardinals,
I show; and say a few words in Latin
—That's to give spice and colour to my sermon—
It also helps to stir them to devotion.
Then I bring out long boxes made of glass,
Chockful of rags and bones, each one a relic,
Or so they think; and I've got, set in brass,
The shoulder bone of one of Jacob's sheep.
'Dearly beloved brethren,' I begin,
'Now listen carefully. Just dip this bone
Into a well; and then if calf or cow,

1. [The root of evil is greed.]

Or sheep or ox, chance to swell up and sicken,
From eating worms, or else from being stung
By serpents, here's all that you have to do:
Take water from that pool, and wash its tongue.
At once it will be cured. And furthermore,
Of pox, of scab, and any kind of sore,
The sheep that drinks its water from this well
Shall be quite healed. Remember this as well:
If once a week the owner of the stock
Should drink, before the crowing of the cock,
A draught of water from this well while fasting,
According to that saintly Jacob's teaching
His cattle and his stock shall multiply.
      " 'Also, gentlemen, it cures jealousy
Should any man fall in a jealous rage,
Make his broth with this water; I'll engage
He never will mistrust his wife again,
Though he may know the truth about her sin,
And she'd had priests for lovers by the dozen!
      " 'And here's a mitten too, as you can see.
Whoever puts his hand inside this mitten
Shall find the grain he sows will multiply,
Whether it's wheat or oats, so long as he
Makes a copper or a silver offering.
Good people, I must warn you of one thing:
If in this church there should be any person
Who has committed sin so horrifying
That he dare not confess to it for shame;
Or if there's any woman, young or old,
Who's turned her husband into a cuckold,
Such persons shall have neither grace nor power
To make an offering to my relics here.
But all who are clear of that kind of sin,
May come and make an offering in God's name
And be absolved, by the authority
This papal mandate here has given me.'
      "And by this dodge I've gained, year after year,
A hundred marks since I was pardoner.
I stand up in my pulpit like a priest;
When the bumpkins have all settled in their seats
I preach just as you've heard me say; and tell
A hundred taradiddles more as well.
And then I do my best to stretch my neck

And bob my head in every direction
Over the folk, now this way, and now that,
Just like a pigeon sitting on a barn.
Both hands and tongue are busy, and so quick
That it's a joy to watch me at my work.
I only preach of avarice and the like,
And in this way induce them to be free
In giving cash—especially to me.
Because my only interest is in gain;
I've none whatever in rebuking sin.
No, none! When they are pushing up the daisies,
Their souls, for all I care, can go to blazes.
No doubt about it, many a good sermon
Is mostly prompted by a bad intention;
Some curry favour and use flattery
To gain advancement through hypocrisy;
Some spring from hate, and some from vanity.
If there's no other way I dare attack,
I can sting with my tongue; and when I preach
I sting so hard, the fellow can't escape
Slander and defamation, if so be
He's wronged my fellow pardoners, or me.
Even if I don't give his actual name,
Yet everybody knows that he's the one
From hints, and other circumstantialities—
That's how I deal with people who annoy us;
That's how I spit out venom, under guise
Of piety, and seem sincerely pious.
"I'll tell you in a word what I'm about:
I preach for money, and for nothing else.
And so my text is what it always was:
Radix malorum est cupiditas.
Thus I know how to preach against the vice
Which masters me—and that is avarice.
Though I myself am guilty of the sin,
I know how to make other people turn
From avarice, and bitterly repent.
But that is not my principal intent.
I only preach for the emolument
But for the present, that's enough of that.
"Next, I tell many parables and fables
Of long ago; these bumpkins love old tales,
They're easy to remember and repeat.

What do you take me for? While I can preach
And earn good money for the things I teach,
Am I to choose to live in poverty?
It's never crossed my mind—not bloody likely!
I mean to preach and beg, and live thereby
Wherever I go, in whatever lands.
You'll never catch me working with my hands—
At begging I can make a better living
Than St. Paul ever did at basketmaking;
He's an apostle I won't imitate.
For I'll have money, wool, and cheese, and wheat,
Though given by the poorest serving lad,
Or by the poorest widow in the place,
Were all her children dying of famine.
No, no! I'll drink the ichor[2] of the vine,
And have a pretty girl in every town.
But hear me out now, gentlemen: in sum,
Your pleasure is that I should tell a tale.
Now that I've had a jar of malty ale,
By God on high, I hope to tell you something
Bound to be reasonably to your liking.
For although I'm a pretty vicious chap,
I can tell a story with a moral to it:
Here's one I preach to bring the money in,
Now if you'll all be quiet, I'll begin."

The Pardoner's Tale

In Flanders there was once a company
Of youngsters wedded to such sin and folly
As gaming, dicing, brothels, and taverns,
Where, night and day, with harps, lutes, and citherns,
They spend their time in dicing and in dancing,
Eating and drinking more than they can carry;
And with these abominable excesses
They offer up the vilest sacrifices
To the devil in these temples of the devil.
Their oaths so blasphemous and terrible,
It makes your flesh creep just to hear them swear.
The body of our blessed Saviour

2. [Liquor.]

They shred to pieces with their oaths, as if
They think the Jews have not rent him enough.
They laugh at one another's wickedness.
And in there come the dainty dancing girls,
Graceful and slim; harpers and procurers,
The young fruit sellers and confectioners,
Who are in fact the devil's officers,
Who light and blow the fire of lechery,
Which is so close conjoined with gluttony.
I take Holy Writ to be my witness,
Lechery springs from wine and drunkenness.
    Think how the drunken Lot, against all nature,
Slept, without knowing it, with both his daughters,
So drunk he did not know what he was doing.
    When Herod (as all know who've read the tale)
Was gorged with wine as he was banqueting,
He gave the order, there at his own table,
To have the guiltless John the Baptist slain.
    And Seneca is doubtless right in saying
There is no difference that he can find
Between a man who's gone out of his mind
And one who's drunk; except it be that madness
Lasts longer, when it comes, than drunkenness.
O accursed Greed, first cause of our undoing!
Origin of our damnation and ruin,
Till Christ redeemed us with his precious blood!
In short, how dearly indeed we've all paid
For that abominable first transgression—
The world corrupted for the sake of Greed!
    Be sure, our father Adam and his wife
For that same sin were driven from paradise
To labour and to woe. While Adam fasted
He was in paradise, as I have read;
But when he ate of the forbidden fruit
Upon the tree, he was at once cast out
Into the world of trouble, pain, and sadness.
We've cause to cry out against Gluttony!
O if men knew how many a malady
Proceeds from gluttony and from excess,
They'd be so much more moderate and frugal
With what they eat when they sit down at table.
O how the short throat and fastidious mouth
Cause men to labour east, west, north, and south

In earth, and air, and water, just to get
A glutton all the choicest food and drink!
St. Paul, you treat the subject best, I think:
"Meat for the belly, and the belly for meats,
But God shall destroy both"—thus St. Paul says.
The Lord knows it's a filthy thing, alas!
To speak its name—yet filthier is the deed,
When a man drinks the white wine and the red
Until he turns his throat into a jakes
Through that accursed and damnable excess!
For the Apostle, with tears in his eyes,
Sadly remarks: "Many walk, of whom I
Have told you often, and now tell you weeping,
That they are enemies of the cross of Christ,
Their end is death, their belly is their god."
O paunch! O belly! O you stinking bag!
Filled full of dung and rotten corruption,
Making a filthy noise at either end,
What an enormous labour and expense
To keep you going! These cooks, how they pound
And strain and grind, and transform and transmute
One thing into another, to placate
Your greedy, gluttonous, lustful appetite!
Out of the very toughest bones they beat
The marrow, since they will throw nothing out
That may slip down the gullet sweet and smooth.
And to give a still better appetite,
With spices culled from leaf and bark and root,
They make delicious sauces. Nonetheless
Be sure that those indulging such delights
Are dead while they are living in that vice!
Wine stirs up lechery and drunkenness,
Is full of quarrelling and wickedness.
You sot, how blotched and altered is your face,
How sour your breath, how beastly your embrace;
And through your drunken nose there seems to come
A noise like "Samson, Samson, Samson, Samson"
—Though Samson never touched a drop of wine!
You fall down like a stuck pig; your tongue's gone;
So has your self-respect; drink is the tomb
Of a man's wit and judgement and discretion.
For no one under the domination
Of drink can keep a secret in his head.

Keep clear of wine then, whether white or red,
Especially from the white wine of Lepe
They have on sale in Fish Street, or Eastcheap.
Because this Spanish wine, in some strange way,
Creeps into other wines that grow near by;
Such vapours rise from it, the man who thinks
He's in Eastcheap at home, after three drinks
Finds he's in Spain, right in the town of Lepe,
And not in Rochelle or in Bordeaux town;
And that's when he starts snorting, "Samson! Samson!"
    But listen, sirs, one word more, if you please!
Let me point out that all the victories,
All the great deeds in the Old Testament
Through grace of God, who is omnipotent,
Were won by means of abstinence and prayer;
Look in the Bible, and you'll find it there.
    Look at Attila, that great conqueror,
Think how he died in shame and dishonour,
And bleeding at the nose in drunken slumber.
I need not say a captain should keep sober.
Give serious consideration, above all,
To that commandment given to Lemuel—
Not Samuel, but Lemuel, I say—
For if you read the Bible you will see
What it lays down on serving wine to those
Who are administrators of justice.
Enough of this; that will, I think, suffice.
    Now that I've said my piece concerning Greed,
Your gambling is the next thing I'll forbid.
Mother of lies! That's what gambling is,
True mother of deceits, damned perjuries,
Manslaughter, abominable blasphemies,
And waste of time and money. Furthermore,
It's a reproach, a matter of dishonour,
To be reputed for a common gambler.
The higher a man's rank may be, the lower
He's thought to sink. And if he be a prince
Who gambles, then the general opinion,
In all that has to do with governing
And politics, holds him in less esteem.
    Stilbon, who was a shrewd ambassador,
Was sent to Corinth with great pomp and splendour
From Sparta, to conclude an alliance;

And on arriving there, he chanced to find
All of the leading citizens of the land
Playing at dice. And so, soon as might be,
He slipped away, back to his own country:
"I will not lose my good name here," said he,
"Nor will I do myself such dishonour
As to ally you with a set of gamblers.
Send other competent ambassadors:
For on my honour I prefer to die
Than to become the instrument whereby
Spartans ally themselves to dice players!
I will not be the agent of a treaty
Between them and you, so glorious in honour!"
That's what he said, that wise philosopher.
    Look at the way the King of Parthia,
As told in *Polycraticus*, sent a pair
Of golden dice to King Demetrius
In scorn, because he gambled; and for this
He held Demetrius's glory and renown
To be of no account, not worth a pin!
Kings can find better ways of killing time.
    A word or two on oaths and perjuries,
As treated by the old authorities;
Swearing and blasphemy are abominable;
Perjury is still more reprehensible.
Almighty God forbade swearing at all—
See what St. Matthew says; and above all,
This saying of the holy Jeremiah:
Speaking of oaths, he laid down: "Thou shalt swear
In truth, in judgement, and in righteousness"
But idle swearing's sinful wickedness.
See the first part of the Table of the Law,
The hallowed commands of the Lord in heaven,
What commandment the second lays down there:
"Thou shalt not take the name of God in vain."
And see how he forbids us all to swear
Before forbidding killing, or worse sin;
This, I say, is the order in which they stand;
As all who comprehend them understand,
It is the second of the Ten Commandments.
And furthermore, I tell you flat that vengeance
Is never going to depart the house

Of him who offers up outrageous oaths:
"By God's own precious blood!" and "By God's nails!"
And "By the blood of Jesus Christ at Hailes!
My throw's a seven, yours a five and three!"
"By God's two arms, if you try cheating me,
I'll run this dagger through your heart and side!"
Such is their fruit, those two damned bits of bone:
Perjury, anger, cheating, homicide.
Now for the love of Christ, who died upon
The cross for us, and for our redemption,
Leave off all swearing, use no oaths at all!
But, gentlemen, I'll now begin my tale.

The three loose-livers of whom I'm to tell,
A long while before the first matin bell
Had seated themselves in tavern, drinking,
And, as they sat, they heard a handbell clinking—
A corpse was being carried to its grave.
At this one of them called his serving lad:
"Ask who it is," said he, "and look alive!
Run and find out whose corpse is passing by:
And see you get his name." "Sir," said the boy,
"There is no need at all for me to go;
I was told before you came, two hours ago.
And he, indeed, was an old friend of yours.
He was killed last night, all of a sudden, as
He sat up on his bench, blind drunk. There came
A softly treading thief, Death is his name,
Who's killing everybody everywhere,
And cut his heart in pieces with a spear,
And thereupon made off without a word.
Thousands he's killed, in the plague raging here.
If I were you, sir, I'd be on my guard
Before I went near such an adversary!
Always be ready to meet him anywhere—
My mother taught me that; I can't say more."

The innkeeper broke in, "By St. Mary!
What the child says is true; he's killed this year
In a big village over a mile from here
Every man, woman, child, workman, and boy.
That's where he's living now, I'm pretty sure.
The wisest thing's to keep a good lookout,
Or else he's like to do a fellow dirt."

"God's arms!" exclaimed one of these debauchees,
"Is the fellow then so dangerous to meet?
In highways and in byways, street by street,
I'll seek him out, I vow it on God's bones.
Now listen, fellows: let us three be one,
Each of us hold his hand up to the other,
And each of us become the other's brother,
And we will kill this black betrayer, Death,
And kill the killer, by God's holy breath,
And that before the sun goes down on us!"
They pledged their word, the three of them together,
That they would live and die for one another,
As though each were the other's own born brother.
And up they jumped in frenzied drunken rage,
Set off in the direction of that village
The innkeeper had spoken of before.
Many and gruesome were the oaths they swore,
Tearing Christ's blessed body limb from limb,
Death shall be dead, if only they can catch him!
When they'd not gone as much as half a mile,
Just as they were about to cross a stile
They met a poor old man, who greeted them
Humbly—"God save and keep you, gentlemen!"
But the most insolent of these three rakes
Answered him back: "Be damned to you, you wretch!
Why so wrapped up, and muffled to the eyes?
And why live on so long in such dotage?"
The old man looked at him hard in the face,
And said, "It is because I cannot find
Anyone, though I walked to the world's end,
In any city or in any village,
Who would exchange his youth for my old age.
And therefore I must stay an old man still
For just so long as it is heaven's will.
Not even Death, alas, will take my life!
So like a restless prisoner I pace,
And on the earth, which is my mother's gate,
Go knocking with my staff early and late,
Saying, 'My dearest mother, let me in!
See how I wither, flesh, and blood, and skin!
Alas, when will my poor bones be at rest?
Dear mother, I would barter my strongbox
That's stood so long a time within my room,

Just for a haircloth shroud to wrap me in!'
But she will not do me that favour yet,
And so I bear a pale and withered face.
"But, sirs, it is not courteous of you
To speak so roughly to an old man, who
Has not offended you by word or deed.
It's there in Holy Writ for you to read:
'Thou shalt rise up before the hoary head
Of an old man'—and therefore do no harm,
I warn you, to an old man while you're young,
Any more than you'd like to have it done
To you in old age, should you live so long.
Now God be with you! I go where I must go."
"By, God you shall not! Not so fast, old fellow,"
The second of the gamblers answered him:
"You shan't get off so easily, by St. John!
You spoke just now about that ruffian Death.
Who's killing all our friends the country round.
My word on it, as sure as you're his spy,
You'd best tell where he is, or else you'll pay,
By God and by his holy sacrament!
It's clear that you and he are in agreement
To kill young folk like us, you bloody cheat."
"Well, gentlemen," said he, "if you're so keen
To find out Death, turn up this winding road,
For on my word I left him in that grove
Under a tree, and there he will abide.
For all your braggadocio he'll not hide.
See that oak there? Right underneath you'll find
Death. God be with you, who redeemed mankind,
And save you and amend!" said the old man.
And thereupon all three began to run
Until they reached the tree, and there they found
Gold florins, newly minted, fine and round,
And near eight bushels of them, so they thought.
Thenceforth it was no longer Death they sought,
Each of them was so happy at the sight,
Those florins looked so beautiful and bright.
They set themselves down by the precious hoard.
It was the worst of them spoke the first word:
"Brothers," he said, "mark what I've got to say:
Although I play the fool, I'm pretty fly.
Upon us Fortune has bestowed this treasure

So we can live in luxury forever.
We'll spend it—easy come, and easy go!
Whew! Holy God, but who could guess or know
That we'd have such a slice of luck today?
If only we could get this gold away,
And carry it to my house, or to yours,
—I needn't say that all this gold is ours—
We'd be in clover, happy as can be!
But obviously it can't be done by day.
People would say that we were downright thieves,
And for our rightful treasure, have us hung!
It is at night this treasure must be moved,
With every care and cunning, if we can.
And therefore this is my advice—let's all
Draw lots, and then see where the lot shall fall;
And he who draws the shortest straw shall run
Fast as he can, rejoicing, to the town,
And on the quiet buy us bread and wine.
The other two must keep a sharp lookout
And guard the gold; and if no time be lost,
We'll carry off the treasure when it's dark,
Take it wherever we decide is best."
The speaker held the straws in his closed fist,
Told them to draw, and see where the luck fell;
And it fell to the youngest of them all,
And he set off at once towards the town.
And thereupon, so soon as he was gone,
One of the two who stayed said to the other:
"You know, of course, that you are my sworn brother.
I'll tell you something that you won't lose by.
As you can see, our friend has gone away,
And here is gold, and that in greatest plenty,
All waiting to be split between us three.
How would it be, if I can work it so
That it is only shared between us two,
Wouldn't I be doing you a friendly turn?"
　　"But," said the other, "how can it be done?
He knows quite well the gold is with us here.
What shall we do? What shall we say to him?"
　　Said the first villain: "Now, can you keep mum?
I'll tell you in a word what's to be done,
All we need do to bring it safely off."

"I'm on," returned the other. "My word on it,
Never you worry, I won't let you down."
"Now," said the first, "you know that we are two,
And two of us are stronger than just one.
Wait till he's settled, and when he sits down
Jump up, as if to grapple him in joke,
And I will skewer him right through the back
While you are scuffling with him as in fun—
And with your dagger see you do the same.
And when it's over, all this gold shall be
Shared out, dear fellow, between you and me.
Then each of us can follow his own bent,
Gaming and dicing to his heart's content."
And thus it was this precious pair agreed,
As you've just heard me tell, to kill the third.
The youngest—the one going to the town—
Keeps turning over and over in his mind
Those lovely shining florins, new and bright.
"O Lord!" exclaimed he, "if I only might
Keep all that treasure for myself alone,
There's none alive beneath the heavenly throne
Of God, who'd live as happily as I!"
And then at last the Fiend, our enemy,
Put it into his head to go and buy
Poison with which to murder both his friends.
You see, such was the life he led, the Fiend
Had leave to bring him to an evil end.
Because it plainly was his fixed intent
To kill them both, and never to repent.
So off he goes with no more loss of time
To find an apothecary in the town.
He asked the man if he would sell him poison,
He wanted it for putting his rats down;
Also there was a polecat in his yard
That had killed all his chickens, so he said;
For if he could he'd like to get back at
The vermin that despoiled him day and night.
The apothecary told him: "You shall have
A thing so strong that, as my soul's to save,
In the whole world there is no living creature
Which, if it swallows any of this mixture,
No bigger amount than a grain of wheat,

But must then lose its life upon the spot;
Yes, it must die, and that in a less while,
Believe me, than it takes to walk a mile:
This poison is so strong and virulent."
    The wretch reached out his hand for it and went,
Taking the poison with him in a box.
He hurried to a man in the next street,
From whom he borrowed three large bottles. Then
He poured the poison into two of them,
And for his own drink kept the third one clean,
Because he had made up his mind to work
Throughout the night at carrying off the gold.
And when—the devil fetch him!—he had filled
His three great bottles to the brim with wine,
He made his way back to his friends again.
    What need is there for sermonizing further?
Just as they'd planned his murder earlier,
They killed him on the spot; when this was done,
The first said to the other, "Let's sit down
And drink and celebrate; and after that
We'll bury him." By chance, as he said this,
He took the bottle where the poison was,
And drank, and gave it to his friend to drink,
And thereupon they both died on the spot.
    Avicenna himself has not set down
In any section of his book, *The Canon
Of Medicine*—or so I would suppose—
Symptoms of poisoning more dire than those
The wretched pair endured in their last hours.
Such was the end of the two murderers,
And of the treacherous poisoner as well.
    Most accursed sin! Iniquitous evil!
Treacherous homicide! O wickedness!
O gambling, greed, and lechery and lust!
You villainous blasphemer against Christ,
With great oaths born of habit and of pride!
Alas, mankind! How does it come about
That to your Maker, by whom you were made,
And by whose precious heart's blood you were bought,
You are so cruel and so false, alas!
    Dear brethren, God forgive you your trespass,
And keep you from the sin of avarice;
My holy pardon here can save you all,

And will, so long as you make offerings
Of gold and silver coin, spoons, brooches, rings—
Bow down your heads before this holy bull!
Come, ladies, make an offering of your wool!
I'll put your name down on my prayer roll,
And you shall enter to the bliss of heaven
I shall absolve you, by my holy power,
You who make offerings, as clean and pure
As you were born!
—There you are, gentlemen!
That's how I preach. And may Jesus Christ
Healer of souls, grant that you may receive
His pardon, for, believe me, that is best.
But, sirs, there's one thing I forgot to add:
I've got relics and pardons in my bag
As good as anybody's in England,
All given to me by the pope's own hand.
If any here should wish, out of devotion,
To make an offering, and have absolution,
Let them come forward now, and kneeling down
Humbly receive my blessing and pardon.
Or take my pardon as we go along,
Take it at every milestone, fresh and new,
Only renew, and yet again renew,
Your offerings in sound gold and silver coin.
It's a great thing for everybody here
To have with you a competent pardoner
As you ride through the land, should occasion
Arise, and anyone need absolution.
Who knows? For one or two of you might fall
Down from his horse and break his neck, that's all.
Think what a safeguard it must be for you
That I, who can absolve both high and low
When soul from body is about to go,
Should chance to fall in with your company!
Let me suggest that our host here begin,
Since he's the one who's most wrapped up in sin.
Step forward, Mister Host—your offering first,
And you can kiss the relics, every one!
All for a penny! Out now with your purse!
"No, not a hope! I'd sooner have Christ's curse!
Lay off!" said he. "Not on your life I won't.
You'd only make me kiss your dirty drawers,

And swear they were the relic of some saint,
Though they were stained all over by your arse!
By the true cross, that St. Helena found,
I'd rather have your ballocks in my hand,
Than any relic in a reliquary.
Let's cut them off, and I'll help you carry
Your balls and have them set in a pig's turd!"
　　But the pardoner answered not a word;
He was so angered that he wouldn't speak.
　　"Well," said our host, "no use to try and joke
With folk like you, who can't keep their hair on."
But at this point the worthy knight cut in,
For he saw the others had begun to laugh.
"Let's have no more of this; that's quite enough!
Now, Mister Pardoner, smile and cheer up!
As for you, Mister Host, come, my dear chap,
I beg you, shake hands with the pardoner.
And you, come over here, Pardoner, pray,
And let's all laugh and have fun as before."
At this they shook hands, and rode on their way.

QUESTIONS

1. Why does the pardoner imply that his collection of relics might not be genuine and admit that he preaches only for money?

2. If the pardoner's "only interest is in gain," as he states, why does he pursue it by preaching against greed? (11)

3. In saying that he knows "how to preach against the vice / Which masters me—and that is avarice," is the pardoner saying that being guilty of a sin is necessary to preach effectively against it? (11)

4. Is the pardoner's success in making "other people turn / From avarice, and bitterly repent" any less laudable because this is not his "principal intent"? (11)

5. At the end of his prologue, the pardoner says he "can tell a story with a moral to it." Does his tale have a moral, and if so, what is it? (12)

6. After the pardoner begins his tale, why does he interrupt it with a sermon denouncing various sins?

7. How does the pardoner's sermon affect our understanding of the tale itself?

8. What is the significance of the three sinners' encounter with the old man?

9. What does the old man say about himself when he says, "Not even Death, alas, will take my life"? (18)

10. Why does the old man tell the three sinners where they can find Death?

11. Why do the three sinners forget about seeking Death after they find the gold?

12. Why does the pardoner tell the story of the three sinners to prompt congregations to "make offerings"? (23)

13. Why does the pardoner say that he is "competent" and capable of granting absolution to the other pilgrims? (23)

14. Why does the pardoner expect the other pilgrims to make offerings to him even though he has admitted that his relics might not be genuine and that his only interest is gain?

FOR FURTHER REFLECTION

1. Is avarice the root of all evil?
2. Is it possible for good acts to be motivated by bad intentions as the pardoner believes of his preaching?
3. Is a person who claims to be free of a vice a better advocate against it than a person who admits to the vice?
4. Do the actions of the three sinners represent human nature or a deviation from it?

DAVID HUME

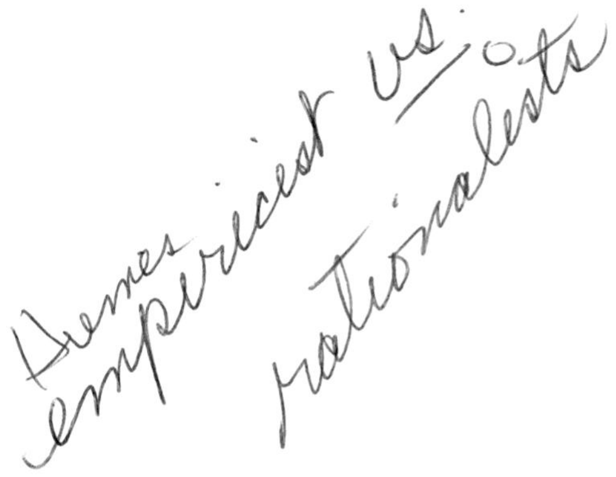

One of the leading philosophers of the Enlightenment, David Hume (1711–1776) was born in Edinburgh, Scotland, and grew up on the family estate at Ninewells. His father died when he was two years old; his mother, who by Hume's later account was a perceptive and devoted woman, quickly recognized her son's intellectual gifts. When he was not quite twelve years old, she sent him to the University of Edinburgh. Hume's family urged him to study law, but he was more interested in the classics and read widely in literature and philosophy. (He would tell a friend in 1735 that "there is nothing to be learnt from a Professor, which is not to be met with in Books.")

In 1734, Hume set aside his scholarly pursuits and took a job in Bristol as a clerk for a sugar importer, but this phase as a businessman lasted for only a few months. He then moved to the village of La Flèche in Anjou, France, and wrote his first major work, *A Treatise of Human Nature*, published anonymously in three parts under the titles *Of the Understanding* (1739), *Of the Passions* (1739), and *Of Morals* (1740). Disappointed by the public's reaction, Hume wrote that it had fallen "dead-born from the Press." However, this wasn't entirely true; it established his reputation in some quarters as a dangerous thinker inclined toward atheism.

Hume returned to Ninewells and published two volumes of *Essays, Moral and Political* (1741–1742), with greater success, but his efforts to gain an academic appointment in ethics and philosophy at the University of Edinburgh several years later met with resounding opposition due to his theological unorthodoxy. In 1751, he tried again, this time for a chair in logic at the University of Glasgow. Rebuffed once more, he took a low-salaried position as the librarian to the Faculty of Advocates at Edinburgh. With the considerable resources of that library at his command, he wrote a six-volume *History of England*, published between 1754 and 1762. It was a critical and commercial success.

Throughout his career, Hume generated controversy. He earned the wrath of the library trustees in 1754 upon being accused of ordering "indecent" books for the collection. The trustees cancelled the orders for the offending volumes. Dismayed, Hume turned over his salary to a close colleague while he managed to retain his chief librarian title—and ongoing access to the collection.

In 1763, Hume became secretary to the British embassy in France. He returned to England three years later with the French philosopher Jean-Jacques Rousseau, who was fleeing persecutors in Switzerland. The friendship with Rousseau ended when the Frenchman's paranoid delusions led him to believe that Hume was plotting against him. Other philosophical contemporaries were deeply influenced by Hume; Immanuel Kant would write that Hume awakened him from his "dogmatic slumbers."

Hume spent his last years in Edinburgh, working on new editions of his writings. As one of his final acts, he arranged for the posthumous publication of his controversial volume *Dialogues Concerning Natural Religion*, which appeared in 1779.

In the period between his two unsuccessful bids for an academic post, Hume revised the central ideas in the first book of his *Treatise*. This revision was eventually published under the title known to modern readers: *An Enquiry Concerning Human Understanding*. In this work, from which the following selection is taken, Hume questions conventional wisdom about cause and effect and about the sources of knowledge in general, thus establishing the framework for contemporary empirical philosophy and method.

DAVID HUME

An Enquiry Concerning Human Understanding (selection)

Of the Origin of Ideas

Everyone will readily allow that there is a considerable difference between the perceptions of the mind, when a man feels the pain of excessive heat or the pleasure of moderate warmth, and when he afterward recalls to his memory this sensation or anticipates it by his imagination. These faculties may mimic or copy the perceptions of the senses, but they never can entirely reach the force and vivacity of the original sentiment. The utmost we say of them, even when they operate with greatest vigour, is that they represent their object in so lively a manner that we could *almost* say we feel or see it. But except the mind be disordered by disease or madness, they never can arrive at such a pitch of vivacity as to render these perceptions altogether undistinguishable. All the colours of poetry, however splendid, can never paint natural objects in such a manner as to make the description be taken for a real landskip. The most lively thought is still inferior to the dullest sensation.

We may observe a like distinction to run through all the other perceptions of the mind. A man in a fit of anger is actuated in a very different manner from one who only thinks of that emotion. If you tell me that any person is in love, I easily understand your meaning and form a just conception of his situation, but never can mistake that conception for the real disorders and agitations of the passion. When we reflect on our past sentiments and affections, our thought is a faithful mirror and copies its objects truly; but the colours which it employs are faint and dull in comparison of those in which our original perceptions were clothed. It requires no nice discernment or metaphysical head to mark the distinction between them.

Here therefore we may divide all the perceptions of the mind into two classes or species, which are distinguished by their different degrees of force and vivacity. The less forcible and lively are commonly denominated *thoughts* or *ideas*. The other species want a name in our language and in most others; I suppose because it was not requisite for any but philosophical purposes to rank them under a general term or appellation. Let us, therefore, use a little freedom and call them *impressions*, employing that word in a sense somewhat different from the usual. By the term *impression*, then, I mean all our more lively perceptions, when we hear or see or feel or love or hate or desire or will. And impressions are distinguished from ideas, which are the less lively perceptions of which we are conscious when we reflect on any of those sensations or movements above mentioned.

Nothing, at first view, may seem more unbounded than the thought of man, which not only escapes all human power and authority, but is not even restrained within the limits of nature and reality. To form monsters, and join incongruous shapes and appearances, costs the imagination no more trouble than to conceive the most natural and familiar objects. And while the body is confined to one planet, along which it creeps with pain and difficulty, the thought can in an instant transport us into the most distant regions of the universe or even beyond the universe, into the unbounded chaos where nature is supposed to lie in total confusion. What never was seen or heard of may yet be conceived; nor is anything beyond the power of thought, except what implies an absolute contradiction.

But though our thought seems to possess this unbounded liberty, we shall find, upon a nearer examination, that it is really confined within very narrow limits, and that all this creative power of the mind amounts to no more than the faculty of compounding, transposing, augmenting, or diminishing the materials afforded us by the senses and experience. When we think of a golden mountain, we only join two consistent ideas, *gold* and *mountain*, with which we were formerly acquainted. A virtuous horse we can conceive, because, from our own feeling, we can conceive virtue; and this we may unite to the figure and shape of a horse, which is an animal familiar to us. In short, all the materials of thinking are derived either from our outward or inward sentiment: the mixture and composition of these belongs alone to the mind and will. Or, to express myself in philosophical language, all our ideas or more feeble perceptions are copies of our impressions or more lively ones.

To prove this, the two following arguments will, I hope, be sufficient. First, when we analyze our thoughts or ideas, however compounded or sublime, we always find that they resolve themselves into such simple ideas as were copied from a precedent feeling or sentiment. Even those ideas which, at first view, seem the most wide of this origin, are found, upon a nearer scrutiny, to be derived from it. The idea of God, as meaning an infinitely intelligent, wise, and good being, arises from reflecting on the operations of our own mind and augmenting, without limit, those qualities of goodness and wisdom. We may prosecute this enquiry to what length we please, where we shall always find that every idea which we examine is copied from a similar impression. Those who would assert that this position is not universally true nor without exception have only one, and that an easy method of refuting it, by producing that idea which, in their opinion, is not derived from this source. It will then be incumbent on us, if we would maintain our doctrine, to produce the impression, or lively perception, which corresponds to it.

Secondly, if it happen, from a defect of the organ, that a man is not susceptible of any species of sensation, we always find that he is as little susceptible of the correspondent ideas. A blind man can form no notion of colours, a deaf man of sounds. Restore either of them that sense in which he is deficient; by opening this new inlet for his sensations, you also open an inlet for the ideas, and he finds no difficulty in conceiving these objects. The case is the same if the object, proper for exciting any sensation, has never been applied to the organ. A Laplander or Negro has no notion of the relish of wine. And though there are few or no instances of a like deficiency in the mind, where a person has never felt or is wholly incapable of a sentiment or passion that belongs to his species, yet we find the same observation to take place in a less degree. A man of mild manners can form no idea of inveterate revenge or cruelty, nor can a selfish heart easily conceive the heights of friendship and generosity. It is readily allowed that other beings may possess many senses of which we can have no conception, because the ideas of them have never been introduced to us in the only manner by which an idea can have access to the mind, to wit, by the actual feeling and sensation.

There is, however, one contradictory phenomenon, which may prove that it is not absolutely impossible for ideas to arise, independent of their correspondent impressions. I believe it will readily be allowed that the several distinct ideas of colour, which enter by the eye, or those of sound, which are conveyed by the ear, are really different from each other, though at the same time resembling. Now if this be true of different colours, it must be no less so of the different shades of the same colour; and each shade produces a distinct idea, independent of the rest. For if this should be denied, it is possible, by the continual gradation of shades, to run a colour insensibly into what is most remote from it; and if you will not allow any of the means to be different, you cannot, without absurdity, deny the extremes to be the same. Suppose, therefore, a person to have enjoyed his sight for thirty years and to have become perfectly acquainted with colours of all kinds except one particular shade of blue, for instance, which it never has been his fortune to meet with. Let all the different shades of that colour except that single one be placed before him, descending gradually from the deepest to the lightest; it is plain that he will perceive a blank where that shade is wanting, and will be sensible that there is a greater distance in that place between the contiguous colour than in any other. Now I ask whether it be possible for him, from his own imagination, to supply this deficiency and raise up to himself the idea of that particular shade, though it had never been conveyed to him by his senses? I believe there are few but will be of opinion that he can; and this may serve as a proof that the simple ideas are not always, in every instance, derived from the correspondent impressions, though this instance is so singular that it is scarcely worth our observing, and does not merit that for it alone we should alter our general maxim.

Here, therefore, is a proposition, which not only seems in itself simple and intelligible, but, if a proper use were made of it, might render every dispute equally intelligible, and banish all that jargon, which has so long taken possession of metaphysical reasonings and drawn disgrace upon them. All ideas, especially abstract ones, are naturally faint and obscure: the mind has but a slender hold of them; they are apt to be confounded with other resembling ideas; and when we have often employed any term, though without a distinct meaning, we are apt to imagine it has a determinate idea annexed to it. On the contrary, all impressions, that is, all sensations, either outward or inward, are strong and vivid; the limits between them are more exactly determined, nor is it easy to fall into any error or mistake with regard to them. When we entertain, therefore, any suspicion that a philosophical term is employed without any meaning or idea (as it is but too frequent), we need but enquire, *from what impression is that supposed idea derived?* And if it be impossible to assign any, this will serve to confirm our suspicion. By bringing ideas into so clear a light we may reasonably hope to remove all dispute which may arise concerning their nature and reality.[1]

1. It is probable that no more was meant by those who denied innate ideas than that all ideas were copies of our impressions; though it must be confessed that the terms which they employed were not chosen with such caution, nor so exactly defined, as to prevent all mistakes about their doctrine. For what is meant by *innate*? If innate be equivalent to natural, then all the perceptions and ideas of the mind must be allowed to be innate or natural, in whatever sense we take the latter word, whether in opposition to what is uncommon, artificial, or miraculous. If by innate be meant contemporary to our birth, the dispute seems to be frivolous; nor is it worthwhile to enquire at what time thinking begins, whether before, at, or after our birth. Again, the word *idea* seems to be commonly taken in a very loose sense, by Locke and others, as standing for any of our perceptions, our sensations and passions, as well as thoughts. Now in this sense I should desire to know, what can be meant by asserting that self-love, or resentment of injuries, or the passion between the sexes is not innate?

But admitting these terms, *impressions* and *ideas*, in the sense above explained, and understanding by *innate* what is original or copied from no precedent perception, then may we assert that all our impressions are innate and our ideas not innate.

To be ingenuous, I must own it to be my opinion that Locke was betrayed into this question by the schoolmen, who, making use of undefined terms, draw out their disputes to a tedious length without ever touching the point in question. A like ambiguity and circumlocution seem to run through that philosopher's reasonings on this as well as most other subjects.

Of the Association of Ideas

It is evident that there is a principle of connexion between the different thoughts or ideas of the mind, and that in their appearance to the memory or imagination, they introduce each other with a certain degree of method and regularity. In our more serious thinking or discourse this is so observable that any particular thought which breaks in upon the regular tract or chain of ideas is immediately remarked and rejected. And even in our wildest and most wandering reveries, nay in our very dreams, we shall find, if we reflect, that the imagination ran not altogether at adventures, but that there was still a connexion upheld among the different ideas which succeeded each other. Were the loosest and freest conversation to be transcribed, there would immediately be observed something which connected it in all its transitions. Or where this is wanting, the person who broke the thread of discourse might still inform you that there had secretly revolved in his mind a succession of thought, which had gradually led him from the subject of conversation. Among different languages, even where we cannot suspect the least connexion or communication, it is found that the words, expressive of ideas, the most compounded, do yet nearly correspond to each other, a certain proof that the simple ideas, comprehended in the compound ones, were bound together by some universal principle, which had an equal influence on all mankind.

Though it be too obvious to escape observation that different ideas are connected together, I do not find that any philosopher has attempted to enumerate or class all the principles of association; a subject, however, that seems worthy of curiosity. To me, there appear to be only three principles of connexion among ideas, namely, *resemblance*, *contiguity* in time or place, and *cause* or *effect*.

That these principles serve to connect ideas will not, I believe, be much doubted. A picture naturally leads our thoughts to the original;[2] the mention of one apartment in a building naturally introduces an enquiry or discourse concerning the others;[3] and if we think of a wound, we can scarcely forbear reflecting on the pain which follows it.[4] But that this enumeration is complete, and that there are no other principles of association except these, may be difficult to prove to the satisfaction of the reader, or even to a man's own satisfaction. All we can do in such cases is to run over several instances and examine carefully the principle which binds the different thoughts to each other, never stopping till we render

2. Resemblance.
3. Contiguity.
4. Cause and effect.

the principle as general as possible.[5] The more instances we examine, and the more care we employ, the more assurance shall we acquire that the enumeration, which we form from the whole, is complete and entire.

Sceptical Doubts Concerning the Operations of the Understanding

All the objects of human reason or enquiry may naturally be divided into two kinds, to wit, *relations of ideas* and *matters of fact*. Of the first kind are the sciences of geometry, algebra, and arithmetic, and in short, every affirmation which is either intuitively or demonstratively certain. *That the square of the hypothenuse is equal to the square of the two sides* is a proposition which expresses a relation between these figures. *That three times five is equal to the half of thirty* expresses a relation between these numbers. Propositions of this kind are discoverable by the mere operation of thought without dependence on what is anywhere existent in the universe. Though there never were a circle or triangle in nature, the truths demonstrated by Euclid would forever retain their certainty and evidence.

Matters of fact, which are the second objects of human reason, are not ascertained in the same manner; nor is our evidence of their truth, however great, of a like nature with the foregoing. The contrary of every matter of fact is still possible, because it can never imply a contradiction, and is conceived by the mind with the same facility and distinctness, as if ever so conformable to reality. *That the sun will not rise tomorrow* is no less intelligible a proposition and implies no more contradiction than the affirmation *that it will rise*. We should in vain, therefore, attempt to demonstrate its falsehood. Were it demonstratively false, it would imply a contradiction, and could never be distinctly conceived by the mind.

It may, therefore, be a subject worthy of curiosity to enquire what is the nature of that evidence which assures us of any real existence and matter of fact beyond the present testimony of our senses or the records of our memory. This part of philosophy, it is observable, has been little cultivated, either by the ancients or moderns; and therefore our doubts and errors in the prosecution of so important an enquiry may be the more excusable, while we march through such difficult paths without any guide or direction. They may even prove useful, by exciting curiosity and destroying that implicit faith and security, which is the bane of all reasoning and free enquiry. The discovery of defects in the common philosophy,

5. For instance, contrast or contrariety is also a connexion among ideas: but it may, perhaps, be considered as a mixture of *causation* and *resemblance*. Where two objects are contrary, the one destroys the other; that is, the cause of its annihilation, and the idea of the annihilation of an object, implies the idea of its former existence.

if any such there be, will not, I presume, be a discouragement, but rather an incitement, as is usual, to attempt something more full and satisfactory than has yet been proposed to the public.

All reasonings concerning matter of fact seem to be founded on the relation of *cause and effect.* By means of that relation alone we can go beyond the evidence of our memory and senses. If you were to ask a man why he believes any matter of fact which is absent, for instance, that his friend is in the country or in France, he would give you a reason; and this reason would be some other fact, as a letter received from him or the knowledge of his former resolutions and promises. A man finding a watch or any other machine in a desert island would conclude that there had once been men in that island. All our reasonings concerning fact are of the same nature. And here it is constantly supposed that there is a connexion between the present fact and that which is inferred from it. Were there nothing to bind them together, the inference would be entirely precarious. The hearing of an articulate voice and rational discourse in the dark assures us of the presence of some person. Why? Because these are the effects of the human make and fabric, and closely connected with it. If we anatomize all the other reasonings of this nature, we shall find that they are founded on the relation of cause and effect, and that this relation is either near or remote, direct or collateral. Heat and light are collateral effects of fire, and the one effect may justly be inferred from the other.

If we would satisfy ourselves, therefore, concerning the nature of that evidence, which assures us of matters of fact, we must enquire how we arrive at the knowledge of cause and effect.

I shall venture to affirm, as a general proposition which admits of no exception, that the knowledge of this relation is not, in any instance, attained by reasonings a priori, but arises entirely from experience, when we find that any particular objects are constantly conjoined with each other. Let an object be presented to a man of ever so strong natural reason and abilities; if that object be entirely new to him, he will not be able, by the most accurate examination of its sensible qualities, to discover any of its causes or effects. Adam, though his rational faculties be supposed, at the very first, entirely perfect, could not have inferred from the fluidity and transparency of water that it would suffocate him or from the light and warmth of fire that it would consume him. No object ever discovers by the qualities which appear to the senses either the causes which produced it or the effects which will arise from it; nor can our reason, unassisted by experience, ever draw any inference concerning real existence and matter of fact.

This proposition, *that causes and effects are discoverable, not by reason but by experience,* will readily be admitted with regard to such objects as we remember to have once been altogether unknown to us, since we must be conscious of the utter inability, which we then lay under, of foretelling what would arise from them. Present two smooth pieces of marble to a man who has no tincture of natural philosophy; he will never discover that they will adhere together in such a manner as to require great force to separate them in a direct line, while they make so small a resistance to a lateral pressure. Such events, as bear little analogy to the common course of nature, are also readily confessed to be known only by experience; nor does any man imagine that the explosion of gunpowder or the attraction of a loadstone could ever be discovered by arguments a priori. In like manner, when an effect is supposed to depend upon an intricate machinery or secret structure of parts, we make no difficulty in attributing all our knowledge of it to experience. Who will assert that he can give the ultimate reason why milk or bread is proper nourishment for a man, not for a lion or a tiger?

But the same truth may not appear, at first sight, to have the same evidence with regard to events which have become familiar to us from our first appearance in the world, which bear a close analogy to the whole course of nature, and which are supposed to depend on the simple qualities of objects, without any secret structure of parts. We are apt to imagine that we could discover these effects by the mere operation of our reason, without experience. We fancy that were we brought on a sudden into this world, we could at first have inferred that one billiard ball would communicate motion to another upon impulse, and that we needed not to have waited for the event, in order to pronounce with certainty concerning it. Such is the influence of custom that where it is strongest it not only covers our natural ignorance, but even conceals itself and seems not to take place, merely because it is found in the highest degree.

But to convince us that all the laws of nature, and all the operations of bodies without exception, are known only by experience, the following reflections may, perhaps, suffice. Were any object presented to us, and were we required to pronounce concerning the effect which will result from it without consulting past observation, after what manner, I beseech you, must the mind proceed in this operation? It must invent or imagine some event which it ascribes to the object as its effect; and it is plain that this invention must be entirely arbitrary. The mind can never possibly find the effect in the supposed cause, by the most accurate scrutiny and examination. For the effect is totally different from the cause, and consequently can never be discovered in it. Motion in the second billiard ball is a quite distinct event from motion in the first; nor is there anything in the one to suggest the smallest hint of the other. A stone or piece of metal raised into the air and left without any support immediately falls; but to consider the matter a priori, is there anything we discover in this situation which can beget the idea of a downward, rather than an upward, or any other motion, in the stone or metal?

And as the first imagination or invention of a particular effect in all natural operations is arbitrary, where we consult not experience, so must we also esteem the supposed tie or connexion between the cause and effect which binds them together and renders it impossible that any other effect could result from the operation of that cause. When I see, for instance, a billiard ball moving in a straight line toward another, even suppose motion in the second ball should by accident be suggested to me, as the result of their contact or impulse, may I not conceive that a hundred different events might as well follow from that cause? May not both these balls remain at absolute rest? May not the first ball return in a straight line or leap off from the second in any line or direction? All these suppositions are consistent and conceivable. Why then should we give the preference to one, which is no more consistent or conceivable than the rest? All our reasonings a priori will never be able to show us any foundation for this preference.

In a word, then, every effect is a distinct event from its cause. It could not, therefore, be discovered in the cause, and the first invention or conception of it, a priori, must be entirely arbitrary. And even after it is suggested, the conjunction of it with the cause must appear equally arbitrary, since there are always many other effects which, to reason, must seem fully as consistent and natural. In vain, therefore, should we pretend to determine any single event or infer any cause or effect without the assistance of observation and experience.

Hence we may discover the reason why no philosopher who is rational and modest has ever pretended to assign the ultimate cause of any natural operation, or to show distinctly the action of that power which produces any single effect in the universe. It is confessed that the utmost effort of human reason is to reduce the principles productive of natural phenomena to a greater simplicity, and to resolve the many particular effects into a few general causes by means of reasonings from analogy, experience, and observation. But as to the causes of these general causes, we should in vain attempt their discovery; nor shall we ever be able to satisfy ourselves, by any particular explication of them. These ultimate springs and principles are totally shut up from human curiosity and enquiry. Elasticity, gravity, cohesion of parts, communication of motion by impulse; these are probably the ultimate causes and principles which we shall ever discover in nature; and we may esteem ourselves sufficiently happy if, by accurate enquiry and reasoning, we can trace up the particular phenomena to, or near to, these general principles. The most perfect philosophy of the natural kind only staves off our ignorance a little longer, as perhaps the most perfect philosophy of the moral or metaphysical kind serves only to discover larger portions of it. Thus the observation of human blindness and weakness is the result of all philosophy and meets us at every turn, in spite of our endeavours to elude or avoid it.

Nor is geometry, when taken into the assistance of natural philosophy, ever able to remedy this defect, or lead us into the knowledge of ultimate causes, by all that accuracy of reasoning for which it is so justly celebrated. Every part of mixed mathematics proceeds upon the supposition that certain laws are established by nature in her operations; and abstract reasonings are employed, either to assist experience in the discovery of these laws or to determine their influence in particular instances where it depends upon any precise degree of distance and quantity. Thus, it is a law of motion, discovered by experience, that the moment or force of any body in motion is in the compound ratio or proportion of its solid contents and its velocity; and consequently, that a small force may remove the greatest obstacle or raise the greatest weight, if, by any contrivance or machinery, we can increase the velocity of that force so as to make it an overmatch for its antagonist. Geometry assists us in the application of this law by giving us the just dimensions of all the parts and figures which can enter into any species of machine; but still the discovery of the law itself is owing merely to experience, and all the abstract reasonings in the world could never lead us one step toward the knowledge of it. When we reason a priori and consider merely any object or cause as it appears to the mind, independent of all observation, it never could suggest to us the notion of any distinct object, such as its effect, much less show us the inseparable and inviolable connexion between them. A man must be very sagacious who could discover by reasoning that crystal is the effect of heat, and ice of cold, without being previously acquainted with the operation of these qualities.

But we have not yet attained any tolerable satisfaction with regard to the question first proposed. Each solution still gives rise to a new question as difficult as the foregoing and leads us on to further enquiries. When it is asked, *What is the nature of all our reasonings concerning matter of fact?* the proper answer seems to be that they are founded on the relation of cause and effect. When again it is asked, *What is the foundation of all our reasonings and conclusions concerning that relation?* it may be replied in one word, experience. But if we still carry on our sifting humour, and ask, *What is the foundation of all conclusions from experience?* this implies a new question, which may be of more difficult solution and explication. Philosophers that give themselves airs of superior wisdom and sufficiency have a hard task when they encounter persons of inquisitive dispositions, who push them from every corner to which they retreat, and who are sure at last to bring them to some dangerous dilemma. The best expedient to prevent this confusion is to be modest in our pretensions, and even to discover the difficulty ourselves before it is objected to us. By this means, we may make a kind of merit of our very ignorance.

I shall content myself, in this section, with an easy task, and shall pretend only to give a negative answer to the question here proposed. I say then that even after we have experience of the operations of cause and effect, our conclusions from that experience are *not* founded on reasoning or any process of the understanding. This answer we must endeavour both to explain and to defend.

It must certainly be allowed that nature has kept us at a great distance from all her secrets, and has afforded us only the knowledge of a few superficial qualities of objects, while she conceals from us those powers and principles on which the influence of those objects entirely depends. Our senses inform us of the colour, weight, and consistency of bread; but neither sense nor reason can ever inform us of those qualities which fit it for the nourishment and support of a human body. Sight or feeling conveys an idea of the actual motion of bodies; but as to that wonderful force or power which would carry on a moving body forever in a continued change of place, and which bodies never lose but by communicating it to others, of this we cannot form the most distant conception. But notwithstanding this ignorance of natural powers[6] and principles, we always presume, when we see like sensible qualities, that they have like secret powers, and expect that effects similar to those which we have experienced will follow from them. If a body of like colour and consistency with that bread which we have formerly eaten be presented to us, we make no scruple of repeating the experiment and foresee, with certainty, like nourishment and support. Now this is a process of the mind or thought of which I would willingly know the foundation. It is allowed on all hands that there is no known connexion between the sensible qualities and the secret powers, and consequently, that the mind is not led to form such a conclusion concerning their constant and regular conjunction by anything which it knows of their nature. As to past *experience*, it can be allowed to give *direct* and *certain* information of those precise objects only, and that precise period of time, which fell under its cognizance; but why this experience should be extended to future times and to other objects, which for aught we know may be only in appearance similar, this is the main question on which I would insist. The bread which I formerly ate nourished me; that is, a body of such sensible qualities was, at that time, endued with such secret powers, but does it follow that other bread must also nourish me at another time, and that like sensible qualities must always be attended with like secret powers? The consequence seems nowise necessary. At least, it must be acknowledged that there is here a consequence drawn by the mind; that there is a certain step taken; a process of thought and an

6. The word *power* is here used in a loose and popular sense. The more accurate explication of it would give additional evidence to this argument.

inference, which wants to be explained. These two propositions are far from being the same: *I have found that such an object has always been attended with such an effect*, and *I foresee that other objects which are, in appearance, similar, will be attended with similar effects.* I shall allow, if you please, that the one proposition may justly be inferred from the other; I know, in fact, that it always is inferred. But if you insist that the inference is made by a chain of reasoning, I desire you to produce that reasoning. The connexion between these propositions is not intuitive. There is required a medium, which may enable the mind to draw such an inference, if indeed it be drawn by reasoning and argument. What that medium is, I must confess, passes my comprehension; and it is incumbent on those to produce it, who assert that it really exists and is the origin of all our conclusions concerning matter of fact.

This negative argument must certainly, in process of time, become altogether convincing, if many penetrating and able philosophers shall turn their enquiries this way and no one be ever able to discover any connecting proposition or intermediate step which supports the understanding in this conclusion. But as the question is yet new, every reader may not trust so far to his own penetration as to conclude, because an argument escapes his enquiry, that therefore it does not really exist. For this reason it may be requisite to venture upon a more difficult task, and enumerating all the branches of human knowledge, endeavour to show that none of them can afford such an argument.

All reasonings may be divided into two kinds, namely, demonstrative reasoning, or that concerning relations of ideas, and moral reasoning, or that concerning matter of fact and existence. That there are no demonstrative arguments in the case seems evident, since it implies no contradiction that the course of nature may change, and that an object, seemingly like those which we have experienced, may be attended with different or contrary effects. May I not clearly and distinctly conceive that a body falling from the clouds, and which in all other respects resembles snow, has yet the taste of salt or feeling of fire? Is there any more intelligible proposition than to affirm that all the trees will flourish in December and January, and decay in May and June? Now whatever is intelligible and can be distinctly conceived implies no contradiction, and can never be proved false by any demonstrative argument or abstract reasoning a priori.

If we be, therefore, engaged by arguments to put trust in past experience and make it the standard of our future judgment, these arguments must be probable only, or such as regard matter of fact and real existence according to the division above mentioned. But that there is no argument of this kind must appear, if our explication of that species of reasoning be admitted as solid and satisfactory. We have said that all arguments concerning existence are founded on the relation of cause and effect, that our knowledge of that relation is derived entirely from experience, and that all our experimental conclusions proceed upon the supposition that the future will be conformable to the past. To endeavour, therefore, the proof of this last supposition by probable arguments or arguments regarding existence, must be evidently going in a circle and taking that for granted which is the very point in question.

In reality, all arguments from experience are founded on the similarity which we discover among natural objects, and by which we are induced to expect effects similar to those which we have found to follow from such objects. And though none but a fool or madman will ever pretend to dispute the authority of experience or to reject that great guide of human life, it may surely be allowed a philosopher to have so much curiosity at least as to examine the principle of human nature, which gives this mighty authority to experience and makes us draw advantage from that similarity which nature has placed among different objects. From causes which appear *similar* we expect similar effects. This is the sum of all our experimental conclusions. Now it seems evident that if this conclusion were formed by reason, it would be as perfect at first and upon one instance, as after ever so long a course of experience. But the case is far otherwise. Nothing so like as eggs; yet no one, on account of this appearing similarity, expects the same taste and relish in all of them. It is only after a long course of uniform experiments in any kind that we attain a firm reliance and security with regard to a particular event. Now where is that process of reasoning which, from one instance, draws a conclusion so different from that which it infers from a hundred instances that are nowise different from that single one? This question I propose as much for the sake of information as with an intention of raising difficulties. I cannot find, I cannot imagine any such reasoning. But I keep my mind still open to instruction, if anyone will vouchsafe to bestow it on me.

Should it be said that from a number of uniform experiments we *infer* a connexion between the sensible qualities and the secret powers, this, I must confess, seems the same difficulty couched in different terms. The question still recurs, on what process of argument this *inference* is founded? Where is the medium, the interposing ideas, which join propositions so very wide of each other? It is confessed that the colour, consistency, and other sensible qualities of bread appear not, of themselves, to have any connexion with the secret powers of nourishment and support. For otherwise we could infer these secret powers from the first appearance of these sensible qualities, without the aid of experience, contrary to the sentiment of all philosophers and contrary to plain matter of fact. Here, then, is our natural state of ignorance with regard to the powers and influence of all objects. How is this remedied by experience? It only shows us a number of uniform effects resulting from certain objects, and teaches us that those particular objects, at that particular time, were endowed with such powers and forces. When a new object, endowed with similar sensible qualities, is produced, we expect similar powers and forces, and look for a like effect. From a body of like colour and consistency with bread we expect like nourishment and support. But this surely is a step or progress of the mind, which wants to be explained. When a man says, *I have found, in all past instances, such sensible qualities conjoined with such secret powers*, and when he says, *Similar sensible qualities will always be conjoined with similar secret powers*, he is not guilty of a tautology, nor are these propositions in any respect the same. You say that the one proposition is an inference from the other. But you must confess that the inference is not intuitive; neither is it demonstrative. Of what nature is it, then? To say it is experimental is begging the question. For all inferences from experience suppose, as their foundation, that the future will resemble the past and that similar powers will be conjoined with similar sensible qualities. If there be any suspicion that the course of nature may change and that the past may be no rule for the future, all experience becomes useless and can give rise to no inference or conclusion. It is impossible, therefore, that any arguments from experience can prove this resemblance of the past to the future, since all these arguments are founded on the supposition of that resemblance. Let the course of things be allowed hitherto ever so regular; that alone, without some new argument or inference, proves not that, for the future, it will continue so. In vain do you pretend to have learned the nature of bodies from your past experience. Their secret nature, and consequently all their effects and influence, may change, without any change in their sensible qualities. This happens sometimes, and with regard to some objects. Why may it not happen always, and with regard to all objects? What logic, what process or argument secures you against this supposition? My practice, you say, refutes my doubts. But you mistake the purport of my question. As an agent, I am quite satisfied in the point; but as a philosopher, who has some share of curiosity, I will not say scepticism, I want to learn the foundation of this inference. No reading, no enquiry has yet been able to remove my difficulty or give me satisfaction in a matter of such importance. Can I do better than propose the difficulty to the public, even though, perhaps, I have small hopes of obtaining a solution? We shall at least, by this means, be sensible of our ignorance, if we do not augment our knowledge.

I must confess that a man is guilty of unpardonable arrogance who concludes, because an argument has escaped his own investigation, that therefore it does not really exist. I must also confess that though all the learned, for several ages, should have employed themselves in fruitless search upon any subject, it may still, perhaps, be rash to conclude positively that the subject must, therefore, pass all human comprehension.

Even though we examine all the sources of our knowledge and conclude them unfit for such a subject, there may still remain a suspicion that the enumeration is not complete or the examination not accurate. But with regard to the present subject, there are some considerations which seem to remove all this accusation of arrogance or suspicion of mistake.

It is certain that the most ignorant and stupid peasants—nay infants, nay even brute beasts—improve by experience and learn the qualities of natural objects by observing the effects which result from them. When a child has felt the sensation of pain from touching the flame of a candle, he will be careful not to put his hand near any candle, but will expect a similar effect from a cause which is similar in its sensible qualities and appearance. If you assert, therefore, that the understanding of the child is led into this conclusion by any process of argument or ratiocination, I may justly require you to produce that argument; nor have you any pretence to refuse so equitable a demand. You cannot say that the argument is abstruse and may possibly escape your enquiry, since you confess that it is obvious to the capacity of a mere infant. If you hesitate, therefore, a moment, or if after reflection you produce any intricate or profound argument, you, in a manner, give up the question and confess that it is not reasoning which engages us to suppose the past resembling the future and to expect similar effects from causes which are, to appearance, similar. This is the proposition which I intended to enforce in the present section. If I be right, I pretend not to have made any mighty discovery. And if I be wrong, I must acknowledge myself to be indeed a very backward scholar, since I cannot now discover an argument which, it seems, was perfectly familiar to me long before I was out of my cradle.

QUESTIONS

1. Why does Hume assert that "the most lively thought is still inferior to the dullest sensation"? (29)

2. Why does Hume imply that feeling "the pain of excessive heat" is similar in some essential quality to experiencing anger or love? (29)

3. If, as Hume argues, all human thought is grounded in sensory experience, how does he explain the apparently "unbounded" nature of human thought? (30)

4. Why does Hume point out that a shade of blue can be imagined in the absence of a preceding impression, and then say that this exception "does not merit that for it alone we should alter our general maxim"? (32)

5. Of what value to Hume is the possibility that the principles of association among different ideas can be reduced to only three—"*resemblance, contiguity* in time or place, and *cause* or *effect*"? (33)

6. How does Hume distinguish between "*relations of ideas*" and "*matters of fact*"? (34)

7. Why does Hume assert, "*That the sun will not rise tomorrow* is no less intelligible a proposition . . . than the affirmation *that it will rise*"? (34)

8. Why does Hume consider "implicit faith and security" to be "the bane of all reasoning and free enquiry"? (34)

9. Why does Hume assert that "all reasonings concerning matter of fact seem to be founded on the relation of *cause and effect*"? (35)

10. Does Hume's philosophy allow for any meaningful assertion of direct cause and effect?

11. According to Hume, does a relationship of cause and effect exist in the objects observed, or in the mind of the observer?

12. Should we conclude from Hume's arguments that nothing can be known about the future?

13. According to Hume, what does experience teach us?

FOR FURTHER REFLECTION

1. What is the value of trying to understand the basis of knowledge?
2. Do we possess any degree of knowledge about the future?
3. Is Hume correct in saying that the supposed "unboundedness" of human thought is in fact "really confined within very narrow limits"?
4. Are there advantages in subscribing to Hume's kind of philosophical skepticism?

PERCY BYSSHE SHELLEY

Percy Bysshe Shelley (1792–1822) was a writer whose life was, in a sense, as much a work of art as anything he wrote—both were an expression of his heartfelt desire to change the world. He was born into an aristocratic English family in Sussex, the son of a wealthy landowner and member of Parliament. From a young age, Shelley felt constrained by convention, and his fierce independence made for a very short university career at Oxford. Shortly after arriving at Oxford in 1810, he became fast friends with Thomas Jefferson Hogg, with whom he wrote *The Necessity of Atheism*, a pamphlet arguing that God's existence could not be empirically proven. Refusing to repudiate it, Shelley and Hogg were immediately expelled. Shelley then moved to London, where he met sixteen-year-old Harriet Westbrook. In 1811, they eloped to Edinburgh and were married.

The couple moved frequently over the next few years, as Shelley wrote poetry and pamphlets and worked to advance various social and political causes. In 1812, Shelley introduced himself to William Godwin, a radical social philosopher whose book *An Enquiry Concerning Political Justice* (1793) became a touchstone in Shelley's life. In 1813, Shelley privately printed his first important work, *Queen Mab*, a long, fantastic poem that ranges through history and envisions a utopian future. The following year, having grown apart from Harriet, he met and fell in love with Mary Wollstonecraft Godwin, the daughter of Godwin and Mary Wollstonecraft, author of *A Vindication of the Rights of Woman* (1792). When Shelley met Mary, she was sixteen and shared many of Shelley's unorthodox opinions, as had been the case with Harriet. Shelley and Mary eloped to France, though he invited Harriet to live with them as if she were a sister.

Upon returning to London several months later, Shelley found himself under siege due to both his radical ideas and his money problems, the latter of which were eased for a short time by the death of his grandfather in 1815. The year 1816 was an eventful one in Shelley's personal life. He began a close friendship with Lord Byron and learned of the death of Harriet who, pregnant by another man, drowned herself. Soon after, Shelley and Mary were married. Shelley was denied custody of the two children he and Harriet had together. Of the children Shelley had with Mary, only one, Percy, born in 1819, survived to adulthood. The first, born in 1815, died after twelve days, and the next two died within nine months of each other in 1818 and 1819.

The family moved to Italy in 1818. There the Shelleys became part of a closely knit group of expatriate writers, and it was during these years marked by deep family tragedy that Mary published *Frankenstein* and Percy wrote what is often considered his greatest work, *Prometheus Unbound* (1820), a dramatic poem that updates the Greek myth. He also wrote many of his best-known lyric poems, such as "Ode to the West Wind." His work from this period was heavily influenced by his reading of ancient Greek authors, John Milton's *Paradise Lost*, and the Bible. He also immersed himself in the writings of the British empiricist philosophers, especially David Hume.

Shelley was not yet thirty when, while sailing on the Gulf of Spezia with a friend, a violent storm struck, sinking their boat. After their bodies washed ashore, Shelley was cremated on the beach and his ashes buried in the Protestant Cemetery in Rome, near the graves of John Keats and Shelley's son William.

"A Defence of Poetry"—Shelley completed only the first of three parts—was a response to "The Four Ages of Poetry," written by a good friend of Shelley's and a fellow poet, Thomas Love Peacock. In his essay, Peacock had suggested, ironically, that the importance and usefulness of poetry and other products of the imagination had diminished in a time of dramatic technological and intellectual advances. Shelley responds, describing his view of how the imagination functions in art and history.

PERCY BYSSHE SHELLEY

A Defence of Poetry (selection)

According to one mode of regarding those two classes of mental action, which are called reason and imagination, the former may be considered as mind contemplating the relations borne by one thought to another, however produced; and the latter, as mind acting upon those thoughts so as to colour them with its own light, and composing from them, as from elements, other thoughts, each containing within itself the principle of its own integrity. The one is the *to poiein*, or the principle of synthesis, and has for its objects those forms which are common to universal nature and existence itself; the other is the *to logizein*, or principle of analysis, and its action regards the relations of things, simply as relations; considering thoughts, not in their integral unity, but as the algebraical representations which conduct to certain general results. Reason is the enumeration of quantities already known; imagination is the perception of the value of those quantities, both separately and as a whole. Reason respects the differences, and imagination the similitudes of things. Reason is to imagination as the instrument to the agent, as the body to the spirit, as the shadow to the substance.

Poetry, in a general sense, may be defined to be "the expression of the imagination": and poetry is connate with the origin of man. Man is an instrument over which a series of external and internal impressions are driven, like the alternations of an ever-changing wind over an Aeolian lyre, which move it by their motion to ever-changing melody. But there is a principle within the human being, and perhaps within all sentient beings, which acts otherwise than in the lyre, and produces not melody alone, but harmony, by an internal adjustment of the sounds or motions thus excited to the impressions which excite them. It is as if the lyre could accommodate its chords to the motions of that which strikes them, in a determined proportion of sound; even as the musician can accommodate his voice to the sound of the lyre. A child at play by itself will express its delight by its voice and motions; and every inflexion of tone and every gesture will bear exact relation to a corresponding antitype in the pleasurable impressions which awakened it; it will be the reflected image of that impression; and as the lyre trembles and sounds after the wind has died away, so the child seeks, by prolonging in its voice and motions the duration of the effect, to prolong also a consciousness of the cause. In relation to the objects which delight a child, these expressions are what poetry is to higher objects. The savage (for the savage is to ages what the child is to years) expresses the emotions produced in him by surrounding objects in a similar manner; and language and gesture, together with plastic or pictorial imitation, become the image of the combined effect of those objects, and of his apprehension of them. Man in society, with all his passions and his pleasures, next becomes the object of the passions and pleasures of man; an additional class of emotions produces an augmented treasure of expressions; and language, gesture, and the imitative arts, become at once the representation and the medium, the pencil and the picture, the chisel and the statue, the chord and the harmony. The social sympathies, or those laws from which as from its elements society results, begin to develop themselves from the moment that two human beings coexist; the future is contained within the present as the plant within the seed; and equality, diversity, unity, contrast, mutual dependence, become the principles alone capable of affording the motives according to which the will of a social being is determined to action, inasmuch as he is social; and constitute pleasure in sensation, virtue in sentiment, beauty in art, truth in reasoning, and love in the intercourse of kind. Hence men, even in the infancy of society, observe a certain order in their words and actions, distinct from that of the objects and the impressions represented by them, all expression being subject to the laws of that from which it proceeds. But let us dismiss those more general considerations which might involve an enquiry into the principles of society itself, and restrict our view to the manner in which the imagination is expressed upon its forms.

In the youth of the world, men dance and sing and imitate natural objects, observing in these actions, as in all others, a certain rhythm or order. And, although all men observe a similar, they observe not the same order, in the motions of the dance, in the melody of the song, in the combinations of language, in the series of their imitations of natural objects. For there is a certain order or rhythm belonging to each of these classes of mimetic representation, from which the hearer and the spectator receive an intenser and purer pleasure than from any other: the sense of an approximation to this order has been called taste, by modern writers. Every man in the infancy of art, observes an order which approximates more or less closely to that from which this highest delight results: but the diversity is not sufficiently marked, as that its gradations should be sensible, except in those instances where the predominance of this faculty of approximation to the beautiful (for so we may be permitted to name the relation between this highest pleasure and its cause) is very great. Those in whom it exists in excess are poets, in the most universal sense of the word; and the pleasure resulting from the manner in which they express the influence of society or nature upon their own minds communicates itself to others, and gathers a sort of reduplication from that community. Their language is vitally metaphorical; that is, it marks the before unapprehended relations of things, and perpetuates their apprehension, until the words which represent them become, through time, signs for portions or classes of thoughts instead of pictures of integral thoughts; and then if no new poets should arise to create afresh the associations which have been thus disorganized, language will be dead to all the nobler purposes of human intercourse. These similitudes or relations are finely said by Lord Bacon to be "the same footsteps of nature impressed upon the various subjects of the world"—and he considers the faculty which perceives them as the storehouse of axioms common to all knowledge. In the infancy of society every author is necessarily a poet, because language itself is poetry, and to be a poet is to apprehend the true and the beautiful, in a word, the good which exists in the relation subsisting, first between existence and perception, and secondly between perception and expression. Every original language near to its source is in itself the chaos of a cyclic poem; the copiousness of lexicography and the distinctions of grammar are the works of a later age, and are merely the catalogue and the form of the creations of poetry.

But poets, or those who imagine and express this indestructible order, are not only the authors of language and of music, of the dance and architecture and statuary and painting; they are the institutors of laws, and the founders of civil society and the inventors of the arts of life and the teachers, who draw into a certain propinquity with the beautiful and the true that partial apprehension of the agencies of the invisible world which is called religion. Hence all original religions are allegorical, or susceptible of allegory, and like Janus have a double face of false and true. Poets, according to the circumstances of the age and nation in which they appeared, were called in the earlier epochs of the world legislators or prophets; a poet essentially comprises and unites both these characters. For he not only beholds intensely the present as it is, and discovers those laws according to which present things ought to be ordered, but he beholds the future in the present, and his thoughts are the germs of the flower and the fruit of latest time. Not that I assert poets to be prophets in the gross sense of the word, or that they can foretell the form as surely as they foreknow the spirit of events: such is the pretence of superstition which would make poetry an attribute of prophecy, rather than prophecy an attribute of poetry. A poet participates in the eternal, the infinite, and the one; as far as relates to his conceptions, time and place and number are not. The grammatical forms which express the moods of time, and the difference of persons, and the distinction of place are convertible with respect to the highest poetry without injuring it as poetry, and the choruses of Aeschylus, and the book of Job, and Dante's *Paradise* would afford, more than any other writings, examples of this fact, if the limits of this essay did not forbid citation. The creations of sculpture, painting, and music are illustrations still more decisive.

Language, colour, form, and religious and civil habits of action are all the instruments and materials of poetry; they may be called poetry by that figure of speech which considers the effect as a synonym of the cause. But poetry in a more restricted sense expresses those arrangements of language, and especially metrical language, which are created by that imperial faculty, whose throne is curtained within the invisible nature of man. And this springs from the nature itself of language, which is a more direct representation of the actions and passions of our internal being, and is susceptible of more various and delicate combinations, than colour, form, or motion, and is more plastic and obedient to the control of that faculty of which it is the creation. For language is arbitrarily produced by the imagination and has relation to thoughts alone; but all other materials, instruments, and conditions of art have relations among each other, which limit and interpose between conception and expression. The former is as a mirror which reflects, the latter as a cloud which enfeebles, the light of which both are mediums of communication. Hence the fame of sculptors, painters, and musicians, although the intrinsic powers of the great masters of these arts may yield in no degree to that of those who have employed language as the hieroglyphic of their thoughts, has never equalled that of poets in the restricted sense of the term; as two performers of equal skill will produce unequal effects from a guitar and a harp. The fame of legislators and founders of religions, so long as their institutions last, alone seems to exceed that of poets in the restricted sense; but it can scarcely be a question whether, if we deduct the celebrity which their flattery of the gross opinions of the vulgar usually conciliates, together with that which belonged to them in their higher character of poets, any excess will remain.

We have thus circumscribed the meaning of the word *poetry* within the limits of that art which is the most familiar and the most perfect expression of the faculty itself. It is necessary however to make the circle still narrower, and to determine the distinction between measured and unmeasured language; for the popular division into prose and verse is inadmissible in accurate philosophy.

Sounds as well as thoughts have relation both between each other and towards that which they represent, and a perception of the order of those relations has always been found connected with a perception of the order of the relations of thoughts. Hence the language of poets has ever affected a certain uniform and harmonious recurrence of sound, without which it were not poetry, and which is scarcely less indispensable to the communication of its influence than the words themselves, without reference to that peculiar order. Hence the vanity of translation; it were as wise to cast a violet into a crucible that you might discover the formal principle of its colour and odour, as seek to transfuse from one language into another the creations of a poet. The plant must spring again from its seed or it will bear no flower—and this is the burthen of the curse of Babel.

An observation of the regular mode of the recurrence of this harmony in the language of poetical minds, together with its relation to music, produced metre, or a certain system of traditional forms of harmony of language. Yet it is by no means essential that a poet should accommodate his language to this traditional form, so that the harmony which is its spirit, be observed. The practise is indeed convenient and popular, and to be preferred, especially in such composition as includes much form and action; but every great poet must inevitably innovate upon the example of his predecessors in the exact structure of his peculiar versification. The distinction between poets and prose writers is a vulgar error. The distinction between philosophers and poets has been anticipated. Plato was essentially a poet—the truth and splendour of his imagery and the melody of his language [are] the most intense that it is possible to conceive. He rejected the measure of the epic, dramatic, and lyrical forms, because he sought to kindle a harmony in thoughts divested of shape and action, and he forbore to invent any regular plan of rhythm which would include, under determinate forms, the varied pauses of his style. Cicero sought to imitate the cadence of his periods but with little success. Lord Bacon was a poet.[1] His language has a sweet and majestic rhythm, which satisfies the sense, no less than the almost superhuman wisdom of his philosophy, satisfies the intellect; it is a strain which distends, and then bursts the circumference of the hearer's mind, and pours itself forth together with it into the universal element with which it has perpetual sympathy. All the authors of revolutions in opinion are not only necessarily poets as they are inventors, nor even as their words unveil the permanent analogy of things by images which participate in the life of truth, but as their periods are harmonious and rhythmical and contain in themselves the elements of verse, being the echo of the eternal music. Nor are those supreme poets, who have employed traditional forms of rhythm on account of the form and action of their subjects, less capable of perceiving and teaching the truth of things than those who have omitted that form. Shakespeare, Dante, and Milton (to confine ourselves to modern writers) are philosophers of the very loftiest power.

1. See the *Filium Labyrinthi* and the "Essay on Death" particularly.

A poem is the very image of life expressed in its eternal truth. There is this difference between a story and a poem, that a story is a catalogue of detached facts, which have no other bond of connexion than time, place, circumstance, cause and effect; the other is the creation of actions according to the unchangeable forms of human nature, as existing in the mind of the creator, which is itself the image of all other minds. The one is partial, and applies only to a definite period of time and a certain combination of events which can never again recur; the other is universal, and contains within itself the germ of a relation to whatever motives or actions have place in the possible varieties of human nature. Time, which destroys the beauty and the use of the story of particular facts, stripped of the poetry which should invest them, augments that of poetry, and forever develops new and wonderful applications of the eternal truth which it contains. Hence epitomes have been called the moths of just history; they eat out the poetry of it. The story of particular facts is as a mirror which obscures and distorts that which should be beautiful; poetry is a mirror which makes beautiful that which is distorted.

The parts of a composition may be poetical, without the composition as a whole being a poem. A single sentence may be considered as a whole though it be found in a series of unassimilated portions; a single word even may be a spark of inextinguishable thought. And thus all the great historians, Herodotus, Plutarch, Livy, were poets; and although the plan of these writers, especially that of Livy, restrained them from developing this faculty in its highest degree, they make copious and ample amends for their subjection, by filling all the interstices of their subjects with living images.

Having determined what is poetry, and who are poets, let us proceed to estimate its effects upon society.

Poetry is ever accompanied with pleasure: all spirits on which it falls open themselves to receive the wisdom which is mingled with its delight. In the infancy of the world, neither poets themselves nor their auditors are fully aware of the excellence of poetry, for it acts in a divine and unapprehended manner, beyond and above consciousness; and it is reserved for future generations to contemplate and measure the mighty cause and effect in all the strength and splendour of their union. Even in modern times, no living poet ever arrived at the fulness of his fame; the jury which sits in judgement upon a poet, belonging as he does to all time, must be composed of his peers; it must be impanelled by time from the selectest of the wise of many generations. A poet is a nightingale, who sits in darkness and sings to cheer its own solitude with sweet sounds; his auditors are as men entranced by the melody of an unseen musician, who feel that they are moved and softened, yet know not whence or why. The poems of Homer and his contemporaries were the delight of infant

Greece; they were the elements of that social system which is the column upon which all succeeding civilization has reposed. Homer embodied the ideal perfection of his age in human character; nor can we doubt that those who read his verses were awakened to an ambition of becoming like to Achilles, Hector, and Ulysses; the truth and beauty of friendship, patriotism, and persevering devotion to an object, were unveiled to the depths in these immortal creations; the sentiments of the auditors must have been refined and enlarged by a sympathy with such great and lovely impersonations, until from admiring they imitated, and from imitation they identified themselves with the objects of their admiration. Nor let it be objected that these characters are remote from moral perfection, and that they can by no means be considered as edifying patterns for general imitation. Every epoch under names more or less specious has deified its peculiar errors; revenge is the naked idol of the worship of a semi-barbarous age; and self-deceit is the veiled image of unknown evil before which luxury and satiety lie prostrate. But a poet considers the vices of his contemporaries as the temporary dress in which his creations must be arrayed, and which cover without concealing the eternal proportions of their beauty. An epic or dramatic personage is understood to wear them around his soul, as he may the ancient armour or the modern uniform around his body; whilst it is easy to conceive a dress more graceful than either. The beauty of the internal nature cannot be so far concealed by its accidental vesture, but that the spirit of its form shall communicate itself to the very disguise, and indicate the shape it hides from the manner in which it is worn. A majestic form and graceful motions will express themselves through the most barbarous and tasteless costume. Few poets of the highest class have chosen to exhibit the beauty of their conceptions in its naked truth and splendour; and it is doubtful whether the alloy of costume, habit, etc., be not necessary to temper this planetary music for mortal ears.

The whole objection, however, of the immorality of poetry rests upon a misconception of the manner in which poetry acts to produce the moral improvement of man. Ethical science arranges the elements which poetry has created, and propounds schemes and proposes examples of civil and domestic life; nor is it for want of admirable doctrines that men hate, and despise, and censure, and deceive, and subjugate one another. But poetry acts in another and diviner manner. It awakens and enlarges the mind itself by rendering it the receptacle of a thousand unapprehended combinations of thought. Poetry lifts the veil from the hidden beauty of the world, and makes familiar objects be as if they were not familiar; it reproduces all that it represents, and the impersonations clothed in its Elysian light stand thenceforward in the minds of those who have once contemplated them, as memorials of that gentle and exalted content, which extends itself over all thoughts and actions with which it coexists. The great secret of morals is love; or a going out of our own nature, and an identification of ourselves with the beautiful which exists in thought, action, or person, not our own. A man, to be greatly good, must imagine intensely and comprehensively; he must put himself in the place of another and of many others; the pains and pleasures of his species must become his own. The great instrument of moral good is the imagination; and poetry administers to the effect by acting upon the cause. Poetry enlarges the circumference of the imagination by replenishing it with thoughts of ever new delight, which have the power of attracting and assimilating to their own nature all other thoughts, and which form new intervals and interstices whose void forever craves fresh food. Poetry strengthens that faculty which is the organ of the moral nature of man, in the same manner as exercise strengthens a limb. A poet therefore would do ill to embody his own conceptions of right and wrong, which are usually those of his place and time, in his poetical creations, which participate in neither. By this assumption of the inferior office of interpreting the effect, in which perhaps after all he might acquit himself but imperfectly, he would resign the glory in a participation in the cause. There was little danger that Homer, or any of the eternal poets, should have so far misunderstood themselves as to have abdicated this throne of their widest dominion. Those in whom the poetical faculty, though great, is less intense, as Euripides, Lucan, Tasso, Spenser, have frequently affected a moral aim, and the effect of their poetry is diminished in exact proportion to the degree in which they compel us to advert to this purpose.

It is difficult to define pleasure in its highest sense; the definition involving a number of apparent paradoxes. For, from an inexplicable defect of harmony in the constitution of human nature, the pain of the inferior is frequently connected with the pleasures of the superior portions of our being. Sorrow, terror, anguish, despair itself are often the chosen expressions of an approximation to the highest good. Our sympathy in tragic fiction depends on this principle; tragedy delights by affording a shadow of the pleasure which exists in pain. This is the source also of the melancholy which is inseparable from the sweetest melody. The pleasure that is in sorrow is sweeter than the pleasure of pleasure itself. And hence the saying, "It is better to go to the house of mourning, than to the house of mirth." Not that this highest species of pleasure is necessarily linked with pain. The delight of love and friendship, the ecstasy of the admiration of nature, the joy of the perception and still more of the creation of poetry is often wholly unalloyed.

The production and assurance of pleasure in this highest sense is true utility. Those who produce and preserve this pleasure are poets or poetical philosophers.

The exertions of Locke, Hume, Gibbon, Voltaire, Rousseau,[2] and their disciples, in favour of oppressed and deluded humanity, are entitled to the gratitude of mankind. Yet it is easy to calculate the degree of moral and intellectual improvement which the world would have exhibited, had they never lived. A little more nonsense would have been talked for a century or two; and perhaps a few more men, women, and children, burnt as heretics. We might not at this moment have been congratulating each other on the abolition of the Inquisition in Spain. But it exceeds all imagination to conceive what would have been the moral condition of the world if neither Dante, Petrarch, Boccaccio, Chaucer, Shakespeare, Calderon, Lord Bacon, nor Milton, had ever existed; if Raphael and Michael Angelo had never been born; if the Hebrew poetry had never been translated; if a revival of the study of Greek literature had never taken place; if no monuments of ancient sculpture had been handed down to us; and if the poetry of the religion of the ancient world had been extinguished together with its belief. The human mind could never, except by the intervention of these excitements, have been awakened to the invention of the grosser sciences, and that application of analytical reasoning to the aberrations of society, which it is now attempted to exalt over the direct expression of the inventive and creative faculty itself.

We have more moral, political, and historical wisdom than we know how to reduce into practice; we have more scientific and economical knowledge than can be accommodated to the just distribution of the produce which it multiplies. The poetry in these systems of thought is concealed by the accumulation of facts and calculating processes. There is no want of knowledge respecting what is wisest and best in morals, government, and political economy, or at least, what is wiser and better than what men now practise and endure. But we let "*I dare not* wait upon *I would*, like the poor cat i' the adage."[3] We want the creative faculty to imagine that which we know; we want the generous impulse to act that which we imagine; we want the poetry of life: our calculations have outrun conception; we have eaten more than we can digest. The cultivation of those sciences which have enlarged the limits of the empire of man over the external world has, for want of the poetical faculty, proportionally circumscribed those of the internal world; and man, having enslaved the elements, remains himself a slave. To what but a cultivation of the mechanical arts in a degree disproportioned to the presence of the creative faculty, which is the basis of all knowledge, is to be attributed the abuse of all invention for abridging and combining labour, to the exasperation of the inequality of mankind? From what other cause has it arisen that these inventions

2. I follow the classification adopted by the author of "Four Ages of Poetry."
But Rousseau was essentially a poet. The others, even Voltaire, were mere reasoners.

3. [Shakespeare, *Macbeth*, 1.7.44–45.]

which should have lightened, have added a weight to the curse imposed on Adam? Poetry, and the principle of self, of which money is the visible incarnation, are the God and Mammon of the world.

The functions of the poetical faculty are two-fold; by one it creates new materials of knowledge and power and pleasure; by the other it engenders in the mind a desire to reproduce and arrange them according to a certain rhythm and order which may be called the beautiful and the good. The cultivation of poetry is never more to be desired than at periods when, from an excess of the selfish and calculating principle, the accumulation of the materials of external life exceed the quantity of the power of assimilating them to the internal laws of human nature. The body has then become too unwieldy for that which animates it.

Poetry is indeed something divine. It is at once the centre and circumference of knowledge; it is that which comprehends all science, and that to which all science must be referred. It is at the same time the root and blossom of all other systems of thought; it is that from which all spring, and that which adorns all; and that which, if blighted, denies the fruit and the seed, and withholds from the barren world the nourishment and the succession of the scions of the tree of life. It is the perfect and consummate surface and bloom of things; it is as the odour and the colour of the rose to the texture of the elements which compose it, as the form and the splendour of unfaded beauty to the secrets of anatomy and corruption. What were virtue, love, patriotism, friendship, etc.—what were the scenery of this beautiful universe which we inhabit—what were our consolations on this side of the grave—and what were our aspirations beyond it—if poetry did not ascend to bring light and fire from those eternal regions where the owl-winged faculty of calculation dare not ever soar? Poetry is not like reasoning, a power to be exerted according to the determination of the will. A man cannot say, "I will compose poetry." The greatest poet even cannot say it; for the mind in creation is as a fading coal which some invisible influence, like an inconstant wind, awakens to transitory brightness; this power arises from within, like the colour of a flower which fades and changes as it is developed, and the conscious portions of our natures are unprophetic either of its approach or its departure. Could this influence be durable in its original purity and force, it is impossible to predict the greatness of the results; but when composition begins, inspiration is already on the decline, and the most glorious poetry that has ever been communicated to the world is probably a feeble shadow of the original conception of the poet. I appeal to the greatest poets of the present day, whether it be not an error to assert that the finest passages of poetry are produced by labour and study. The toil and the delay recommended by critics can be justly interpreted to mean no more than a careful observation of the inspired moments, and an artificial connexion of the spaces between their suggestions by the intertexture of conventional expressions; a necessity only imposed by the limitedness of the poetical faculty itself. For Milton conceived the *Paradise Lost* as a whole before he executed it in portions. We have his own authority also for the muse having "dictated" to him the "unpremeditated song," and let this be an answer to those who would allege the fifty-six various readings of the first line of the *Orlando Furioso*. Compositions so produced are to poetry what mosaic is to painting. This instinct and intuition of the poetical faculty is still more observable in the plastic and pictorial arts: a great statue or picture grows under the power of the artist as a child in the mother's womb; and the very mind which directs the hands in formation is incapable of accounting to itself for the origin, the gradations, or the media of the process.

Poetry is the record of the best and happiest moments of the happiest and best minds. We are aware of evanescent visitations of thought and feeling sometimes associated with place or person, sometimes regarding our own mind alone, and always arising unforeseen and departing unbidden, but elevating and delightful beyond all expression: so that even in the desire and the regret they leave, there cannot but be pleasure, participating as it does in the nature of its object. It is as it were the interpenetration of a diviner nature through our own; but its footsteps are like those of a wind over a sea, where the coming calm erases, and whose traces remain only as on the wrinkled sand which paves it. These and corresponding conditions of being are experienced principally by those of the most delicate sensibility and the most enlarged imagination; and the state of mind produced by them is at war with every base desire. The enthusiasm of virtue, love, patriotism, and friendship is essentially linked with these emotions; and whilst they last, self appears as what it is, an atom to a universe. Poets are not only subject to these experiences as spirits of the most refined organization, but they can colour all that they combine with the evanescent hues of this ethereal world; a word, or a trait in the representation of a scene or a passion, will touch the enchanted chord and reanimate, in those who have ever experienced these emotions, the sleeping, the cold, the buried image of the past. Poetry thus makes immortal all that is best and most beautiful in the world; it arrests the vanishing apparitions which haunt the interlunations of life, and veiling them, or in language or in form, sends them forth among mankind, bearing sweet news of kindred joy to those with whom their sisters abide—abide, because there is no portal of expression from the caverns of the spirit which they inhabit into the universe of things. Poetry redeems from decay the visitations of the divinity in man.

Poetry turns all things to loveliness; it exalts the beauty of that which is most beautiful, and it adds beauty to that which is most deformed; it marries exultation and horror, grief and pleasure, eternity and change; it subdues to union under its light yoke all irreconcilable things. It transmutes all that it touches, and every form moving within the radiance of its presence is changed by wondrous sympathy to an incarnation of the spirit which it breathes; its secret alchemy turns to potable gold the poisonous waters which flow from death through life; it strips the veil of familiarity from the world, and lays bare the naked and sleeping beauty which is the spirit of its forms.

All things exist as they are perceived—at least in relation to the percipient. "The mind is its own place, and of itself can make a heaven of hell, a hell of heaven." But poetry defeats the curse which binds us to be subjected to the accident of surrounding impressions. And whether it spreads its own figured curtain or withdraws life's dark veil from before the scene of things, it equally creates for us a being within our being. It makes us the inhabitants of a world to which the familiar world is a chaos. It reproduces the common universe of which we are portions and percipients, and it purges from our inward sight the film of familiarity which obscures from us the wonder of our being. It compels us to feel that which we perceive, and to imagine that which we know. It creates anew the universe after it has been annihilated in our minds by the recurrence of impressions blunted by reiteration. It justifies that bold and true word of Tasso: *Non merita nome di creatore, se non Iddio ed il Poeta.*[4]

A poet, as he is the author to others of the highest wisdom, pleasure, virtue, and glory, so he ought personally to be the happiest, the best, the wisest, and the most illustrious of men. As to his glory, let time be challenged to declare whether the fame of any other institutor of human life be comparable to that of a poet. That he is the wisest, the happiest, and the best, inasmuch as he is a poet, is equally incontrovertible; the greatest poets have been men of the most spotless virtue, of the most consummate prudence, and, if we could look into the interior of their lives, the most fortunate of men; and the exceptions, as they regard those who possessed the poetic faculty in a high yet inferior degree, will be found on consideration to confirm rather than destroy the rule. Let us for a moment stoop to the arbitration of popular breath, and usurping and uniting in our own persons the incompatible characters of accuser, witness, judge, and executioner, let us decide without trial, testimony, or form that certain motives of those who are "there sitting where we dare not soar" are reprehensible. Let us assume that Homer was a drunkard, that Virgil was a flatterer, that Horace was a coward, that Tasso was a madman, that Lord Bacon was a peculator, that Raphael was a libertine, that Spenser was a poet laureate. It is inconsistent with this division of our subject to cite living poets, but posterity has done ample justice to the great names now referred to.

4. [No one merits the name of creator except God and the poet.]

Their errors have been weighed and found to have been dust in the balance; if their sins "were as scarlet, they are now white as snow"; they have been washed in the blood of the mediator and the redeemer time. Observe in what a ludicrous chaos the imputations of real or fictitious crime have been confused in the contemporary calumnies against poetry and poets; consider how little is as it appears—or appears as it is; look to your own motives, and judge not, lest ye be judged.

Poetry, as has been said, in this respect differs from logic, that it is not subject to the control of the active powers of the mind, and that its birth and recurrence has no necessary connexion with consciousness or will. It is presumptuous to determine that these are the necessary conditions of all mental causation, when mental effects are experienced insusceptible of being referred to them. The frequent recurrence of the poetical power, it is obvious to suppose, may produce in the mind an habit of order and harmony correlative with its own nature and with its effects upon other minds. But in the intervals of inspiration, and they may be frequent without being durable, a poet becomes a man, and is abandoned to the sudden reflux of the influences under which others habitually live. But as he is more delicately organized than other men, and sensible to pain and pleasure, both his own and that of others, in a degree unknown to them, he will avoid the one and pursue the other with an ardour proportioned to this difference. And he renders himself obnoxious to calumny, when he neglects to observe the circumstances under which these objects of universal pursuit and flight have disguised themselves in one another's garments.

But there is nothing necessarily evil in this error, and thus cruelty, envy, revenge, avarice, and the passions purely evil, have never formed any portion of the popular imputations on the lives of poets.

I have thought it most favourable to the cause of truth to set down these remarks according to the order in which they were suggested to my mind, by a consideration of the subject itself, instead of following that of the treatise that excited me to make them public. Thus although devoid of the formality of a polemical reply, if the view they contain be just, they will be found to involve a refutation of the doctrines of the "Four Ages of Poetry," so far at least as regards the first division of the subject. I can readily conjecture what should have moved the gall of the learned and intelligent author of that paper; I confess myself, like him, unwilling to be stunned by the Theseids of the hoarse Codri of the day. Bavius and Maevius undoubtedly are, as they ever were, insufferable persons. But it belongs to a philosophical critic to distinguish rather than confound.

The first part of these remarks has related to poetry in its elements and principles; and it has been shown, as well as the narrow limits assigned them would permit, that what is called poetry, in a restricted sense, has a common source with all other forms of order and of beauty according to which the materials of human life are susceptible of being arranged, and which is poetry in an universal sense.

The second part will have for its object an application of these principles to the present state of the cultivation of poetry, and a defence of the attempt to idealize the modern forms of manners and opinions, and compel them into a subordination to the imaginative and creative faculty. For the literature of England, an energetic development of which has ever preceded or accompanied a great and free development of the national will, has arisen as it were from a new birth. In spite of the low-thoughted envy which would undervalue contemporary merit, our own will be a memorable age in intellectual achievements, and we live among such philosophers and poets as surpass beyond comparison any who have appeared since the last national struggle for civil and religious liberty. The most unfailing herald, companion, and follower of the awakening of a great people to work a beneficial change in opinion or institution, is poetry. At such periods there is an accumulation of the power of communicating and receiving intense and impassioned conceptions respecting man and nature. The persons in whom this power resides, may often, as far as regards many portions of their nature, have little apparent correspondence with that spirit of good of which they are the ministers. But even whilst they deny and abjure, they are yet compelled to serve the power which is seated upon the throne of their own soul. It is impossible to read the compositions of the most celebrated writers of the present day without being startled with the electric life which burns within their words. They measure the circumference and sound the depths of human nature with a comprehensive and all-penetrating spirit, and they are themselves perhaps the most sincerely astonished at its manifestations, for it is less their spirit than the spirit of the age. Poets are the hierophants of an unapprehended inspiration, the mirrors of the gigantic shadows which futurity casts upon the present, the words which express what they understand not; the trumpets which sing to battle, and feel not what they inspire; the influence which is moved not, but moves. Poets are the unacknowledged legislators of the world.

QUESTIONS

1. Why does Shelley say that "in the infancy of society every author is necessarily a poet, because language itself is poetry"? (51)
2. What does Shelley mean when he says that poets "foreknow the spirit of events"? (51)
3. According to Shelley, what enables a poet to participate "in the eternal, the infinite, and the one"? (51)
4. What does Shelley mean when he says that language "is as a mirror which reflects" while other forms of artistic expression are "as a cloud which enfeebles"? (52)
5. Why does Shelley claim that "the distinction between poets and prose writers is a vulgar error"? (53)
6. According to Shelley, what unites poets and philosophers?
7. In Shelley's opinion, how is a poet, who is confined to a particular place and time, able to express eternal truths?
8. Why does Shelley assert that "no living poet ever arrived at the fulness of his fame"? (54)
9. What does Shelley believe to be the relationship between poetry and morality?
10. What does Shelley mean when he says that "man, having enslaved the elements, remains himself a slave"? (57)
11. Why does Shelley consider poetry and "the principle of self" as being in opposition to each other? (58)
12. How is Shelley's larger argument regarding the importance of poetry advanced by his belief that a poem is created not "according to the determination of the will," but rather its creation depends on an unpredictable force that "arises from within"? (58)
13. What does Shelley mean when he says that poetry "compels us to feel that which we perceive, and to imagine that which we know"? (60)

14. Is Shelley saying that the character of great poets can be deduced from the art they created, or that any defects in their character must be judged in light of the art they created?

15. According to Shelley, do poets determine the future or reveal it?

FOR FURTHER REFLECTION

1. Is art as much of an influence on today's world as it was on Shelley's? Do you agree with his concluding statement that "poets are the unacknowledged legislators of the world"?

2. Are there any absolute criteria that must be taken into account in determining the value of a work of art?

3. Does art bring about change or only represent it?

4. Do you agree with Shelley when he asserts that poetry "is not subject to the control of the active powers of the mind" and that the creation of poetry is not related to consciousness or will?

HONORÉ DE BALZAC

Although better known as a novelist, Honoré de Balzac (1799–1850) wrote nearly fifty short stories, most of them early in his career. "The Unknown Masterpiece" (1831) is both a portrait of a painter tormented by the artistic enterprise and an inquiry into the nature of art. The story explores art's various functions, the conditions that enable or hinder its creation, and the difficulty of establishing the value of any given work.

Balzac was born in Tours, France, to a civil-servant father and a neurotic mother whose interest in mysticism was an early influence on her son. Like his father, Balzac adopted the aristocratic particle *de* even though he had no legitimate right to it. After attending boarding school at Vendôme, he studied law and worked as a law clerk in Paris. He obtained his license in 1819 but decided to pursue a career in literature.

For the next ten years, Balzac wrote with the principal goal of making money. He contributed to magazines and produced sensational potboiler novels at a rapid pace, under a pseudonym and often in collaboration with other writers. Balzac briefly tried his hand at the publishing business, but the venture was a disaster that left him in considerable debt, a condition he would rarely escape for the rest of his life. In 1829, he published *Les Chouans*, a novel about Breton peasants and their involvement in the French Revolution. The novel's success put him on the road to literary celebrity. Balzac was as intent on cutting a dashing figure in Paris society as he was on becoming a successful author, and his extravagant, self-indulgent lifestyle was matched in its intensity by his legendary work habits. With the help of great quantities of coffee, Balzac would write for fourteen or sixteen hours a day, often beginning at midnight after only a few hours of sleep.

In the mid-1830s, Balzac began to conceive of his fiction as a single, vast portrait of French society between the beginning of the French Revolution in 1789, and the July Revolution and the ascendance of Louis-Philippe to the throne in 1830. By 1840, he had decided to call it *La comédie humaine*. The work spans every class and profession and is populated by more than two thousand characters, some appearing in several books. Balzac carries forward some elements of romanticism, such as the primacy of the individual and the power of the imagination. But in depicting individuals who struggle against larger social forces, he helped lay the groundwork for the realism found in later nineteenth-century novels. *Eugénie Grandet* (1833), *Le Père Goriot* (1835), *Les illusions perdues* (1837–1843), and *La Cousine Bette* (1847) are all part of *La comédie humaine* and are among Balzac's most highly regarded novels.

In 1832, Balzac met Éveline Hanska, a married Polish countess who was an admirer of his writing. The following year, she became his mistress. They decided to marry when her husband died. That finally occurred in 1842, but Hanska was put off by Balzac's indebtedness, which he tried to reverse by writing at an ever more feverish pace. Balzac and Hanska's intermittent meetings continued over the next six years. Meanwhile, Balzac's health gradually declined until, quite ill, he went to live with Hanska at her chateau in 1848. Finally, in 1850, she agreed to marry him, and they moved to Paris. Balzac died five months later.

HONORÉ DE BALZAC

The Unknown Masterpiece

1. Gillette

Toward the end of the year 1612, on a cold December morning, a young man whose clothing looked very thin was walking to and fro in front of the door to a house located on the rue des Grands-Augustins in Paris. After walking on that street for quite some time with the indecision of a lover who lacks the courage to visit his first mistress, no matter how easy her virtue, he finally crossed the threshold of that door and asked whether Master François Porbus was at home. On the affirmative reply made by an old woman busy sweeping a downstairs room, the young man slowly climbed the steps, stopping from stair to stair like some recently appointed courtier worried about how the king will receive him. When he reached the top of the spiral staircase, he remained on the landing for a while, unsure about seizing the grotesque knocker that decorated the door to the studio in which Henri IV's painter, abandoned by Marie de Médicis in favor of Rubens, was no doubt working. The young man was experiencing that profound emotion that must have stirred the heart of all the great artists when, at the height of their youth and love of art, they approached a man of genius or some masterpiece. There exists in all human feelings a pristine purity, engendered by a noble enthusiasm, that gradually grows weaker until happiness is only a memory, and glory a lie. Among these delicate emotions, the one most resembling love is the youthful ardor of an artist beginning the delicious torture of his destiny of glory and misfortune, an ardor full of audacity and shyness, of vague beliefs and inevitable discouragements. The man who, short of money but of budding genius, has never felt a sharp thrill when introducing himself to a master, will always be lacking a string in his heart, some stroke of the brush, a certain feeling in his work, some poetic expressiveness. If a few braggarts, puffed up with themselves, believe in their future too soon, only fools consider them wise. Judging by this, the young stranger seemed to possess real merit, if talent can be measured by that initial shyness, by that indefinable modesty that men slated for glory are prone to lose during the practice of their art, just as pretty women lose theirs in the habits of coquetry. Being accustomed to triumph lessens one's self-doubt, and modesty may be a form of doubt.

Overwhelmed with poverty and, at that moment, surprised at his own presumptuousness, the poor novice wouldn't have entered the studio of the painter to whom we owe the admirable portrait of Henri IV if it hadn't been for an unusual helping hand sent his way by chance. An old man came up the stairs. From the oddness of his clothes, from the magnificence of his lace collar, from the exceptional self-assurance of his gait, the young man guessed that this person must be the painter's protector or friend; he moved back on the landing to give him room and studied him with curiosity, hoping to find in him the good nature of an artist or the helpful disposition of an art lover; but he discerned something diabolical in that face, and especially that indefinable something which attracts artists. Imagine a bald, convex, jutting forehead, sloping down to a small, flat nose turned up at the end like Rabelais's or Socrates'; a smiling, wrinkled mouth; a short chin, lifted proudly and adorned with a gray beard cut in a point; sea-green eyes apparently dimmed by age but which, through the contrast of the pearly white in which the irises swam, must sometimes cast hypnotic looks at the height of anger or enthusiasm. In addition, his face was singularly withered by the labors of old age, and still more by the kind of thoughts that hollow out both the soul and the body. His eyes had no more lashes, and only a few traces of eyebrows could be made out above their protruding ridges. Place this head on a thin, weak body, encircle it with sparkling-white lace of openwork like that of a fish slice, throw onto the old man's black doublet a heavy gold chain, and you will have an imperfect picture of that character, whom the feeble daylight of the staircase lent an additional tinge of the fantastic. You would have thought him a Rembrandt painting, walking silently without a frame in the dark atmosphere which that great painter made all his own. The old man cast a glance imbued with wisdom at the young man, knocked three times at the door, and said to the sickly man of about forty, who opened it: "Good day, master."

Porbus bowed respectfully; he let the young man in, thinking the old man had brought him along, and didn't trouble himself over him, especially since the novice was under the spell that born painters must undergo at the view of the first studio they've seen, where they can discover some of the practical methods of their art. A skylight in the vaulted ceiling illuminated Master Porbus's studio. Falling directly onto a canvas attached to the easel, on which only three or four white lines had been placed, the daylight didn't reach the black depths of the corners of that vast room; but a few stray reflections in that russet shadow ignited a silvery flash on the belly of a knight's breastplate hung on the wall; streaked with a sudden furrow of light the carved, waxed cornice of an antique sideboard laden with curious platters; or jabbed with brilliant dots the grainy weave of some old curtains of gold brocade with large, sharp folds, thrown there as models. Plaster anatomical figures, fragments and torsos of ancient goddesses, lovingly polished by the kisses of the centuries, were strewn over the shelves and consoles. Innumerable sketches, studies in three colors of crayon, in sanguine, or in pen and ink, covered the walls up to the ceiling. Paintboxes, bottles of oil and turpentine, and overturned stools left only a narrow path to reach the aureole projected by the tall window, whose beams fell directly onto Porbus's pale face and the peculiar man's ivory-colored cranium. The young man's attention was soon claimed exclusively by a painting which, in that time of chaos and revolutions, had already become famous and was visited by some of those obstinate men to whom we owe the preservation of the sacred fire in dark days. That beautiful canvas depicted Saint Mary of Egypt preparing to pay her boat fare. That masterpiece, painted for Marie de Médicis, was sold by her when she had become destitute.

"I like your saint," the old man said to Porbus, "and I'd pay ten gold écus for it over and above what the queen is paying; but, compete with her? Never!"

"You find it good?"

"Hm, hm!" said the old man. "Good? Yes and no. Your lady isn't badly set up, but she's not alive. You people think you've done it all when you've drawn a figure correctly and you've put everything in the right place according to the laws of anatomy! You color in that outline with a flesh tone prepared in advance on your palette, making sure to keep one side darker than the other, and because from time to time you look at a naked woman standing on a table, you think you've copied nature, you imagine you're painters and that you've stolen God's secrets! Brrr! To be a great poet, it's not enough to have a full command of syntax and avoid solecisms of language! Look at your saint, will you, Porbus? At first glance she seems admirable; but at the second look, you notice that she's glued to the background and that you could never walk all around her. She's a silhouette with only one side, she's a cutout likeness, an image that couldn't turn around or shift position. I feel no air between this arm and the field of the picture; space and depth are lacking; and yet the perspective is quite correct, and the atmospheric gradation of tones is precisely observed; but, despite such laudable efforts, I can't believe that that beautiful body is animated by the warm breath of life. It seems to me that, if I placed my hand on that bosom so firm and round, I'd find it as cold as marble! No, my friend, the blood isn't flowing beneath that ivory skin, life is not swelling with its crimson dew the veins and capillaries that intertwine in networks beneath the transparent amber of the temples and chest. This spot is throbbing, but this other spot is rigid; life and death are locked in combat in every detail: here she's a woman, there she's a statue, over there she's a corpse. Your creation is incomplete. You've been able to breathe only a portion of your soul into your beloved work. Prometheus's torch has gone out more than once in your hands, and many places in your painting haven't been touched by the heavenly flame."

"But why is that, dear master?" Porbus respectfully asked the old man, while the youngster had difficulty repressing a strong urge to strike him.

"Ah! This is it," said the little old man. "You've wavered indecisively between the two systems, between drawing and color, between the painstaking stolidity and precise stiffness of the old German masters and the dazzling fervor and felicitous richness of the Italian painters. You wanted to imitate Hans Holbein and Titian, Albrecht Dürer and Paolo Veronese, at the same time. Certainly that was a magnificent ambition! But what happened? You haven't achieved either the austere charm of dryness or the deceptive magic of chiaroscuro. In this spot here, like molten bronze cracking a mold that's too weak for it, Titian's rich, blond color has smashed through the thin outline à la Dürer into which you had poured it. In other places, the outline resisted, and restrained the magnificent outpouring of the Venetian palette. Your figure is neither perfectly drawn nor perfectly painted, and everywhere it bears the traces of that unfortunate indecisiveness. If you didn't feel strong enough to weld together in the flame of your genius the two competing manners, you should have opted openly for one or the other, so you could achieve that unity which simulates one of the conditions of life. You are true only in the interior sections; your outlines are false, they fail to join up properly, and they don't indicate that there's anything behind them. There's truth here," said the old man, pointing to the saint's chest. "And then here," he continued, indicating the place on the painting where the shoulder ended. "But here," he said, returning to the center of the bosom, "everything is false. Let's not analyze it, it would drive you to despair."

The old man sat down on a stool, held his head in his hands, and fell silent.

"Master," Porbus said to him, "all the same, I studied that bosom from a nude live model; but, to our misfortune, there are true effects in nature that are no longer lifelike on the canvas . . ."

"The mission of art is not to copy nature but to express it! You're not a cheap copyist but a poet!" the old man exclaimed hotly, interrupting Porbus with a lordly gesture. "Otherwise a sculptor would be through with all his labors if he just took a cast of a woman! Well now, just try taking a cast of your sweetheart's hand and setting it down in front of you; you'll find a hideous corpse that's not at all like the real thing, and you'll be compelled to seek out the chisel of a man who wouldn't copy it exactly for you, but would depict its movement and its life for you. Our job is to grasp the spirit, the soul, the face of objects and living beings. Effects! Effects! They're merely the incidental phenomena of life, not life itself. A hand, since I've chosen that example, a hand isn't merely part of a body, it expresses and prolongs an idea that must be grasped and rendered. Neither the painter, nor the poet, nor the sculptor should separate the effect from the cause, since they're inevitably interconnected! The real struggle is there! Many painters achieve an instinctive sort of success without knowing that theme of art. You draw a woman, but you don't see her! That's not the way to make nature yield up her secrets. Your hand, without any thought on your part, reproduces the model you had copied in your teacher's studio. You don't delve sufficiently into the intimate depths of the form, you don't pursue it with sufficient love and perseverance through its twists and turns and its elusive maneuvers. Beauty is something austere and difficult that cannot be attained that way; you have to wait for the right moment, spy it out, seize it, and hug it tight to force it to surrender. Form is a Proteus much more unseizable and rich in hidden secrets than the Proteus of legend; it's only after lengthy struggles that you can compel it to show itself in its true guise; all of you are satisfied with the first semblance it yields to you, or at most the second, or the third; that's not how victorious fighters go about it! Those unvanquished painters don't allow themselves to be deceived by all those subterfuges; they persevere until nature is forced to show itself bare, in its true spirit. That's how Raphael went about it," said the old man, taking off his black velvet cap to show the respect he felt for the king of art; "his great superiority is due to the intimate sense which, in his works, seems set on breaking through form. In his figures, form is what it is in us, an interpreter of ideas and feelings, a great poetry. Every figure is a world, a portrait whose model appeared in a sublime vision, colored by light, pointed out by an inner voice, stripped bare by a heavenly finger that showed the sources of expression within the past of an entire lifetime. You make beautiful robes of flesh for your women, beautiful draperies of hair, but where is the blood that produces either calm or passion and causes particular effects? Your saint is a brunette, but this here, my poor Porbus, is suitable for a blond! And so your figures are pale, colored-in phantoms that you trot out before us, and you call that painting and art. Because you've produced something that looks more like a woman than like a house, you think you've hit the mark; and, really proud because you no longer need to label your figures *currus venustus* or *pulcher homo*, the way the earliest painters did, you imagine you're wonderful artists! Ha, ha! You're not there yet, my worthy friends, you'll have to use up many a crayon and cover many a canvas before you get there. Of course, a woman carries her head this way, she holds her skirt like that, her eyes grow languid and melt with that air of resigned gentleness, that's the way that the fluttering shadow of her lashes hovers over her cheeks! It's right, and it isn't. What's missing? A trifle, but that trifle is everything. You have the semblance of life, but you aren't expressing its overflowing superabundance, that indefinable something, which may be the soul, hovering like a cloud above the outer husk; in short, that bloom of life which Titian and Raphael captured. Starting out from where you've left off, some excellent painting might be achieved; but you get tired too soon. The layman admires you, but the true connoisseur merely smiles. Oh Mabuse, my teacher," that odd character added, "you're a thief, you stole life when you died!—Aside from that," he resumed, "this canvas is better than the paintings of that brute Rubens, with his mountains of Flemish meat, sprinkled with vermilion, his tidal waves of red hair, and his glaring colors. At least you've got color, feeling, and drawing there, the three essential components of art."

"But that saint is sublime, my good man!" the young man called out loudly, emerging from his deep daydreams. "These two figures, the saint and the boatman, have a subtlety of purpose that the Italian painters have no notion of; I don't know one of them who could have created the indecisiveness of the boatman."

"Does this little rascal belong to you?" Porbus asked the old man.

"Alas, master, forgive my boldness," replied the novice, blushing. "I'm a nobody, a dauber of pictures by instinct who has recently arrived in this city, which is the fount of all knowledge."

"Get to work!" Porbus said to him, offering him a red crayon and a sheet of paper.

The stranger nimbly made a line copy of the Saint Mary.

"Oh, ho!" cried the old man. "Your name?"

The young man signed "Nicolas Poussin" at the bottom.

"That's not bad for a beginner," said the odd character who had been speaking so extravagantly. "I see that it's possible to talk about painting in your presence. I don't blame you for having admired Porbus's saint. It's a masterpiece for the world at large, and only those initiated into the deepest secrets of art can discover what's wrong with it. But, since you're worthy of the lesson, and able to understand, I'm going to show you just how little it would take to complete this picture. Be all eyes and give me complete attention; another opportunity to teach you like this may never occur again! Your palette, Porbus?"

Porbus went to get a palette and brushes. The little old man rolled up his sleeves in a convulsively brusque fashion, stuck his thumb into the palette, mottled and laden with paints, that Porbus held out to him; he not so much took as ripped from his hands a fistful of brushes of all sizes, and his pointy beard suddenly started bobbing in menacing motions that expressed the urgings of an ardent imagination. While loading his brush with paint, he muttered between his teeth: "Here are tints that are only good enough to be thrown out the window along with the man who mixed them; they're revoltingly crude and false, how can I paint with this?" Then, with feverish energy, he dipped the tip of his brush into the various gobs of paint, at times running through their entire gamut more rapidly than a cathedral organist races from one end of his keyboard to another during the Easter "O Filii."

Porbus and Poussin remained motionless on either side of the canvas, sunk in the most vehement contemplation.

"Do you see, young man," said the old man without turning away, "do you see how, with three or four strokes and a little bluish glaze, it was possible to make the air circulate around the head of this poor saint, who must have been stifled, trapped in that thick atmosphere? See how this drapery now flutters and how one now realizes that the breeze is lifting it! Before, it looked like a starched cloth held up by pins. Do you notice how the gleaming gloss I've just put on her chest reproduces the plump suppleness of a girl's skin, and how the tint blended of red-brown and burnt ocher warms up the gray chill of this large shadow, in which the blood was coagulating instead of flowing? Young man, young man, what I'm showing you here, no master could teach vou. Mabuse alone possessed the secret of giving figures life. Mabuse had only one pupil: me. I never had any, and I'm old! You have enough intelligence to guess the rest from what I allow you to glimpse."

While speaking, the old man was placing strokes on every part of the painting: here two brushstrokes, there just one, but always so felicitously that you would have said it was a different picture, one bathed in light. He worked with such passionate fervor that beads of sweat stood out on his hairless brow, he moved so rapidly, with short movements that were so impatient and jerky, that it seemed to young Poussin as if the body of that peculiar character contained a demon acting through his hands, seizing them eerily as if against the man's will. The preternatural brightness of his eyes, the convulsions that looked like the effects of resistance, lent that notion a semblance of truth that had to affect a young imagination. The old man kept saying: "Bang, bang, bang! That's how it takes on consistency, young man! Come, little brushstrokes, make that icy tint grow red for me! Let's go!—Boom, boom, boom!" he would say, while adding warmth to the areas he had accused of lacking life, while eliminating the differences in feeling with a few patches of color, and restoring the unity of tone that an ardent Egyptian woman demanded.

"You see, youngster, it's only the final brushstroke that counts. Porbus laid on a hundred and I've laid on just one. No one is going to thank us for what's underneath. Remember that!"

Finally that demon halted and, turning around to address Porbus and Poussin, who were speechless with admiration, he said: "This is still not as good as my *Quarrelsome Beauty*, and yet it would be possible to put one's name at the bottom of a picture like this. Yes, I'd sign it," he added, standing up to fetch a mirror, in which he looked at it. "Now let's go dine," he said. "Both of you come to my house. I have smoked ham, I have good wine! Ho, ho! Despite the unfortunate era we live in, we'll chat about painting! We're equally matched. Here's a little fellow," he added, tapping Nicolas Poussin on the shoulder, "who has some aptitude."

Then, catching sight of the Norman's wretched coat, he drew a leather purse from his belt, rummaged in it, drew out two gold coins, and, showing them to him, said: "I'll buy your drawing."

"Take it," said Porbus to Poussin, seeing him give a start and blush with shame, for that young adept had a poor man's pride. "Go on and take it; he's got enough in his moneybag to ransom two kings!"

The three of them left the studio and walked, conversing about the arts, until they reached a beautiful wooden house located near the Saint-Michel Bridge; its decorations, its door knocker, the frames of its casement windows, its arabesques, all amazed Poussin. The aspiring painter suddenly found himself in a downstairs room, in front of a good fire, near a table laden with appetizing food, and, by unusual good fortune, in the company of two great artists who were exceptionally good-natured.

"Young man," Porbus said to him, seeing him dumbfounded in front of a painting, "don't look at that picture too long, or it will drive you to despair."

It was the *Adam* that Mabuse painted to get out of the prison where his creditors kept him so long. Indeed, that figure gave such a strong impression of being real that, from that moment on, Nicolas Poussin began to understand the true meaning of the confused words the old man had uttered. The old man looked at the picture with seeming satisfaction, but without enthusiasm, and appeared to be saying: "I've done better!"

"There's life in it," he said. "My poor master outdid himself in it; but there was still a little truth missing in the background of the picture. The man is really alive; he's getting up and is going to approach us. But the air, sky, and wind that we breathe, see, and feel aren't there. Besides, he's still just a man! Now, the only man who ever came directly from the hands of God ought to have something divine about him, which is missing. Mabuse used to say so himself, with vexation, when he wasn't drunk."

Poussin was looking back and forth between the old man and Porbus with restless curiosity. He came up to Porbus as if to ask him their host's name; but the painter put a finger to his lips with an air of mystery, and the young man, though keenly interested, kept silent, hoping that sooner or later some remark would allow him to learn the name of his host, whose wealth and talents were sufficiently attested to by the respect Porbus showed him and by the wonders assembled in that room.

Seeing a magnificent portrait of a woman on the somber oak paneling, Poussin exclaimed: "What a beautiful Giorgione!"

"No," replied the old man, "you're looking at one of my first smears."

"Damn! Then I'm in the home of the god of painting," Poussin said naively.

The old man smiled like a man long accustomed to such praise.

"Master Frenhofer," said Porbus, "could you possibly send for a little of your good Rhenish wine for me?"

"Two casks," replied the old man. "One to repay you for the pleasure I had this morning looking at your pretty sinner, and the other as a present to a friend."

"Oh, if I weren't always under the weather," continued Porbus, "and if you were willing to let me see your *Quarrelsome Beauty*, I could paint some tall, wide, deep picture in which the figures were life-size."

"Show my painting!" cried the old man, quite upset. "No, no, I still have to perfect it. Yesterday, toward evening," he said, "I thought I had finished it. Her eyes seemed moist to me, her flesh was stirring. The locks of her hair were waving. She was breathing! Even though I've found the way to achieve nature's relief and three-dimensionality on a flat canvas, this morning, when it got light, I realized my mistake. Oh, to achieve this glorious result, I've studied thoroughly the great masters of color, I've analyzed and penetrated layer by layer the paintings of Titian, that king of light; like that sovereign painter, I sketched in my figure in a light tint with a supple, heavily loaded brush—for shadow is merely an incidental phenomenon, remember that, youngster. Then I went back over my work and, by means of gradations and glazes that I made successively less transparent, I rendered the heaviest shadows and even the deepest blacks; for the shadows of ordinary painters are of a different nature from their bright tints; they're wood, bronze, or whatever you want, except flesh in shadow. You feel that, if their figure shifted position, the areas in shadow would never be cleared up and wouldn't become bright. I avoided that error, into which many of the most illustrious have fallen, and in my picture the whiteness can be discerned beneath the opacity of even the most dense shadow! Unlike that pack of ignoramuses who imagine they're drawing correctly because they produce a line carefully shorn of all rough edges, I haven't indicated the outer borders of my figure in a dry manner, bringing out even the slightest detail of the anatomy, because the human body isn't bounded by lines. In that area, sculptors can come nearer the truth than we can. Nature is comprised of a series of solid shapes that dovetail into one another. Strictly speaking, there's no such thing as drawing! Don't laugh, young man! As peculiar as that remark may sound to you, you'll understand the reasons behind it some day. Line is the means by which man renders the effect of light on objects; but there are no lines in nature, where everything is continuous: it's by modeling that we draw; that is, we separate things from the medium in which they exist; only the distribution of the light gives the body its appearance! Thus, I haven't fixed any outlines, I've spread over the contours a cloud of blond, warm intermediate tints in such a way that no one can put his finger on the exact place where the contours meet the background. From close up, this work looks fleecy and seems lacking in precision, but, at two paces, everything firms up, becomes fixed, and stands out; the body turns, the forms project, and you feel the air circulating all around them. And yet I'm still not satisfied, I have some doubts. Perhaps it's wrong to draw a single line, perhaps it would be better to attack a figure from the center, first concentrating on the projecting areas that catch most of the light, and only then moving on to the darker sections. Isn't that how the sun operates, that divine painter of the universe? Oh nature, nature, who has ever captured you in your inmost recesses? You see, just like ignorance, an excess of knowledge leads to a negation. I have doubts about my painting!"

The old man paused, then resumed: "It's ten years now, young man, that I've been working on it; but what are ten short years when it's a question of struggling with nature? We don't know how long it took Sir Pygmalion to make the only statue that ever walked!"

The old man dropped into deep musing, and sat there with fixed eyes, mechanically playing with his knife.

"Now he's in converse with his 'spirit,'" said Porbus quietly.

At that word, Nicholas Poussin felt himself under the power of an unexplainable artistic curiosity. That old man with white eyes, attentive and in a stupor, had become more than a man to him; he seemed like a whimsical genius living in an unknown sphere. He awakened a thousand confused ideas in his soul. The moral phenomenon of that type of fascination can no more be defined than one can render in words the emotion caused by a song that reminds an exiled man's heart of his homeland. The scorn this old man affected to express for beautiful artistic endeavors, his wealth, his ways, Porbus's deference toward him, that painting kept a secret for so long—a labor of patience, a labor of genius, no doubt, if one were to judge by the head of the Virgin that young Poussin had so candidly admired, and which, still beautiful even alongside Mabuse's *Adam*, bespoke the imperial talents of one of the princes of art—everything about that old man exceeded the boundaries of human nature. The clear, perceivable image that Nicholas Poussin's rich imagination derived from his observation of that preternatural being was a total image of the artistic nature, that irrational nature to which such great powers have been entrusted, and which all too often abuses those powers, leading cool reason, the bourgeois, and even some connoisseurs over a thousand rocky roads where there is nothing for them, while that white-winged lass, a madcap of fantasies, discovers there epics, castles, works of art. Nature—mocking and kind, fertile and poor! And so, for the enthusiastic Poussin, that old man, through a sudden transformation, had become art itself, art with its secrets, its passions, and its daydreams.

"Yes, my dear Porbus," Frenhofer resumed, "up to now I've been unable to find a flawless woman, a body whose contours are perfectly beautiful, and whose complexion . . . But," he said, interrupting himself, where is she in the living flesh, that undiscoverable Venus of the ancients, so often sought for, and of whose beauty we scarcely come across even a few scattered elements here and there? Oh, if I could see for a moment, just once, that divine, complete nature—in short, that ideal—I'd give my entire fortune; but I'd go after you in the underworld, heavenly beauty! Like Orpheus, I'd descend to the Hades of art to bring back life from there."

"We can leave," said Porbus to Poussin; "he can't hear us anymore or see us anymore!"

"Let's go to his studio," replied the amazed young man.

"Oh, the sly old customer has taken care to block all entry to it. His treasures are too well guarded for us to reach them. I didn't wait for your suggestion or your fancies to attempt an attack on the mystery."

"So there is a mystery?"

"Yes," Porbus replied. "Old Frenhofer is the only pupil Mabuse was ever willing to train. Having become his friend, his rescuer, his father, Frenhofer sacrificed the largest part of his treasures in satisfying Mabuse's passions; in exchange, Mabuse transmitted to him the secret of three-dimensionality, the power to give figures that extraordinary life, that natural bloom, which is our eternal despair, but the technique of which he possessed so firmly that, one day, having sold for drink the flowered damask with which he was supposed to make garments to wear at Emperor Charles V's visit to the city, he accompanied his patron wearing paper clothing painted like damask. The particular brilliance of the material worn by Mabuse surprised the emperor, who, wanting to compliment the old drunkard's protector on it, discovered the deception. Frenhofer is a man who's impassioned over our art, who sees higher and farther than other painters. He has meditated profoundly on color, on the absolute truth of line; but, by dint of so much investigation, he has come to have his doubts about the very thing he was investigating. In his moments of despair, he claims that there is no such thing as drawing and that only geometric figures can be rendered in line; that is going beyond the truth, because with line and with black, which isn't a color, we can create a figure; which proves that our art, like nature, is made up of infinite elements: drawing supplies a skeleton, color supplies life; but life without the skeleton is even more incomplete than the skeleton without life. Lastly, there's something truer than all this: practice and observation are everything to a painter, and if reasoning and poetry pick a fight with our brushes, we wind up doubting like this fellow here, who is as much a lunatic as he is a painter. Although a sublime painter, he had the misfortune of being born into wealth, and that allowed his mind to wander. Don't imitate him! Work! Painters shouldn't meditate unless they have their brushes in their hand."

"We'll make our way in!" cried Poussin, no longer listening to Porbus and no longer troubled by doubts.

Porbus smiled at the young stranger's enthusiasm, and left him, inviting him to come and see him.

Nicolas Poussin went back slowly toward the rue de la Harpe, walking past the modest hostelery in which he lodged, without noticing it. Climbing his wretched staircase with restless speed, he reached an upstairs room located beneath a half-timbered roof, that naive, lightweight covering of old Parisian houses. Near the dark window, the only one in his room, he saw a girl, who, at the sound of the door, suddenly stood up straight, prompted by her love; she had recognized the painter by the way he had jiggled the latch.

"What's the matter?" she asked.

"The matter, the matter," he cried, choking with pleasure, "is that I really felt I was a painter! I had doubted myself up to now, but this morning I began to believe in myself! I can be a great man! Come, Gillette, we'll be rich and happy! There's gold in these brushes."

But he suddenly fell silent. His serious, energetic face lost its expression of joy when he compared the immensity of his hopes to the insignificance of his resources. The walls were covered with plain pieces of paper full of crayon sketches. He didn't own four clean canvases. Paints were expensive at the time, and the poor gentleman's palette was nearly bare. Living in such destitution, he possessed and was aware of incredible riches of the heart and the superabundance of a devouring genius. Brought to Paris by a nobleman who had befriended him, or perhaps by his own talent, he had suddenly found a sweetheart there, one of those noble, generous souls who accept suffering at the side of a great man, adopting his poverty and trying to understand his whims; brave in poverty and love just as other women are fearless in supporting luxury and making a public show of their lack of feelings. The smile that played on Gillette's lips gilded that garret, competing with the brightness of the sky. The sun didn't always shine, whereas she was always there, communing with his passion, devoted to his happiness and his suffering, consoling the genius that overflowed with love before seizing art.

"Listen, Gillette, come."

The joyful, obedient girl leaped onto the painter's knees. She was all grace, all beauty, lovely as springtime, adorned with all feminine riches and illumining them with the flame of a beautiful soul.

"Oh, God!" he cried, "I'll never have the courage to tell her."

"A secret?" she asked. "I want to hear it."

Poussin remained quiet, lost in thought.

"Well, talk."

"Gillette, my poor sweetheart!"

"Oh, you want something from me?"

"Yes."

"If you want me to pose for you again the way I did the other day," she continued in a rather sulky way, "I'll never agree to it again, because, at times like that, your eyes no longer tell me anything. You no longer think about me, even though you're looking at me."

"Would you prefer to see me drawing another woman?"

"Maybe," she said, "if she were good and ugly."

"So, then," Poussin went on in a serious tone, "what if, for my future glory, in order to make me a great painter, it were necessary to pose for someone else?"

"You want to test me," she said. "You know very well I wouldn't go." Poussin's head dropped onto his chest, like that of a man succumbing to a joy or sorrow too strong for his soul.

"Listen," she said, tugging the sleeve of Poussin's threadbare doublet, "I've told you, Nick, that I'd give my life for you; but I've never promised you to give up my love for you while I was alive."

"Give it up?" cried Poussin.

"If I showed myself that way to somebody else, you wouldn't love me anymore. And I myself would feel unworthy of you. Isn't catering to your whims a natural, simple thing? In spite of myself, I'm happy, and even proud to do everything you ask me to. But for somebody else—oh, no."

"Forgive me, Gillette," said the painter, falling on his knees. "I'd rather be loved than famous. For me you're more beautiful than wealth and honors. Go, throw away my brushes, burn those sketches. I was wrong. My calling is to love you. I'm not a painter, I'm a lover. Art and all its secrets can go hang!"

She admired him, she was happy, delighted! She ruled supreme, she felt instinctively that the arts were forgotten for her sake and cast at her feet like a grain of incense.

"And yet he's only an old man," Poussin continued. "He'll only be able to see the woman in you. You're so perfect!"

"I've got to love you!" she cried, prepared to sacrifice her romantic scruples to reward her lover for all the sacrifices he made for her. "But," she went on, "it would mean ruining me. Ah, to ruin myself for you! Yes, it's a beautiful thing, but you'll forget me. Oh, what a terrible idea you've come up with!"

"I've come up with it, and I love you," he said with a kind of contrition, "but it makes me a scoundrel."

"Shall we consult Father Hardouin?" she asked.

"Oh, no. Let it be a secret between the two of us."

"All right, I'll go; but you mustn't be there," she said. "Remain outside the door, armed with your dagger; if I scream, come in and kill the painter."

No longer seeing anything but his art, Poussin crushed Gillette in his arms.

"He doesn't love me anymore!" Gillette thought when she was alone.

She already regretted her decision. But she soon fell prey to a fear that was even crueler than her regret; she did her best to drive away an awful thought that was taking shape in her heart. She was thinking that she already loved the painter less, suspecting him of being less estimable than before.

2. Catherine Lescault

Three months after Poussin and Porbus first met, Porbus paid a visit to Master Frenhofer. The old man was at the time a prey to one of those spontaneous fits of deep discouragement, the cause of which, if one is to believe the firm opinions of traditional doctors, is indigestion, the wind, heat, or some bloating of the hypochondriac regions; but, according to psychologists, is really the imperfection of our moral nature. The man was suffering from fatigue, pure and simple, after trying to finish his mysterious painting. He was seated languidly in an enormous chair of carved oak trimmed with black leather; and, without abandoning his melancholy attitude, he darted at Porbus the glance of a man who had settled firmly into his distress.

"Well, master," Porbus said, "was the ultramarine you went to Bruges for bad? Weren't you able to grind your new white? Is your oil defective, or your brushes stiff?"

"Alas!" exclaimed the old man, "for a moment I thought my picture was finished; but now I'm sure I was wrong about a few details, and I won't be calm until I've dispelled my doubts. I've decided to take a trip to Turkey, Greece, and Asia to look for a model and compare my picture to different types of natural beauties. Maybe," he went on, with a smile of satisfaction, "I've got nature herself upstairs. Sometimes I'm almost afraid that a breath of air might wake up that woman and she might disappear."

Then he suddenly rose, as if to depart.

"Oh, oh," Porbus replied, "I've come just in time to save you the expense and fatigue of the journey."

"How so?" asked Frenhofer in surprise.

"Young Poussin has a sweetheart whose incomparable beauty is totally flawless. But, dear master, if he agrees to lend her to you, at the very least you'll have to show us your canvas."

The old man just stood there, motionless, in a state of complete stupefaction.

"What!" he finally cried in sorrow. "Show my creation, my wife? Rend the veil with which I've chastely covered my happiness? But that would be a terrible prostitution! For ten years now I've been living with this woman; she's mine, only mine, she loves me. Hasn't she smiled at me at each brushstroke I've given her? She has a soul, the soul that I endowed her with. She would blush if anyone's eyes but mine were fixed on her. Show her! But where is the husband or lover so vile as to lead his wife to dishonor? When you paint a picture for the royal court, you don't put your whole soul into it; all you're selling to the courtiers is colored dummies. My kind of painting isn't painting, it's emotion, passion! She was born in my studio, she must remain there as a virgin, she can only leave when fully dressed. Poetry and women only surrender themselves naked to their lovers! Do we possess Raphael's model, Ariosto's Angelica, Dante's Beatrice? No, we only see their forms! Well, the picture I have under lock and key upstairs is something exceptional in our art. It isn't a canvas, it's a woman!—a woman with whom I weep, laugh, converse, and think. Do you want me suddenly to throw away ten years' happiness the way one throws off a coat? Do you want me suddenly to leave off being a father, a lover, God? That woman isn't a single creature, she's all of creation. Let your young man come; I'll give him my treasures, I'll give him pictures by Correggio, Michelangelo, Titian; I'll kiss the print of his feet in the dust; but make him my rival? Shame upon me! Ha, ha, I'm even more of a lover than I am a painter. Yes, I'll have the strength to burn my *Quarrelsome Beauty* with my dying breath; but to expose her to the eyes of a man, a young man, a painter? No, no! If anyone sullied her with a glance, I'd kill him the next day! I'd kill you on the spot, you, my friend, if you didn't salute her on your knees! Now do you want me to submit my idol to the cold eyes and stupid criticisms of imbeciles? Oh, love is a mystery, it lives only in the depths of our heart, and everything is ruined when a man says, even to his friend, 'This is the woman I love!'"

The old man seemed to have become young again; his eyes shone and were full of life; his pale cheeks were mottled with a vivid red, and his hands were trembling. Porbus, astonished at the passionate vehemence with which those words were uttered, had nothing to say in reply to a sentiment that was as novel as it was profound. Was Frenhofer in his right mind or mad? Was he under the spell of some artistic fancy, or were the ideas he had expressed the result of that indescribable fanaticism produced in us by the long gestation of a great work? Could one ever hope to come to terms with that odd passion?

A prey to all these thoughts, Porbus said to the old man, "But isn't it one woman for another? Isn't Poussin exposing his sweetheart to your eyes?"

"Some sweetheart!" Frenhofer replied. "She'll betray him sooner or later. Mine will always be faithful to me!"

"All right," Porbus continued, "let's drop the subject. But before you find, even in Asia, a woman as beautiful and perfect as the one I'm talking about, you may die without finishing your picture."

"Oh, it's finished," said Frenhofer. "Anyone who looked at it would imagine he saw a woman lying on a velvet bed beneath curtains. Near her, a golden tripod emits incense. You'd be tempted to take hold of the tassel of the cords that hold back the curtains, and you'd think you saw the bosom of Catherine Lescault, a beautiful courtesan nicknamed the *Quarrelsome Beauty*, heaving with her breath. And yet, I'd like to be sure . . ."

"Well, go to Asia," Porbus replied, detecting a sort of hesitation in Frenhofer's eyes.

And Porbus took a few steps toward the door of the room.

At that moment, Gillette and Nicolas Poussin had arrived near Frenhofer's dwelling. As the girl was about to go in, she freed herself from the painter's arm and recoiled as if gripped by some sudden presentiment.

"But what am I coming here for?" she asked her lover in deep tones, staring at him.

"Gillette, I've left it all up to you, and I want to obey you in all ways. You are my conscience and my glory. Go back to our room; I'll be happier, maybe, than if you . . ."

"Am I my own mistress when you speak to me that way? Oh, no, I'm only a child.—Let's go," she added, seeming to make a violent effort; "if our love dies and I'm laying in long days of regret for myself, won't your fame be the reward for my obedience to your wishes? Let's go in; being a kind of eternal memory on your palette will be like being still alive."

On opening the door to the house, the two lovers came upon Porbus; amazed at the beauty of Gillette, whose eyes were full of tears at the moment, he took hold of her as she stood there trembling and, leading her in to the old man, said, "Now, isn't she worth all the masterpieces in the world?"

Frenhofer gave a start. There was Gillette, in the naive, simple attitude of an innocent, frightened girl of Caucasian Georgia who has been kidnapped and is being presented by brigands to a slave dealer. A modest blush gave color to her face, she lowered her eyes, her hands hung at her sides, her strength seemed to desert her, and tears protested against the violence being done to her modesty. At that moment, Poussin, in despair at having let that beautiful treasure out of his garret, cursed himself. He became a lover foremost and an artist next; a thousand scruples tortured his heart when he saw the rejuvenated eyes of the old man, who, as painters do, was mentally undressing the girl, divining her most secret forms. Then he reverted to the fierce jealousy of true love.

"Gillette, let's go!" he cried.

At that tone, at that cry, his joyful sweetheart raised her eyes in his direction, saw him, and rushed into his arms.

"Oh, you do love me!" she replied, bursting into tears.

After having had the energy to be silent about her suffering, she had no more strength left to conceal her happiness.

"Oh, leave her with me for just a while," said the old painter, "and you'll compare her to my Catherine. Yes, I consent."

There was still love in Frenhofer's cry. He seemed to have a lover's vanity for his painted woman and to be enjoying in advance the victory that his virgin's beauty would win over that of a real girl.

"Don't let him go back on his word!" cried Porbus, tapping Poussin on the shoulder. "The fruits of love are quickly gone, those of art are immortal."

Looking hard at Poussin and Porbus, Gillette replied, "Am I nothing more than a woman to him?" She raised her head proudly; but when, after darting a fierce glance at Frenhofer, she saw her lover busy contemplating once again the portrait he had recently taken for a Giorgione, she said, "Ah! Let's go upstairs! He's never looked at me that way."

"Old man," Poussin resumed, torn from his meditation by Gillette's voice, "do you see this blade? I'll thrust it into your heart at the first word of complaint this girl utters; I'll set fire to your house, and no one will get out alive. Understand?"

Nicolas Poussin was somber, and his words were awesome. This attitude, and especially the young painter's gesture, consoled Gillette, who almost forgave him for sacrificing her to the art of painting and his glorious future. Porbus and Poussin remained at the studio door, looking at each other in silence. If at first the painter of St. Mary of Egypt permitted himself a few exclamations—"Ah, she's getting undressed; he's asking her to stand in the daylight! He's comparing her!"—soon he fell silent at the sight of Poussin, whose face showed deep sadness. And, even though elderly painters no longer feel such petty scruples in the presence of art, he admired them for being so naive and charming. The young man kept his hand on his dagger's hilt and his ear almost glued to the door. The two of them, standing there in the darkness, they looked like two conspirators awaiting the moment when they would strike down a tyrant.

"Come in, come in," called the old man, beaming with happiness. "My picture is perfect, and now I can show it with pride. Never will a painter, brushes, paints, canvas, or light create any rival to Catherine Lescault, the beautiful courtesan."

Prey to a keen curiosity, Porbus and Poussin rushed into the midst of a vast studio covered with dust, in which everything was in disorder, in which they saw here and there pictures hung on the walls. They first stopped in front of a life-size woman's figure, half draped, for which they were overcome with admiration.

"Oh, don't bother about that," said Frenhofer, "it's a canvas I daubed over to study a pose, it's a worthless picture. Here are my mistakes," he went on, showing them captivating compositions hanging on the walls all around them.

At these words, Porbus and Poussin, dumbfounded at this contempt for works of that merit, looked for the portrait they had been told about, but failed to catch sight of it.

"Well, here it is!" said the old man, whose hair was mussed, whose face was inflamed with a preternatural excitement, whose eyes sparkled, and who was panting like a young man drunk with love. "Ah, ha!" he cried. "You weren't expecting so much perfection! You're standing in front of a woman, and looking for a picture. There's such great depth to this canvas, the air in it is so real, that you can no longer distinguish it from the air that surrounds us. Where is art? Lost, vanished! Here are the very forms of a girl. Haven't I really captured her coloring, the lifelikeness of the line that seems to bound her body? Isn't it the same phenomenon that's offered to us by objects that exist within the atmosphere just as fish live in water? Don't you admire the way the contours stand out from the background? Don't you imagine that you could run your hand down that back? Thus, for seven years, I studied the effects of the mating of daylight and objects. And that hair, doesn't the light inundate it? . . . But she drew a breath, I think! . . . That bosom, see? Oh, who wouldn't want to worship her on his knees? The flesh is throbbing. She's going to stand up, just wait."

"Can you make out anything?" Poussin asked Porbus.

"No. What about you?"

"Not a thing."

The two painters left the old man to his ecstasy and looked to see whether the light, falling vertically onto the canvas he was showing them, wasn't neutralizing all its effects. Then they examined the painting, placing themselves to the right, to the left, straight in front of it, stooping down and getting up again in turns.

"Yes, yes, it's really a canvas," Frenhofer said to them, misunderstanding the purpose of that careful scrutiny. "Look, here's the stretcher, the easel; finally, here are my paints, my brushes."

And he took hold of a brush that he showed them in a naive gesture.

"The sly old fox is having a joke with us," said Poussin, coming back in front of the so-called painting. "All I see there is colors in a jumbled heap, contained within a multitude of peculiar lines that form a wall of paint."

"We're wrong. See?" Porbus said.

Coming closer, they could discern in a corner of the canvas the tip of a bare foot emerging from that chaos of colors, tints, and vague nuances, a sort of shapeless mist; but a delicious foot, a living foot! They stood awestruck with admiration before that fragment, which had escaped from an unbelievable, slow, and progressive destruction. That foot appeared there like the torso of some Parisian marble Venus rising up out of the ruins of a city that had been burned to the ground.

"There's a woman underneath all this!" cried Porbus, indicating to Poussin the layers of paint that the old painter had set down one over the other, in the belief that he was making his painting perfect.

The two painters spontaneously turned toward Frenhofer, beginning to understand, though only vaguely, the state of ecstasy in which he existed.

"He's speaking in good faith," said Porbus.

"Yes, my friend," replied the old man, awakening, "one must have faith, faith in art, and one must live with one's work for a long time in order to produce a creation like this. Some of these shadows cost me many labors. Look, on the cheek, beneath the eyes, there's a light penumbra that, if you observe it in nature, will seem all but uncapturable to you. Well, do you think that that effect didn't cost me unheard-of pains to reproduce? But also, dear Porbus, look at my piece attentively and you'll understand more fully what I was telling you about the way to handle modeling and contours. Look at the light on the bosom and see how, by a series of strokes and highlights done in heavy impasto, I succeeded in catching true daylight and combining it with the gleaming whiteness of the illuminated areas; and how, to achieve the converse effect, eliminating the ridges and grain of the paint, I was able, by dint of caressing the figure's contour, which is submerged in demitints, to remove the very notion of a drawn line and such artificial procedures, and to give it the very look and solidity of nature. Come close, you'll see better how I worked. From a distance, it can't be seen. There! In this spot, I think, it's highly remarkable."

And with the tip of his brush he pointed out a blob of bright paint to the two artists.

Porbus tapped the old man on the shoulder, turning toward Poussin. "Do you know that we have a very great painter in him?" he said.

"He's even more of a poet than a painter," Poussin replied gravely.

"This," continued Porbus, touching the canvas, "is the extreme limit of our art on earth."

"And from there it gets lost in the skies," said Poussin.

"How many pleasures in this bit of canvas!" exclaimed Porbus.

The old man, absorbed, wasn't listening to them but was smiling at that imaginary woman.

"But sooner or later he'll notice that there's nothing on his canvas!" cried Poussin.

"Nothing on my canvas!" said Frenhofer, looking by turns at the two painters and at his so-called picture.

"What have you done?" Porbus replied to Poussin.

The old man gripped the young man's arm violently, saying: "You see nothing, vagabond, good-for-nothing, cad, catamite! Why did you come up here, anyway?—My dear Porbus," he went on, turning to that painter, "could you too be making fun of me? Answer me! I'm your friend; tell me, have I really spoiled my picture?"

Porbus, undecided, didn't dare say a thing; but the anxiety depicted on the old man's pallid face was so cruel that he pointed to the canvas and said, "Just look!"

Frenhofer studied his picture for a moment and tottered.

"Nothing, nothing! And after working ten years on it!"

He sat down and began weeping.

"So I'm just an imbecile, a lunatic! So I have no talent, no ability; I'm just a rich man who, when he does something, merely does it! So I haven't created anything!"

He studied his canvas through his tears. Suddenly he stood up with pride and darted a furious glance at the two painters.

"By the blood, body, and head of Christ, you are envious men trying to make me believe that she's ruined, so you can steal her from me! *I* can see her!" he cried. "She's wonderfully beautiful."

At that moment, Poussin heard the weeping of Gillette, who had been forgotten in a corner.

"What's wrong, angel?" the painter asked her, suddenly becoming a lover again.

"Kill me!" she said. "I'd be a low creature if I still loved you, because I have contempt for you. I admire you, and you horrify me. I love you, and I think I hate you already."

While Poussin was listening to Gillette, Frenhofer was covering up his Catherine with a green serge, as gravely calm as a jeweler locking up his drawers because he thinks that skillful thieves are present. He threw the two painters a profoundly crafty look, full of scorn and suspicion, and silently turned them out of his studio, with convulsive haste. Then, on the threshold of his home, he said to them, "Farewell, my little friends."

That leave-taking chilled the hearts of the two painters. The next day, Porbus, worried, came to see Frenhofer again, and was informed that he had died during the night after burning his canvases.

QUESTIONS

1. What does Frenhofer mean when he says to Porbus, "The mission of art is not to copy nature but to express it"? (70)

2. While Frenhofer works on Porbus's painting, why does it appear to Poussin as if Frenhofer's body contains "a demon acting through his hands, seizing them eerily as if against the man's will"? (73)

3. Why is Frenhofer able to improve Porbus's painting with such assurance, while remaining plagued with doubt about his own painting?

4. Why does Poussin's experience with Frenhofer and Porbus make him begin to believe in himself and see himself as a painter?

5. Why does Poussin think that it will make him a great painter if Gillette poses for Frenhofer?

6. Why does Gillette agree to pose for another painter? Why does she love Poussin less after agreeing to his request?

7. What relationship does the story suggest between Gillette and the woman depicted in *Quarrelsome Beauty*?

8. Are we supposed to think that Frenhofer is "in his right mind" or "mad"? (82) According to the story, does madness play a role in the creation of great art?

9. Why won't Frenhofer allow anyone to see *Quarrelsome Beauty*?

10. Why does Frenhofer agree to show Porbus and Poussin the painting if Gillette poses for him?

11. Upon seeing *Quarrelsome Beauty*, what do Porbus and Poussin begin "to understand, though only vaguely," about "the state of ecstasy" in which Frenhofer exists? (85)

12. What does Porbus mean when he says that Frenhofer's painting is "the extreme limit of our art on earth"? (86)

13. Why does Frenhofer burn his canvases?

FOR FURTHER REFLECTION

1. What does *Quarrelsome Beauty* suggest about the nature of art?
2. Is there a relationship between art and madness?
3. Must artists hold their artistic aspirations in higher regard than their relationships with other people in order to produce great art?
4. Is it possible to establish objective criteria for evaluating a work of art?

LEO TOLSTOY

Count Leo Tolstoy (1828–1910), the fourth of five children, was born on his family's estate at Yasnaya Polyana, Russia. His mother died when he was two, and his father when he was nine; Tolstoy and his siblings were subsequently raised by a distant relative. Tolstoy was privately tutored, and at the age of sixteen he entered the Kazan University, where he showed some ability in the study of languages, but transferred to law. However, he was often distracted from his studies by his interest in drinking and gambling and his pursuit of women. In 1847, he left the university without a degree and returned home to manage the family estate, which he had inherited from his father.

Tolstoy was restless, though, and in the next few years he found himself spending most of his time in Moscow, about one hundred miles to the north, and in St. Petersburg, where he resumed study of the law. He also began to write, composing *Childhood,* the first volume of his autobiographical trilogy. He joined an older brother in the Caucasus in 1851 and volunteered to serve in the Russian army the next year, seeing combat against the Chechen insurgency. In 1854, during the Crimean War, he helped defend Sevastopol against British and French forces. Between 1852 and 1857 his autobiographical trilogy appeared in print.

After retiring from the service in 1856 and traveling in Europe for several years, Tolstoy returned to Russia, and in 1862 he married Sofya Andreyevna Behrs, the well-educated daughter of a Moscow doctor. The couple would have thirteen children. Over the next decade and a half, Tolstoy wrote the works that would establish his literary reputation: *The Cossacks* (1863), *War and Peace* (in six volumes, 1868–1869), and *Anna Karenina* (serialized, 1875–1877), the latter two novels generally considered among the greatest written in any language.

After *Anna Karenina*, Tolstoy turned increasingly toward a form of radical Christianity based on a literal interpretation of Christ's teachings. His pacifism and rejection of the notion of private property put him at odds with both the

Russian Orthodox Church, from which he was finally excommunicated in 1901, and his own family. He wrote voluminously during this period, mostly theological and moral works, but significant literature also continued to flow from his pen, including the classic story "The Death of Ivan Ilyich" (1886).

In his later years, Tolstoy was estranged from his wife, who thought that his utopian ideas were causing him to abdicate fiscal responsibility for his family and estate. Against his will, she took over the copyright to his works published before 1880, and oversaw the ongoing profitable publication of his most famous works.

At the age of eighty-two, after talking and writing for many years about the path of ascetic mysticism, Tolstoy determined to follow it. He left home in the middle of winter, and, several days later, died of pneumonia at the train station at Astapovo.

In addition to his sympathy for the plight of Russia's peasant class, Tolstoy developed deeply philosophical views about the nature of history. In *War and Peace*, Tolstoy depicts the lives of individual characters in the context of Napoleon's invasion of Russia. He believed this perspective to be truer to history's real mechanism than the simple claims that the commands of rulers or the force of abstract ideals determine historical events and outcomes. "The Second Epilogue to *War and Peace*" is Tolstoy's effort to articulate fully these ideas.

LEO TOLSTOY

Second Epilogue to *War and Peace*

History is the life of nations and of humanity. To seize and put into words, to describe directly the life of humanity or even of a single nation, appears impossible.

The ancient historians all employed one and the same method to describe and seize the apparently elusive—the life of a people. They described the activity of individuals who ruled the people, and regarded the activity of those men as representing the activity of the whole nation.

The question: how did individuals make nations act as they wished and by what was the will of these individuals themselves guided? The ancients met by recognizing a divinity which subjected the nations to the will of a chosen man, and guided the will of that chosen man so as to accomplish ends that were predestined.

For the ancients these questions were solved by a belief in the direct participation of the Deity in human affairs.

Modern history, in theory, rejects both these principles.

It would seem that having rejected the belief of the ancients in man's subjection to the Deity and in a predetermined aim toward which nations are led, modern history should study not the manifestations of power but the causes that produce it. But modern history has not done this. Having in theory rejected the view held by the ancients, it still follows them in practice.

Instead of men endowed with divine authority and directly guided by the will of God, modern history has given us either heroes endowed with extraordinary, superhuman capacities, or simply men of very various kinds, from monarchs to journalists, who lead the masses. Instead of the former divinely appointed aims of the Jewish, Greek, or Roman nations, which ancient historians regarded as representing the progress of humanity, modern history has postulated its own aims—the welfare of the French, German, or English people, or, in its highest abstraction, the welfare and civilization of humanity in general, by which is usually meant that of the peoples occupying a small northwesterly portion of a large continent.

Modern history has rejected the beliefs of the ancients without replacing them by a new conception, and the logic of the situation has obliged the historians, after they had apparently rejected the divine authority of the kings and the "fate" of the ancients, to reach the same conclusion by another road, that is, to recognize (1) nations guided by individual men, and (2) the existence of a known aim to which these nations and humanity at large are tending.

At the basis of the works of all the modern historians from Gibbon to Buckle, despite their seeming disagreements and the apparent novelty of their outlooks, lie those two old, unavoidable assumptions.

In the first place the historian describes the activity of individuals who in his opinion have directed humanity (one historian considers only monarchs, generals, and ministers as being such men, while another includes also orators, learned men, reformers, philosophers, and poets). Secondly, it is assumed that the goal toward which humanity is being led is known to the historians: to one of them this goal is the greatness of the Roman, Spanish, or French realm; to another it is liberty, equality, and a certain kind of civilization of a small corner of the world called Europe.

In 1789 a ferment arises in Paris; it grows, spreads, and is expressed by a movement of peoples from west to east. Several times it moves eastward and collides with a countermovement from the east westward. In 1812 it reaches its extreme limit, Moscow, and then, with remarkable symmetry, a countermovement occurs from east to west, attracting to it, as the first movement had done, the nations of middle Europe. The countermovement reaches the starting point of the first movement in the west—Paris—and subsides.

During that twenty-year period an immense number of fields were left untilled, houses were burned, trade changed its direction, millions of men migrated, were impoverished, or were enriched, and millions of Christian men professing the law of love of their fellows slew one another.

What does all this mean? Why did it happen? What made those people burn houses and slay their fellow men? What were the causes of these events? What force made men act so? These are the instinctive, plain, and most legitimate questions humanity asks itself when it encounters the monuments and tradition of that period.

For a reply to these questions the common sense of mankind turns to the science of history, whose aim is to enable nations and humanity to know themselves.

If history had retained the conception of the ancients it would have said that God, to reward or punish his people, gave Napoleon power and directed his will to the fulfillment of the divine ends, and that reply would have been clear and complete. One might believe or disbelieve in the divine significance of Napoleon, but for anyone believing in it there would have been nothing unintelligible in the history of that period, nor would there have been any contradictions.

But modern history cannot give that reply. Science does not admit the conception of the ancients as to the direct participation of the Deity in human affairs, and therefore history ought to give other answers.

Modern history replying to these questions says: you want to know what this movement means, what caused it, and what force produced these events? Then listen:

"Louis XIV was a very proud and self-confident man; he had such and such mistresses and such and such ministers and he ruled France badly. His descendants were weak men and they too ruled France badly. And they had such and such favorites and such and such mistresses. Moreover, certain men wrote some books at that time. At the end of the eighteenth century there were a couple of dozen men in Paris who began to talk about all men being free and equal. This caused people all over France to begin to slash at and drown one another. They killed the king and many other people. At that time there was in France a man of genius—Napoleon. He conquered everybody everywhere—that is, he killed many people because he was a great genius. And for some reason he went to kill Africans, and killed them so well and was so cunning and wise that when he returned to France he ordered everybody to obey him, and they all obeyed him. Having become an emperor he again went out to kill people in Italy, Austria, and Prussia. And there too he killed a great many. In Russia there was an emperor, Alexander, who decided to restore order in Europe and therefore fought against Napoleon. In 1807 he suddenly made friends with him, but in 1811 they again quarreled and again began killing many people. Napoleon led six hundred thousand men into Russia and captured Moscow; then he suddenly ran away from Moscow, and the Emperor Alexander, helped by the advice of Stein and others, united Europe to arm against the disturber of its peace. All Napoleon's allies suddenly became his enemies and their forces advanced against the fresh forces he raised. The Allies defeated Napoleon, entered Paris, forced Napoleon to abdicate, and sent him to the island of Elba, not depriving him of the title of emperor and showing him every respect, though five years before and one year later they all regarded him as an outlaw and a brigand. Then Louis XVIII, who till then had been the laughingstock both of the French and the Allies, began to reign. And Napoleon, shedding tears before his Old Guards, renounced the throne and went into exile. Then the skillful statesmen and diplomatists (especially Talleyrand, who managed to sit down in a particular chair before anyone else and thereby extended the frontiers of France) talked in Vienna and by these conversations made the nations happy or unhappy. Suddenly the diplomatists and monarchs nearly quarreled and were on the point of again ordering their armies to kill one another, but just then Napoleon arrived in France with a battalion, and the French, who had been hating him, immediately all submitted to him. But the Allied monarchs were angry at this and went to fight the French once more. And they defeated the genius Napoleon and, suddenly recognizing him as a brigand, sent him to the island of St. Helena. And the exile, separated from the beloved France so dear to his heart, died a lingering death on that rock and bequeathed his great deeds to posterity. But in Europe a reaction occurred and the sovereigns once again all began to oppress their subjects."

It would be a mistake to think that this is ironic—a caricature of the historical accounts. On the contrary it is a very mild expression of the contradictory replies, not meeting the questions, which *all* the historians give, from the compilers of memoirs and the histories of separate states to the writers of general histories and the new histories of the *culture* of that period.

The strangeness and absurdity of these replies arise from the fact that modern history, like a deaf man, answers questions no one has asked.

If the purpose of history be to give a description of the movement of humanity and of the peoples, the first question—in the absence of a reply to which all the rest will be incomprehensible—is: what is the power that moves peoples? To this, modern history laboriously replies either that Napoleon was a great genius, or that Louis XIV was very proud, or that certain writers wrote certain books.

All that may be so and mankind is ready to agree with it, but it is not what was asked. All that would be interesting if we recognized a divine power based on itself and always consistently directing its nations through Napoleons, Louis-es, and writers; but we do not acknowledge such a power, and therefore before speaking about Napoleons, Louis-es, and authors, we ought to be shown the connection existing between these men and the movement of the nations.

If instead of a divine power some other force has appeared, it should be explained in what this new force consists, for the whole interest of history lies precisely in that force.

History seems to assume that this force is self-evident and known to everyone. But in spite of every desire to regard it as known, anyone reading many historical works cannot help doubting whether this new force, so variously understood by the historians themselves, is really quite well known to everybody.

What force moves the nations?

Biographical historians and historians of separate nations understand this force as a power inherent in heroes and rulers. In their narration events occur solely by the will of a Napoleon, an Alexander, or in general, of the persons they describe. The answers given by this kind of historian to the question of what force causes events to happen are satisfactory only as long as there is but one historian to each event. As soon as historians of different nationalities and tendencies begin to describe the same event, the replies they give immediately lose all meaning, for this force is understood by them all not only differently but often in quite contradictory ways. One historian says that an event was produced by Napoleon's power, another that it was produced by Alexander's, a third that it was due to the power of some other person. Besides this, historians of that kind contradict each other even in their statement as to the force on which the authority of some particular person was based. Thiers, a Bonapartist, says that Napoleon's power was based on his virtue and genius. Lanfrey, a Republican, says it was based on his trickery and deception of the people. So the historians of this class, by mutually destroying one another's positions, destroy the understanding of the force which produces events, and furnish no reply to history's essential question.

Writers of universal history who deal with all the nations seem to recognize how erroneous is the specialist historians' view of the force which produces events. They do not recognize it as a power inherent in heroes and rulers, but as the resultant of a multiplicity of variously directed forces. In describing a war or the subjugation of a people, a general historian looks for the cause of the event not in the power of one man, but in the interaction of many persons connected with the event.

According to this view the power of historical personages, represented as the product of many forces, can no longer, it would seem, be regarded as a force that itself produces events. Yet in most cases universal historians still employ the conception of power as a force that itself produces events, and treat it as their cause. In their exposition, a historic character is first the product of his time, and his power only the resultant of various forces, and then his power is itself a force producing events. Gervinus, Schlosser, and others, for instance, at one time prove Napoleon to be a product of the Revolution, of the ideas of 1789 and so forth, and at another plainly say that the campaign of 1812 and other things they do not like were simply the product of Napoleon's misdirected will, and that the very ideas of 1789 were arrested in their development by Napoleon's caprice. The ideas of the Revolution and the general temper of the age produced Napoleon's power. But Napoleon's power suppressed the ideas of the Revolution and the general temper of the age.

This curious contradiction is not accidental. Not only does it occur at every step, but the universal historians' accounts are all made up of a chain of such contradictions. This contradiction occurs because after entering the field of analysis the universal historians stop halfway.

To find component forces equal to the composite or resultant force, the sum of the components must equal the resultant. This condition is never observed by the universal historians, and so to explain the resultant forces they are obliged to admit, in addition to the insufficient components, another unexplained force affecting the resultant action.

Specialist historians describing the campaign of 1813 or the restoration of the Bourbons plainly assert that these events were produced by the will of Alexander. But the universal historian Gervinus, refuting this opinion of the specialist historian, tries to prove that the campaign of 1813 and the restoration of the Bourbons were due to other things beside Alexander's will—such as the activity of Stein, Metternich, Madame de Staël, Talleyrand, Fichte, Chateaubriand, and others. The historian evidently decomposes Alexander's power into the components: Talleyrand, Chateaubriand, and the rest—but the sum of the components, that is, the interactions of Chateaubriand, Talleyrand, Madame de Staël, and the others, evidently does not equal the resultant, namely the phenomenon of millions of Frenchmen submitting to the Bourbons. That Chateaubriand, Madame de Staël, and others spoke certain words to one another only affected their mutual relations but does not account for the submission of millions. And therefore to explain how from these relations of theirs the submission of millions of people resulted—that is, how component forces equal to one *A* gave a resultant equal to a thousand times *A*—the historian is again obliged to fall back on power—the force he had denied—and to recognize it as the resultant of the forces, that is, he has to admit an unexplained force acting on the resultant. And that is just what the universal historians do, and consequently they not only contradict the specialist historians but contradict themselves.

Peasants having no clear idea of the cause of rain, say, according to whether they want rain or fine weather: "The wind has blown the clouds away," or, "The wind has brought up the clouds." And in the same way the universal historians sometimes, when it pleases them and fits in with their theory, say that power is the result of events, and sometimes, when they want to prove something else, say that power produces events.

A third class of historians—the so-called historians of culture—following the path laid down by the universal historians who sometimes accept writers and ladies as forces producing events—again take that force to be something quite different. They see it in what is called culture—in mental activity.

The historians of culture are quite consistent in regard to their progenitors, the writers of universal histories, for if historical events may be explained by the fact that certain persons treated one another in such and such ways, why not explain them by the fact that such and such people wrote such and such books? Of the immense number of indications accompanying every vital phenomenon, these historians select the indication of intellectual activity and say that this indication is the cause. But despite their endeavors to prove that the cause of events lies in intellectual activity, only by a great stretch can one admit that there is any connection between intellectual activity and the movement of peoples, and in no case can one admit that intellectual activity controls people's actions, for that view is not confirmed by such facts as the very cruel murders of the French Revolution resulting from the doctrine of the equality of man, or the very cruel wars and executions resulting from the preaching of love.

But even admitting as correct all the cunningly devised arguments with which these histories are filled—admitting that nations are governed by some undefined force called an *idea*—history's essential question still remains unanswered, and to the former power of monarchs and to the influence of advisers and other people introduced by the universal historians, another, newer force—the *idea*—is added, the connection of which with the masses needs explanation. It is possible to understand that Napoleon had power and so events occurred; with some effort one may even conceive that Napoleon together with other influences was the cause of an event; but how a book, *Le contrat social*, had the effect of making Frenchmen begin to drown one another cannot be understood without an explanation of the casual nexus of this new force with the event.

Undoubtedly some relation exists between all who live contemporaneously, and so it is possible to find some connection between the intellectual activity of men and their historical movements, just as such a connection may be found between the movements of humanity and commerce, handicraft, gardening, or anything else you please. But why intellectual activity is considered by the historians of culture to be the cause or expression of the whole historical movement is hard to understand. Only the following considerations can have led the historians to such a conclusion: (1) that history is written by learned men, and so it is natural and agreeable for them to think that the activity of their class supplies the basis of the movement of all humanity, just as a similar belief is natural and agreeable to traders, agriculturists, and soldiers (if they do not express it, that is merely because traders and soldiers do not write history); and (2) that spiritual activity, enlightenment, civilization, culture, ideas, are all indistinct, indefinite conceptions under whose banner it is very easy to use words having a still less definite meaning, and which can therefore be readily introduced into any theory.

But not to speak of the intrinsic quality of histories of this kind (which may possibly even be of use to someone for something) the histories of culture, to which all general histories tend more and more to approximate, are significant from the fact that after seriously and minutely examining various religious, philosophic, and political doctrines as causes of events, as soon as they have to describe an actual historic event such as the campaign of 1812 for instance, they involuntarily describe it as resulting from an exercise of power—and say plainly that that campaign was the result of Napoleon's will. Speaking so, the historians of culture involuntarily contradict themselves, and show that the new force they have devised does not account for what happens in history, and that history can only be explained by introducing a power which they apparently do not recognize.

A locomotive is moving. Someone asks: "What moves it?" A peasant says the devil moves it. Another man says the locomotive moves because its wheels go round. A third asserts that the cause of its movement lies in the smoke which the wind carries away.

The peasant is irrefutable. He has devised a complete explanation. To refute him someone would have to prove to him that there is no devil, or another peasant would have to explain to him that it is not the devil but a German who moves the locomotive. Only then, as a result of the contradiction, will they see that they are both wrong. But the man who says that the movement of the wheels is the cause refutes himself, for having once begun to analyze he ought to go on and explain further why the wheels go round; and till he has reached the ultimate cause of the movement of the locomotive in the pressure of steam in the boiler, he has no right to stop in his search for the cause. The man who explains the movement of the locomotive by the smoke that is carried back has noticed that the wheels do not supply an explanation and has taken the first sign that occurs to him and in his turn has offered that as an explanation.

The only conception that can explain the movement of the locomotive is that of a force commensurate with the movement observed.

The only conception that can explain the movement of the peoples is that of some force commensurate with the whole movement of the peoples.

Yet to supply this conception various historians take forces of different kinds, all of which are incommensurate with the movement observed. Some see it as a force directly inherent in heroes, as the peasant sees the devil in the locomotive; others as a force resulting from several other forces, like the movement of the wheels; others again as an intellectual influence, like the smoke that is blown away.

So long as histories are written of separate individuals, whether Caesars, Alexanders, Luthers, or Voltaires, and not the histories of *all*, absolutely *all* those who take part in an event, it is quite impossible to describe the movement of humanity without the conception of a force compelling men to direct their activity toward a certain end. And the only such conception known to historians is that of power.

This conception is the one handle by means of which the material of history, as at present expounded, can be dealt with, and anyone who breaks that handle off, as Buckle did, without finding some other method of treating historical material, merely deprives himself of the one possible way of dealing with it. The necessity of the conception of power as an explanation of historical events is best demonstrated by the universal historians and historians of culture themselves, for they professedly reject that conception but inevitably have recourse to it at every step.

In dealing with humanity's inquiry, the science of history up to now is like money in circulation—paper money and coin. The biographies and special national histories are like paper money. They can be used and can circulate and fulfill their purpose without harm to anyone and even advantageously, as long as no one asks what is the security behind them. You need only forget to ask how the will of heroes produces events, and such histories as Thiers's will be interesting and instructive and may perhaps even possess a tinge of poetry. But just as doubts of the real value of paper money arise either because, being easy to make, too much of it gets made or because people try to exchange it for gold, so also doubts concerning the real value of such histories arise either because too many of them are written or because in his simplicity of heart someone inquires: by what force did Napoleon do this?—that is, wants to exchange the current paper money for the real gold of actual comprehension.

The writers of universal histories and of the history of culture are like people who, recognizing the defects of paper money, decide to substitute for it money made of metal that has not the specific gravity of gold. It may indeed make jingling coin, but will do no more than that. Paper money may deceive the ignorant, but nobody is deceived by tokens of base metal that have no value but merely jingle. As gold is gold only if it is serviceable not merely for exchange but also for use, so universal historians will be valuable only when they can reply to history's essential question: what is power? The universal historians give contradictory replies to that question, while the historians of culture evade it and answer something quite different. And as counters of imitation gold can be used only among a group of people who agree to accept them as gold, or among those who do not know the nature of gold, so universal historians and historians of culture, not answering humanity's essential question, serve as currency for some purposes of their own, only in universities and among the mass of readers who have a taste for what they call "serious reading."

Having abandoned the conception of the ancients as to the divine subjection of the will of a nation to some chosen man and the subjection of that man's will to the Deity, history cannot without contradictions take a single step till it has chosen one of two things: either a return to the former belief in the direct intervention of the Deity in human affairs or a definite explanation of the meaning of the force producing historical events and termed *power*.

A return to the first is impossible, the belief has been destroyed; and so it is essential to explain what is meant by power.

Napoleon ordered an army to be raised and go to war. We are so accustomed to that idea and have become so used to it that the question: why did six hundred thousand men go to fight when Napoleon uttered certain words, seems to us senseless. He had the power and so what he ordered was done.

This reply is quite satisfactory if we believe that the power was given him by God. But as soon as we do not admit that, it becomes essential to determine what is this power of one man over others.

It cannot be the direct physical power of a strong man over a weak one—a domination based on the application or threat of physical force, like the power of Hercules; nor can it be based on the effect of moral force, as in their simplicity some historians think who say that the leading figures in history are heroes, that is, men gifted with a special strength of soul and mind called genius. This power cannot be based on the predominance of moral strength, for, not to mention heroes such as Napoleon about whose moral qualities opinions differ widely, history shows us that neither a Louis XI nor a Metternich, who ruled over millions of people, had any particular moral qualities, but on the contrary were generally morally weaker than any of the millions they ruled over.

If the source of power lies neither in the physical nor in the moral qualities of him who possesses it, it must evidently be looked for elsewhere—in the relation to the people of the man who wields the power.

And that is how power is understood by the science of jurisprudence, that exchange bank of history which offers to exchange history's understanding of power for true gold.

Power is the collective will of the people transferred, by expressed or tacit consent, to their chosen rulers.

In the domain of jurisprudence, which consists of discussions of how a state and power might be arranged were it possible for all that to be arranged, it is all very clear; but when applied to history that definition of power needs explanation.

The science of jurisprudence regards the state and power as the ancients regarded fire—namely, as something existing absolutely. But for history, the state and power are merely phenomena, just as for modern physics fire is not an element but a phenomenon.

From this fundamental difference between the view held by history and that held by jurisprudence, it follows that jurisprudence can tell minutely how in its opinion power should be constituted and what power—existing immutably outside time—is, but to history's questions about the meaning of the mutations of power *in* time it can answer nothing.

If power be the collective will of the people transferred to their ruler, was Pugachëv a representative of the will of the people? If not, then why was Napoleon I? Why was Napoleon III a criminal when he was taken prisoner at Boulogne, and why, later on, were those criminals whom he arrested?

Do palace revolutions—in which sometimes only two or three people take part—transfer the will of the people to a new ruler? In international relations, is the will of the people also transferred to their conqueror? Was the will of the Confederation of the Rhine transferred to Napoleon in 1806? Was the will of the Russian people transferred to Napoleon in 1809, when our army in alliance with the French went to fight the Austrians?

To these questions three answers are possible:

Either to assume (1) that the will of the people is always unconditionally transferred to the ruler or rulers they have chosen, and that therefore every emergence of a new power, every struggle against the power once appointed, should be absolutely regarded as an infringement of the real power; or (2) that the will of the people is transferred to the rulers conditionally, under definite and known conditions, and to show that all limitations, conflicts, and even destructions of power result from a nonobservance by the rulers of the conditions under which their power was entrusted to them; or (3) that the will of the people is delegated to the rulers conditionally, but that the conditions are unknown and indefinite, and that the appearance of several authorities, their struggles and their falls, result solely from the greater or lesser fulfillment by the rulers of these unknown conditions on which the will of the people is transferred from some people to others.

And these are the three ways in which the historians do explain the relation of the people to their rulers.

Some historians—those biographical and specialist historians already referred to—in their simplicity failing to understand the question of the meaning of power, seem to consider that the collective will of the people is unconditionally transferred to historical persons, and therefore when describing some single state they assume that particular power to be the one absolute and real power, and that any other force opposing this is not a power but a violation of power—mere violence.

Their theory, suitable for primitive and peaceful periods of history, has the inconvenience—in application to complex and stormy periods in the life of nations during which various powers arise simultaneously and struggle with one another—that a Legitimist historian will prove that the National Convention, the Directory, and Bonaparte were mere infringers of the true power, while a Republican and a Bonapartist will prove: the one that the Convention and the other that the Empire was the real power, and that all the others were violations of power. Evidently the explanations furnished by these historians being mutually contradictory can only satisfy young children.

Recognizing the falsity of this view of history, another set of historians say that power rests on a conditional delegation of the will of the people to their rulers, and that historical leaders have power only conditionally on carrying out the program that the will of the people has by tacit agreement prescribed to them. But what this program consists in these historians do not say, or if they do they continually contradict one another.

Each historian, according to his view of what constitutes a nation's progress, looks for these conditions in the greatness, wealth, freedom, or enlightenment of the citizens of France or some other country. But not to mention the historians' contradictions as to the nature of this program—or even admitting that some one general program of these conditions exists—the facts of history almost always contradict that theory. If the conditions under which power is entrusted consist in the wealth, freedom, and enlightenment of the people, how is it that Louis XIV and Ivan the Terrible end their reigns tranquilly, while Louis XVI and Charles I are executed by their people? To this question historians reply that Louis XIV's activity, contrary to the program, reacted on Louis XVI. But why did it not react on Louis XIV or on Louis XV—why should it react just on Louis XVI? And what is the time limit for such reactions? To these questions there are and can be no answers. Equally little does this view explain why for several centuries the collective will is not withdrawn from certain rulers and their heirs, and then suddenly during a period of fifty years is transferred to the Convention, to the Directory, to Napoleon, to Alexander, to Louis XVIII, to Napoleon again, to Charles X, to Louis Philippe, to a Republican government, and to Napoleon III. When explaining these rapid transfers of the people's will from one individual to another, especially in view of international relations, conquests, and alliances, the historians are obliged to admit that some of these transfers are not normal delegations of the people's will but are accidents dependent on cunning, on mistakes, on craft, or on the weakness of a diplomatist, a ruler, or a party leader. So that the greater part of the events of history—civil wars, revolutions, and conquests—are presented by these historians not as the results of free transferences of the people's will, but as results of the ill-directed will of one or more individuals, that is, once again, as usurpations of power. And so these historians also see and admit historical events which are exceptions to the theory.

These historians resemble a botanist who, having noticed that some plants grow from seeds producing two cotyledons, should insist that all that grows does so by sprouting into two leaves, and that the palm, the mushroom, and even the oak, which blossom into full growth and no longer resemble two leaves, are deviations from the theory.

Historians of the third class assume that the will of the people is transferred to historic personages conditionally, but that the conditions are unknown to us. They say that historical personages have power only because they fulfill the will of the people which has been delegated to them.

But in that case, if the force that moves nations lies not in the historic leaders but in the nations themselves, what significance have those leaders?

The leaders, these historians tell us, express the will of the people; the activity of the leaders represents the activity of the people.

But in that case the question arises whether all the activity of the leaders serves as an expression of the people's will, or only some part of it. If the whole activity of the leaders serves as the expression of the people's will, as some historians suppose, then all the details of the court scandals contained in the biographies of a Napoleon or a Catherine serve to express the life of the nation, which is evident nonsense; but if it is only some particular side of the activity of an historical leader which serves to express the people's life, as other so-called philosophical historians believe, then to determine which side of the activity of a leader expresses the nation's life, we have first of all to know in what the nation's life consists.

Met by this difficulty historians of that class devise some most obscure, impalpable, and general abstraction which can cover all conceivable occurrences, and declare this abstraction to be the aim of humanity's movement. The most usual generalizations adopted by almost all the historians are: freedom, equality, enlightenment, progress, civilization, and culture. Postulating some generalization as the goal of the movement of humanity, the historians study the men of whom the greatest number of monuments have remained: kings, ministers, generals, authors, reformers, popes, and journalists, to the extent to which in their opinion these persons have promoted or hindered that abstraction. But as it is in no way proved that the aim of humanity does consist in freedom, equality, enlightenment, or civilization, and as the connection of the people with the rulers and enlighteners of humanity is only based on the arbitrary assumption that the collective will of the people is always transferred to the men whom we have noticed, it happens that the activity of the millions who migrate, burn houses, abandon agriculture, and destroy one another never is expressed in the account of the activity of some dozen people who did not burn houses, practice agriculture, or slay their fellow creatures.

History proves this at every turn. Is the ferment of the peoples of the west at the end of the eighteenth century and their drive eastward explained by the activity of Louis XIV, XV, and XVI, their mistresses and ministers, and by the lives of Napoleon, Rousseau, Diderot, Beaumarchais, and others?

Is the movement of the Russian people eastward to Kazan and Siberia expressed by details of the morbid character of Ivan the Terrible and by his correspondence with Kurbsky?

Is the movement of the peoples at the time of the Crusades explained by the life and activity of the Godfreys and the Louis-es and their ladies? For us that movement of the peoples from west to east, without leaders, with a crowd of vagrants, and with Peter the Hermit, remains incomprehensible. And yet more incomprehensible is the cessation of that movement when a rational and sacred aim for the Crusade—the deliverance of Jerusalem—had been clearly defined by historic leaders. Popes, kings, and knights incited the peoples to free the Holy Land; but the people did not go, for the unknown cause which had previously impelled them to go no longer existed. The history of the Godfreys and the Minnesingers can evidently not cover the life of the peoples. And the history of the Godfreys and the Minnesingers has remained the history of Godfreys and Minnesingers, but the history of the life of the peoples and their impulses has remained unknown.

Still less does the history of authors and reformers explain to us the life of the peoples.

The history of culture explains to us the impulses and conditions of life and thought of a writer or a reformer. We learn that Luther had a hot temper and said such and such things; we learn that Rousseau was suspicious and wrote such and such books; but we do not learn why after the Reformation the peoples massacred one another, nor why during the French Revolution they guillotined one another.

If we unite both these kinds of history, as is done by the newest historians, we shall have the history of monarchs and writers, but not the history of the life of the peoples.

The life of the nations is not contained in the lives of a few men, for the connection between those men and the nations has not been found. The theory that this connection is based on the transference of the collective will of a people to certain historical personages is a hypothesis unconfirmed by the experience of history.

The theory of the transference of the collective will of the people to historic persons may perhaps explain much in the domain of jurisprudence and be essential for its purposes, but in its application to history, as soon as revolutions, conquests, or civil wars occur—that is, as soon as history begins—that theory explains nothing.

The theory seems irrefutable just because the act of transference of the people's will cannot be verified, for it never occurred.

Whatever happens and whoever may stand at the head of affairs, the theory can always say that such and such a person took the lead because the collective will was transferred to him.

The replies this theory gives to historical questions are like the replies of a man who, watching the movements of a herd of cattle and paying no attention to the varying quality of the pasturage in different parts of the field, or to the driving of the herdsman, should attribute the direction the herd takes to what animal happens to be at its head.

"The herd goes in that direction because the animal in front leads it and the collective will of all the other animals is vested in that leader." This is what historians of the first class say—those who assume the unconditional transference of the people's will.

"If the animals leading the herd change, this happens because the collective will of all the animals is transferred from one leader to another, according to whether the animal is or is not leading them in the direction selected by the whole herd." Such is the reply of historians who assume that the collective will of the people is delegated to rulers under conditions which they regard as known. (With this method of observation it often happens that the observer, influenced by the direction he himself prefers, regards those as leaders who, owing to the people's change of direction, are no longer in front, but on one side, or even in the rear.)

"If the animals in front are continually changing and the direction of the whole herd is constantly altered, this is because in order to follow a given direction the animals transfer their will to the animals that have attracted our attention, and to study the movements of the herd we must watch the movements of all the prominent animals moving on all sides of the herd." So say the third class of historians who regard all historical persons, from monarchs to journalists, as the expression of their age.

The theory of the transference of the will of the people to historic persons is merely a paraphrase—a restatement of the question in other words.

What causes historical events? Power. What is power? Power is the collective will of the people transferred to one person. Under what condition is the will of the people delegated to one person? On condition that that person expresses the will of the whole people. That is, power is power: in other words, power is a word the meaning of which we do not understand.

If the realm of human knowledge were confined to abstract reasoning, then having subjected to criticism the explanation of power that juridical science gives us, humanity would conclude that power is merely a word and has no real existence. But to understand phenomena man has, besides abstract reasoning, experience by which he verifies his reflections. And experience tells us that power is not merely a word but an actually existing phenomenon.

Not to speak of the fact that no description of the collective activity of men can do without the conception of power, the existence of power is proved both by history and by observing contemporary events.

Whenever an event occurs a man appears or men appear, by whose will the event seems to have taken place. Napoleon III issues a decree and the French go to Mexico. The King of Prussia and Bismarck issue decrees and an army enters Bohemia. Napoleon I issues a decree and an army enters Russia. Alexander I gives a command and the French submit to the Bourbons. Experience shows us that whatever event occurs it is always related to the will of one or of several men who have decreed it.

The historians, in accord with the old habit of acknowledging divine intervention in human affairs, want to see the cause of events in the expression of the will of someone endowed with power, but that supposition is not confirmed either by reason or by experience.

On the one side reflection shows that the expression of a man's will—his words—are only part of the general activity expressed in an event, as for instance in a war or a revolution, and so without assuming an incomprehensible, supernatural force—a miracle—one cannot admit that words can be the immediate cause of the movements of millions of men. On the other hand, even if we admitted that words could be the cause of events, history shows that the expression of the will of historical personages does not in most cases produce any effect, that is to say, their commands are often not executed, and sometimes the very opposite of what they order occurs.

Without admitting divine intervention in the affairs of humanity we cannot regard power as the cause of events.

Power, from the standpoint of experience, is merely the relation that exists between the expression of someone's will and the execution of that will by others.

To explain the conditions of that relationship we must first establish a conception of the expression of will, referring it to man and not to the Deity.

If the Deity issues a command, expresses his will, as ancient history tells us, the expression of that will is independent of time and is not caused by anything, for the Divinity is not controlled by an event. But speaking of commands that are the expression of the will of men acting in time and in relation to one another, to explain the connection of commands with events we must restore (1) the condition of all that takes place—the continuity of movement in time both of the events and of the person who commands, and (2) the inevitability of the connection between the person commanding and those who execute his command.

Only the expression of the will of the Deity, not dependent on time, can relate to a whole series of events occurring over a period of years or centuries, and only the Deity, independent of everything, can by his sole will determine the direction of humanity's movement; but man acts in time and himself takes part in what occurs.

Reinstating the first condition omitted, that of time, we see that no command can be executed without some preceding order having been given rendering the execution of the last command possible.

No command ever appears spontaneously, or itself covers a whole series of occurrences; but each command follows from another, and never refers to a whole series of events but always to one moment only of an event.

When, for instance, we say that Napoleon ordered armies to go to war, we combine in one simultaneous expression a whole series of consecutive commands dependent one on another. Napoleon could not have commanded an invasion of Russia and never did so. Today he ordered such and such papers to be written to Vienna, to Berlin, and to Petersburg; tomorrow such and such decrees and orders to the army, the fleet, the commissariat, and so on and so on—millions of commands, which formed a whole series corresponding to a series of events which brought the French armies into Russia.

If throughout his reign Napoleon gave commands concerning an invasion of England and expended on no other undertaking so much time and effort, and yet during his whole reign never once attempted to execute that design but undertook an expedition into Russia, with which country he considered it desirable to be in alliance (a conviction he repeatedly expressed)—this came about because his commands did not correspond to the course of events in the first case, but did so correspond in the latter.

For an order to be certainly executed, it is necessary that a man should order what can be executed. But to know what can and what cannot be executed is impossible, not only in the case of Napoleon's invasion of Russia in which millions participated, but even in the simplest event, for in either case millions of obstacles may arise to prevent its execution. Every order executed is always one of an immense number unexecuted. All the impossible orders inconsistent with the course of events remain unexecuted. Only the possible ones get linked up with a consecutive series of commands corresponding to a series of events, and are executed.

Our false conception that an event is caused by a command which precedes it is due to the fact that when the event has taken place and out of thousands of others those few commands which were consistent with that event have been executed, we forget about the others that were not executed because they could not be. Apart from that, the chief source of our error in this matter is due to the fact that in the historical accounts a whole series of innumerable, diverse, and petty events, such for instance as all those which led the French armies to Russia, is generalized into one event in accord with the result produced by that series of events, and corresponding with this generalization the whole series of commands is also generalized into a single expression of will.

We say that Napoleon wished to invade Russia and invaded it. In reality in all Napoleon's activity we never find anything resembling an expression of that wish, but find a series of orders, or expressions of his will, very variously and indefinitely directed. Amid a long series of unexecuted orders of Napoleon's one series, for the campaign of 1812, was carried out—not because those orders differed in any way from the other, unexecuted orders but because they coincided with the course of events that led the French army into Russia; just as in stencil work this or that figure comes out not because the color was laid on from this side or in that way, but because it was laid on from all sides over the figure cut in the stencil.

So that examining the relation in time of the commands to the events, we find that a command can never be the cause of the event, but that a certain definite dependence exists between the two.

To understand in what this dependence consists it is necessary to reinstate another omitted condition of every command proceeding not from the Deity but from a man, which is, that the man who gives the command himself takes part in the event.

This relation of the commander to those he commands is just what is called power. This relation consists in the following:

For common action people always unite in certain combinations, in which regardless of the difference of the aims set for the common action, the relation between those taking part in it is always the same.

Men uniting in these combinations always assume such relations toward one another that the larger number take a more direct share, and the smaller number a less direct share, in the collective action for which they have combined.

Of all the combinations in which men unite for collective action one of the most striking and definite examples is an army.

Every army is composed of lower grades of the service—the rank and file—of whom there are always the greatest number; of the next higher military rank—corporals and noncommissioned officers of whom there are fewer, and of still-higher officers of whom there are still fewer, and so on to the highest military command which is concentrated in one person.

A military organization may be quite correctly compared to a cone, of which the base with the largest diameter consists of the rank and file; the next higher and smaller section of the cone consists of the next higher grades of the army, and so on to the apex, the point of which will represent the commander in chief.

The soldiers, of whom there are the most, form the lower section of the cone and its base. The soldier himself does the stabbing, hacking, burning, and pillaging, and always receives orders for these actions from men above him; he himself never gives an order. The noncommissioned officers (of whom there are fewer) perform the action less frequently than the soldiers, but they already give commands. An officer still less often acts directly himself, but commands still more frequently. A general does nothing but command the troops, indicates the objective, and hardly ever uses a weapon himself. The commander in chief never takes direct part in the action itself, but only gives general orders concerning the movement of the mass of the troops. A similar relation of people to one another is seen in every combination of men for common activity—in agriculture, trade, and every administration.

And so without particularly analyzing all the contiguous sections of a cone and of the ranks of an army, or the ranks and positions in any administrative or public business whatever from the lowest to the highest, we see a law by which men, to take associated action, combine in such relations that the more directly they participate in performing the action the less they can command and the more numerous they are, while the less their direct participation in the action itself, the more they command and the fewer of them there are; rising in this way from the lowest ranks to the man at the top, who takes the least direct share in the action and directs his activity chiefly to commanding.

This relation of the men who command to those they command is what constitutes the essence of the conception called power.

Having restored the condition of time under which all events occur, we find that a command is executed only when it is related to a corresponding series of events. Restoring the essential condition of relation between those who command and those who execute, we find that by the very nature of the case those who command take the smallest part in the action itself and that their activity is exclusively directed to commanding.

When an event is taking place people express their opinions and wishes about it and as the event results from the collective activity of many people, some one of the opinions or wishes expressed is sure to be fulfilled if but approximately. When one of the opinions expressed is fulfilled, that opinion gets connected with the event as a command preceding it.

Men are hauling a log. Each of them expresses his opinion as to how and where to haul it. They haul the log away, and it happens that this is done as one of them said. He *ordered* it. There we have command and power in their primary form. The man who worked most with his hands could not think so much about what he was doing, or reflect on or command what would result from the common activity; while the man who commanded more would evidently work less with his hands on account of his greater verbal activity.

When some larger concourse of men direct their activity to a common aim there is a yet sharper division of those who, because their activity is given to directing and commanding, take less part in the direct work.

When a man works alone he always has a certain set of reflections which, as it seems to him, directed his past activity, justify his present activity, and guide him in planning his future actions. Just the same is done by a concourse of people, allowing those who do not take a direct part in the activity to devise considerations, justifications, and surmises concerning their collective activity.

For reasons known or unknown to us, the French began to drown and kill one another. And corresponding to the event its justification appears in people's belief that this was necessary for the welfare of France, for liberty, and for equality. People ceased to kill one another, and this event was accompanied by its justification in the necessity for a centralization of power, resistance to Europe, and so on. Men went from the west to the east killing their fellow men, and the event was accompanied by phrases about the glory of France, the baseness of England, and so on. History shows us that these justifications of the events have no common sense and are all contradictory, as in the case of killing a man as the result of recognizing his rights, and the killing of millions in Russia for the humiliation of England. But these justifications have a very necessary significance in their own day.

These justifications release those who produce the events from moral responsibility. These temporary aims are like the broom fixed in front of a locomotive to clear the snow from the rails in front: they clear men's moral responsibilities from their path.

Without such justification there would be no reply to the simplest question that presents itself when examining each historical event. How is it that millions of men commit collective crimes—make war, commit murder, and so on?

With the present complex forms of political and social life in Europe, can any event that is not prescribed, decreed, or ordered by monarchs, ministers, parliaments, or newspapers be imagined? Is there any collective action which cannot find its justification in political unity, in patriotism, in the balance of power, or in civilization? So that every event that occurs inevitably coincides with some expressed wish and, receiving a justification, presents itself as the result of the will of one man or of several men.

In whatever direction a ship moves, the flow of the waves it cuts will always be noticeable ahead of it. To those on board the ship the movement of those waves will be the only perceptible motion.

Only by watching closely moment by moment the movement of that flow and comparing it with the movement of the ship do we convince ourselves that every bit of it is occasioned by the forward movement of the ship, and that we were led into error by the fact that we ourselves were imperceptibly moving.

We see the same if we watch moment by moment the movement of historical characters (that is, reestablish the inevitable condition of all that occurs—the continuity of movement in time) and do not lose sight of the essential connection of historical persons with the masses.

When the ship moves in one direction there is one and the same wave ahead of it, when it turns frequently the wave ahead of it also turns frequently. But wherever it may turn there always will be the wave anticipating its movement.

Whatever happens it always appears that just that event was foreseen and decreed. Wherever the ship may go, the rush of water which neither directs nor increases its movement foams ahead of it, and at a distance seems to us not merely to move of itself but to govern the ship's movement also.

Examining only those expressions of the will of historical persons which, as commands, were related to events, historians have assumed that the events depended on those commands. But examining the events themselves and the connection in which the historical persons stood to the people, we have found that they and their orders were dependent on events. The incontestable proof of this deduction is that, however many commands were issued, the event does not take place unless there are other causes for it, but as soon as an event occurs—be it what it may—then out of all the continually expressed wishes of different people some will always be found which by their meaning and their time of utterance are related as commands to the events.

Arriving at this conclusion we can reply directly and positively to these two essential questions of history:

(1) What is power?

(2) What force produces the movement of the nations?

(1) Power is the relation of a given person to other individuals, in which the more this person expresses opinions, predictions, and justifications of the collective action that is performed, the less is his participation in that action.

(2) The movement of nations is caused not by power, nor by intellectual activity, nor even by a combination of the two, as historians have supposed, but by the activity of *all* the people who participate in the events, and who always combine in such a way that those taking the largest direct share in the event take on themselves the least responsibility and vice versa.

Morally the wielder of power appears to cause the event; physically it is those who submit to the power. But as the moral activity is inconceivable without the physical, the cause of the event is neither in the one nor in the other but in the union of the two.

Or in other words, the conception of a cause is inapplicable to the phenomena we are examining.

In the last analysis we reach the circle of infinity—that final limit to which in every domain of thought man's reason arrives if it is not playing with the subject. Electricity produces heat, heat produces electricity. Atoms attract each other and atoms repel one another.

Speaking of the interaction of heat and electricity and of atoms, we cannot say why this occurs, and we say that it is so because it is inconceivable otherwise, because it must be so and that it is a law. The same applies to historical events. Why war and revolution occur we do not know. We only know that to produce the one or the other action, people combine in a certain formation in which they all take part, and we say that this is so because it is unthinkable otherwise, or in other words that it is a law.

If history dealt only with external phenomena, the establishment of this simple and obvious law would suffice and we should have finished our argument. But the law of history relates to man. A particle of matter cannot tell us that it does not feel the law of attraction or repulsion and that that law is untrue, but man, who is the subject of history, says plainly: I am free and am therefore not subject to the law.

The presence of the problem of man's free will, though unexpressed, is felt at every step of history.

All seriously thinking historians have involuntarily encountered this question. All the contradictions and obscurities of history and the false path historical science has followed are due solely to the lack of a solution of that question.

If the will of every man were free, that is, if each man could act as he pleased, all history would be a series of disconnected incidents.

If in a thousand years even one man in a million could act freely, that is, as he chose, it is evident that one single free act of that man's in violation of the laws governing human action would destroy the possibility of the existence of any laws for the whole of humanity.

If there be a single law governing the actions of men, free will cannot exist, for then man's will is subject to that law.

In this contradiction lies the problem of free will, which from most ancient times has occupied the best human minds and from most ancient times has been presented in its whole tremendous significance.

The problem is that regarding man as a subject of observation from whatever point of view—theological, historical, ethical, or philosophic—we find a general law of necessity to which he (like all that exists) is subject. But regarding him from within ourselves as what we are conscious of, we feel ourselves to be free.

This consciousness is a source of self-cognition quite apart from and independent of reason. Through his reason man observes himself, but only through consciousness does he know himself.

Apart from consciousness of self no observation or application of reason is conceivable.

To understand, observe, and draw conclusions, man must first of all be conscious of himself as living. A man is only conscious of himself as a living being by the fact that he wills, that is, is conscious of his volition. But his will—which forms the essence of his life—man recognizes (and can but recognize) as free.

If, observing himself, man sees that his will is always directed by one and the same law (whether he observes the necessity of taking food, using his brain, or anything else), he cannot recognize this never-varying direction of his will otherwise than as a limitation of it. Were it not free it could not be limited. A man's will seems to him to be limited just because he is not conscious of it except as free.

You say: I am not free. But I have lifted my hand and let it fall. Everyone understands that this illogical reply is an irrefutable demonstration of freedom.

That reply is the expression of a consciousness that is not subject to reason.

If the consciousness of freedom were not a separate and independent source of self-consciousness it would be subject to reasoning and to experience, but in fact such subjection does not exist and is inconceivable.

A series of experiments and arguments proves to every man that he, as an object of observation, is subject to certain laws, and man submits to them and never resists the laws of gravity or impermeability once he has become acquainted with them. But the same series of experiments and arguments proves to him that the complete freedom of which he is conscious in himself is impossible, and that his every action depends on his organization, his character, and the motives acting upon him; yet man never submits to the deductions of these experiments and arguments. Having learned from experiment and argument that a stone falls downwards, a man indubitably believes this and always expects the law that he has learned to be fulfilled.

But learning just as certainly that his will is subject to laws, he does not and cannot believe this.

However often experiment and reasoning may show a man that under the same conditions and with the same character he will do the same thing as before, yet when under the same conditions and with the same character he approaches for the thousandth time the action that always ends in the same way, he feels as certainly convinced as before the experiment that he can act as he pleases. Every man, savage or sage, however incontestably reason and experiment may prove to him that it is impossible to imagine two different courses of action in precisely the same conditions, feels that without this irrational conception (which constitutes the essence of freedom) he cannot imagine life. He feels that however impossible it may be, it is so, for without this conception of freedom not only would he be unable to understand life, but he would be unable to live for a single moment.

He could not live, because all man's efforts, all his impulses to life, are only efforts to increase freedom. Wealth and poverty, fame and obscurity, power and subordination, strength and weakness, health and disease, culture and ignorance, work and leisure, repletion and hunger, virtue and vice, are only greater or lesser degrees of freedom.

A man having no freedom cannot be conceived of except as deprived of life.

If the conception of freedom appears to reason to be a senseless contradiction like the possibility of performing two actions at one and the same instant of time, or of an effect without a cause, that only proves that consciousness is not subject to reason.

This unshakable, irrefutable consciousness of freedom, uncontrolled by experiment or argument, recognized by all thinkers and felt by everyone without exception, this consciousness without which no conception of man is possible constitutes the other side of the question.

Man is the creation of an all-powerful, all-good, and all-seeing God. What is sin, the conception of which arises from the consciousness of man's freedom? That is a question for theology.

The actions of men are subject to general immutable laws expressed in statistics. What is man's responsibility to society, the conception of which results from the conception of freedom? That is a question for jurisprudence.

Man's actions proceed from his innate character and the motives acting upon him. What is conscience and the perception of right and wrong in actions that follows from the consciousness of freedom? That is a question for ethics.

Man in connection with the general life of humanity appears subject to laws that determine that life. But the same man apart from that connection appears to be free. How should the past life of nations and of humanity be regarded—as the result of the free, or as the result of the constrained, activity of man? That is a question for history.

Only in our self-confident day of the popularization of knowledge—thanks to that most powerful engine of ignorance, the diffusion of printed matter—has the question of the freedom of will been put on a level on which the question itself cannot exist. In our time the majority of so-called advanced people—that is, the crowd of ignoramuses—have taken the work of the naturalists who deal with one side of the question for a solution of the whole problem.

They say and write and print that the soul and freedom do not exist, for the life of man is expressed by muscular movements and muscular movements are conditioned by the activity of the nerves; the soul and free will do not exist because at an unknown period of time we sprang from the apes. They say this, not at all suspecting that thousands of years ago that same law of necessity which with such ardor they are now trying to prove by physiology and comparative zoology was not merely acknowledged by all the religions and all the thinkers, but has never been denied. They do not see that the role of the natural sciences in this matter is merely to serve as an instrument for the illumination of one side of it. For the fact that, from the point of view of observation, reason and the will are merely secretions of the brain, and that man following the general law may have developed from lower animals at some unknown period of time, only explains from a fresh side the truth admitted thousands of years ago by all the religious and philosophic theories—that from the point of view of reason man is subject to the law of necessity; but it does not advance by a hair's breadth the solution of the question, which has another, opposite, side, based on the consciousness of freedom.

If men descended from the apes at an unknown period of time, that is as comprehensible as that they were made from a handful of earth at a certain period of time (in the first case the unknown quantity is the time, in the second case it is the origin); and the question of how man's consciousness of freedom is to be reconciled with the law of necessity to which he is subject cannot be solved by comparative physiology and zoology, for in a frog, a rabbit, or an ape, we can observe only the muscular nervous activity, but in man we observe consciousness as well as the muscular and nervous activity.

The naturalists and their followers, thinking they can solve this question, are like plasterers set to plaster one side of the walls of a church who, availing themselves of the absence of the chief superintendent of the work, should in an excess of zeal plaster over the windows, icons, woodwork, and still unbuttressed walls, and should be delighted that from their point of view as plasterers, everything is now so smooth and regular.

For the solution of the question of free will or inevitability, history has this advantage over other branches of knowledge in which the question is dealt with, that for history this question does not refer to the essence of man's free will but to its manifestation in the past and under certain conditions.

In regard to this question, history stands to the other sciences as experimental science stands to abstract science.

The subject for history is not man's will itself but our presentation of it.

And so for history, the insoluble mystery presented by the incompatibility of free will and inevitability does not exist as it does for theology, ethics, and philosophy. History surveys a presentation of man's life in which the union of these two contradictions has already taken place.

In actual life each historic event, each human action, is very clearly and definitely understood without any sense of contradiction, although each event presents itself as partly free and partly compulsory.

To solve the question of how freedom and necessity are combined and what constitutes the essence of these two conceptions, the philosophy of history can and should follow a path contrary to that taken by other sciences. Instead of first defining the conceptions of freedom and inevitability in themselves, and then ranging the phenomena of life under those definitions, history should deduce a definition of the conception of freedom and inevitability themselves from the immense quantity of phenomena of which it is cognizant and that always appear dependent on these two elements.

Whatever presentation of the activity of many men or of an individual we may consider, we always regard it as the result partly of man's free will and partly of the law of inevitability.

Whether we speak of the migration of the peoples and the incursions of the barbarians, or of the decrees of Napoleon III, or of someone's action an hour ago in choosing one direction out of several for his walk, we are unconscious of any contradiction. The degree of freedom and inevitability governing the actions of these people is clearly defined for us.

Our conception of the degree of freedom often varies according to differences in the point of view from which we regard the event, but every human action appears to us as a certain combination of freedom and inevitability. In every action we examine we see a certain measure of freedom and a certain measure of inevitability. And always the more freedom we see in any action the less inevitability do we perceive, and the more inevitability the less freedom.

The proportion of freedom to inevitability decreases and increases according to the point of view from which the action is regarded, but their relation is always one of inverse proportion.

A sinking man who clutches at another and drowns him; or a hungry mother exhausted by feeding her baby, who steals some food; or a man trained to discipline who on duty at the word of command kills a defenseless man—seem less guilty, that is, less free and more subject to the law of necessity, to one who knows the circumstances in which these people were placed, and more free to one who does not know that the man was himself drowning, that the mother was hungry, that the soldier was in the ranks, and so on. Similarly a man who committed a murder twenty years ago and has since lived peaceably and harmlessly in society seems less guilty and his action more due to the law of inevitability, to someone who considers his action after twenty years have elapsed, than to one who examined it the day after it was committed. And in the same way every action of an insane, intoxicated, or highly excited man appears less free and more inevitable to one who knows the mental condition of him who committed the action, and seems more free and less inevitable to one who does not know it. In all these cases the conception of freedom is increased or diminished and the conception of compulsion is correspondingly decreased or increased, according to the point of view from which the action is regarded. So that the greater the conception of necessity the smaller the conception of freedom and vice versa.

Religion, the common sense of mankind, the science of jurisprudence, and history itself understand alike this relation between necessity and freedom.

All cases without exception in which our conception of freedom and necessity is increased and diminished depend on three considerations: (1) the relation to the external world of the man who commits the deeds, (2) his relation to time, and (3) his relation to the causes leading to the action.

The first consideration is the clearness of our perception of the man's relation to the external world and the greater or lesser clearness of our understanding of the definite position occupied by the man in relation to everything coexisting with him. This is what makes it evident that a drowning man is less free and more subject to necessity than one standing on dry ground, and that makes the actions of a man closely connected with others in a thickly populated district, or of one bound by family, official, or business duties, seem certainly less free and more subject to necessity than those of a man living in solitude and seclusion.

If we consider a man alone, apart from his relation to everything around him, each action of his seems to us free. But if we see his relation to anything around him, if we see his connection with anything whatever—with a man who speaks to him, a book he reads, the work on which he is engaged, even with the air he breathes or the light that falls on the things about him—we see that each of these circumstances has an influence on him and controls at least some side of his activity. And the more we perceive of these influences the more our conception of his freedom diminishes and the more our conception of the necessity that weighs on him increases.

The second consideration is the more or less evident time relation of the man to the world and the clearness of our perception of the place the man's action occupies in time. That is the ground which makes the fall of the first man, resulting in the production of the human race, appear evidently less free than a man's entry into marriage today. It is the reason why the life and activity of people who lived centuries ago and are connected with me in time cannot seem to me as free as the life of a contemporary, the consequences of which are still unknown to me.

The degree of our conception of freedom or inevitability depends in this respect on the greater or lesser lapse of time between the performance of the action and our judgment of it.

If I examine an act I performed a moment ago in approximately the same circumstances as those I am in now, my action appears to me undoubtedly free. But if I examine an act performed a month ago, then being in different circumstances, I cannot help recognizing that if that act had not been committed much that resulted from it—good, agreeable, and even essential—would not have taken place. If I reflect on an action still more remote, ten years ago or more, then the consequences of my action are still plainer to me and I find it hard to imagine what would have happened had that action not been performed. The farther I go back in memory, or what is the same thing the farther I go forward in my judgment, the more doubtful becomes my belief in the freedom of my action.

In history we find a very similar progress of conviction concerning the part played by free will in the general affairs of humanity. A contemporary event seems to us to be indubitably the doing of all the known participants, but with a more remote event we already see its inevitable results which prevent our considering anything else possible. And the farther we go back in examining events the less arbitrary do they appear.

The Austro-Prussian war appears to us undoubtedly the result of the crafty conduct of Bismarck, and so on. The Napoleonic wars still seem to us, though already questionably, to be the outcome of their heroes' will. But in the Crusades we already see an event occupying its definite place in history and without which we cannot imagine the modern history of Europe, though to the chroniclers of the Crusades that event appeared as merely due to the will of certain people. In regard to the migration of the peoples it does not enter anyone's head today to suppose that the renovation of the European world depended on Attila's caprice. The farther back in history the object of our observation lies, the more doubtful does the free will of those concerned in the event become and the more manifest the law of inevitability.

The third consideration is the degree to which we apprehend that endless chain of causation inevitably demanded by reason, in which each phenomenon comprehended, and therefore man's every action, must have its definite place as a result of what has gone before and as a cause of what will follow.

The better we are acquainted with the physiological, psychological, and historical laws deduced by observation and by which man is controlled, and the more correctly we perceive the physiological, psychological, and historical causes of the action, and the simpler the action we are observing and the less complex the character and mind of the man in question, the more subject to inevitability and less free do our actions and those of others appear.

When we do not at all understand the cause of an action, whether a crime, a good action, or one that is simply nonmoral, we ascribe a greater amount of freedom to it. In the case of a crime, we most urgently demand the punishment for such an act; in the case of a virtuous act, we rate its merit most highly. In an indifferent case, we recognize in it more individuality, originality, and independence. But if even one of the innumerable causes of the act is known to us we recognize a certain element of necessity and are less insistent on punishment for the crime, or the acknowledgment of the merit of the virtuous act, or the freedom of the apparently original action. That a criminal was reared among malefactors mitigates his fault in our eyes. The self-sacrifice of a father or a mother, or self-sacrifice with the possibility of a reward, is more comprehensible than gratuitous self-sacrifice, and therefore seems less deserving of sympathy and less the result of free will. The founder of a sect or party, or an inventor, impresses us less when we know how or by what the way was prepared for his activity. If we have a large range of examples, if our observation is constantly directed to seeking the correlation of cause and effect in people's actions, their actions appear to us more under compulsion and less free the more correctly we connect the effects with the causes. If we examined simple actions and had a vast number of such actions under observation, our conception of their inevitability would still be greater. The dishonest conduct of the son of a dishonest father, the misconduct of a woman who had fallen into bad company, a drunkard's relapse into drunkenness, and so on are actions that seem to us less free the better we understand their cause. If the man whose actions we are considering is on a very low stage of mental development, like a child, a madman, or a simpleton—then, knowing the causes of the act and the simplicity of the character and intelligence in question, we see so large an element of necessity and so little free will that as soon as we know the cause prompting the action we can foretell the result.

On these three considerations alone is based the conception of irresponsibility for crimes and the extenuating circumstances admitted by all legislative codes. The responsibility appears greater or less according to our greater or lesser knowledge of the circumstances in which the man was placed whose action is being judged, and according to the greater or lesser interval of time between the commission of the action and its investigation, and according to the greater or lesser understanding of the causes that led to the action.

Thus our conception of free will and inevitability gradually diminishes or increases according to the greater or lesser connection with the external world, the greater or lesser remoteness of time, and the greater or lesser dependence on the causes in relation to which we contemplate a man's life.

So that if we examine the case of a man whose connection with the external world is well known, where the time between the action and its examination is great, and where the causes of the action are most accessible, we get the conception of a maximum of inevitability and a minimum of free will. If we examine a man little dependent on external conditions, whose action was performed very recently, and the causes of whose action are beyond our ken, we get the conception of a minimum of inevitability and a maximum of freedom.

In neither case—however we may change our point of view, however plain we may make to ourselves the connection between the man and the external world, however inaccessible it may be to us, however long or short the period of time, however intelligible or incomprehensible the causes of the action may be—can we ever conceive either complete freedom or complete necessity.

(1) To whatever degree we may imagine a man to be exempt from the influence of the external world, we never get a conception of freedom in space. Every human action is inevitably conditioned by what surrounds

him and by his own body. I lift my arm and let it fall. My action seems to me free; but asking myself whether I could raise my arm in every direction, I see that I raised it in the direction in which there was least obstruction to that action either from the things around me or from the construction of my own body. I chose one out of all the possible directions because in it there were fewest obstacles. For my action to be free it was necessary that it should encounter no obstacles. To conceive of a man being free we must imagine him outside space, which is evidently impossible.

(2) However much we approximate the time of judgment to the time of the deed, we never get a conception of freedom in time. For if I examine an action committed a second ago I must still recognize it as not being free, for it is irrevocably linked to the moment at which it was committed. Can I lift my arm? I lift it, but ask myself: could I have abstained from lifting my arm at the moment that has already passed? To convince myself of this I do not lift it the next moment. But I am not now abstaining from doing so at the first moment when I asked the question. Time has gone by which I could not detain, the arm I then lifted is no longer the same as the arm I now refrain from lifting, nor is the air in which I lifted it the same that now surrounds me. The moment in which the first movement was made is irrevocable, and at that moment I could make only one movement, and whatever movement I made would be the only one. That I did not lift my arm a moment later does not prove that I could have abstained from lifting it then. And since I could make only one movement at that single moment of time, it could not have been any other. To imagine it as free, it is necessary to imagine it in the present, on the boundary between the past and the future—that is, outside time, which is impossible.

(3) However much the difficulty of understanding the causes may be increased, we never reach a conception of complete freedom, that is, an absence of cause. However inaccessible to us may be the cause of the expression of will in any action, our own or another's, the first demand of reason is the assumption of and search for a cause, for without a cause no phenomenon is conceivable. I raise my arm to perform an action independently of any cause, but my wish to perform an action without a cause is the cause of my action.

But even if—imagining a man quite exempt from all influences, examining only his momentary action in the present, unevoked by any cause—we were to admit so infinitely small a remainder of inevitability as equaled zero, we should even then not have arrived at the conception of complete freedom in man, for a being uninfluenced by the external world, standing outside of time and independent of cause, is no longer a man.

In the same way we can never imagine the action of a man quite devoid of freedom and entirely subject to the law of inevitability.

(1) However we may increase our knowledge of the conditions of space in which man is situated, that knowledge can never be complete, for the number of those conditions is as infinite as the infinity of space. And therefore so long as not *all* the conditions influencing men are defined, there is no complete inevitability but a certain measure of freedom remains.

(2) However we may prolong the period of time between the action we are examining and the judgment upon it, that period will be finite, while time is infinite, and so in this respect too there can never be absolute inevitability.

(3) However accessible may be the chain of causation of any action, we shall never know the whole chain since it is endless, and so again we never reach absolute inevitability.

But besides this, even if, admitting the remaining minimum of freedom to equal zero, we assumed in some given case—as for instance in that of a dying man, an unborn babe, or an idiot—complete absence of freedom, by so doing we should destroy the very conception of man in the case we are examining, for as soon as there is no freedom there is also no man. And so the conception of the action of a man subject solely to the law of inevitability without any element of freedom is just as impossible as the conception of a man's completely free action.

And so to imagine the action of a man entirely subject to the law of inevitability without any freedom, we must assume the knowledge of an *infinite* number of space relations, an *infinitely* long period of time, and an *infinite* series of causes.

To imagine a man perfectly free and not subject to the law of inevitability, we must imagine him all alone, *beyond space*, *beyond time*, and *free from dependence on cause*.

In the first case, if inevitability were possible without freedom we should have reached a definition of inevitability by the laws of inevitability itself, that is, a mere form without content.

In the second case, if freedom were possible without inevitability we should have arrived at unconditioned freedom beyond space, time, and cause, which by the fact of its being unconditioned and unlimited would be nothing or mere content without form.

We should in fact have reached those two fundamentals of which man's whole outlook on the universe is constructed—the incomprehensible essence of life, and the laws defining that essence.

Reason says: (1) Space with all the forms of matter that give it visibility is infinite, and cannot be imagined otherwise. (2) Time is infinite motion without a moment of rest and is unthinkable otherwise. (3) The connection between cause and effect has no beginning and can have no end.

Consciousness says: (1) I alone am, and all that exists is but me, consequently I include space. (2) I measure flowing time by the fixed moment of the present in which alone I am conscious of myself as living, consequently I am outside time. (3) I am beyond cause, for I feel myself to be the cause of every manifestation of my life.

Reason gives expression to the laws of inevitability. Consciousness gives expression to the essence of freedom.

Freedom not limited by anything is the essence of life, in man's consciousness. Inevitability without content is man's reason in its three forms.

Freedom is the thing examined. Inevitability is what examines. Freedom is the content. Inevitability is the form.

Only by separating the two sources of cognition, related to one another as form to content, do we get the mutually exclusive and separately incomprehensible conceptions of freedom and inevitability.

Only by uniting them do we get a clear conception of man's life.

Apart from these two concepts which in their union mutually define one another as form and content, no conception of life is possible.

All that we know of the life of man is merely a certain relation of free will to inevitability, that is, of consciousness to the laws of reason.

All that we know of the external world of nature is only a certain relation of the forces of nature to inevitability, or of the essence of life to the laws of reason.

The great natural forces lie outside us and we are not conscious of them; we call those forces gravitation, inertia, electricity, animal force, and so on, but we are conscious of the force of life in man and we call that freedom.

But just as the force of gravitation, incomprehensible in itself but felt by every man, is understood by us only to the extent to which we know the laws of inevitability to which it is subject (from the first knowledge that all bodies have weight, up to Newton's law), so too the force of free will, incomprehensible in itself but of which everyone is conscious, is intelligible to us only in as far as we know the laws of inevitability to which it is subject (from the fact that every man dies, up to the knowledge of the most complex economic and historic laws).

All knowledge is merely a bringing of this essence of life under the laws of reason.

Man's free will differs from every other force in that man is directly conscious of it, but in the eyes of reason it in no way differs from any other force. The forces of gravitation, electricity, or chemical affinity are only distinguished from one another in that they are differently defined by reason. Just so the force of man's free will is distinguished by reason from the other forces of nature only by the definition reason gives it. Freedom, apart from necessity, that is, apart from the laws of reason that define it, differs in no way from gravitation, or heat, or the force that makes things grow; for reason, it is only a momentary undefinable sensation of life.

And as the undefinable essence of the force moving the heavenly bodies, the undefinable essence of the forces of heat and electricity or of chemical affinity, or of the vital force, forms the content of astronomy, physics, chemistry, botany, zoology, and so on, just in the same way does the force of free will form the content of history. But just as the subject of every science is the manifestation of this unknown essence of life while that essence itself can only be the subject of metaphysics, even so the manifestation of the force of free will in human beings in space, in time, and in dependence on cause forms the subject of history, while free will itself is the subject of metaphysics.

In the experimental sciences, what we know we call the laws of inevitability, what is unknown to us we call vital force. Vital force is only an expression for the unknown remainder over and above what we know of the essence of life.

So also in history what is known to us we call laws of inevitability, what is unknown we call free will. Free will is for history only an expression for the unknown remainder of what we know about the laws of human life.

History examines the manifestations of man's free will in connection with the external world in time and in dependence on cause, that is, it defines this freedom by the laws of reason, and so history is a science only in so far as this free will is defined by those laws.

The recognition of man's free will as something capable of influencing historical events, that is, as not subject to laws, is the same for history as the recognition of a free force moving the heavenly bodies would be for astronomy.

That assumption would destroy the possibility of the existence of laws, that is, of any science whatever. If there is even a single body moving freely, then the laws of Kepler and Newton are negatived and no conception of the movement of the heavenly bodies any longer exists. If any single action is due to free will, then not a single historical law can exist, nor any conception of historical events.

For history, lines exist of the movement of human wills, one end of which is hidden in the unknown but at the other end of which a consciousness of man's will in the present moves in space, time, and dependence on cause.

The more this field of motion spreads out before our eyes, the more evident are the laws of that movement. To discover and define those laws is the problem of history.

From the standpoint from which the science of history now regards its subject on the path it now follows, seeking the causes of events in man's free will, a scientific enunciation of those laws is impossible, for however man's free will may be restricted, as soon as we recognize it as a force not subject to law, the existence of law becomes impossible.

Only by reducing this element of free will to the infinitesimal, that is, by regarding it as an infinitely small quantity, can we convince ourselves of the absolute inaccessibility of the causes, and then instead of seeking causes, history will take the discovery of laws as its problem.

The search for these laws has long been begun and the new methods of thought which history must adopt are being worked out simultaneously with the self-destruction toward which—ever dissecting and dissecting the causes of phenomena—the old method of history is moving.

All human sciences have traveled along that path. Arriving at infinitesimals, mathematics, the most exact of sciences, abandons the process of analysis and enters on the new process of the integration of unknown, infinitely small, quantities. Abandoning the conception of cause, mathematics seeks law, that is, the property common to all unknown, infinitely small, elements.

In another form but along the same path of reflection the other sciences have proceeded. When Newton enunciated the law of gravity he did not say that the sun or the earth had a property of attraction; he said that all bodies from the largest to the smallest have the property of attracting one another, that is, leaving aside the question of the cause of the movement of the bodies, he expressed the property common to all bodies from the infinitely large to the infinitely small. The same is done by the natural sciences: leaving aside the question of cause, they seek for laws. History stands on the same path. And if history has for its object the study of the movement of the nations and of humanity and not the narration of episodes in the lives of individuals, it too, setting aside the conception of cause, should seek the laws common to all the inseparably interconnected infinitesimal elements of free will.

From the time the law of Copernicus was discovered and proved, the mere recognition of the fact that it was not the sun but the earth that moves sufficed to destroy the whole cosmography of the ancients. By disproving that law it might have been possible to retain the old conception of the movements of the bodies, but without disproving it, it would seem impossible to continue studying the Ptolemaic worlds. But even after the discovery of the law of Copernicus the Ptolemaic worlds were still studied for a long time.

From the time the first person said and proved that the number of births or of crimes is subject to mathematical laws, and that this or that mode of government is determined by certain geographical and economic conditions, and that certain relations of population to soil produce migrations of peoples, the foundations on which history had been built were destroyed in their essence.

By refuting these new laws the former view of history might have been retained; but without refuting them it would seem impossible to continue studying historic events as the results of man's free will. For if a certain mode of government was established or certain migrations of peoples took place in consequence of such and such geographic, ethnographic, or economic conditions, then the free will of those individuals who appear to us to have established that mode of government or occasioned the migrations can no longer be regarded as the cause.

And yet the former history continues to be studied side by side with the laws of statistics, geography, political economy, comparative philology, and geology, which directly contradict its assumptions.

The struggle between the old views and the new was long and stubbornly fought out in physical philosophy. Theology stood on guard for the old views and accused the new of violating revelation. But when truth conquered, theology established itself just as firmly on the new foundation.

Just as prolonged and stubborn is the struggle now proceeding between the old and the new conception of history, and theology in the same way stands on guard for the old view, and accuses the new view of subverting revelation.

In the one case as in the other, on both sides the struggle provokes passion and stifles truth. On the one hand there is fear and regret for the loss of the whole edifice constructed through the ages, on the other is the passion for destruction.

To the men who fought against the rising truths of physical philosophy, it seemed that if they admitted that truth it would destroy faith in God, in the creation of the firmament, and in the miracle of Joshua the son of Nun. To the defenders of the laws of Copernicus and Newton, to Voltaire for example, it seemed that the laws of astronomy destroyed religion, and he utilized the law of gravitation as a weapon against religion.

Just so it now seems as if we have only to admit the law of inevitability, to destroy the conception of the soul, of good and evil, and all the institutions of state and church that have been built up on those conceptions.

So too, like Voltaire in his time, uninvited defenders of the law of inevitability today use that law as a weapon against religion, though the law of inevitability in history, like the law of Copernicus in astronomy, far from destroying, even strengthens the foundation on which the institutions of state and church are erected.

As in the question of astronomy then, so in the question of history now, the whole difference of opinion is based on the recognition or nonrecognition of something absolute, serving as the measure of visible phenomena. In astronomy it was the immovability of the earth, in history it is the independence of personality—free will.

As with astronomy the difficulty of recognizing the motion of the earth lay in abandoning the immediate sensation of the earth's fixity and of the motion of the planets, so in history the difficulty of recognizing the subjection of personality to the laws of space, time, and cause lies in renouncing the direct feeling of the independence of one's own personality. But as in astronomy the new view said: "It is true that we do not feel the movement of the earth, but by admitting its immobility we arrive at absurdity, while by admitting its motion (which we do not feel) we arrive at laws," so also in history the new view says; "It is true that we are not conscious of our dependence, but by admitting our free will we arrive at absurdity, while by admitting our dependence on the external world, on time, and on cause, we arrive at laws."

In the first case it was necessary to renounce the consciousness of an unreal immobility in space and to recognize a motion we did not feel; in the present case it is similarly necessary to renounce a freedom that does not exist, and to recognize a dependence of which we are not conscious.

QUESTIONS

1. According to Tolstoy, how is history "the life of nations and of humanity"? (93) Why does Tolstoy say that it appears impossible to put this history into words?

2. Why does Tolstoy think that traditional views of history are flawed?

3. According to Tolstoy, why isn't power an adequate explanation of historical events?

4. What influence does Tolstoy think great commanders have on those they command?

5. Why does Tolstoy repeatedly make analogies to physics and mathematics as he tries to form an explanation of historical events?

6. What is Tolstoy's purpose in introducing a discussion of the philosophical problem of free will and necessity into an attempt to explain history?

7. For Tolstoy, what respective weight do freedom and necessity have in the unfolding of historical events?

8. Does Tolstoy's theory of history apply only to massive events, like Napoleon's invasion of Russia, or to smaller human affairs as well?

9. Does Tolstoy think that the course of history can ever be exactly predicted?

FOR FURTHER REFLECTION

1. Why do all people seem to have a need to preserve a record of their history?
2. Is it possible to create a written history that does not imply an explanation and interpretation of historical events?
3. Do historians always have an obligation to try to depict the truth, or are there times when histories should be written to create beliefs that might be important to the morale and well-being of the community?
4. Can the course of historical events be adequately explained by reducing everything to one discipline, for example, biology, economics, or religion?
5. Is it possible to verify that any action of an individual arises entirely from an exercise of free will?

RUDYARD KIPLING

A man who became known to both friends and detractors as "the poet of Empire," Rudyard Kipling (1865–1936) had established himself by the beginning of the twentieth century as one of the most widely read writers in the English-speaking world. His short stories, poems, novels, and children's books, drawing on his international experience and delivered in a vivid, condensed style, earned him popular and critical acclaim. In 1907 he received the Nobel Prize in Literature.

Kipling was born in Bombay (now Mumbai), India, where his father was an artist, sculptor, and teacher. His mother, the musically gifted Alice Macdonald, had two younger sisters who married pre-Raphaelite painters. Much of Kipling's early childhood was spent in the company of his Indian ayah, and as a result he spoke Hindustani as his first language. When he was five, Kipling and his three-year-old sister were sent away from India to a foster home in Southsea, England, where they lived miserably for the next five years. In his memoirs, Kipling would describe the foster home as "the House of Desolation." At the age of twelve, Kipling went to boarding school in north Devon. There his schoolmasters encouraged him to read widely; he also edited the school magazine.

In 1882 he returned to India and, just sixteen years old, took a job as assistant editor at the *Civil and Military Gazette* in Lahore, in the Punjab region of India (now a part of Pakistan). From his vantage point at the paper, Kipling was able to reflect on the policies and practices of the British Empire. His wide knowledge of both local Indian life and British expatriates, including soldiers, missionaries, and other adventurers, served him well when he began to write fiction and poems. Many of his early literary works were published in the newspaper under the headline "Plain Tales from the Hills." The book published in 1888 under the same title signaled that a powerful new voice had arrived in English fiction. Within a few short years, Kipling had published more than half a dozen paperback volumes, consisting mostly of short stories. These gained him popularity, first among readers of English on the Indian subcontinent and then among the British reading public in England. When Kipling returned to England in 1889, he was a famous man.

In 1892 Kipling married an American, Caroline Balestier, and they settled in Vermont. Eventually they returned to England, but Kipling spent considerable time in South Africa, in the company of his good friend, the statesman and diamond tycoon Cecil Rhodes. Kipling's wealth and connections made his globetrotting existence possible, but did not protect him from criticism. By the early 1900s, many writers in the literary establishment had openly begun to accuse him of jingoism and scorned his embrace of British imperialism. Such charges were based partly on poems such as "Recessional," brought out on the occasion of Queen Victoria's Diamond Jubilee in 1897, and "The White Man's Burden," a notorious exhortation to the United States to impose its will upon the Philippine Islands following victory in the Spanish-American War. Although Kipling's fame would decrease from its peak in the 1890s, his literary output continued unabated, including the brilliant novel *Kim* (1901) and numerous volumes of short stories, some of which have prompted literary scholars in recent years to reappraise Kipling, categorizing him as a modernist literary innovator.

"The Man Who Would Be King," narrated by a British newspaper correspondent in India, relates the experiences of two adventurers in Afghanistan. It was first published in 1888 in Allahabad, India, in a volume of stories titled *The Phantom 'Rickshaw.*

RUDYARD KIPLING

The Man Who Would Be King

Brother to a Prince and fellow to a beggar
if he be found worthy.

The Law, as quoted, lays down a fair conduct of life, and one not easy to follow. I have been fellow to a beggar again and again under circumstances which prevented either of us finding out whether the other was worthy. I have still to be brother to a Prince, though I once came near to kinship with what might have been a veritable King and was promised the reversion of a Kingdom—army, law-courts, revenue, and policy all complete. But, to-day, I greatly fear that my King is dead, and if I want a crown I must go hunt it for myself.

The beginning of everything was in a railway train upon the road to Mhow from Ajmir. There had been a Deficit in the Budget, which necessitated travelling, not Second-class, which is only half as dear as First-class, but by Intermediate, which is very awful indeed. There are no cushions in the Intermediate class, and the population are either Intermediate, which is Eurasian, or native, which for a long night journey is nasty, or Loafer, which is amusing though intoxicated. Intermediates do not buy from refreshment-rooms. They carry their food in bundles and pots, and buy sweets from the native sweetmeat-sellers, and drink the roadside water. That is why in hot weather Intermediates are taken out of the carriages dead, and in all weathers are most properly looked down upon.

My particular Intermediate happened to be empty till I reached Nasirabad, when a big black-browed gentleman in shirt-sleeves entered, and, following the custom of Intermediates, passed the time of day. He was a wanderer and a vagabond like myself, but with an educated taste for whiskey. He told tales of things he had seen and done, of out-of-the-way corners of the Empire into which he had penetrated, and of adventures in which he risked his life for a few days' food.

"If India was filled with men like you and me, not knowing more than the crows where they'd get their next day's rations, it isn't seventy millions of revenue the land would be paying—it's seven hundred millions," said he; and as I looked at his mouth and chin I was disposed to agree with him.

We talked politics—the politics of Loaferdom, that sees things from the underside where the lath and plaster are not smoothed off—and we talked postal arrangements because my friend wanted to send a telegram back from the next station to Ajmir, the turning-off place from the Bombay to the Mhow line as you travel westward. My friend had no money beyond eight annas which he wanted for dinner, and I had no money at all, owing to the hitch in the Budget before mentioned. Further, I was going into a wilderness where, though I should resume touch with the Treasury, there were no telegraph offices. I was, therefore, unable to help him in any way.

"We might threaten a Station-master, and make him send a wire on tick," said my friend, "but that'd mean enquiries for you and for me, and *I*'ve got my hands full these days. Did you say you were travelling back along this line within any days?"

"Within ten," I said.

"Can't you make it eight?" said he. "Mine is rather urgent business."

"I can send your telegram within ten days if that will serve you," I said.

"I couldn't trust the wire to fetch him now I think of it. It's this way. He leaves Delhi on the 23rd for Bombay. That means he'll be running through Ajmir about the night of the 23rd."

"But I'm going into the Indian Desert," I explained.

"Well *and* good," said he. "You'll be changing at Marwar Junction to get into Jodhpore territory—you must do that—and he'll be coming through Marwar Junction in the early morning of the 24th by the Bombay Mail. Can you be at Marwar Junction on that time? 'Twon't be inconveniencing you because I know that there's precious few pickings to be got out of these Central India States—even though you pretend to be correspondent of the *Backwoodsman*."

"Have you ever tried that trick?" I asked.

"Again and again, but the Residents find you out, and then you get escorted to the Border before you've time to get your knife into them. But about my friend here. I *must* give him a word o' mouth to tell him what's come to me, or else he won't know where to go. I would take it more than kind of you if you was to come out of Central India in time to catch him at Marwar Junction, and say to him: 'He has gone South for the week.' He'll know what that means. He's a big man with a red beard, and a great swell he is. You'll find him sleeping like a gentleman with all his luggage round him in a Second-class apartment. But don't you be afraid. Slip down the window and say: 'He has gone South for the week,' and he'll tumble. It's only cutting your time of stay in those parts by two days. I ask you as a stranger—going to the West," he said with emphasis.

"Where have *you* come from?" said I.

"From the East," said he, "and I am hoping that you will give him the message on the Square—for the sake of my Mother as well as your own."

Englishmen are not usually softened by appeals to the memory of their mothers; but for certain reasons, which will be fully apparent, I saw fit to agree.

"It's more than a little matter," said he, "and that's why I asked you to do it—and now I know that I can depend on you doing it. A Second-class carriage at Marwar Junction, and a red-haired man asleep in it. You'll be sure to remember. I get out at the next station, and I must hold on there till he comes or sends me what I want."

"I'll give the message if I catch him," I said, "and for the sake of your Mother as well as mine I'll give you a word of advice. Don't try to run the Central India States just now as the correspondent of the *Backwoodsman*. There's a real one knocking about here, and it might lead to trouble."

"Thank you," said he simply, "and when will the swine be gone? I can't starve because he's ruining my work. I wanted to get hold of the Degumber Rajah down here about his father's widow, and give him a jump."

"What did he do to his father's widow, then?"

"Filled her up with red pepper and slippered her to death as she hung from a beam. I found that out myself, and I'm the only man that would dare going into the State to get hush-money for it. They'll try to poison me, same as they did in Chortumna when I went on the loot there. But you'll give the man at Marwar Junction my message?"

He got out at a little roadside station, and I reflected. I had heard, more than once, of men personating correspondents of newspapers and bleeding small Native States with threats of exposure, but I had never met any of the caste before. They lead a hard life, and generally die with great suddenness. The Native States have a wholesome horror of English newspapers, which may throw light on their peculiar methods of government, and do their best to choke correspondents with champagne, or drive them out of their mind with four-in-hand barouches. They do not understand that nobody cares a straw for the internal administration of Native States so long as oppression and crime are kept within decent limits, and the ruler is not drugged, drunk, or diseased from one end of the year to the other. They are the dark places of the earth, full of unimaginable cruelty, touching the Railway and the Telegraph on one side, and, on the other, the days of Harun-al-Raschid. When I left the train I did business with divers Kings, and in eight days passed through many changes of life. Sometimes I wore dress-clothes and consorted with Princes and Politicals, drinking from crystal and eating from silver. Sometimes I lay out upon the ground and devoured what I could get, from a plate made of leaves, and drank the running water, and slept under the same rug as my servant. It was all in the day's work.

Then I headed for the Great Indian Desert upon the proper date, as I had promised, and the night Mail set me down at Marwar Junction, where a funny, little, happy-go-lucky, native-managed railway runs to Jodhpore. The Bombay Mail from Delhi makes a short halt at Marwar. She arrived as I got in, and I had just time to hurry to her platform and go down the carriages. There was only one Second-class on the train. I slipped the window and looked down upon a flaming red beard, half covered by a railway rug. That was my man, fast asleep, and I dug him gently in the ribs. He woke with a grunt, and I saw his face in the light of the lamps. It was a great and shining face.

"Tickets again?" said he.

"No," said I. "I am to tell you that he is gone South for the week. He has gone South for the week!"

The train had begun to move out. The red man rubbed his eyes. "He has gone South for the week," he repeated. "Now that's just like his impidence. Did he say that I was to give you anything? 'Cause I won't."

"He didn't," I said, and dropped away, and watched the red lights die out in the dark. It was horribly cold because the wind was blowing off the sands. I climbed into my own train—not an Intermediate carriage this time—and went to sleep.

If the man with the beard had given me a rupee I should have kept it as a memento of a rather curious affair. But the consciousness of having done my duty was my only reward.

Later on I reflected that two gentlemen like my friends could not do any good if they foregathered and personated correspondents of newspapers, and might, if they blackmailed one of the little rat-trap states of Central India or Southern Rajputana, get themselves into serious difficulties. I therefore took some trouble to describe them as accurately as I could remember to people who would be interested in deporting them: and succeeded, so I was later informed, in having them headed back from the Degumber borders.

Then I became respectable, and returned to an Office where there were no Kings and no incidents outside the daily manufacture of a newspaper. A newspaper office seems to attract every conceivable sort of person, to the prejudice of discipline. Zenana-mission ladies arrive, and beg that the Editor will instantly abandon all his duties to describe a Christian prize-giving in a back slum of a perfectly inaccessible village;

Colonels who have been overpassed for command sit down and sketch the outline of a series of ten, twelve, or twenty-four leading articles on Seniority versus Selection; missionaries wish to know why they have not been permitted to escape from their regular vehicles of abuse and swear at a brother-missionary under special patronage of the editorial We; stranded theatrical companies troop up to explain that they cannot pay for their advertisements, but on their return from New Zealand or Tahiti will do so with interest; inventors of patent punkah-pulling machines, carriage couplings, and unbreakable swords and axle-trees call with specifications in their pockets and hours at their disposal; tea-companies enter and elaborate their prospectuses with the office pens; secretaries of ball-committees clamour to have the glories of their last dance more fully described; strange ladies rustle in and say: "I want a hundred lady's cards printed *at once*, please," which is manifestly part of an Editor's duty; and every dissolute ruffian that ever tramped the Grand Trunk Road makes it his business to ask for employment as a proof-reader. And, all the time, the telephone-bell is ringing madly, and Kings are being killed on the Continent, and Empires are saying—"you're another," and Mr. Gladstone is calling down brimstone upon the British Dominions, and the little black copy-boys are whining, "*kaa-pi chay-ha-yeh*" (copy wanted) like tired bees, and most of the paper is as blank as Modred's shield.

But that is the amusing part of the year. There are six other months when none ever come to call, and the thermometer walks inch by inch up to the top of the glass, and the office is darkened to just above reading-light, and the press-machines are red-hot of touch, and nobody writes anything but accounts of amusements in the Hill-stations or obituary notices. Then the telephone becomes a tinkling terror, because it tells you of the sudden deaths of men and women that you knew intimately, and the prickly-heat covers you with a garment, and you sit down and write: "A slight increase of sickness is reported from the Khuda Janta Khan District. The outbreak is purely sporadic in its nature, and, thanks to the energetic efforts of the District authorities, is now almost at an end. It is, however, with deep regret we record the death," etc.

Then the sickness really breaks out, and the less recording and reporting the better for the peace of the subscribers. But the Empires and the Kings continue to divert themselves as selfishly as before, and the Foreman thinks that a daily paper really ought to come out once in twenty-four hours, and all the people at the Hill-stations in the middle of their amusements say: "Good gracious! Why can't the paper be sparkling? I'm sure there's plenty going on up here."

That is the dark half of the moon, and, as the advertisements say, "must be experienced to be appreciated."

It was in that season, and a remarkably evil season, that the paper began running the last issue of the week on Saturday night, which is to say Sunday morning, after the custom of a London paper. This was a great convenience, for immediately after the paper was put to bed, the dawn would lower the thermometer from 96° to almost 84° for half an hour, and in that chill—you have no idea how cold is 84° on the grass until you begin to pray for it—a very tired man could get off to sleep ere the heat roused him.

One Saturday night it was my pleasant duty to put the paper to bed alone. A King or courtier or a courtesan or a Community was going to die or get a new Constitution, or do something that was important on the other side of the world, and the paper was to be held open till the latest possible minute in order to catch the telegram.

It was a pitchy-black night, as stifling as a June night can be, and the *loo*, the red-hot wind from the westward, was booming among the tinder-dry trees and pretending that the rain was on its heels. Now and again a spot of almost boiling water would fall on the dust with the flop of a frog, but all our weary world knew that was only pretence. It was a shade cooler in the press-room than the office, so I sat there, while the type ticked and clicked, and the night-jars hooted at the windows, and the all but naked compositors wiped the sweat from their foreheads, and called for water. The thing that was keeping us back, whatever it was, would not come off, though the *loo* dropped and the last type was set, and the whole round earth stood still in the choking heat, with its finger on its lip, to wait the event. I drowsed, and wondered whether the telegraph was a blessing, and whether this dying man, or struggling people, might be aware of the inconvenience the delay was causing. There was no special reason beyond the heat and worry to make tension, but, as the clock-hands crept up to three o'clock and the machines spun their fly-wheels two and three times to see that all was in order, before I said the word that would set them off, I could have shrieked aloud.

Then the roar and rattle of the wheels shivered the quiet into little bits. I rose to go away, but two men in white clothes stood in front of me. The first one said: "It's him!" The second said: "So it is!" And they both laughed almost as loudly as the machinery roared, and mopped their foreheads. "We seed there was a light burning across the road, and we were sleeping in that ditch there for coolness, and I said to my friend here, 'The office is open. Let's come along and speak to him as turned us back from the Degumber State,'" said the smaller of the two. He was the man I had met in the Mhow train, and his fellow was the red-bearded man of Marwar Junction. There was no mistaking the eyebrows of the one or the beard of the other.

I was not pleased, because I wished to go to sleep, not to squabble with loafers. "What do you want?" I asked.

"Half an hour's talk with you, cool and comfortable, in the office," said the red-bearded man. "We'd *like* some drink—the Contrack doesn't begin yet, Peachey, so you needn't look—but what we really want is advice. We don't want money. We ask you as a favour, because we found out you did us a bad turn about Degumber State."

I led from the press-room to the stifling office with the maps on the walls, and the red-haired man rubbed his hands. "That's something like," said he. "This was the proper shop to come to. Now, Sir, let me introduce to you Brother Peachey Carnehan, that's him, and Brother Daniel Dravot, that is *me*, and the less said about our professions the better, for we have been most things in our time. Soldier, sailor, compositor, photographer, proof-reader, street-preacher, and correspondents of the *Backwoodsman* when we thought the paper wanted one. Carnehan is sober, and so am I. Look at us first, and see that's sure. It will save you cutting into my talk. We'll take one of your cigars apiece, and you shall see us light up."

I watched the test. The men were absolutely sober, so I gave them each a tepid whiskey and soda.

"Well *and* good," said Carnehan of the eyebrows, wiping the froth from his moustache. "Let me talk now, Dan. We have been all over India, mostly on foot. We have been boiler-fitters, engine-drivers, petty contractors, and all that, and we have decided that India isn't big enough for such as us."

They certainly were too big for the office. Dravot's beard seemed to fill half the room and Carnehan's shoulders the other half, as they sat on the big table. Carnehan continued: "The country isn't half worked out because they that governs it won't let you touch it. They spend all their blessed time in governing it, and you can't lift a spade, nor chip a rock, nor look for oil, nor anything like that without all the Government saying—'Leave it alone, and let us govern.' Therefore, such *as* it is, we will let it alone, and go away to some other place where a man isn't crowded and can come to his own. We are not little men, and there is nothing that we are afraid of except Drink, and we have signed a Contrack on that. *Therefore*, we are going away to be Kings."

"Kings in our own right," muttered Dravot.

"Yes, of course," I said. "You've been tramping in the sun, and it's a very warm night, and hadn't you better sleep over the notion? Come to-morrow."

"Neither drunk nor sunstruck," said Dravot. "We have slept over the notion half a year, and require to see Books and Atlases, and we have decided that there is only one place now in the world that two strong men can Sar-a-*whack*. They call it Kafiristan. By my reckoning it's the top right-hand corner of Afghanistan, not more than three hundred miles from Peshawar. They have two-and-thirty heathen idols there, and we'll be the thirty-third and -fourth. It's a mountainous country, and the women of those parts are very beautiful."

"But that is provided against in the Contrack," said Carnehan. "Neither Woman nor Liqu-or, Daniel."

"And that's all we know, except that no one has gone there, and they fight, and in any place where they fight a man who knows how to drill men can always be a King. We shall go to those parts and say to any King we find—'D'you want to vanquish your foes?' and we will show him how to drill men; for that we know better than anything else. Then we will subvert that King and seize his Throne and establish a Dy-nasty."

"You'll be cut to pieces before you're fifty miles across the Border," I said. "You have to travel through Afghanistan to get to that country. It's one mass of mountains and peaks and glaciers, and no Englishman has been through it. The people are utter brutes, and even if you reached them you couldn't do anything."

"That's more like," said Carnehan. "If you could think us a little more mad we would be more pleased. We have come to you to know about this country, to read a book about it, and to be shown maps. We want you to tell us that we are fools and to show us your books." He turned to the book-cases.

"Are you at all in earnest?" I said.

"A little," said Dravot sweetly. "As big a map as you have got, even if it's all blank where Kafiristan is, and any books you've got. We can read, though we aren't very educated."

I uncased the big thirty-two-miles-to-the-inch map of India, and two smaller Frontier maps, hauled down volume INF–KAN of the *Encyclopaedia Britannica*, and the men consulted them.

"See here!" said Dravot, his thumb on the map. "Up to Jagdallak, Peachey and me know the road. We was there with Roberts' Army. We'll have to turn off to the right at Jagdallak through Laghmann territory. Then we get among the hills—fourteen thousand feet—fifteen thousand—it will be cold work there, but it don't look very far on the map."

I handed him Wood on the *Sources of the Oxus*. Carnehan was deep in the *Encyclopaedia*.

"They're a mixed lot," said Dravot reflectively; "and it won't help us to know the names of their tribes. The more tribes the more they'll fight, and the better for us. From Jagdallak to Ashang. H'mm!"

"But all the information about the country is as sketchy and inaccurate as can be," I protested. "No one knows anything about it really. Here's the file of the *United Services' Institute*. Read what Bellew says."

"Blow Bellew!" said Carnehan. "Dan, they're a stinkin' lot of heathens, but this book here says they think they're related to us English."

I smoked while the men pored over Raverty, Wood, the maps, and the *Encyclopaedia*.

"There is no use your waiting," said Dravot politely. "It's about four o'clock now. We'll go before six o'clock if you want to sleep, and we won't steal any of the papers. Don't you sit up. We're two harmless lunatics, and if you come tomorrow evening down to the Serai we'll say good-bye to you."

"You *are* two fools," I answered. "You'll be turned back at the Frontier or cut up the minute you set foot in Afghanistan. Do you want any money or a recommendation down-country? I can help you to the chance of work next week."

"Next week we shall be hard at work ourselves, thank you," said Dravot. "It isn't so easy being a King as it looks. When we've got our Kingdom in going order we'll let you know, and you can come up and help us to govern it."

"Would two lunatics make a Contrack like that?" said Carnehan, with subdued pride, showing me a greasy half-sheet of notepaper on which was written the following. I copied it, then and there, as a curiosity—

This Contract between me and you persuing witnesseth in the name of God—Amen and so forth.

(One) That me and you will settle this matter together; i. e., to be Kings of Kafiristan.

(Two) That you and me will not, while this matter is being settled, look at any Liquor, nor any Woman black, white, or brown, so as to get mixed up with one or the other harmful.

(Three) That we conduct ourselves with Dignity and Discretion, and if one of us gets into trouble the other will stay by him.

Signed by you and me this day.

Peachey Taliaferro Carnehan.
Daniel Dravot.
Both Gentlemen at Large.

"There was no need for the last article," said Carnehan, blushing modestly; "but it looks regular. Now you know the sort of men that loafers are—we *are* loafers, Dan, until we get out of India—and *do* you think that we would sign a Contrack like that unless we was in earnest? We have kept away from the two things that make life worth having."

"You won't enjoy your lives much longer if you are going to try this idiotic adventure. Don't set the office on fire," I said, "and go away before nine o'clock."

I left them still poring over the maps and making notes on the back of the "Contrack." "Be sure to come down to the Serai to-morrow," were their parting words.

The Kumharsen Serai is the great four-square sink of humanity where the strings of camels and horses from the North load and unload. All the nationalities of Central Asia may be found there, and most of the folk of India proper. Balkh and Bokhara there meet Bengal and Bombay, and try to draw eye-teeth. You can buy ponies, turquoises, Persian pussy-cats, saddle-bags, fat-tailed sheep, and musk in the Kumharsen Serai, and get many strange things for nothing. In the afternoon I went down to see whether my friends intended to keep their word or were lying there drunk.

A priest attired in fragments of ribbons and rags stalked up to me, gravely twisting a child's paper whirligig. Behind him was his servant bending under the load of a crate of mud toys. The two were loading up two camels, and the inhabitants of the Serai watched them with shrieks of laughter.

"The priest is mad," said a horse-dealer to me. "He is going up to Kabul to sell toys to the Amir. He will either be raised to honour or have his head cut off. He came in here this morning and has been behaving madly ever since."

"The witless are under the protection of God," stammered a flat-cheeked Usbeg in broken Hindi. "They foretell future events."

"Would they could have foretold that my caravan would have been cut up by the Shinwaris almost within shadow of the Pass!" grunted the Eusufzai agent of a Rajputana trading-house whose goods had been diverted into the hands of other robbers just across the Border, and whose misfortunes were the laughing-stock of the bazar. "Ohé, priest, whence come you and whither do you go?"

"From Roum have I come," shouted the priest, waving his whirligig; "from Roum, blown by the breath of a hundred devils across the sea! O thieves, robbers, liars, the blessing of Pir Khan on pigs, dogs, and perjurers! Who will take the Protected of God to the North to sell charms that are never still to the Amir? The camels shall not gall, the sons shall not fall sick, and the wives shall remain faithful while they are away, of the men who give me place in their caravan. Who will assist me to slipper the King of the Roos with a golden slipper with a silver heel? The protection of Pir Khan be upon his labours!" He spread out the skirts of his gaberdine and pirouetted between the lines of tethered horses.

"There starts a caravan from Peshawar to Kabul in twenty days, *Hazrut*," said the Eusufzai trader. "My camels go therewith. Do thou also go and bring us good luck."

"I will go even now!" shouted the priest. "I will depart upon my winged camels, and be at Peshawar in a day! Ho! Hazar Mir Khan," he yelled to his servant, "drive out the camels, but let me first mount my own."

He leaped on the back of his beast as it knelt, and, turning round to me, cried: "Come thou also, Sahib, a little along the road, and I will sell thee a charm—an amulet that shall make thee King of Kafiristan."

Then the light broke upon me, and I followed the two camels out of the Serai till we reached open road and the priest halted.

"What d'you think o' that?" said he in English. "Carnehan can't talk their patter, so I've made him my servant. He makes a handsome servant. 'Tisn't for nothing that I've been knocking about the country for fourteen years. Didn't I do that talk neat? We'll hitch on to a caravan at Peshawar till we get to Jagdallak, and then we'll see if we can get donkeys for our camels, and strike into Kafiristan. Whirligigs for the Amir, O Lor! Put your hand under the camel-bags and tell me what you feel."

I felt the butt of a Martini, and another and another.

"Twenty of 'em," said Dravot placidly. "Twenty of 'em and ammunition to correspond, under the whirligigs and the mud dolls."

"Heaven help you if you are caught with those things!" I said. "A Martini is worth her weight in silver among the Pathans."

"Fifteen hundred rupees of capital—every rupee we could beg, borrow, or steal—are invested on these two camels," said Dravot. "We won't get caught. We're going through the Khaiber with a regular caravan. Who'd touch a poor mad priest?"

"Have you got everything you want?" I asked, overcome with astonishment.

"Not yet, but we shall soon. Give us a memento of your kindness, *Brother*. You did me a service yesterday, and that time in Marwar. Half my Kingdom shall you have, as the saying is." I slipped a small charm compass from my watch-chain and handed it up to the priest.

"Good-bye," said Dravot, giving me his hand cautiously. "It's the last time we'll shake hands with an Englishman these many days. Shake hands with him, Carnehan," he cried, as the second camel passed me.

Carnehan leaned down and shook hands. Then the camels passed away along the dusty road, and I was left alone to wonder. My eye could detect no failure in the disguises. The scene in the Serai proved that they were complete to the native mind. There was just the chance, therefore, that Carnehan and Dravot would be able to wander through Afghanistan without detection. But, beyond, they would find death—certain and awful death.

Ten days later a native correspondent, giving me the news of the day from Peshawar, wound up his letter with: "There has been much laughter here on account of a certain mad priest who is going in his estimation to sell petty gauds and insignificant trinkets which he ascribes as great charms to H. H. the Amir of Bokhara. He passed through Peshawar and associated himself to the Second Summer caravan that goes to Kabul. The merchants are pleased because through superstition they imagine that such mad fellows bring good fortune."

The two, then, were beyond the Border. I would have prayed for them, but, that night, a real King died in Europe, and demanded an obituary notice.

The wheel of the world swings through the same phases again and again. Summer passed and winter thereafter, and came and passed again. The daily paper continued, and I with it, and upon the third summer there fell a hot night, a night-issue, and a strained waiting for something to be telegraphed from the other side of the world, exactly as had happened before. A few great men had died in the past two years, the machines worked with more clatter, and some of the trees in the Office garden were a few feet taller. But that was all the difference.

I passed over to the press-room, and went through just such a scene as I have already described. The nervous tension was stronger than it had been two years before, and I felt the heat more acutely. At three o'clock I cried, "Print off," and turned to go, when there crept to my chair what was left of a man. He was bent into a circle, his head was sunk between his shoulders, and he moved his feet one over the other like a bear. I could hardly see whether he walked or crawled—this rag-wrapped, whining cripple who addressed me by name, crying that he was come back. "Can you give me a drink?" he whimpered. "For the Lord's sake, give me a drink!"

I went back to the office, the man following with groans of pain, and I turned up the lamp.

"Don't you know me?" he gasped, dropping into a chair, and he turned his drawn face, surmounted by a shock of gray hair, to the light.

I looked at him intently. Once before had I seen eyebrows that met over the nose in an inch-broad black band, but for the life of me I could not tell where.

"I don't know you," I said, handing him the whiskey. "What can I do for you?"

He took a gulp of the spirit raw, and shivered in spite of the suffocating heat.

"I've come back," he repeated; "and I was the King of Kafiristan—me and Dravot—crowned Kings we was! In this office we settled it—you setting there and giving us the books. I am Peachey—Peachey Taliaferro Carnehan, and you've been setting here ever since—O Lord!"

I was more than a little astonished, and expressed my feelings accordingly.

"It's true," said Carnehan, with a dry cackle, nursing his feet, which were wrapped in rags. "True as gospel. Kings we were, with crowns upon our heads—me and Dravot—poor Dan—oh poor, poor Dan, that would never take advice, not though I begged of him!"

"Take the whiskey," I said, "and take your own time. Tell me all you can recollect of everything from beginning to end. You got across the border on your camels. Dravot dressed as a mad priest and you his servant. Do you remember that?"

"I ain't mad—yet, but I shall be that way soon. Of course I remember. Keep looking at me, or maybe my words will go all to pieces. Keep looking at me in my eyes, and don't say anything."

I leaned forward and looked into his face as steadily as I could. He dropped one hand upon the table and I grasped it by the wrist. It was twisted like a bird's claw, and upon the back was a ragged, red, diamond-shaped scar.

"No, don't look there. Look at *me*," said Carnehan. "That comes afterwards, but for the Lord's sake don't distrack me! We left with that caravan, me and Dravot playing all sorts of antics to amuse the people we were with. Dravot used to make us laugh in the evenings when all the people was cooking their dinners—cooking their dinners, and . . . what did they do then? They lit little fires with sparks that went into Dravot's beard, and we all laughed—fit to die. Little red fires they was, going into Dravot's big red beard—so funny." His eyes left mine, and he smiled foolishly.

"You went as far as Jagdallak with that caravan," I said at a venture, "after you had lit those fires. To Jagdallak, where you turned off to try to get into Kafiristan."

"No, we didn't neither. What are you talking about? We turned off before Jagdallak, because we heard the roads was good. But they wasn't good enough for our two camels—mine and Dravot's. When we left the caravan, Dravot took off all his clothes and mine too, and said we would be heathen, because the Kafirs didn't allow Mohammedans to talk to them. So we dressed betwixt and between, and such a sight as Daniel Dravot I never saw yet nor expect to see again. He burned half his beard, and slung a sheep-skin over his shoulder, and shaved his head into patterns. He shaved mine, too, and made me wear outrageous things to look like a heathen. That was in a most mountainous country, and our camels couldn't go along anymore because of the mountains. They were tall and black, and coming home I saw them fight like wild goats—there are lots of goats in Kafiristan. And these mountains, they never keep still, no more than the goats. Always fighting they are, and don't let you sleep at night."

"Take some more whiskey," I said very slowly. "What did you and Daniel Dravot do when the camels could go no further because of the rough roads that led into Kafiristan?"

"What did which do? There was a party called Peachey Taliaferro Carnehan that was with Dravot. Shall I tell you about him? He died out there in the cold. Slap from the bridge fell old Peachey, turning and twisting in the air like a penny whirligig that you can sell to the Amir. No; they was two for three ha'pence, those whirligigs, or I am much mistaken and woeful sore, . . . And then these camels were no use, and Peachey said to Dravot—'For the Lord's sake let's get out of this before our heads are chopped off,' and with that they killed the camels all among the mountains, not having anything in particular to eat, but first they took off the boxes with the guns and the ammunition, till two men came along driving four mules. Dravot up and dances in front of them, singing—'Sell me four mules.' Says the first man—'If you are rich enough to buy, you are rich enough to rob'; but before ever he could put his hand to his knife, Dravot breaks his neck over his knee, and the other party runs away. So Carnehan loaded the mules with the rifles that was taken off the camels, and together we starts forward into those bitter cold mountainous parts, and never a road broader than the back of your hand."

He paused for a moment, while I asked him if he could remember the nature of the country through which he had journeyed.

"I am telling you as straight as I can, but my head isn't as good as it might be. They drove nails through it to make me hear better how Dravot died. The country was mountainous and the mules were most contrary, and the inhabitants was dispersed and solitary. They went up and up, and down and down, and that other party, Carnehan, was imploring of Dravot not to sing and whistle so loud, for fear of bringing down the tremenjus avalanches. But Dravot says that if a King couldn't sing it wasn't worth being King, and whacked the mules over the rump, and never took no heed for ten cold days. We came to a big level valley all among the mountains, and the mules were near dead, so we killed them, not having anything in special for them or us to eat. We sat upon the boxes, and played odd and even with the cartridges that was jolted out.

"Then ten men with bows and arrows ran down that valley, chasing twenty men with bows and arrows, and the row was tremenjus. They was fair men—fairer than you or me—with yellow hair and remarkable well built. Says Dravot, unpacking the guns—'This is the beginning of the business. We'll fight for the ten men,' and with that he fires two rifles at the twenty men, and drops one of them at two hundred yards from the rock where he was sitting. The other men began to run, but Carnehan and Dravot sits on the boxes picking them off at all ranges, up and down the valley. Then we goes up to the ten men that had run across the snow too, and they fires a footy little arrow at us. Dravot he shoots above their heads, and they all falls down flat. Then he walks over them and kicks them, and then he lifts them up and shakes hands all round to make them friendly like. He calls them and gives them the boxes to carry, and waves his hand for all the world as though he was King already. They takes the boxes and him across the valley and up the hill into a pine wood on the top, where there was half a dozen big stone idols. Dravot he goes to the biggest—a fellow they call Imbra—and lays a rifle and a cartridge at his feet, rubbing his nose respectful with his own nose, patting him on the head, and saluting in front of it. He turns round to the men and nods his head, and says—'That's all right. I'm in the know too, and all these old jimjams are my friends.' Then he opens his mouth and points down it, and when the first man brings him food, he says—'No'; and when the second man brings him food he says—'No'; but when one of the old priests and the boss of the village brings him food, he says—'Yes,' very haughty, and eats it slow. That was how we came to our first village, without any trouble, just as though we had tumbled from the skies. But we tumbled from one of those damned rope-bridges, you see, and—you couldn't expect a man to laugh much after that?"

"Take some more whiskey and go on," I said. "That was the first village you came into. How did you get to be King?"

"I wasn't King," said Carnehan. "Dravot he was the King, and a handsome man he looked with the gold crown on his head, and all. Him and the other party stayed in that village, and every morning Dravot sat by the side of old Imbra, and the people came and worshipped. That was Dravot's order. Then a lot of men came into the valley, and Carnehan and Dravot picks them off with the rifles before they knew where they was, and runs down into the valley and up again the other side and finds another village, same as the first one, and the people all falls down flat on their faces, and Dravot says—'Now what is the trouble between you two villages?' and the people points to a woman, as fair as you or me, that was carried off, and Dravot takes her back to the first village and counts up the dead—eight there was. For each dead man Dravot pours a little milk on the ground and waves his arms like a whirligig, and 'That's all right,' says he. Then he and Carnehan takes the big boss of each village by the arm and walks them down into the valley, and shows them how to scratch a line with a spear right down the valley, and gives each a sod of turf from both sides of the line. Then all the people comes down and shouts like the devil and all, and Dravot says—'Go and dig the land, and be fruitful and multiply,' which they did, though they didn't understand. Then we asks the names of things in their lingo—bread and water and fire and idols and such, and Dravot leads the priest of each village up to the idol, and says he must sit there and judge the people, and if anything goes wrong he is to be shot.

"Next week they was all turning up the land in the valley as quiet as bees and much prettier, and the priests heard all the complaints and told Dravot in dumb show what it was about. 'That's just the beginning,' says Dravot. 'They think we're Gods.' He and Carnehan picks out twenty good men and shows them how to click off a rifle, and form fours, and advance in line, and they was very pleased to do so, and clever to see the hang of it. Then he takes out his pipe and his baccy-pouch and leaves one at one village, and one at the other, and off we two goes to see what was to be done in the next valley. That was all rock, and there was a little village there, and Carnehan says—'Send 'em to the old valley to plant,' and takes 'em there and gives 'em some land that wasn't took before. They were a poor lot, and we blooded 'em with a kid before letting 'em into the new Kingdom. That was to impress the people, and then they settled down quiet, and Carnehan went back to Dravot, who had got into another valley, all snow and ice and most mountainous. There was no people there, and the Army got afraid, so Dravot shoots one of them, and goes on till he finds some people in a village, and the Army explains that unless the people wants to be killed they had better not shoot their little matchlocks; for they had matchlocks. We makes friends with the priest, and I stays there alone with two of the Army, teaching the men how to drill; and a thundering big Chief comes across the snow with kettle-drums and horns twanging, because he heard there was a new God kicking about. Carnehan sights for the brown of the men half a mile across the snow and wings one of them. Then he sends a message to the Chief that, unless he wished to be killed, he must come and shake hands with me and leave his arms behind. The Chief comes alone first, and Carnehan shakes hands with him and whirls his arms about, same as Dravot used, and very much surprised that Chief was, and strokes my eyebrows. Then Carnehan goes alone to the Chief, and asks him in dumb show if he had an enemy he hated. 'I have,' says the Chief. So Carnehan weeds out the pick of his men, and sets the two of the Army to show them drill, and at the end of two weeks the men can maneuver about as well as Volunteers. So he marches with the Chief to a great big plain on the top of a mountain, and the Chief's men rushes into a village and takes it; we three Martinis firing into the brown of the enemy. So we took that village too, and I gives the Chief a rag from my coat and says, 'Occupy till I come,' which was scriptural. By way of a reminder, when me and the Army was eighteen hundred yards away, I drops a bullet near him standing on the snow, and all the people falls flat on their faces. Then I sends a letter to Dravot wherever he be by land or by sea."

At the risk of throwing the creature out of train, I interrupted— "How could you write a letter up yonder?"

"The letter?—Oh!—The letter! Keep looking at me between the eyes, please. It was a string-talk letter, that we'd learned the way of it from a blind beggar in the Punjab."

I remember that there had once come to the office a blind man with a knotted twig and a piece of string which he wound round the twig according to some cipher of his own. He could, after the lapse of days or hours, repeat the sentence which he had reeled up. He had reduced the alphabet to eleven primitive sounds; and he tried to teach me his method, but I could not understand.

"I sent that letter to Dravot," said Carnehan, "and told him to come back because this Kingdom was growing too big for me to handle, and then I struck for the first valley, to see how the priests were working. They called the village we took along with the Chief, Bashkai, and the first village we took, Er-Heb. The priests at Er-Heb was doing all right, but they had a lot of pending cases about land to show me, and some men from another village had been firing arrows at night. I went out and looked for that village, and fired four rounds at it from a thousand yards. That used all the cartridges I cared to spend, and I waited for Dravot, who had been away two or three months, and I kept my people quiet.

"One morning I heard the devil's own noise of drums and horns, and Dan Dravot marches down the hill with his Army and a tail of hundreds of men, and, which was the most amazing, a great gold crown on his head. 'My Gord, Carnehan,' says Daniel, 'this is a tremenjus business, and we've got the whole country as far as it's worth having. I am the son of Alexander by Queen Semiramis, and you're my younger brother and a God too! It's the biggest thing we've ever seen. I've been marching and fighting for six weeks with the Army, and every footy little village for fifty miles has come in rejoiceful; and more than that, I've got the key of the whole show, as you'll see, and I've got a crown for you! I told 'em to make two of 'em at a place called Shu, where the gold lies in the rock like suet in mutton. Gold I've seen, and turquoise I've kicked out of the cliffs, and there's garnets in the sands of the river, and here's a chunk of amber that a man brought me. Call up all the priests and, here, take your crown.'

"One of the men opens a black hair bag, and I slips the crown on. It was too small and too heavy, but I wore it for the glory. Hammered gold it was—five pound weight, like a hoop of a barrel.

" 'Peachey,' says Dravot, 'we don't want to fight no more. The Craft's the trick, so help me!' and he brings forward that same Chief that I left at Bashkai—Billy Fish we called him afterwards, because he was so like Billy Fish that drove the big tank-engine at Mach on the Bolan in the old days. 'Shake hands with him,' says Dravot, and I shook hands and nearly dropped, for Billy Fish gave me the Grip. I said nothing, but tried him with the Fellow Craft Grip. He answers all right, and I tried the Master's Grip, but that was a slip. 'A Fellow Craft he is!' I says to Dan. 'Does he know the word?'—'He does,' says Dan, 'and all the priests know. It's a miracle! The Chiefs and the priests can work a Fellow Craft Lodge in a way that's very like ours, and they've cut the marks on the rocks, but they don't know the Third Degree, and they've come to find out. It's Gord's Truth. I've known these long years that the Afghans knew up to the Fellow Craft Degree, but this is a miracle. A God and a Grand-Master of the Craft am I, and a Lodge in the Third Degree I will open, and we'll raise the head priests and the Chiefs of the villages.'

"'It's against all the law,' I says, 'holding a Lodge without warrant from any one; and you know we never held office in any Lodge.'

"'It's a master-stroke o' policy,' says Dravot. 'It means running the country as easy as a four-wheeled bogie on a down grade. We can't stop to enquire now, or they'll turn against us. I've forty Chiefs at my heel, and passed and raised according to their merit they shall be. Billet these men on the villages, and see that we run up a Lodge of some kind. The temple of Imbra will do for the Lodge-room. The women must make aprons as you show them. I'll hold a levee of Chiefs to-night and Lodge to-morrow.'

"I was fair run off my legs, but I wasn't such a fool as not to see what a pull this Craft business gave us. I showed the priests' families how to make aprons of the degrees, but for Dravot's apron the blue border and marks was made of turquoise lumps on white hide, not cloth. We took a great square stone in the temple for the Master's chair, and little stones for the officers' chairs, and painted the black pavement with white squares, and did what we could to make things regular.

"At the levee which was held that night on the hillside with big bonfires, Dravot gives out that him and me were Gods and sons of Alexander, and Past Grand-Masters in the Craft, and was come to make Kafiristan a country where every man should eat in peace and drink in quiet, and 'specially obey us. Then the Chiefs come round to shake hands, and they were so hairy and white and fair it was just shaking hands with old friends. We gave them names according as they was like men we had known in India—Billy Fish, Holly Dilworth, Pikky Kergan, that was Bazar-master when I was at Mhow, and so on, and so on.

"*The* most amazing miracles was at Lodge next night. One of the old priests was watching us continuous, and I felt uneasy, for I knew we'd have to fudge the Ritual, and I didn't know what the men knew. The old priest was a stranger come in from beyond the village of Bashkai. The minute Dravot puts on the Master's apron that the girls had made for him, the priest fetches a whoop and a howl, and tries to overturn the stone that Dravot was sitting on. 'It's all up now,' I says. 'That comes of meddling with the Craft without warrant!' Dravot never winked an eye, not when ten priests took and tilted over the Grand-Master's chair—which was to say the stone of Imbra. The priest begins rubbing the bottom end of it to clear away the black dirt, and presently he shows all the other priests the Master's Mark, same as was on Dravot's apron, cut into the stone. Not even the priests of the temple of Imbra knew it was there. The old chap falls flat on his face at Dravot's feet and kisses 'em. 'Luck again,' says Dravot, across the Lodge to me; 'they say it's the missing Mark that no one could understand the why of. We're more than safe now.' Then he bangs the butt of his gun for a gavel and says: 'By virtue of the authority vested in me by my own right hand and the help of Peachey, I declare myself Grand-Master of all Freemasonry in Kafiristan in this the Mother Lodge o' the country, and King of Kafiristan equally with Peachey!' At that he puts on his crown and I puts on mine—I was doing Senior Warden—and we opens the Lodge in most ample form. It was a amazing miracle! The priests moved in Lodge through the first two degrees almost without telling, as if the memory was coming back to them. After that, Peachey and Dravot raised such as was worthy—high priests and Chiefs of far-off villages. Billy Fish was the first, and I can tell you we scared the soul out of him. It was not in any way according to Ritual, but it served our turn. We didn't raise more than ten of the biggest men, because we didn't want to make the Degree common. And they was clamouring to be raised.

"'In another six months,' says Dravot, 'we'll hold another Communication, and see how you are working.' Then he asks them about their villages, and learns that they was fighting one against the other, and were sick and tired of it. And when they wasn't doing that they was fighting with the Mohammedans. 'You can fight those when they come into our country,' says Dravot. 'Tell off every tenth man of your tribes for a Frontier guard, and send two hundred at a time to this valley to be drilled. Nobody is going to be shot or speared anymore so long as he does well, and I know that you won't cheat me, because you're white people—sons of Alexander—and not like common, black Mohammedans. You are *my* people, and by God,' says he, running off into English at the end—'I'll make a damned fine Nation of you, or I'll die in the making!'

"I can't tell all we did for the next six months, because Dravot did a lot I couldn't see the hang of, and he learned their lingo in a way I never could. My work was to help the people plough, and now and again go out with some of the Army and see what the other villages were doing, and make 'em throw rope-bridges across the ravines which cut up the country horrid. Dravot was very kind to me, but when he walked up and down in the pine wood pulling that bloody red beard of his with both fists I knew he was thinking plans I could not advise about, and I just waited for orders.

"But Dravot never showed me disrespect before the people. They were afraid of me and the Army, but they loved Dan. He was the best of friends with the priests and the Chiefs; but anyone could come across the hills with a complaint, and Dravot would hear him out fair, and call four priests together and say what was to be done. He used to call in Billy Fish from Bashkai, and Pikky Kergan from Shu, and an old Chief we called Kafoozelum—it was like enough to his real name—and hold councils with 'em when there was any fighting to be done in small villages. That was his Council of War, and the four priests of Bashkai, Shu, Khawak, and Madora was his Privy Council. Between the lot of 'em they sent me, with forty men and twenty rifles, and sixty men carrying turquoises, into the Ghorband country to buy those handmade Martini rifles, that come out of the Amir's workshops at Kabul, from one of the Amir's Herati regiments that would have sold the very teeth out of their mouths for turquoises.

"I stayed in Ghorband a month, and gave the Governor there the pick of my baskets for hush-money, and bribed the Colonel of the regiment some more, and, between the two and the tribes-people, we got more than a hundred hand-made Martinis, a hundred good Kohat Jezails that'll throw to six hundred yards, and forty man-loads of very bad ammunition for the rifles. I came back with what I had, and distributed 'em among the men that the Chiefs sent in to me to drill. Dravot was too busy to attend to those things, but the old Army that we first made helped me, and we turned out five hundred men that could drill, and two hundred that knew how to hold arms pretty straight. Even those corkscrewed, hand-made guns was a miracle to them. Dravot talked big about powder-shops and factories, walking up and down in the pine wood when the winter was coming on.

"'I won't make a Nation,' says he; 'I'll make an Empire! These men aren't niggers; they're English! Look at their eyes—look at their mouths. Look at the way they stand up. They sit on chairs in their own houses. They're the Lost Tribes, or something like it, and they've grown to be English. I'll take a census in the spring if the priests don't get frightened. There must be a fair two million of 'em in these hills. The villages are full o' little children. Two million people—two hundred and fifty thousand fighting men—and all English! They only want the rifles and a little drilling. Two hundred and fifty thousand men ready to cut in on Russia's right flank when she tries for India! Peachey, man,' he says, chewing his beard in great hunks, 'we shall be Emperors—Emperors of the Earth! Rajah Brooke will be a suckling to us. I'll treat with the Viceroy on equal terms. I'll ask him to send me twelve picked English—twelve that I know of—to help us govern a bit. There's Mackray, Sergeant-pensioner at Segowli—many's the good dinner he's given me, and his wife a pair of trousers. There's Donkin, the Warder of Tounghoo Jail; there's hundreds that I could lay my hand on if I was in India. The Viceroy shall do it for me; I'll send a man through in the spring for those men, and I'll write for a dispensation from the Grand Lodge for what I've done as Grand-Master. That—and all the Sniders that'll be thrown out when the native troops in India take up the Martini. They'll be worn smooth, but they'll do for fighting in these hills. Twelve English, a hundred thousand Sniders run through the Amir's country in driblets—I'd be content with twenty thousand in one year—and we'd be an Empire. When everything was shipshape, I'd hand over the crown—this crown I'm wearing now—to Queen Victoria on my knees, and she'd say: "Rise up, Sir Daniel Dravot." Oh, it's big! It's big, I tell you! But there's so much to be done in every place—Bashkai, Khawak, Shu, and everywhere else.'

" 'What is it?' I says. 'There are no more men coming in to be drilled this autumn. Look at those fat, black clouds. They're bringing the snow.'

" 'It isn't that,' says Daniel, putting his hand very hard on my shoulder; 'and I don't wish to say anything that's against you, for no other living man would have followed me and made me what I am as you have done. You're a first-class Commander-in-Chief, and the people know you; but—it's a big country, and somehow you can't help me, Peachey, in the way I want to be helped.'

" 'Go to your blasted priests, then!' I said, and I was sorry when I made that remark, but it did hurt me sore to find Daniel talking so superior when I'd drilled all the men, and done all he told me.

" 'Don't let's quarrel, Peachey,' says Daniel, without cursing. 'You're a King too, and the half of this Kingdom is yours; but can't you see, Peachey, we want cleverer men than us now—three or four of 'em, that we can scatter about for our Deputies. It's a hugeous great State, and I can't always tell the right thing to do, and I haven't time for all I want to do, and here's the winter coming on, and all.' He put half his beard into his mouth, all red like the gold of his crown.

" 'I'm sorry, Daniel,' says I. 'I've done all I could. I've drilled the men and shown the people how to stack their oats better; and I've brought in those tinware rifles from Ghorband—but I know what you're driving at. I take it Kings always feel oppressed that way.'

" 'There's another thing too,' says Dravot, walking up and down. 'The winter's coming, and these people won't be giving much trouble, and if they do we can't move about. I want a wife.'

" 'For Gord's sake leave the women alone!' I says. 'We've both got all the work we can, though I *am* a fool. Remember the Contrack, and keep clear o' women.'

" 'The Contrack only lasted till such time as we was Kings; and Kings we have been these months past,' says Dravot, weighing his crown in his hand. 'You go get a wife too, Peachey—a nice, strappin', plump girl that'll keep you warm in the winter. They're prettier than English girls, and we can take the pick of 'em. Boil 'em once or twice in hot water, and they'll come out like chicken and ham.'

" 'Don't tempt me!' I says. 'I will not have any dealings with a woman not till we are a dam' side more settled than we are now. I've been doing the work o' two men, and you've been doing the work o' three. Let's lie off a bit, and see if we can get some better tobacco from Afghan country and run in some good liquor; but no women.'

"'Who's talking o' *women*?' says Dravot. 'I said *wife*—a Queen to breed a King's son for the King. A Queen out of the strongest tribe, that'll make them your blood-brothers, and that'll lie by your side and tell you all the people thinks about you and their own affairs. That's what I want.'

"'Do you remember that Bengali woman I kept at Mogul Serai when I was a plate-layer?' says I. 'A fat lot o' good she was to me. She taught me the lingo and one or two other things; but what happened? She ran away with the Station-master's servant and half my month's pay. Then she turned up at Dadur Junction in tow of a half-caste, and had the impidence to say I was her husband—all among the drivers in the running-shed too!'

"'We've done with that,' says Dravot; 'these women are whiter than you or me, and a Queen I will have for the winter months.'

"'For the last time o' asking, Dan, do *not*,' I says. 'It'll only bring us harm. The Bible says that Kings ain't to waste their strength on women, especially when they've got a new raw Kingdom to work over.'

"'For the last time of answering, I will,' said Dravot, and he went away through the pine-trees looking like a big red devil, the sun being on his crown and beard and all.

"But getting a wife was not as easy as Dan thought. He put it before the Council, and there was no answer till Billy Fish said that he'd better ask the girls. Dravot damned them all round. 'What's wrong with me?' he shouts, standing by the idol Imbra. 'Am I a dog or am I not enough of a man for your wenches? Haven't I put the shadow of my hand over this country? Who stopped the last Afghan raid?' It was me really, but Dravot was too angry to remember. 'Who bought your guns? Who repaired the bridges? Who's the Grand-Master of the sign cut in the stone?' says he, and he thumped his hand on the block that he used to sit on in Lodge, and at Council, which opened like Lodge always. Billy Fish said nothing, and no more did the others. 'Keep your hair on, Dan,' said I; 'and ask the girls. That's how it's done at Home, and these people are quite English.'

"'The marriage of the King is a matter of State,' says Dan, in a white-hot rage, for he could feel, I hope, that he was going against his better mind. He walked out of the Council-room, and the others sat still, looking at the ground.

"'Billy Fish,' says I to the Chief of Bashkai, 'what's the difficulty here? A straight answer to a true friend.'

"'You know,' says Billy Fish. 'How should a man tell you who knows everything? How can daughters of men marry Gods or Devils? It's not proper.'

"I remembered something like that in the Bible; but if, after seeing us as long as they had, they still believed we were Gods, it wasn't for me to undeceive them.

"'A God can do anything,' says I. 'If the King is fond of a girl he'll not let her die.'

"'She'll have to,' said Billy Fish. 'There are all sorts of Gods and Devils in these mountains, and now and again a girl marries one of them and isn't seen anymore. Besides, you two know the Mark cut in the stone. Only the Gods know that. We thought you were men till you showed the sign of the Master.'

"I wished then that we had explained about the loss of the genuine secrets of a Master-Mason at the first go-off; but I said nothing. All that night there was a blowing of horns in a little dark temple half-way down the hill, and I heard a girl crying fit to die. One of the priests told us that she was being prepared to marry the King.

"'I'll have no nonsense of that kind,' says Dan. 'I don't want to interfere with your customs, but I'll take my own wife.'

"'The girl's a little bit afraid,' says the priest. 'She thinks she's going to die, and they are a-heartening of her up down in the temple.'

"'Hearten her very tender, then,' says Dravot, 'or I'll hearten you with the butt of a gun so you'll never want to be heartened again.' He licked his lips, did Dan, and stayed up walking about more than half the night, thinking of the wife that he was going to get in the morning. I wasn't any means comfortable, for I knew that dealings with a woman in foreign parts, though you was a crowned King twenty times over, could not but be risky. I got up very early in the morning while Dravot was asleep, and I saw the priests talking together in whispers, and the Chiefs talking together too, and they looked at me out of the corners of their eyes.

"'What is up, Fish?' I says to the Bashkai man, who was wrapped up in his furs and looking splendid to behold.

"'I can't rightly say,' says he; 'but if you can make the King drop all this nonsense about marriage, you'll be doing him and me and yourself a great service.'

"'That I do believe,' says I. 'But sure, you know, Billy, as well as me, having fought against and for us, that the King and me are nothing more than two of the finest men that God Almighty ever made. Nothing more, I do assure you.'

"'That may be,' says Billy Fish, 'and yet I should be sorry if it was.' He sinks his head upon his great fur cloak for a minute and thinks. 'King,' says he, 'be you man or God or Devil, I'll stick by you to-day. I have twenty of my men with me, and they will follow me. We'll go to Bashkai until the storm blows over.'

"A little snow had fallen in the night, and everything was white except the greasy fat clouds that blew down and down from the North. Dravot came out with his crown on his head, swinging his arms and stamping his feet, and looking more pleased than Punch.

"'For the last time, drop it, Dan,' says I in a whisper; 'Billy Fish here says that there will be a row.'

"'A row among my people!' says Dravot. 'Not much. Peachey, you're a fool not to get a wife too. Where's the girl?' says he with a voice as loud as the braying of a jackass. 'Call up all the Chiefs and priests, and let the Emperor see if his wife suits him.'

"There was no need to call anyone. They were all there leaning on their guns and spears round the clearing in the centre of the pine wood. A lot of priests went down to the little temple to bring up the girl, and the horns blew fit to wake the dead. Billy Fish saunters round and gets as close to Daniel as he could, and behind him stood his twenty men with matchlocks. Not a man of them under six feet. I was next to Dravot, and behind me was twenty men of the regular Army. Up comes the girl, and a strapping wench she was, covered with silver and turquoises, but white as death, and looking back every minute at the priests.

"'She'll do,' said Dan, looking her over. 'What's to be afraid of, lass? Come and kiss me.' He puts his arm round her. She shuts her eyes, gives a bit of a squeak, and down goes her face in the side of Dan's flaming red beard.

"'The slut's bitten me!' says he, clapping his hand to his neck, and, sure enough, his hand was red with blood. Billy Fish and two of his matchlock-men catches hold of Dan by the shoulders and drags him into the Bashkai lot, while the priests howls in their lingo—'Neither God nor Devil, but a man!' I was all taken aback, for a priest cut at me in front, and the Army behind began firing into the Bashkai men.

"'God A'mighty!' says Dan. 'What is the meaning o' this?'

"'Come back! Come away!' says Billy Fish. 'Ruin and Mutiny is the matter. We'll break for Bashkai if we can.'

"I tried to give some sort of orders to my men—the men o' the regular Army—but it was no use, so I fired into the brown of 'em with an English Martini and drilled three beggars in a line. The valley was full of shouting, howling creatures, and every soul was shrieking, 'Not a God nor a Devil, but only a man!' The Bashkai troops stuck to Billy Fish all they were worth, but their matchlocks wasn't half as good as the Kabul breech-loaders, and four of them dropped. Dan was bellowing like a bull, for he was very wrathy; and Billy Fish had a hard job to prevent him running out at the crowd.

"'We can't stand,' says Billy Fish. 'Make a run for it down the valley! The whole place is against us.' The matchlock-men ran, and we went down the valley in spite of Dravot. He was swearing horrible and crying out he was a King. The priests rolled great stones on us, and the regular Army fired hard, and there wasn't more than six men, not counting Dan, Billy Fish, and me, that came down to the bottom of the valley alive.

"Then they stopped firing, and the horns in the temple blew again. 'Come away—for Gord's sake come away!' says Billy Fish. 'They'll send runners out to all the villages before ever we get to Bashkai. I can protect you there, but I can't do anything now.'

"My own notion is that Dan began to go mad in his head from that hour. He stared up and down like a stuck pig. Then he was all for walking back alone and killing the priests with his bare hands; which he could have done. 'An Emperor am I,' says Daniel, 'and next year I shall be a Knight of the Queen.'

" 'All right, Dan,' says I; 'but come along now while there's time.'

" 'It's your fault,' says he, 'for not looking after your Army better. There was mutiny in the midst, and you didn't know—you damned engine-driving, plate-laying, missionary's-pass-hunting hound!' He sat upon a rock and called me every foul name he could lay tongue to. I was too heart-sick to care, though it was all his foolishness that brought the smash.

" 'I'm sorry, Dan,' says I, 'but there's no accounting for natives. This business is our 'Fifty-Seven. Maybe we'll make something out of it yet, when we've got to Bashkai.'

" 'Let's get to Bashkai, then,' says Dan, 'and, by God, when I come back here again I'll sweep the valley so there isn't a bug in a blanket left!'

"We walked all that day, and all that night Dan was stumping up and down on the snow, chewing his beard and muttering to himself.

" 'There's no hope o' getting clear,' said Billy Fish. 'The priests will have sent runners to the villages to say that you are only men. Why didn't you stick on as Gods till things was more settled? I'm a dead man,' says Billy Fish, and he throws himself down on the snow and begins to pray to his Gods.

"Next morning we was in a cruel bad country—all up and down, no level ground at all, and no food either. The six Bashkai men looked at Billy Fish hungry-way as if they wanted to ask something, but they said never a word. At noon we came to the top of a flat mountain all covered with snow, and when we climbed up into it, behold, there was an Army in position waiting in the middle!

" 'The runners have been very quick,' says Billy Fish, with a little bit of a laugh. 'They are waiting for us.'

"Three or four men began to fire from the enemy's side, and a chance shot took Daniel in the calf of the leg. That brought him to his senses. He looks across the snow at the Army, and sees the rifles that we had brought into the country.

"'We're done for,' says he. 'They are Englishmen, these people,—and it's my blasted nonsense that has brought you to this. Get back, Billy Fish, and take your men away; you've done what you could, and now cut for it. Carnehan,' says he, 'shake hands with me and go along with Billy. Maybe they won't kill you. I'll go and meet 'em alone. It's me that did it. Me, the King!'

"'Go!' says I. 'Go to Hell, Dan. I'm with you here. Billy Fish, you clear out, and we two will meet those folk.'

"'I'm a Chief' says Billy Fish, quite quiet. 'I stay with you. My men can go.'

"The Bashkai fellows didn't wait for a second word, but ran off; and Dan and me and Billy Fish walked across to where the drums were drumming and the horns were horning. It was cold—awful cold. I've got that cold in the back of my head now. There's a lump of it there."

The punkah-coolies had gone to sleep. Two kerosene lamps were blazing in the office, and the perspiration poured down my face and splashed on the blotter as I leaned forward. Carnehan was shivering, and I feared that his mind might go. I wiped my face, took a fresh grip of the piteously mangled hands, and said: "What happened after that?"

The momentary shift of my eyes had broken the clear current.

"What was you pleased to say?" whined Carnehan. "They took them without any sound. Not a little whisper all along the snow, not though the King knocked down the first man that set hand on him—not though old Peachey fired his last cartridge into the brown of 'em. Not a single solitary sound did those swines make. They just closed up tight, and I tell you their furs stunk. There was a man called Billy Fish, a good friend of us all, and they cut his throat, Sir, then and there, like a pig; and the King kicks up the bloody snow and says: 'We've had a dashed fine run for our money. What's coming next?' But Peachey, Peachey Taliaferro, I tell you, Sir, in confidence as betwixt two friends, he lost his head, Sir. No, he didn't neither. The King lost his head, so he did, all along o' one of those cunning rope-bridges. Kindly let me have the paper-cutter, Sir. It tilted this way. They marched him a mile across that snow to a rope-bridge over a ravine with a river at the bottom. You may have seen such. They prodded him behind like an ox. 'Damn your eyes!' says the King. 'D'you suppose I can't die like a gentleman?' He turns to Peachey—Peachey that was crying like a child. 'I've brought you to this, Peachey,' says he. 'Brought you out of your happy life to be killed in Kafiristan, where you was late Commander-in-Chief of the Emperor's forces. Say you forgive me, Peachey.'—'I do,' says Peachey. 'Fully and freely do I forgive you, Dan.'—'Shake hands, Peachey,' says he. 'I'm going now.' Out he goes, looking neither right nor left, and when he was plumb in the middle of those dizzy dancing ropes, 'Cut, you beggars,' he shouts; and they cut, and old Dan fell, turning round and round and round, twenty thousand miles, for he took half an hour to fall till he struck the water, and I could see his body caught on a rock with the gold crown close beside.

"But do you know what they did to Peachey between two pine-trees? They crucified him, Sir, as Peachey's hands will show. They used wooden pegs for his hands and his feet; and he didn't die. He hung there and screamed, and they took him down next day, and said it was a miracle that he wasn't dead. They took him down—poor old Peachey that hadn't done them any harm—that hadn't done them any—"

He rocked to and fro and wept bitterly, wiping his eyes with the back of his scarred hands and moaning like a child for some ten minutes.

"They was cruel enough to feed him up in the temple, because they said he was more of a God than old Daniel that was a man. Then they turned him out on the snow, and told him to go home, and Peachey came home in about a year, begging along the roads quite safe; for Daniel Dravot he walked before and said: 'Come along, Peachey. It's a big thing we're doing.' The mountains they danced at night, and the mountains they tried to fall on Peachey's head, but Dan he held up his hand, and Peachey came along bent double. He never let go of Dan's hand, and he never let go of Dan's head. They gave it to him as a present in the temple, to remind him not to come again, and though the crown was pure gold, and Peachey was starving, never would Peachey sell the same. You knew Dravot, Sir! You knew Right Worshipful Brother Dravot! Look at him now!"

He fumbled in the mass of rags round his bent waist; brought out a black horsehair bag embroidered with silver thread; and shook therefrom on to my table—the dried, withered head of Daniel Dravot! The morning sun that had long been paling the lamps struck the red beard and blind, sunken eyes; struck, too, a heavy circlet of gold studded with raw turquoises, that Carnehan placed tenderly on the battered temples.

"You be'old now," said Carnehan, "the Emperor in his 'abit as he lived—the King of Kafiristan with his crown upon his head. Poor old Daniel that was a monarch once!"

I shuddered, for, in spite of defacements manifold, I recognised the head of the man of Marwar Junction. Carnehan rose to go. I attempted to stop him. He was not fit to walk abroad. "Let me take away the whiskey, and give me a little money," he gasped. "I was a King once. I'll go to the Deputy Commissioner and ask to set in the Poorhouse till I get my health. No, thank you, I can't wait till you get a carriage for me. I've urgent private affairs—in the South—at Marwar."

He shambled out of the office and departed in the direction of the Deputy Commissioner's house. That day at noon I had occasion to go down the blinding hot Mall, and I saw a crooked man crawling along the white dust of the roadside, his hat in his hand, quavering dolorously after the fashion of street-singers at Home. There was not a soul in sight, and he was out of all possible earshot of the houses. And he sang through his nose, turning his head from right to left:—

"The Son of Man goes forth to war,
A golden crown to gain;
His blood-red banner streams afar—
Who follows in his train?"

I waited to hear no more, but put the poor wretch into my carriage and drove him off to the nearest missionary for eventual transfer to the Asylum. He repeated the hymn twice while he was with me, whom he did not in the least recognise, and I left him singing it to the missionary.

Two days later I enquired after his welfare of the Superintendent of the Asylum.

"He was admitted suffering from sun-stroke. He died early yesterday morning," said the Superintendent. "Is it true that he was half an hour bareheaded in the sun at mid-day?"

"Yes," said I, "but do you happen to know if he had anything upon him by any chance when he died?"

"Not to my knowledge," said the Superintendent.

And there the matter rests.

QUESTIONS

1. Why, after agreeing to serve as a trusted messenger between Dravot and Carnehan, does the narrator report them to the authorities in Degumber State?

2. Why do Dravot and Carnehan bind themselves to the "Contrack" even though they dislike bureaucratic rules and laws? (142)

3. What does Dravot mean when he says, "We're two harmless lunatics"? (143)

4. Why do Dravot and Carnehan agree to keep "away from the two things that make life worth having"? (143)

5. Why is Dravot so confident that he and Carnehan will succeed in becoming kings?

6. At the end of the story, why does Carnehan say, "I was a King once," when earlier in his tale he says he wasn't king, but "Dravot he was the King"? (161, 149)

7. Why does Carnehan sometimes refer to himself in the third person when he tells his story to the narrator three years after going to Kafiristan?

8. Why does Dravot claim to be the son of Alexander and Queen Semiramis as he leads his army in Kafiristan?

9. Why is Carnehan concerned with violating the law when Dravot says he wants to establish a lodge?

10. What does Dravot mean when he says to the Kafiristan people, "You are *my* people"? Why does he want to "make a damned fine Nation" of them? (153)

11. Why does Carnehan tell Chief Billy Fish that he and Dravot "are nothing more than two of the finest men that God Almighty ever made" when the Kafiristan people believe that Carnehan and Dravot are gods? (157)

12. Why do the Kafiristan people drop Dravot from a bridge but crucify Carnehan?

13. Why do the Kafiristan people say that Carnehan "was more of a God than old Daniel that was a man"? (161)

14. Why does Carnehan return to tell the narrator his story and bring him Dravot's head?

15. Why does Carnehan sing a song about "the Son of Man" before he dies? (162)

16. Why does the enterprise of Dravot and Carnehan ultimately fail?

17. To whom does the title, "The Man Who Would Be King," refer?

FOR FURTHER REFLECTION

1. Is the story a cautionary tale of the pitfalls of imperial ambition and a criticism of British colonial attitudes and practices, or is it a description of how a criminal enterprise implodes?

2. What is the narrator's attitude toward the native populations in the story?

3. Which is more important in this story, class or race?

4. What influences Dravot and Carnehan the most as they pursue their imperial project in Afghanistan: "the Law," "the Contrack," the rules for secret lodges, or the Bible?

5. What does the story tell us about Kipling's attitude toward the British Empire?

6. Does the narrator of the story convey a moral point of view?

LUIGI PIRANDELLO

Luigi Pirandello (1867–1936) was born in Girgenti (now Agrigento), a town in southern Sicily. At that time, Italy was in the process of uniting from separate states into a single nation; both his parents' families were actively engaged in the struggle for unification. Pirandello's father, Stefano, a middle-class merchant in the sulfur trade, wanted his son to enter business, but a brief stint in the sulfur-mining industry dissuaded Pirandello from this pursuit. Pirandello finished high school in Palermo, the capital of Sicily, where his family had moved in 1880, and during this time he also began to write poetry. In 1887, he went to study at the University of Rome. He published his first collection of poems, *Mal giocondo*, in 1889, and he completed a doctorate in philology at the University of Bonn, Germany, in 1891.

Pirandello's first collection of short stories, *Amori senza amore*, appeared in 1894. That same year, his father arranged his marriage to Antonietta Portulano, the daughter of a wealthy business associate. The dowry was invested heavily in the sulfur industry, and it gave Pirandello the financial independence to live in Rome and pursue his literary goals, but when a landslide shut down the mines in 1903, the family fortune was devastated. For income, Pirandello sold stories and taught Italian and German in Rome.

The sudden impoverishment emotionally unhinged Pirandello's wife. Her mental illness was characterized by paranoia, intense jealousy of her husband, and, eventually, physical violence. Pirandello committed her to an asylum in 1919, and she remained in institutional care until her death in 1959.

Antonietta's illness had an enormous impact on Pirandello's life and work. He began to write about his troubled domestic situation shortly after her breakdown, and his serialized novel, *Il fu Mattia Pascal* (1904), was an immediate success. In the book, Pirandello explored issues of the subconscious, and the mercurial roles that emotions and experiences play in shaping personality. When he wrote *Six Characters in Search of an Author*, in 1921, he used drama to articulate his view that—unlike art—neither life nor personality are fixed, stable entities. Jarringly unconventional, the play was poorly received when it was first performed in Rome, but the crowds in Milan loved it. Over time, its groundbreaking importance was recognized, and its influence is evident in many works of twentieth-century absurdist and existentialist theater.

Pirandello became a member of the Fascist Party in 1923, and received Benito Mussolini's support in founding the Teatro d'Arte di Roma, but the theater closed in 1928 due to financial difficulties. In his later years, Pirandello grew disillusioned with Mussolini and with fascism.

Before the work of Sigmund Freud was widely known, Pirandello studied the writings of Alfred Binet, a French experimental psychologist. Using this knowledge to explore the underlying motivations of people's actions, Pirandello became an insightful observer of the illusions that individuals create in order to cope with life—its monotony, relationships, and challenges. In *Six Characters*, he focuses on the distinction between character, as embodied by the eponymous six, and personality, investigating the question of whether all the people who share an experience also share the same reality.

Pirandello was one of the great modernist writers and was a pioneer in using the new science of psychology to inform his artistic drama. He won the Nobel Prize in Literature in 1934.

LUIGI PIRANDELLO

Six Characters in Search of an Author

CHARACTERS OF THE PLAY-IN-THE-MAKING

THE FATHER

THE MOTHER

THE SON, AGED 22

THE STEPDAUGHTER, 18

THE BOY, 14

THE LITTLE GIRL, 4

MADAM PACE

ACTORS OF THE COMPANY

THE DIRECTOR

LEADING LADY

LEADING MAN

SECOND ACTRESS

INGENUE

JUVENILE LEAD

OTHER ACTORS AND ACTRESSES

STAGE MANAGER

PROMPTER

PROPERTY MAN

TECHNICIAN

DIRECTOR'S SECRETARY

STAGE DOOR MAN

STAGE CREW

THE PLACE: *The stage of a playhouse.*

The play has neither acts nor scenes. The performance should be interrupted twice: first—without any lowering of the curtain—when the Director and the chief among the Characters retire to put the scenario together and the Actors leave the stage; second, when the Technician lets the curtain down by mistake.

When the audience arrives in the theater, the curtain is raised and the stage, as normally in the daytime, is without wings or scenery and almost completely dark and empty. From the beginning we are to receive the impression of an unrehearsed performance.

Two stairways, left and right respectively, connect the stage with the auditorium.

On stage the dome of the prompter's box has been placed on one side of the box itself. On the other side, at the front of the stage, a small table and an armchair with its back to the audience, for the Director.

Two other small tables of different sizes with several chairs around them have also been placed at the front of the stage, ready as needed for the rehearsal. Other chairs here and there, left and right, for the actors, and at the back, a piano, on one side and almost hidden.

As soon as the houselights dim, the Technician is seen entering at the door on stage. He is wearing a blue shirt, and a tool bag hangs from his belt. From a corner at the back he takes several stage braces, then arranges them on the floor downstage, and kneels down to hammer some nails in. At the sound of the hammering, the Stage Manager comes running from the door that leads to the dressing rooms.

STAGE MANAGER. Oh! What are you doing?

TECHNICIAN. What am I doing? Hammering.

STAGE MANAGER. At this hour? (*He looks at the clock.*) It's ten-thirty already. The Director will be here any moment. For the rehearsal.

TECHNICIAN. I gotta have time to work, too, see.

STAGE MANAGER. You will have. But not now.

TECHNICIAN. When?

STAGE MANAGER. Not during rehearsal hours. Now move along, take all this stuff away, and let me set the stage for the second act of, um, *The Game of Role Playing.*

Muttering, grumbling, the Technician picks up the stage braces and goes away. Meanwhile, from the door on stage, the Actors of the Company start coming in, both men and women, one at a time at first, then in twos, at random, nine or ten of them, the number one would expect as the cast in rehearsals of Pirandello's play The Game of Role Playing, *which is the order of the day. They enter, greet the Stage Manager and each other, all saying good-morning to all. Several go to their dressing rooms. Others, among them the Prompter, who has a copy of the script rolled up under his arm, stay on stage, waiting for the Director to begin the rehearsal. Meanwhile, either seated in conversational groups, or standing, they exchange a few words among themselves. One lights a cigarette, one complains about the part he has been assigned, one reads aloud to his companions items of news from a theater journal. It would be well if both the Actresses and the Actors wore rather gay and brightly colored clothes and if this first improvised scene combined vivacity with naturalness. At a certain point, one of the actors can sit down at the piano and strike up a dance tune. The younger Actors and Actresses start dancing.*

STAGE MANAGER, *clapping his hands to call them to order.* All right, that's enough of that. The Director's here.

The noise and the dancing stop at once. The Actors turn and look toward the auditorium from the door of which the Director is now seen coming. A bowler hat on his head, a walking stick under his arm, and a big cigar in his mouth, he walks down the aisle and, greeted by the Actors, goes on stage by one of the two stairways. The Secretary hands him his mail: several newspapers and a script in a wrapper.

DIRECTOR. Letters?

SECRETARY. None. That's all the mail there is.

DIRECTOR, *handing him the script.* Take this to my room. (*Then, looking around and addressing himself to the Stage Manager.*) We can't see each other in here. Want to give us a little light?

STAGE MANAGER. OK.

He goes to give the order, and shortly afterward, the whole left side of the stage where the Actors are is lit by a vivid white light. Meanwhile, the Prompter has taken up his position in his box. He uses a small lamp and has the script open in front of him.

DIRECTOR, *clapping his hands.* Very well, let's start. (*To the Stage Manager.*) Someone missing?

STAGE MANAGER. The Leading Lady.

DIRECTOR. As usual! (*He looks at the clock.*) We're ten minutes late already. Fine her for that, would you, please? Then she'll learn to be on time.

He has not completed his rebuke when the voice of the Leading Lady is heard from the back of the auditorium.

LEADING LADY. No, no, for heaven's sake! I'm here! I'm here! (*She is dressed all in white with a big, impudent hat on her head and a cute little dog in her arms. She runs down the aisle and climbs one of the sets of stairs in great haste.*)

DIRECTOR. You've sworn an oath always to keep people waiting.

LEADING LADY. You must excuse me. Just couldn't find a taxi. But you haven't even begun, I see. And I'm not on right away. (*Then, calling the Stage Manager by name, and handing the little dog over to him.*) Would you please shut him in my dressing room?

DIRECTOR, *grumbling.* And the little dog to boot! As if there weren't enough dogs around here. (*He claps his hands again and turns to the Prompter.*) Now then, the second act of *The Game of Role Playing.* (*As he sits down in his armchair.*) Quiet, gentlemen. Who's on stage?

The Actresses and Actors clear the front of the stage and go and sit on one side, except for the three who will start the rehearsal and the Leading Lady who, disregarding the Director's request, sits herself down at one of the two small tables.

DIRECTOR, *to the Leading Lady.* You're in this scene, are you?

LEADING LADY. Me? No, no.

DIRECTOR, *irritated.* Then how about getting up, for heaven's sake?

The Leading Lady rises and goes and sits beside the other Actors who have already gone to one side.

DIRECTOR, *to the Prompter.* Start, start.

PROMPTER, *reading from the script.* "In the house of Leone Gala. A strange room, combined study and dining room."

DIRECTOR, *turning to the Stage Manager.* We'll use the red room.

STAGE MANAGER, *making a note on a piece of paper.* Red room. Very good.

PROMPTER, *continuing to read from the script.* "The table is set and the desk has books and papers on it. Shelves with books on them, and cupboards with lavish tableware. Door in the rear through which one goes to Leone's bedroom. Side door on the left through which one goes to the kitchen. The main entrance is on the right."

DIRECTOR, *rising and pointing.* All right, now listen carefully. That's the main door. This is the way to the kitchen. (*Addressing himself to the Actor playing the part of Socrates.*) You will come on and go out on this side. (*To the Stage Manager.*) The compass at the back. And curtains. (*He sits down again.*)

STAGE MANAGER, *making a note.* Very good.

PROMPTER, *reading as before.* "Scene One. Leone Gala, Guido Venanzi, Filippo called Socrates." (*To the Director.*) Am I supposed to read the stage directions, too?

DIRECTOR. Yes, yes, yes! I've told you that a hundred times!

PROMPTER, *reading as before.* "At the rise of the curtain, Leone Gala, wearing a chef's hat and apron, is intent on beating an egg in a saucepan with a wooden spoon. Filippo, also dressed as a cook, is beating another egg. Guido Venanzi, seated, is listening."

LEADING ACTOR, *to the Director.* Excuse me, but do I really have to wear a chef's hat?

DIRECTOR, *annoyed by this observation.* I should say so! It's in the script. (*And he points at it.*)

LEADING ACTOR. But it's ridiculous, if I may say so.

DIRECTOR, *leaping to his feet, furious.* Ridiculous, ridiculous! What do you want me to do? We never get a good play from France anymore, so we're reduced to producing plays by Pirandello, a fine man and all that, but neither the actors, the critics, nor the audience are ever happy with his plays, and if you ask me, he does it all on purpose. (*The Actors laugh. And now he rises and coming over to the Leading Actor shouts:*) A cook's hat, yes, my dear man! And you beat eggs. And you think you have nothing more on your hands than the beating of eggs? Guess again. You symbolize the shell of those eggs.

(*The Actors resume their laughing, and start making ironical comments among themselves.*) Silence! And pay attention while I explain. (*Again addressing himself to the Leading Actor.*) Yes, the shell: that is to say, the empty *form* of reason without the *content* of instinct, which is blind. You are reason, and your wife is instinct in the game of role-playing. You play the part assigned you, and you're your own puppet—of your own free will. Understand?

LEADING ACTOR, *extending his arms, palms upward.* Me? No.

DIRECTOR, *returning to his place.* Nor do I. Let's go on. Wait and see what I do with the ending. (*In a confidential tone.*) I suggest you face three-quarters front. Otherwise, what with the abstruseness of the dialogue, and an audience that can't hear you, goodbye play! (*Again clapping.*) Now, again, order! Let's go.

PROMPTER. Excuse me, sir, may I put the top back on the prompter's box? There's rather a draft.

DIRECTOR. Yes, yes, do that.

The Stage Door Man has entered the auditorium in the meanwhile, his braided cap on his head. Proceeding down the aisle, he goes up on stage to announce to the Director the arrival of the Six Characters, who have also entered the auditorium, and have started following him at a certain distance, a little lost and perplexed, looking around them.

Whoever is going to try and translate this play into scenic terms must take all possible measures not *to let these Six Characters get confused with the Actors of the Company. Placing both groups correctly, in accordance with the stage directions, once the Six are on stage, will certainly help, as will lighting the two groups in contrasting colors. But the most suitable and effective means to be suggested here is the use of special masks for the Characters: masks specially made of material which doesn't go limp when sweaty and yet masks which are not too heavy for the Actors wearing them, cut out and worked over so they leave eyes, nostrils, and mouth free. This will also bring out the inner significance of the play. The Characters in fact should not be presented as ghosts but as created realities, unchanging constructs of the imagination, and therefore more solidly real than the Actors with their fluid naturalness. The masks will help to give the impression of figures constructed by art, each one unchangeably fixed in the expression of its own fundamental sentiment, thus:* remorse *in the case of the Father;* revenge *in the case of the Stepdaughter;* disdain *in the case of the Son;* grief *in the case of the Mother, who should have wax tears fixed in the rings under her eyes and on her cheeks, as with the sculpted and painted images of the* mater dolorosa *in church. Their clothes should be of special material and design, without extravagance, with rigid, full folds like a statue, in short not suggesting a material you might buy at any store in town, cut out and tailored at any dressmaker's.*

The Father is a man of about fifty, hair thin at the temples, but not bald, thick mustache coiled round a still youthful mouth that is often open in an uncertain, pointless smile. Pale, most notably on his broad forehead; blue eyes, oval, very clear and piercing; dark jacket and light trousers; at times gentle and smooth, at times he has hard, harsh outbursts.

The Mother seems scared and crushed by an intolerable weight of shame and self-abasement. Wearing a thick black crepe widow's veil, she is modestly dressed in black, and when she lifts the veil, the face does not show signs of suffering, and yet seems made of wax. Her eyes are always on the ground.

The Stepdaughter, eighteen, is impudent, almost insolent. Very beautiful, and also in mourning, but mourning of a showy elegance. She shows contempt for the timid, afflicted, almost humiliated manner of her little brother, rather a mess of a Boy, fourteen, also dressed in black, but a lively tenderness for her little sister, a Little Girl of around four, dressed in white with black silk sash round her waist.

The Son, twenty-two, tall, almost rigid with contained disdain for the Father and supercilious indifference toward the Mother, wears a mauve topcoat and a long green scarf wound round his neck.

STAGE DOOR MAN, *beret in hand.* Excuse me, your honor.

DIRECTOR, *rudely jumping on him.* What is it now?

STAGE DOOR MAN, *timidly.* There are some people here asking for you.

The Director and the Actors turn in astonishment to look down into the auditorium.

DIRECTOR, *furious again.* But I'm rehearsing here! And you know perfectly well no one can come in during rehearsal! (*Turning again toward the house.*) Who are these people? What do they want?

FATHER, *stepping forward, followed by the others, to one of the two little stairways to the stage.* We're here in search of an author.

DIRECTOR, *half angry, half astounded.* An author? What author?

FATHER. Any author, sir.

DIRECTOR. There's no author here at all. It's not a new play we're rehearsing.

STEPDAUGHTER, *very vivaciously as she rushes up the stairs.* Then so much the better, sir! *We* can be your new play!

ONE OF THE ACTORS, *among the racy comments and laughs of the others.* Did you hear that?

FATHER, *following the Stepdaughter onstage.* Certainly, but if the author's not here . . . (*To the Director.*) Unless *you'd* like to be the author?

The Mother, holding the Little Girl by the hand, and the Boy climb the first steps of the stairway and remain there waiting. The Son stays morosely below.

DIRECTOR. Is this your idea of a joke?

FATHER. Heavens, no! Oh, sir, on the contrary, we bring you a painful drama.

STEPDAUGHTER. We can make your fortune for you.

DIRECTOR. Do me a favor and leave. We have no time to waste on madmen.

FATHER, *wounded, smoothly.* Oh, sir, you surely know that life is full of infinite absurdities which, brazenly enough, do not need to appear probable, because they're true.

DIRECTOR. What in God's name are you saying?

FATHER. I'm saying it can actually be considered madness, sir, to force oneself to do the opposite: that is, to give probability to things so they will seem true. But permit me to observe that, if this is madness, it is also the raison d'être of your profession.

The Actors become agitated and indignant.

DIRECTOR, *rising and looking him over.* It is, is it? It seems to you an affair for madmen, our profession?

FATHER. Well, to make something seem true which is not true . . . without any need, sir, just for fun . . . Isn't it your job to give life on stage to creatures of fantasy?

DIRECTOR, *immediately, making himself spokesman for the growing indignation of his Actors.* Let me tell you something, my good sir. The actor's profession is a very noble one. If, as things go nowadays, our new playwrights give us nothing but stupid plays, with puppets in them instead of men, it is our boast, I'd have you know, to have given life—on these very boards—to immortal works of art.

Satisfied, the Actors approve and applaud their Director.

FATHER, *interrupting and bearing down hard.* Exactly! That's just it. You have created living beings—*more* alive than those that breathe and wear clothes! Less real, perhaps, but more true! We agree completely!

The Actors look at each other, astounded.

DIRECTOR. What? You were saying just now . . .

FATHER. No, no, don't misunderstand me. You shouted that you hadn't time to waste on madmen. So I wanted to tell you that no one knows better than you that Nature employs the human imagination to carry her work of creation on to a higher plane!

DIRECTOR. All right, all right. But what are you getting at, exactly?

FATHER. Nothing, sir. I only wanted to show that one may be born to this life in many modes, in many forms: as tree, as rock, water or butterfly . . . or woman. And that . . . characters are born too.

DIRECTOR, *his amazement ironically feigned.* And you—with these companions of yours—were born a character?

FATHER. Right, sir. And alive, as you see.

The Director and the Actors burst out laughing as at a joke.

FATHER, *wounded.* I'm sorry to hear you laugh, because, I repeat, we carry a painful drama within us, as you all might deduce from the sight of that lady there, veiled in black.

As he says this, he gives his hand to the Mother to help her up the last steps and, still holding her by the hand, he leads her with a certain tragic solemnity to the other side of the stage, which is suddenly bathed in fantastic light. The Little Girl and the Boy follow the Mother; then the Son, who stands on one side at the back; then the Stepdaughter who also detaches herself from the others—downstage and leaning against the proscenium arch. At first astonished at this development, then overcome with admiration, the Actors now burst into applause as at a show performed for their benefit.

DIRECTOR, *bowled over at first, then indignant.* Oh, stop this! Silence please! (*Then, turning to the Characters.*) And you, leave! Get out of here! (*To the Stage Manager.*) For God's sake, get them out!

STAGE MANAGER, *stepping forward but then stopping, as if held back by a strange dismay.* Go! Go!

FATHER, *to the Director.* No, look, we, um—

DIRECTOR, *shouting.* I tell you we've got to work!

LEADING MAN. It's not right to fool around like this . . .

FATHER, *resolute, stepping forward.* I'm amazed at your incredulity! You're accustomed to seeing the created characters of an author spring to life, aren't you, right here on this stage, the one confronting the other? Perhaps the trouble is there's no script *there* (*pointing to the Prompter's box*) with us in it?

STEPDAUGHTER, *going right up to the Director, smiling, coquettish.* Believe me, we really are six characters, sir. Very interesting ones at that. But lost. Adrift.

FATHER, *brushing her aside.* Very well: lost, adrift. (*Going right on.*) In the sense, that is, that the author who created us, made us live, did not wish, or simply and materially was not able, to place us in the world of art. And that was a real crime, sir, because whoever has the luck to be born a living character can also laugh at death. He will never die! The man will die, the writer, the instrument of creation; the creature will never die! And to have eternal life it doesn't even take extraordinary gifts, nor the performance of miracles. Who was Sancho Panza? Who was Don Abbondio? But they live forever because, as live germs, they have the luck to find a fertile matrix, an imagination which knew how to raise and nourish them, make them live through all eternity!

DIRECTOR. That's all well and good. But what do you people want here?

FATHER. We want to live, sir.

DIRECTOR, *ironically.* Through all eternity?

FATHER. No, sir. But for a moment at least. In you.

AN ACTOR. Well, well, well!

LEADING LADY. They want to live in us.

JUVENILE LEAD, *pointing to the Stepdaughter.* Well, I've no objection, so long as I get that one.

FATHER. Now look, look. The play is still in the making. (*To the Director.*) But if you wish, and your actors wish, we can make it right away. Acting in concert.

LEADING MAN, *annoyed.* Concert? We don't put on concerts! We do plays, dramas, comedies!

FATHER. Very good. That's why we came.

DIRECTOR. Well, where's the script?

FATHER. Inside us, sir. (*The Actors laugh.*) The drama is inside us. It *is* us. And we're impatient to perform it. According to the dictates of the passion within us.

STEPDAUGHTER, *scornful, with treacherous grace, deliberate impudence.* My passion—if you only knew, sir! My passion—for him! (*She points to the Father and makes as if to embrace him but then breaks into a strident laugh.*)

FATHER, *an angry interjection.* You keep out of this now. And please don't laugh that way!

STEPDAUGHTER. No? Then, ladies and gentlemen, permit me. A two months' orphan, I shall dance and sing for you all. Watch how! (*She mischievously starts to sing "Beware of Chu Chin Chow" by Dave Stamper, reduced to a fox trot or slow one-step by Francis Salabert: the first verse, accompanied by a step or two of dancing. While she sings and dances, the Actors, especially the young ones, as if drawn by some strange fascination, move toward her and half raise their hands as if to take hold of her. She runs away and when the Actors burst into applause she just stands there, remote, abstracted, while the Director protests.*)

ACTORS AND ACTRESSES, *laughing and clapping.* Brava! Fine! Splendid!

DIRECTOR, *annoyed.* Silence! What do you think this is, a night spot? (*Taking the Father a step or two to one side, with a certain amount of consternation.*) Tell me something. Is she crazy?

FATHER. Crazy? Of course not. It's much worse than that.

STEPDAUGHTER, *running over at once to the Director.* Worse! Worse! Not crazy but worse! Just listen: I'll play it for you right now, this drama, and at a certain point you'll see me—when this dear little thing—(*she takes the Little Girl who is beside the Mother by the hand and leads her to the Director*)—isn't she darling? (*Takes her in her arms and kisses her.*) Sweetie! Sweetie! (*Puts her down again and adds with almost involuntary emotion.*) Well, when God suddenly takes this little sweetheart away from her poor mother, and that idiot there—(*thrusting the Boy forward, rudely seizing him by a sleeve*) does the stupidest of things, like the nitwit that he is, (*with a shove she drives him back toward the Mother*) then you will see me take to my heels. Yes, ladies and gentlemen, take to my heels! I can hardly wait for that moment. For after what happened between him and me—(*she points to the Father with a horrible wink)* something very intimate, you understand—I can't stay in such company any longer, witnessing the anguish of our mother on account of that fool there. (*She points to the Son.*) Just look at him, look at him!—how indifferent, how frozen, because he is the legitimate son, that's what he is, full of contempt for me, for him (*the Boy*), and for that little creature (*the Little Girl*), because we three are bastards, d'you see? bastards. (*Goes to the Mother and embraces her.*) And this poor mother, the common mother of us all, he—well, he doesn't want to acknowledge her as *his* mother too, and he looks down on her, that's what he does, looks on her as only the mother of us three bastards, the wretch! (*She says this rapidly in a state of extreme excitement. Her voice swells to the word "bastards!" and descends again to the final "wretch," almost spitting it out.)*

MOTHER, *to the Director, with infinite anguish.* In the name of these two small children, sir, I implore you . . . (*She grows faint and sways.*) Oh, heavens . . .

FATHER, *rushing over to support her with almost all the Actors who are astonished and scared.* Please! Please, a chair, a chair for this poor widow!

ACTORS, *rushing over.*—Is it true then?—She's *really* fainting?

DIRECTOR. A chair!

One of the Actors proffers a chair. The others stand around, ready to help. The Mother, seated, tries to stop the Father from lifting the veil that hides her face.

FATHER, *to the Director.* Look at her, look at her . . .

MOTHER. Heavens, no, stop it!

FATHER. Let them see you. (*He lifts her veil.*)

MOTHER, *rising and covering her face with her hands, desperate.* Oh, sir, please stop this man from carrying out his plan. It's horrible for me!

DIRECTOR, *surprised, stunned.* I don't know where we're at! What's this all about? (*To the Father.*) Is this your wife?

FATHER, *at once.* Yes, sir, my wife.

DIRECTOR. Then how is she a widow, if you're alive?

The Actors relieve their astonishment in a loud burst of laughter.

FATHER, *wounded, with bitter resentment.* Don't laugh! Don't laugh like that! Please! Just that is her drama, sir. She had another man. Another man who should be here!

MOTHER, *with a shout.* No! No!

STEPDAUGHTER. He had the good luck to die. Two months ago, as I told you. We're still in mourning, as you see.

FATHER. But he's absent, you see, not just because he's dead. He's absent—take a look at her, sir, and you will understand at once!—Her drama wasn't in the love of two men for whom she was incapable of feeling anything—except maybe a little gratitude (not to me, but to him)—She is not a woman, she is a mother!—And her drama—a powerful one, very powerful—is in fact all in those four children which she bore to her two men.

MOTHER. *My* men? Have you the gall to say I wanted two men? It was him, sir. He forced the other man on me. Compelled—yes, compelled—me to go off with him!

STEPDAUGHTER, *cutting in, roused.* It's not true!

MOTHER, *astounded.* How d'you mean, not true?

STEPDAUGHTER. It's not true! It's not true!

MOTHER. And what can you know about it?

STEPDAUGHTER. It's not true. (*To the Director.*) Don't believe it. Know why she says it? For his sake. (*Pointing to the Son.*) His indifference tortures her, destroys her. She wants him to believe that, if she abandoned him when he was two, it was because he (*the Father*) compelled her to.

MOTHER, *with violence.* He did compel me, he did compel me, as God is my witness! (*To the Director.*) Ask him if that isn't true. (*Her husband.*) Make him tell you himself. She couldn't know anything about it.

STEPDAUGHTER. With my father, while he lived, I know you were always happy and content. Deny it if you can.

MOTHER. I don't deny it, I don't . . .

STEPDAUGHTER. He loved you, he cared for you! (*To the Boy, with rage.*) Isn't that so? Say it! Why don't you speak, you dope?

MOTHER. Leave the poor boy alone. Why d'you want to make me out ungrateful, daughter? I have no wish to offend your father! I told him (*the Father*) I didn't abandon my son and my home for my own pleasure. It wasn't my fault.

FATHER. That's true, sir. It was mine.

Pause.

LEADING MAN, *to his companions.* What a show!

LEADING LADY. And *they* put it on—for us.

JUVENILE LEAD. Quite a change!

DIRECTOR, *who is now beginning to get very interested.* Let's listen to this, let's listen! (*And saying this, he goes down one of the stairways into the auditorium, and stands in front of the stage, as if to receive a spectator's impression of the show.*)

SON, *without moving from his position, cold, quiet, ironic.* Oh yes, you can now listen to the philosophy lecture. He will tell you about the Demon of Experiment.

FATHER. You are a cynical idiot, as I've told you a hundred times. (*To the Director, now in the auditorium.*) He mocks me, sir, on account of that phrase I found to excuse myself with.

SON, *contemptuously.* Phrases!

FATHER. Phrases! Phrases! As if they were not a comfort to everyone: in the face of some unexplained fact, in the face of an evil that eats into us, to find a word that says nothing but at least quiets us down!

STEPDAUGHTER. Quiets our guilt feelings too. That above all.

FATHER. Our guilt feelings? Not so. I have never quieted my guilt feelings with words alone.

STEPDAUGHTER. It took a little money as well, didn't it, it took a little dough! The hundred lire he was going to pay me, ladies and gentlemen!

Movement of horror among the Actors.

SON, *with contempt toward the Stepdaughter.* That's filthy.

STEPDAUGHTER. Filthy? The dough was there. In a small pale blue envelope on the mahogany table in the room behind the shop. Madam Pace's (*she pronounces it "Pah-chay"*) shop. One of those Madams who lure us poor girls from good families into their ateliers under the pretext of selling *Robes et Manteaux.*

SON. And with those hundred lire he was going to pay she has bought the right to tyrannize over us all. Only it so happens I'd have you know—that he never actually incurred the debt.

STEPDAUGHTER. Oh, oh, but we were really going to it, I assure you! (*She bursts out laughing.*)

MOTHER, *rising in protest.* Shame, daughter! Shame!

STEPDAUGHTER, *quickly.* Shame? It's my revenge! I am frantic, sir, frantic to live it, live that scene! The room . . . here's the shop window with the coats in it; there's the bed-sofa, the mirror, a screen; and in front of the window the little mahogany table with the hundred lire in the pale blue envelope. I can see it. I could take it. But you men should turn away now: I'm almost naked. I don't blush anymore. It's he that blushes now. (*Points to the Father.*) But I assure you he was very pale, very pale, at that moment. (*To the Director.*) You must believe me, sir.

DIRECTOR. You lost me some time ago.

FATHER. Of course! Getting it thrown at you like that! Restore a little order, sir, and let *me* speak. And never mind this ferocious girl. She's trying to heap opprobrium on me by withholding the relevant explanations!

STEPDAUGHTER. This is no place for long-winded narratives!

FATHER. I said—explanations.

STEPDAUGHTER. Oh, certainly. Those that suit your turn.

At this point, the Director returns to the stage to restore order.

FATHER. But that's the whole root of the evil. Words. Each of us has, inside him, a world of things—to everyone, his world of things. And how can we understand each other, sir, if, in the words I speak, I put the sense and value of things as they are inside me, whereas the man who hears them inevitably receives them in the sense and with the value they have for him, the sense and value of the world inside him? We think we understand each other but we never do. Consider: the compassion, all the compassion I feel for this woman (*the Mother*) has been received by her as the most ferocious of cruelties!

MOTHER. You ran me out of the house.

FATHER. Hear that? Ran her out. It *seemed to her* that I ran her out.

MOTHER. You can talk; I can't . . . But, look, sir, after he married me . . . and who knows why he did? I was poor, of humble birth . . .

FATHER. And that's why. I married you for your . . . humility. I loved you for it, believing . . . (*He breaks off, seeing her gestured denials; seeing the impossibility of making himself understood by her, he opens his arms wide in a gesture of despair, and turns to the Director.*) See that? She says no. It's scarifying, isn't it, sir, scarifying, this deafness of hers, this mental deafness! She has a heart, oh yes, where her children are concerned! But she's deaf, deaf in the brain, deaf, sir, to the point of desperation!

STEPDAUGHTER, *to the Director.* All right, but now make him tell you what his intelligence has ever done for us.

FATHER. If we could only foresee all the evil that can result from the good we believe we're doing!

At this point, the Leading Lady, who has been on hot coals seeing the Leading Man flirt with the Stepdaughter, steps forward and asks of the Director:

LEADING LADY. Excuse me, is the rehearsal continuing?

DIRECTOR. Yes, of course! But let me listen a moment.

JUVENILE LEAD. This is something quite new.

INGENUE. Very interesting!

LEADING LADY. If that sort of thing interests you. (*And she darts a look at the Leading Man.*)

DIRECTOR, *to the Father.* But you must give us *clear* explanations. (*He goes and sits down.*)

FATHER. Right. Yes. Listen. There was a man working for me. A poor man. As my secretary. Very devoted to me. Understood *her* (*the Mother*) very well. There was mutual understanding between them. Nothing wrong in it. They thought no harm at all. Nothing off-color about it. No, no, he knew his place, as she did. They didn't do anything wrong. Didn't even think it.

STEPDAUGHTER. So he thought it *for* them. And did it.

FATHER. It's not true! I wanted to do them some good. And myself too, oh yes, I admit. I'd got to this point, sir: I couldn't say a word to either of them but they would exchange a significant look. The one would consult the eyes of the other, asking how what I had said should be taken, if they didn't want to put me in a rage. That sufficed, you will understand, to keep me continually in a rage, in a state of unbearable exasperation.

DIRECTOR. Excuse me, why didn't you fire him, this secretary?

FATHER. Good question! That's what I did do, sir. But then I had to see that poor woman remain in my house, a lost soul. Like an animal without a master that one takes pity on and carries home.

MOTHER. No, no, it's—

FATHER, *at once, turning to her to get it in first.* Your son? Right?

MOTHER. He'd already snatched my son from me.

FATHER. But not from cruelty. Just so he'd grow up strong and healthy. In touch with the soil.

STEPDAUGHTER, *pointing at the latter, ironic.* And just look at him!

FATHER, *at once.* Uh? Is it also my fault if he then grew up this way? I sent him to a wet nurse, sir, in the country, a peasant woman. I didn't find her (*the Mother*) strong enough, despite her humble origin. I'd married her for similar reasons, as I said. All nonsense maybe, but there we are. I always had these confounded aspirations toward a certain solidity, toward what is morally sound. (*Here the Stepdaughter bursts out laughing.*) Make her stop that! It's unbearable!

DIRECTOR. Stop it. I can't hear, for heaven's sake!

Suddenly, again, as the Director rebukes her, she is withdrawn and remote, her laughter cut off in the middle. The Director goes down again from the stage to get an impression of the scene.

FATHER. I couldn't bear to be with that woman anymore. (*Points to the Mother.*) Not so much, believe me, because she irritated me, and even made me feel physically ill, as because of the pain—a veritable anguish—that I felt on her account.

MOTHER. And he sent me away!

FATHER. Well provided for. And to that man. Yes, sir. So she could be free of me.

MOTHER. And so *he* could be free.

FATHER. That, too. I admit it. And much evil resulted. But I intended good. And more for her than for me, I swear it! (*He folds his arms across his chest. Then, suddenly, turning to the Mother.*) I never lost sight of you, never lost sight of you till, from one day to the next, unbeknownst to me, he carried you off to another town. He noticed I was interested in her, you see, but that was silly, because my interest was absolutely pure, absolutely without ulterior motive. The interest I took in her new family, as it grew up, had an unbelievable tenderness to it. Even she should bear witness to that! (*He points to the Stepdaughter.*)

STEPDAUGHTER. Oh, very much so! I was a little sweetie. Pigtails over my shoulders. Panties coming down a little bit below my skirt. A little sweetie. He would see me coming out of school, at the gate. He would come and see me as I grew up . . .

FATHER. This is outrageous. You're betraying me!

STEPDAUGHTER. I'm not! What do you mean?

FATHER. Outrageous. Outrageous. (*Immediately, still excited, he continues in a tone of explanation, to the Director.*) My house, sir, when she had left it, at once seemed empty. (*Points to the Mother.*) She was an incubus. But she filled my house for me. Left alone, I wandered through these rooms like a fly without a head. This fellow here (*the Son*) was raised away from home. Somehow, when he got back, he didn't seem mine anymore. Without a mother between me and him, he grew up on his own, apart, without any relationship to me, emotional or intellectual. And then—strange, sir, but true—first I grew curious, then I was gradually attracted toward *her* family, which I had brought into being. The thought of *this* family began to fill the void around me. I had to—really had to—believe she was at peace, absorbed in the simplest cares of life, lucky to be away and far removed from the complicated torments of my spirit. And to have proof of this, I would go and see that little girl at the school gate.

STEPDAUGHTER. Correct! He followed me home, smiled at me and, when I was home, waved to me, like this! I would open my eyes wide and look at him suspiciously. I didn't know who it was. I told mother. And she guessed right away it was him. (*The Mother nods.*) At first she didn't want to send me back to school for several days. When I did go, I saw him again at the gate—the clown!—with a brown paper bag in his hand. He came up to me, caressed me, and took from the bag a lovely big Florentine straw hat with a ring of little May roses round it—for me!

DIRECTOR. You're making too long a story of this.

SON, *contemptuously.* Story is right! Fiction! Literature!

FATHER. Literature? This is life, sir. Passion!

DIRECTOR. Maybe! But not actable!

FATHER. I agree. This is all preliminary. I wouldn't *want* you to act it. As you see, in fact, she (*the Stepdaughter*) is no longer that little girl with pigtails—

STEPDAUGHTER. —and the panties showing below her skirt!

FATHER. The drama comes now, sir. Novel, complex—

STEPDAUGHTER, *gloomy, fierce, steps forward.* —What my father's death meant for us was—

FATHER, *not giving her time to continue.* —poverty, sir. They returned, unbeknownst to me. She's so thickheaded. (*Pointing to the Mother.*) It's true she can hardly write herself, but she could have had her daughter write, or her son, telling me they were in need!

MOTHER. But, sir, how could I have guessed he felt the way he did?

FATHER. Which is just where you always went wrong. You could never guess how I felt about anything!

MOTHER. After so many years of separation, with all that had happened . . .

FATHER. And is it my fault if that fellow carried you off as he did? (*Turning to the Director.*) From one day to the next, as I say. He'd found some job someplace. I couldn't even trace them. Necessarily, then, my interest dwindled, with the years. The drama breaks out, sir, unforeseen and violent, at their return. When I, alas, was impelled by the misery of my still living flesh . . . Oh, and what misery that is for a man who is alone, who has not wanted to form debasing relationships, not yet old enough to do without a woman, and no longer young enough to go and look for one without shame! Misery? It's horror, horror, because no woman can give him love anymore.—Knowing this, one should go without! Well, sir, on the outside, when other people are watching, each man is clothed in dignity; but, on the inside, he knows what unconfessable things are going on within him. One gives way, gives way to temptation, to rise again, right afterward, of course, in a great hurry to put our dignity together again, complete, solid, a stone on a grave that hides and buries from our eyes every sign of our shame and even the very memory of it! It's like that with everybody. Only the courage to say it is lacking—to say certain things.

STEPDAUGHTER. The courage to do them, though—everybody's got that.

FATHER. Everybody. But in secret. That's why it takes more courage to say them. A man only has to say them and it's all over; he's labeled a cynic. But, sir, he isn't! He's just like everybody else. Better! He's better because he's not afraid to reveal, by the light of intelligence, the red stain of shame, there, in the human beast, which closes its eyes to it. Woman—yes, woman—what is she like, actually? She looks at us, inviting, tantalizing. You take hold of her. She's no sooner in your arms than she shuts her eyes. It is the sign of her submission. The sign with which she tells the man: blind yourself for I am blind.

STEPDAUGHTER. How about when she no longer keeps them shut? When she no longer feels the need to hide the red stain of shame from herself by closing her eyes, and instead, her eyes dry now and impassive, sees the shame of the man, who has blinded himself even without love? They make me vomit, all those intellectual elaborations, this philosophy that begins by revealing the beast and then goes on to excuse it and save its soul . . . I can't bear to hear about it! Because when a man feels obliged to *reduce* life this way, reduce it all to "the beast," throwing overboard every vestige of the truly human, every aspiration after chastity, all feelings of purity, of the ideal, of duties, of modesty, of shame, then nothing is more contemptible, more nauseating than his wretched guilt feelings! Crocodile tears!

DIRECTOR. Let's get to the facts, to the facts! This is just discussion.

FATHER. Very well. But a fact is like a sack. When it's empty, it won't stand up. To make it stand up you must first pour into it the reasons and feelings by which it exists. I couldn't know that—when that man died and they returned here in poverty—she went out to work as a dressmaker to support the children, nor that the person she went to work for was that . . . that Madam Pace!

STEPDAUGHTER. A high-class dressmaker, if you'd all like to know! To all appearances, she serves fine ladies, but then she arranges things so that the fine ladies serve *her* . . . without prejudice to ladies not so fine!

MOTHER. Believe me, sir, I never had the slightest suspicion that that old witch hired me because she had her eye on my daughter . . .

STEPDAUGHTER. Poor mama! Do you know, sir, what the woman did when I brought her my mother's work? She would point out to me the material she'd ruined by giving it to my mother to sew. And she deducted for that, she deducted. And so, you understand, *I* paid, while that poor creature thought she was making sacrifices for me and those two by sewing, even at night, Madam Pace's material!

Indignant movements and exclamations from the Actors.

DIRECTOR, *without pause.* And there, one day, you met—

STEPDAUGHTER, *pointing to the Father.* —him, him, yes sir! An old client! Now there's a scene for you to put on! Superb!

FATHER. Interrupted by her—the mother—

STEPDAUGHTER, *without pause, treacherously.* —almost in time!—

FATHER, *shouting.* No, no, *in* time! Because, luckily, I recognized the girl in time. And I took them all back, sir, into my home. Now try to visualize my situation and hers, the one confronting the other—she as you see her now, myself unable to look her in the face anymore.

STEPDAUGHTER. It's too absurd! But—afterward—was it possible for me to be a modest little miss, virtuous and well-bred, in accordance with those confounded aspirations toward a certain solidity, toward what is morally sound?

FATHER. And therein lies the drama, sir, as far as I'm concerned: in my awareness that each of us thinks of himself as *one* but that, well, it's not true, each of us is many, oh so many, sir, according to the possibilities of being that are in us. We are one thing for this person, another for that! Already *two* utterly different things! And with it all, the illusion of being always one thing for all men, and always this one thing in every single action. It's not true! Not true! We realize as much when, by some unfortunate chance, in one or another of our acts, we find ourselves suspended, hooked. We see, I mean, that we are not wholly in that act, and that therefore it would be abominably unjust to judge us by that act alone, to hold us suspended, hooked, in the pillory, our whole life long, as if our life were summed up in that act! Now do you understand this girl's treachery? She surprised me in a place, in an act, in which she should never have had to know me—I couldn't be that way for her. And she wants to give me a reality such as I could never have expected I would have to assume for her, the reality of a fleeting moment, a shameful one, in my life! This, sir, this is what I feel most strongly. And you will see that the drama will derive tremendous value from this. But now add the situation of the others! His . . . (*He points to the Son.*)

SON, *shrugging contemptuously.* Leave me out of this! It's none of my business.

FATHER. What? None of your business?

SON. None. And I *want* to be left out. I wasn't made to be one of you, and you know it.

STEPDAUGHTER. We're common, aren't we?—And he's so refined.—But from time to time I give him a hard, contemptuous look, and he looks down at the ground. You may have noticed that, sir. He looks down at the ground. For he knows the wrong he's done me.

SON, *hardly looking at her.* Me?

STEPDAUGHTER. You! You! I'm on the streets because of you! (*A movement of horror from the Actors.*) Did you or did you not, by your attitude, deny us—I won't say the intimacy of home but even the hospitality which puts guests at their ease? We were the intruders, coming to invade the kingdom of your legitimacy! I'd like to have you see, sir, certain little scenes between just him and me! He says I tyrannized over them all. But it was entirely because of his attitude that I started to exploit the situation he calls filthy, a situation which had brought me into his home with my mother, who is also *his* mother, *as its mistress*!

SON, *coming slowly forward.* They can't lose, sir, three against one, an easy game. But figure to yourself a son, sitting quietly at home, who one fine day sees a young woman arrive, an impudent type with her nose in the air, asking for his father, with whom she has heaven knows what business; and then he sees her return, in the same style, accompanied by that little girl over there; and finally he sees her treat his father—who can say why?—in a very ambiguous and cool manner, demanding money, in a tone that takes for granted that he *has* to give it, has to, is obligated—

FATHER. —but I *am* obligated; it's for your mother!

SON. How would I know? When, sir, (*to the Director*) have I ever seen her? When have I ever heard her spoken of. One day I see her arrive with her, (*the Stepdaughter*) with that boy, with that little girl. They say to me: "It's your mother too, know that?" I manage to figure out from her carryings-on (*pointing at the Stepdaughter*) why they arrived in our home from one day to the next . . . What I'm feeling and experiencing I can't put into words, and wouldn't want to. I wouldn't want to confess it, even to myself. It cannot therefore result in any action on my part. You can see that. Believe me, sir, I'm a character that, dramatically speaking, remains unrealized. I'm out of place in their company. So please leave me out of it all!

FATHER. What? But it's just because you're so—

SON, *in violent exasperation.* —I'm so what? How would *you* know? When did you ever care about me?

FATHER. Touché! Touché! But isn't even that a dramatic situation? This withdrawnness of yours, so cruel to me, and to your mother who, on her return home is seeing you almost for the first time, a grown man she doesn't recognize, though she knows you're her son . . . (*Pointing out the Mother to the Director.*) Just look at her, she's crying.

STEPDAUGHTER, *angrily, stamping her foot.* Like the fool she is!

FATHER, *pointing her out to the Director.* And she can't abide him, you know. (*Again referring to the Son.*)—He says it's none of his business. The truth is he's almost the pivot of the action. Look at that little boy, clinging to his mother all the time, scared, humiliated . . . It's all because of *him.* (*The Son.*) Perhaps the most painful situation of all is that little boy's: he feels alien, more than all the others, and the poor little thing is so mortified, so anguished at being taken into our home—out of charity, as it were . . . (*Confidentially.*) He's just like his father: humble, doesn't say anything . . .

DIRECTOR. He won't fit anyway. You've no idea what a nuisance children are on stage.

FATHER. But he wouldn't be a nuisance for long. Nor would the little girl, no, she's the first to go . . .

DIRECTOR. Very good, yes! The whole thing interests me very much indeed. I have a hunch, a definite hunch, that there's material here for a fine play!

STEPDAUGHTER, *trying to inject herself.* With a character like me in it!

FATHER, *pushing her to one side in his anxiety to know what the Director will decide.* You be quiet!

DIRECTOR, *going right on, ignoring the interruption.* Yes, it's new stuff . . .

FATHER. Very new!

DIRECTOR. You had some gall, though, to come and throw it at me this way . . .

FATHER. Well, you see, sir, born as we are to the stage . . .

DIRECTOR. You're amateurs, are you?

FATHER. No. I say: "born to the stage" because . . .

DIRECTOR. Oh, come on, you must have done some acting!

FATHER. No, no, sir, only as every man acts the part assigned to him—by himself or others—in this life. In me you see passion itself, which—in almost all people, as it rises—invariably becomes a bit theatrical . . .

DIRECTOR. Well, never mind! Never mind about that!—You see, my dear sir, without the author . . . I could direct you to an author . . .

FATHER. No, no, look: you be the author!

DIRECTOR. Me? What are you talking about?

FATHER. Yes, you. You. Why not?

DIRECTOR. Because I've never been an author, that's why not!

FATHER. Couldn't you be one now, hm? There's nothing to it. Everyone's doing it. And your job is made all the easier by the fact that you have us—here—alive—right in front of your nose!

DIRECTOR. It wouldn't be enough.

FATHER. Not enough? Seeing us live our own drama . . .

DIRECTOR. I know, but you always need someone to write it!

FATHER. No. Just someone to take it down, maybe, since you have us here—in action—scene by scene. It'll be enough if we piece together a rough sketch for you, then you can rehearse it.

DIRECTOR, *tempted, goes up on stage again.* Well, I'm almost, almost tempted . . . Just for kicks . . . We could actually rehearse . . .

FATHER. Of course you could! What scenes you'll see emerge! I can list them for you right away.

DIRECTOR. I'm tempted . . . I'm tempted . . . Let's give it a try . . . Come to my office. (*Turns to the Actors.*) Take a break, will you? But don't go away. We'll be back in fifteen or twenty minutes. (*To the Father.*) Let's see what we can do . . . Maybe we can get something very extraordinary out of all this . . .

FATHER. We certainly can. Wouldn't it be better to take *them* along? *(He points to the Characters.)*

DIRECTOR. Yes, let them all come. (*Starts going off, then comes back to address the Actors.*) Now don't forget. Everyone on time. Fifteen minutes.

Director and Six Characters cross the stage and disappear. The Actors stay there and look at one another in amazement.

LEADING MAN. Is he serious? What's he going to do?

JUVENILE. This is outright insanity.

A THIRD ACTOR. We have to improvise a drama right off the bat?

JUVENILE LEAD. That's right. Like commedia dell'arte.

LEADING LADY. Well, if he thinks *I'm* going to lend myself to that sort of thing . . .

INGENUE. Count me out.

A FOURTH ACTOR, *alluding to the Characters.* I'd like to know who those people are.

A THIRD ACTOR. Who would they be? Madmen or crooks!

JUVENILE LEAD. And he's going to pay attention to them?

INGENUE. Carried away by vanity! Wants to be an author now . . .

LEADING MAN. It's out of this world. If this is what the theater is coming to, my friends . . .

A FIFTH ACTOR. I think it's rather fun.

A THIRD ACTOR. Well! We shall see. We shall see. (*And chatting thus among themselves, the Actors leave the stage, some using the little door at the back, others returning to their dressing rooms.*)

The curtain remains raised. The performance is interrupted by a twenty-minute intermission.

Bells ring. The performance is resumed.

From dressing rooms, from the door, and also from the house, the Actors, the Stage Manager, the Technician, the Prompter, the Property Man return to the stage; at the same time the Director and the Six Characters emerge from the office.

As soon as the house lights are out, the stage lighting is as before.

DIRECTOR. Let's go, everybody! Is everyone here? Quiet! We're beginning. (*Calls the Technician by name.*)

TECHNICIAN. Here!

DIRECTOR. Set the stage for the parlor scene. Two wings and a backdrop with a door in it will do, quickly please!

The Technician at once runs to do the job, and does it while the Director works things out with the Stage Manager, the Property Man, the Prompter, and the Actors. This indication of a set consists of two wings, a drop with a door in it, all in pink and gold stripes.

DIRECTOR, *to the Property Man.* See if we have some sort of bed-sofa in the prop room.

PROPERTY MAN. Yes, sir, there's the green one.

STEPDAUGHTER. No, no, not green! It was yellow, flowered, plush, and very big. Extremely comfortable.

PROPERTY MAN. Well, we have nothing like that.

DIRECTOR. But it doesn't matter. Bring the one you have.

STEPDAUGHTER. Doesn't matter? Madam Pace's famous chaise lounge!

DIRECTOR. This is just for rehearsal. Please don't meddle! (*To the Stage Manager.*) See if we have a display case—long and rather narrow.

STEPDAUGHTER. The table, the little mahogany table for the pale blue envelope!

STAGE MANAGER, *to the Director.* There's the small one. Gilded.

DIRECTOR. All right. Get that one.

FATHER. A large mirror.

STEPDAUGHTER. And the screen. A screen, please, or what'll I do?

STAGE MANAGER. Yes, ma'am, we have lots of screens, don't worry.

DIRECTOR, *to the Stepdaughter.* A few coat hangers?

STEPDAUGHTER. A great many, yes.

DIRECTOR, *to the Stage Manager.* See how many we've got, and have them brought on.

STAGE MANAGER. Right, sir, I'll see to it.

The Stage Manager also hurries to do his job and while the Director goes on talking with the Prompter and then with the Characters and the Actors, has the furniture carried on by stagehands and arranges it as he thinks fit.

DIRECTOR, *to the Prompter.* Meanwhile you can get into position. Look, this is the outline of the scenes, act by act. (*He gives him several sheets of paper.*) You'll have to be a bit of a virtuoso today.

PROMPTER. Shorthand?

DIRECTOR, *pleasantly surprised.* Oh, good! You know shorthand?

PROMPTER. I may not know prompting, but shorthand . . . (*Turning to a stagehand.*) Get me some paper from my room—quite a lot—all you can find!

The stagehand runs off and returns a little later with a wad of paper which he gives to the Prompter.

DIRECTOR, *going right on, to the Prompter.* Follow the scenes line by line as we play them, and try to pin down the speeches, at least the most important ones. (*Then, turning to the Actors.*) Clear the stage please, everyone! Yes, come over to this side and pay close attention. (*He indicates the left.*)

LEADING LADY. Excuse me but—

DIRECTOR, *forestalling.* There'll be no improvising, don't fret.

LEADING MAN. Then what are we to do?

DIRECTOR. Nothing. For now, just stop, look, and listen. Afterward you'll be given written parts. Right now we'll rehearse. As best we can. With them doing the rehearsing for us. (*He points to the Characters.*)

FATHER, *amid all the confusion on stage, as if he'd fallen from the clouds. We're* rehearsing? How d'you mean?

DIRECTOR. Yes, for them. You rehearse for them. (*Indicates the Actors.*)

FATHER. But if we are the characters . . .

DIRECTOR. All right, you're characters, but, my dear sir, characters don't perform here, actors perform here. The characters are there, in the script (*he points to the Prompter's box*)—when there *is* a script!

FATHER. Exactly! Since there isn't, and you gentlemen have the luck to have them right here, alive in front of you, those characters . . .

DIRECTOR. Oh, great! Want to do it all yourselves? Appear before the public, do the acting yourselves?

FATHER. Of course. Just as we are.

DIRECTOR, *ironically.* I'll bet you'd put on a splendid show!

LEADING MAN. Then what's the use of staying?

DIRECTOR, *without irony, to the Characters.* Don't run away with the idea that you can act! That's laughable . . . (*And in fact the Actors laugh.*) Hear that? They're laughing. (*Coming back to the point.*) I was forgetting. I must cast the show. It's quite easy. It casts itself. (*To the Second Actress.*) You, ma'am, will play the Mother. (*To the Father.*) You'll have to find her a name.

FATHER. Amalia, sir.

DIRECTOR. But that's this lady's real name. We wouldn't want to call her by her real name!

FATHER. Why not? If that is her name . . . But of course, if it's to be this lady . . . (*He indicates the Second Actress with a vague gesture.*) To me she (*the Mother*) is Amalia. But suit yourself . . . (*He is getting more and more confused.*) I don't know what to tell you . . . I'm beginning to . . . oh, I don't know . . . to find my own words ringing false, they sound different somehow.

DIRECTOR. Don't bother about that, just don't bother about it. We can always find the right sound. As for the name, if you say Amalia, Amalia it shall be; or we'll find another. For now, we'll designate the characters thus: (*to the Juvenile Lead*) you're the Son. (*To the Leading Lady.*) You, ma'am, are of course the Stepdaughter.

STEPDAUGHTER, *excitedly*. What, what? That one there is me? (*She bursts out laughing.*)

DIRECTOR, *mad*. What is there to laugh at?

LEADING LADY, *aroused*. No one has ever dared laugh at me! I insist on respect—or I quit!

STEPDAUGHTER. But, excuse me, I'm not laughing at you.

DIRECTOR, *to the Stepdaughter*. You should consider yourself honored to be played by . . .

LEADING LADY, *without pause, contemptuously*. —"That one there!"

STEPDAUGHTER. But I wasn't speaking of you, believe me. I was speaking of me. I don't see me in you, that's all. I don't know why . . . I guess you're just not like me!

FATHER. That's it, exactly, my dear sir! What is *expressed* in us . . .

DIRECTOR. Expression, expression! You think that's your business? Not at all!

FATHER. Well, but what *we* express . . .

DIRECTOR. But you don't. You don't express. You provide us with raw material. The actors give it body and face, voice and gesture. They've given expression to much loftier material, let me tell you. Yours is on such a small scale that, if it stands up on stage at all, the credit, believe me, should all go to my actors.

FATHER. I don't dare contradict you, sir, but it's terribly painful for us who are as you see us—with these bodies, these faces—

DIRECTOR, *cutting in, out of patience.* —that's where makeup comes in, my dear sir, for whatever concerns the face, the remedy is makeup!

FATHER. Yes. But the voice, gesture—

DIRECTOR. Oh, for heaven's sake! You can't exist here! Here the actor acts you, and that's that!

FATHER. I understand, sir. But now perhaps I begin to guess also why our author who saw us, alive as we are, did not want to put us on stage. I don't want to offend your actors. God forbid! But I feel that seeing myself acted . . . I don't know by whom . . .

LEADING MAN, *rising with dignity and coming over, followed by the gay young Actresses who laugh.* By me, if you've no objection.

FATHER, *humble, smooth.* I'm very honored, sir. (*He bows.*) But however much art and willpower the gentleman puts into absorbing me into himself . . . (*He is bewildered now.*)

LEADING MAN. Finish. Finish.

The Actresses laugh.

FATHER. Well, the performance he will give, even forcing himself with makeup to resemble me, well, with that figure (*all the Actors laugh*) he can hardly play me as I am. I shall rather be—even apart from the face—what he interprets me to be, as he feels I am—if he feels I am anything—and not as I feel myself inside myself. And it seems to me that whoever is called upon to judge us should take this into account.

DIRECTOR. So now you're thinking of what the critics will say? And I was still listening! Let the critics say what they want. We will concentrate on putting on your play! (*He walks away a little, and looks around.*) Come on, come on. Is the set ready? (*To the Actors and the Characters.*) Don't clutter up the stage, I want to be able to see! (*He goes down from the stage.*) Let's not lose any more time! (*To the Stepdaughter.*) Does the set seem pretty good to you?

STEPDAUGHTER. Oh! But I can't recognize it!

DIRECTOR. Oh my God, don't tell me we should reconstruct Madam Pace's back room for you! (*To the Father.*) Didn't you say a parlor with flowered wallpaper?

FATHER. Yes, sir. White.

DIRECTOR. It's not white. Stripes. But it doesn't matter. As for furniture we're in pretty good shape. That little table—bring it forward a bit! (*Stagehands do this. To the Property Man.*) Meanwhile you get an envelope, possibly a light blue one, and give it to the gentleman. (*Indicating the Father.*)

PROPERTY MAN. A letter envelope?

DIRECTOR AND FATHER. Yes, a letter envelope.

PROPERTY MAN. I'll be right back. (*He exits.*)

DIRECTOR. Come on, come on. It's the young lady's scene first. (*The Leading Lady comes forward.*) No, no, wait. I said the young lady. (*Indicating the Stepdaughter.*) You will just watch—

STEPDAUGHTER, *adding, without pause.* —watch me live it!

LEADING LADY, *resenting this.* I'll know how to live it too, don't worry, once I put myself in the role!

DIRECTOR, *raising his hands to his head.* Please! No more chatter! Now, scene one. The young lady with Madam Pace. Oh, and how about this Madam Pace? (*Bewildered, looking around him, he climbs back on stage.*)

FATHER. She isn't with us, sir.

DIRECTOR. Then what do we do?

FATHER. But she's alive. She's alive too.

DIRECTOR. Fine. But where?

FATHER. I'll tell you. (*Turning to the Actresses.*) If you ladies will do me the favor of giving me your hats for a moment.

THE ACTRESSES, *surprised a little, laughing a little, in chorus.* —What? Our hats?—What does he say?—Why?—Oh, dear!

DIRECTOR. What are you going to do with the ladies' hats?

The Actors laugh.

FATHER. Oh, nothing. Just put them on these coat hooks for a minute. And would some of you be so kind as to take your coats off too?

ACTORS, *as before.* Their coats too?—And then?—He's nuts!

AN ACTRESS OR TWO, *as above.* —But why?—Just the coats?

FATHER. Just so they can be hung there for a moment. Do me this favor. Will you?

ACTRESSES, *taking their hats off, and one or two of them their coats, too, continuing to laugh, and going to hang the hats here and there on the coat hooks.* —Well, why not?—There!—This is getting to be really funny!—Are we to put them on display?

FATHER. Exactly! That's just right, ma'am, on display!

DIRECTOR. May one inquire *why* you are doing this?

FATHER. Yes, sir. If we set the stage better, who knows but she may come to us, drawn by the objects of her trade . . . (*Inviting them to look toward the entrance at the back.*) Look! Look!

The entrance at the back opens, and Madam Pace walks a few paces downstage, a hag of enormous fatness with a pompous wig of carrot-colored wool and a fiery red rose on one side of it, à l'espagnole, *heavily made up, dressed with gauche elegance in garish red silk, a feathered fan in one hand and the other hand raised to hold a lighted cigarette between two fingers. At the sight of this apparition, the Director and the Actors at once dash off the stage with a yell of terror, rushing down the stairs and making as if to flee up the aisle. The Stepdaughter, on the other hand, runs to Madam Pace—deferentially, as to her boss.*

STEPDAUGHTER, *running to her.* Here she is, here she is!

FATHER, *beaming.* It's she! What did I tell you? Here she is!

DIRECTOR, *overcoming his first astonishment, and incensed now.* What tricks are these?

The next four speeches are more or less simultaneous.

LEADING MAN. What goes on around here?

JUVENILE LEAD. Where on earth did she come from?

INGENUE. They must have been holding her in reserve.

LEADING LADY. Hocus pocus! Hocus pocus!

FATHER, *dominating these protests.* Excuse me, though! Why, actually, would you want to destroy this prodigy in the name of vulgar truth, this miracle of a reality that is born of the stage itself—called into being by the stage, drawn here by the stage, and shaped by the stage—and which has more right to live on the stage than you have because it is much truer? Which of you actresses will later re-create Madam Pace? This lady *is* Madam Pace. You must admit that the actress who re-creates her will be less true than this lady—who is Madam Pace. Look, my daughter recognized her, and went right over to her. Stand and watch the scene!

Hesitantly, the Director and the Actors climb back on stage. But the scene between the Stepdaughter and Madam Pace has begun during the protest of the Actors and the Father's answer, sotto voce, very quietly, in short naturally—as would never be possible on a stage. When, called to order by the Father, the Actors turn again to watch, they hear Madam Pace, who has just placed her hand under the Stepdaughter's chin in order to raise her head, talk unintelligibly. After trying to hear for a moment, they just give up.

DIRECTOR. Well?

LEADING MAN. What's she saying?

LEADING LADY. One can't hear a thing.

JUVENILE LEAD. Louder!

STEPDAUGHTER, *leaving Madam Pace, who smiles a priceless smile, and walking down toward the Actors.* Louder, huh? How d'you mean, louder? These aren't things that can be said louder. I was able to say them loudly—to shame him (*indicating the Father*)—that was my revenge. For Madam, it's different, my friends: it would mean—jail.

DIRECTOR. Oh my God! It's like that, is it? But, my dear young lady, in the theater one must be heard. And even we couldn't hear you, right here on the stage. How about an audience out front? There's a scene to be done. And anyway you *can* speak loudly—it's just between yourselves, we won't be standing here listening like now. Pretend you're alone. In a room. The back room of the shop. No one can hear you. (*The Stepdaughter charmingly and with a mischievous smile tells him no with a repeated movement of the finger.*) Why not?

STEPDAUGHTER, *sotto voce, mysteriously.* There's someone who'll hear if she (*Madam Pace*) speaks loudly.

DIRECTOR, *in consternation.* Is someone else going to pop up now?

The Actors make as if to quit the stage again.

FATHER. No, no, sir. She means me. I'm to be there—behind the door—waiting. And Madam knows. So if you'll excuse me. I must be ready for my entrance. (*He starts to move.*)

DIRECTOR, *stopping him.* No, wait. We must respect the exigencies of the theater. Before you get ready—

STEPDAUGHTER, *interrupting him.* Let's get on with it, I tell you I'm dying with desire to live it, to live that scene! If he's ready, I'm more than ready!

DIRECTOR, *shouting.* But first we have to get that scene out of you and her! (*Indicating Madam Pace.*) Do you follow me?

STEPDAUGHTER. Oh dear, oh dear, she was telling me things you already know—that my mother's work had been badly done once again, the material is ruined, and I'm going to have to bear with her if I want her to go on helping us in our misery.

MADAM PACE, *coming forward with a great air of importance.* Sí, sí, señor, porque yo no want profit. No advantage, no.

DIRECTOR, *almost scared.* What, what? She talks like *that*?

All the Actors loudly burst out laughing.

STEPDAUGHTER, *also laughing.* Yes, sir, she talks like that—halfway between Spanish and English—very funny, isn't it?

MADAM PACE. Now that is not good manners, no, that you laugh at me! Yo hablo the English as good I can, señor!

DIRECTOR. And it *is* good! Yes! Do talk that way, ma'am! It's a sure-fire effect! There couldn't be anything better to, um, soften the crudity of the situation! Do talk that way! It's fine!

STEPDAUGHTER. Fine! Of course! To have certain propositions put to you in a lingo like that. Sure-fire, isn't it? Because, sir, it seems almost a joke. When I hear there's "an old señor" who wants to "have good time conmigo," I start to laugh—don't I, Madam Pace?

MADAM PACE. Old, viejo, no. Viejito—leetle beet old, sí, darling? Better like that: if he no give you fun, he bring you prudencia.

MOTHER, *jumping up, to the stupefaction and consternation of all the Actors, who had been taking no notice of her, and who now respond to her shouts with a start and, smiling, try to restrain her, because she has grabbed Madam Pace's wig and thrown it on the floor*). Witch! Witch! Murderess! My daughter!

STEPDAUGHTER, *running over to restrain her Mother.* No, no, Mama, no, please!

FATHER, *running over too at the same time.* Calm down, calm down! Sit here.

MOTHER. Then send that woman away!

STEPDAUGHTER, *to the Director, who also has run over.* It's not possible, not possible that my mother should be here!

FATHER, *also to the Director.* They can't be together. That's why, you see, the woman wasn't with us when we came. Their being together would spoil it, you understand.

DIRECTOR. It doesn't matter, doesn't matter at all. This is just a preliminary sketch. Everything helps. However confusing the elements, I'll piece them together somehow. (*Turning to the Mother and sitting her down again in her place.*) Come along, come along, ma'am, calm down, sit down again.

STEPDAUGHTER, *who meanwhile has moved center stage again. Turning to Madam Pace.* All right, let's go!

MADAM PACE. Ah, no! No thank you! Yo aquí no do nada with your mother present.

STEPDAUGHTER. Oh, come on! Bring in that old señor who wants to have good time conmigo! (*Turning imperiously to all the others.*) Yes, we've got to have it, this scene!—Come on, let's go! (*To Madam Pace.*) You may leave.

MADAM PACE. Ah sí, I go, I go, go seguramente . . . (*She makes her exit furiously, putting her wig back on, and looking haughtily at the Actors who applaud mockingly.*)

STEPDAUGHTER, *to the Father.* And you can make your entrance. No need to go out and come in again. Come here. Pretend, you're already in. Right. Now I'm here with bowed head, modest, huh? Let's go! Speak up! With a different voice, the voice of someone just in off the street: "Hello, miss."

DIRECTOR, *by this time out front again.* Now look, are you directing this, or am I? (*To the Father who looks undecided and perplexed.*) Do it, yes. Go to the back. Don't leave the stage, though. And then come forward.

The Father does it, almost dismayed. Very pale; but already clothed in the reality of his created life, he smiles as he approaches from the back, as if still alien to the drama which will break upon him. The Actors now pay attention to the scene which is beginning.

DIRECTOR, *softly, in haste, to the Prompter in the box.* And you, be ready now, ready to write!

THE SCENE

FATHER, *coming forward, with a different voice.* Hello, miss.

STEPDAUGHTER, *with bowed head and contained disgust.* Hello.

FATHER, *scrutinizing her under her hat which almost hides her face and noting that she is very young, exclaims, almost to himself, a little out of complaisance and a little out of fear of compromising himself in a risky adventure.* Oh . . . —Well, I was thinking, it wouldn't be the first time, hm? The first time you came here.

STEPDAUGHTER, *as above.* No, sir.

FATHER. You've been here other times? (*And when the Stepdaughter nods.*) More than one? (*He waits a moment for her to answer, then again scrutinizes her under her hat, smiles, then says:*) Well then, hm . . . it shouldn't any longer be so . . . May I take this hat off for you?

STEPDAUGHTER, *without pause, to forestall him, not now containing her disgust.* No, sir, *I* will take it off! (*And she does so in haste, convulsed.*)

The Mother, watching the scene with the Son and with the two others, smaller and more her own, who are close to her all the time, forming a group at the opposite side of the stage from the Actors, is on tenterhooks as she follows the words and actions of Father and Stepdaughter with varied expression: grief, disdain, anxiety, horror, now hiding her face, now emitting a moan.

MOTHER. Oh God! My God!

FATHER, *is momentarily turned to stone by the moaning; then he reassumes the previous tone.* Now give it to me: I'll hang it up for you. (*He takes the hat from her hands.*) But I could wish for a little hat worthier of such a dear, lovely little head! Would you like to help me choose one? From the many Madam has?—You wouldn't?

INGENUE, *interrupting.* Oh now, come on, those are *our* hats!

DIRECTOR, *without pause, very angry.* Silence, for heaven's sake, don't try to be funny!—This is the stage. (*Turning back to the Stepdaughter.*) Would you begin again, please?

STEPDAUGHTER, *beginning again.* No, thank you, sir.

FATHER. Oh, come on now, don't say no. Accept one from me. To please me . . . There are some lovely ones you know. And we would make Madam happy. Why else does she put them on display?

STEPDAUGHTER. No, no, sir, look, I wouldn't even be able to wear it.

FATHER. You mean because of what the family would think when they saw you come home with a new hat on? Think nothing of it. Know how to handle that? What to tell them at home?

STEPDAUGHTER, *breaking out, at the end of her rope.* But that's not why, sir. I couldn't wear it because I'm . . . as you see me. You might surely have noticed! (*Points to her black attire.*)

FATHER. In mourning, yes. Excuse me. It's true, I do see it. I beg your pardon. I'm absolutely mortified, believe me.

STEPDAUGHTER, *forcing herself and plucking up courage to conquer her contempt and nausea.* Enough! Enough! It's for me to thank you, it is not for you to be mortified or afflicted. Please pay no more attention to what I said. Even for me, you understand . . . (*She forces herself to smile and adds:*) I need to forget I am dressed like this.

DIRECTOR, *interrupting, addressing himself to the Prompter in his box, and going up on stage again.* Wait! Wait! Don't write. Leave that last sentence out, leave it out! (*Turning to the Father and Stepdaughter.*) It's going very well indeed. (*Then to the Father alone.*) This is where you go into the part we prepared. (*To the Actors.*) Enchanting, that little hat scene, don't you agree?

STEPDAUGHTER. Oh, but the best is just coming. Why aren't we continuing?

DIRECTOR. Patience one moment. (*Again addressing himself to the Actors.*) Needs rather delicate handling, of course . . .

LEADING MAN. —With a certain *ease*—

LEADING LADY. Obviously. But there's nothing to it. (*To the Leading Man.*) We can rehearse it at once, can't we?

LEADING MAN. As far as I'm . . . Very well, I'll go out and make my entrance. (*And he does go out by the back door, ready to reenter.*)

DIRECTOR, *to the Leading Lady.* And so, look, your scene with that Madam Pace is over. I'll write it up later. You are standing . . . Hey, where are you going?

LEADING LADY. Wait. I'm putting my hat back on . . . (*She does so, taking the hat from the hook.*)

DIRECTOR. Oh yes, good. —Now, you're standing here with your head bowed.

STEPDAUGHTER, *amused.* But she's not wearing black!

LEADING LADY. I shall wear black! And I'll carry it better than you!

DIRECTOR, *to the Stepdaughter.* Keep quiet, please! Just watch. You can learn something. (*Claps his hands.*) Get going, get going! The entrance! (*And he goes back out front to get an impression of the stage.*)

The door at the back opens, and the Leading Man comes forward, with the relaxed, waggish manner of an elderly Don Juan. From the first speeches, the performance of the scene by the Actors is quite a different thing, without, however, having any element of parody in it—rather, it seems corrected, set to rights. Naturally, the Stepdaughter and the Father, being quite unable to recognize themselves in this Leading Lady and Leading Man but hearing them speak their own words, express in various ways, now with gestures, now with smiles, now with open protests, their surprise, their wonderment, their suffering, etc., as will be seen forthwith.

The Prompter's voice is clearly heard from the box.

LEADING MAN. Hello, miss.

FATHER, *without pause, unable to contain himself.* No, no!

The Stepdaughter, seeing how the Leading Man makes his entrance, has burst out laughing.

DIRECTOR, *coming from the proscenium, furious.* Silence here! And stop that laughing at once! We can't go ahead till it stops.

STEPDAUGHTER, *coming from the proscenium.* How can I help it? This lady (*the Leading Lady*) just stands there. If she's supposed to be me, let me tell you that if anyone said hello to me in that manner and that tone of voice, I'd burst out laughing just as I actually did!

FATHER, *coming forward a little too.* That's right . . . the manner, the tone . . .

DIRECTOR. Manner! Tone! Stand to one side now, and let me see the rehearsal.

LEADING MAN, *coming forward.* If I'm to play an old man entering a house of ill—

DIRECTOR. Oh, pay no attention, please. Just begin again. It was going fine. (*Waiting for the Actor to resume.*) Now then . . .

LEADING MAN. Hello, miss.

LEADING LADY. Hello.

LEADING MAN, *re-creating the Father's gesture of scrutinizing her under her hat, but then expressing very distinctly first the complaisance and then the fear.* Oh . . . Well . . . I was thinking it wouldn't be the first time, I hope . . .

FATHER, *unable to help correcting him.* Not "I hope." "Would it?" "Would it?"

DIRECTOR. He says: "would it?" A question.

LEADING MAN, *pointing to the Prompter.* I heard: "I hope."

DIRECTOR. Same thing! "Would it." Or "I hope." Continue, continue.— Now, maybe a bit less affected . . . Look, I'll do it for you. Watch me . . . (*Returns to the stage, then repeats the bit since the entrance.*)— Hello, miss.

LEADING LADY. Hello.

DIRECTOR. Oh, well . . . I was thinking . . . (*Turning to the Leading Man to have him note how he has looked at the Leading Lady under her hat.*) Surprise . . . fear and complaisance. (*Then, going on, and turning to the Leading Lady.*) It wouldn't be the first time, would it? The first time you came here. (*Again turning to the Leading Man with an inquiring look.*) Clear? (*To the Leading Lady.*) Then you say: No, sir. (*Back to the Leading Man.*) How shall I put it? Plasticity! (*Goes back out front.*)

LEADING LADY. No, sir.

LEADING MAN. You came here other times? More than one?

DIRECTOR. No, no, wait. (*Indicating the Leading Lady.*) First let her nod. "You came here other times?"

The Leading Lady raises her head a little, closes her eyes painfully as if in disgust, then nods twice at the word "Down" from the Director.

STEPDAUGHTER, *involuntarily.* Oh, my God! (*And she at once puts her hand on her mouth to keep the laughter in.*)

DIRECTOR, *turning round.* What is it?

STEPDAUGHTER, *without pause.* Nothing, nothing.

DIRECTOR, *to the Leading Man.* That's your cue. Go straight on.

LEADING MAN. More than one? Well then, hm . . . it shouldn't any longer be so . . . May I take this little hat off for you?

The Leading Man says this last speech in such a tone and accompanies it with such a gesture that the Stepdaughter, her hands on her mouth, much as she wants to hold herself in, cannot contain her laughter, which comes bursting out through her fingers irresistibly and very loud.

LEADING LADY, *returning to her place, enraged.* Now look, I'm not going to be made a clown of by that person!

LEADING MAN. Nor am I. Let's stop.

DIRECTOR, *to the Stepdaughter, roaring.* Stop it! Stop it!

STEPDAUGHTER. Yes, yes. Forgive me, forgive me . . .

DIRECTOR. You have no manners! You're presumptuous! So there!

FATHER, *seeking to intervene.* That's true, yes, that's true, sir, but forgive . . .

DIRECTOR, *on stage again.* Forgive nothing! It's disgusting!

FATHER. Yes, sir. But believe me, it has such a strange effect—

DIRECTOR. Strange? Strange? What's strange about it?

FATHER. I admire your actors, sir, I really admire them, this gentleman (*Leading Man*) and that lady (*Leading Lady*) but assuredly . . . well, they're not us . . .

DIRECTOR. So what? How *could* they be you, if they're the actors?

FATHER. Exactly, the actors! And they play our parts well, both of them. But of course, to us, they seem something else—that tries to be the same but simply isn't!

DIRECTOR. How d'you mean, isn't? What is it then?

FATHER. Something that . . . becomes theirs. And stops being ours.

DIRECTOR. Necessarily! I explained that to you!

FATHER. Yes. I understand, I do under—

DIRECTOR. Then that will be enough! (*Turning to the Actors.*) We'll be rehearsing by ourselves as we usually do. Rehearsing with authors present has always been hell, in my experience. There's no satisfying them. (*Turning to the Father and the Stepdaughter.*) Come along then. Let's resume. And let's hope you find it possible not to laugh this time.

STEPDAUGHTER. Oh, no, I won't be laughing this time around. My big moment comes up now. Don't worry!

DIRECTOR. Very well, when she says: "Please pay no more attention to what I said . . . Even for me—you understand . . ." (*Turning to the Father.*) You'll have to cut right in with: "I understand, oh yes, I understand . . ." and ask her right away—

STEPDAUGHTER, *interrupting.* Oh? Ask me what?

DIRECTOR. —why she is in mourning.

STEPDAUGHTER. No, no, look, when I told him I needed to forget I was dressed like this, do you know what his answer was? "Oh, good! Then let's take that little dress right off, shall we?"

DIRECTOR. Great! Terrific! It'll knock 'em right out of their seats!

STEPDAUGHTER. But it's the truth.

DIRECTOR. Truth, is it? Well, well, well. This is the theater! Our motto is: truth up to a certain point!

STEPDAUGHTER. Then what would you propose?

DIRECTOR. You'll see. You'll see it. Just leave me alone.

STEPDAUGHTER. Certainly not. From my nausea—from all the reasons one more cruel than another why I am what I am, why I am "that one there"—you'd like to cook up some romantic, sentimental concoction, wouldn't you? He asks me why I'm in mourning, and I tell him, through my tears, that Papa died two months ago! No, my dear sir! He has to say what he did say: "Then let's take that little dress right off, shall we?" And I, with my two-months mourning in my heart, went back there—you see? Behind that screen—and—my fingers quivering with shame, with loathing—I took off my dress, took off my corset . . .

DIRECTOR, *running his hands through his hair.* Good God, what are you saying?

STEPDAUGHTER, *shouting frantically.* The truth, sir, the truth!

DIRECTOR. Well, yes, of course, that must be the truth . . . and I quite understand your horror, young lady. Would you try to understand that all that is impossible *on the stage*?

STEPDAUGHTER. Impossible? Then, thanks very much, I'm leaving.

DIRECTOR. No, no, look . . .

STEPDAUGHTER. I'm leaving, I'm leaving! You went in that room, you two, didn't you, and figured out "what is possible on the stage"? Thanks very much. I see it all. He wants to skip to the point where he can act out his (*exaggerating*) spiritual travail! But I want to play my drama. Mine!

DIRECTOR, *annoyed, and shrugging haughtily.* Oh well, *your* drama. This is not just your drama, if I may say so. How about the drama of the others? His drama (*the Father*), hers (*the Mother*)? We can't let one character hog the limelight, just taking the whole stage over, and overshadowing all the others! Everything must be placed within the frame of one harmonious picture! We must perform only what is performable! I know as well as you do that each of us has a whole life of his own inside him and would like to bring it all out. But the difficult thing is this: to bring out only as much as is needed—in relation to the others—and in this to *imply* all the rest, *suggest* what remains inside! Oh, it would be nice if every character could come down to the footlights and tell the audience just what is brewing inside him—in a fine monologue or, if you will, a lecture! (*Good-natured, conciliatory.*) Miss, you will have to contain yourself. And it will be in your interest. It could make a bad impression—let me warn you—this tearing fury, this desperate disgust—since, if I may say so, you confessed having been with others at Madam Pace's—before him—more than once!

STEPDAUGHTER, *lowering her head, pausing to recollect, a deeper note in her voice.* It's true. But to me the others are also *him*, all of them equally!

DIRECTOR, *not getting it.* The others? How d'you mean?

STEPDAUGHTER. People "go wrong." And wrong follows on the heels of wrong. Who is responsible, if not whoever it was who first brought them down? Isn't that always the case? And for me that is him. Even before I was born. Look at him, and see if it isn't so.

DIRECTOR. Very good. And if he has so much to feel guilty about, can't you appreciate how it must weigh him down? So let's at least permit him to act it out.

STEPDAUGHTER. And how, may I ask, how could he act out all that "noble" guilt, all those so "moral" torments, if you propose to spare him the horror of one day finding in his arms—after having bade her take off the black clothes that marked her recent loss—a woman now, and already gone wrong—that little girl, sir, that little girl whom he used to go watch coming out of school?

She says these last words in a voice trembling with emotion. The Mother, hearing her say this, overcome with uncontrollable anguish, which comes out first in suffocated moans and subsequently bursts out in bitter weeping. The emotion takes hold of everyone. Long pause.

STEPDAUGHTER, *as soon as the Mother gives signs of calming down, somber, determined.* We're just among ourselves now. Still unknown to the public. Tomorrow you will make of us the show you have in mind. You will put it together in your way. But would you like to really see—our drama? Have it explode—the real thing?

DIRECTOR. Of course. Nothing I'd like better. And I'll use as much of it as I possibly can!

STEPDAUGHTER. Very well. Have this Mother here go out.

MOTHER, *ceasing to weep, with a loud cry.* No, no! Don't allow this, don't allow it!

DIRECTOR. I only want to take a look, ma'am.

MOTHER. I can't, I just can't!

DIRECTOR. But if it's already happened? Excuse me but I just don't get it.

MOTHER. No, no, it's happening now. It's always happening. My torment is not a pretense! I am alive and present—always, in every moment of my torment—it keeps renewing itself, it too is alive and always present. But those two little ones over there—have you heard them speak? They cannot speak, sir, not anymore! They still keep clinging to me—to keep my torment alive and present. For themselves they don't exist, don't exist any longer. And she (*the Stepdaughter*), she just fled, ran away from me, she's lost, lost . . . If I see her before me now, it's for the same reason: to renew the torment, keep it always alive and present forever—the torment I've suffered on her account too—forever!

FATHER, *solemn.* The eternal moment, sir, as I told you. She (*the Stepdaughter*) is here to catch me, fix me, hold me there in the pillory, hanging there forever, hooked, in that single fleeting shameful moment of my life! She cannot give it up. And, actually, sir, *you* cannot spare me.

DIRECTOR. But I didn't say I wouldn't use that. On the contrary, it will be the nucleus of the whole first act. To the point where she (*the Mother*) surprises you.

FATHER. Yes, exactly. Because that is the sentence passed upon me: all our passion which has to culminate in her (*the Mother's*) final cry!

STEPDAUGHTER. It still rings in my ears. It's driven me out of my mind, that cry!—You can present me as you wish, sir, it doesn't matter. Even dressed. As long as at least my arms—just my arms—are bare. Because it was like this. (*She goes to the Father and rests her head on his chest.)* I was standing like this with my head on his chest and my arms round his neck like this. Then I saw something throbbing right here on my arm. A vein. Then, as if it was just this living vein that disgusted me, I jammed my eyes shut, like this, d'you see?—and buried my head on his chest. (*Turning to the Mother.*) Scream, scream, Mama! (*Buries her head on the Father's chest and with her shoulders raised as if to avoid hearing the scream she adds in a voice stifled with torment.*) Scream as you screamed then!

MOTHER, *rushing forward to part them.* No! My daughter! My daughter! (*Having pulled her from him.*) Brute! Brute! It's my daughter, don't you see—my daughter!

DIRECTOR, *the outburst having sent him reeling to the footlights, while the Actors show dismay.* Fine! Splendid! And now, curtain, curtain!

FATHER, *running to him, convulsed.* Right! Yes! Because that, sir, is how it actually was!

DIRECTOR, *in admiration and conviction.* Yes, yes, of course! Curtain! Curtain!

Hearing this repeated cry of the Director, the Technician lets down the curtain, trapping the Director and the Father between curtain and footlights.

DIRECTOR, *looking up, with raised arms.* What an idiot! I say "Curtain," meaning that's how the act should end, and they let down the actual curtain! (*He lifts a corner of the curtain so he can get back on stage. To the Father.*) Yes, yes, fine, splendid! Absolutely surefire! Has to end that way. I can vouch for the first act. (*Goes behind the curtain with the Father.*)

When the curtain rises we see that the stagehands have struck that first indication of a set, and have put on stage in its stead a small garden fountain. On one side of the stage, the Actors are sitting in a row, and on the other are the Characters. The Director is standing in the middle of the stage, in the act of meditating with one hand, fist clenched, on his mouth.

DIRECTOR, *shrugging after a short pause.* Yes, well then, let's get to the second act. Just leave it to me as we agreed beforehand and everything will be all right.

STEPDAUGHTER. Our entrance into his house (*the Father*) in spite of him (*the Son*).

DIRECTOR, *losing patience*. Very well. But leave it all to me, I say.

STEPDAUGHTER. In spite of him. Just let that be clear.

MOTHER, *shaking her head from her corner*. For all the good that's come out of it . . .

STEPDAUGHTER, *turning quickly on her*. It doesn't matter. The more damage to us, the more guilt feelings for him.

DIRECTOR, *still out of patience*. I understand, I understand. All this will be taken into account, especially at the beginning. Rest assured.

MOTHER, *supplicatingly*. Do make them understand, I beg you, sir, for my conscience sake, for I tried in every possible way—

STEPDAUGHTER, *continuing her Mother's speech, contemptuously*. To placate me, to advise me not to give him trouble. (*To the Director*.) Do what she wants, do it because it's true. I enjoy the whole thing very much because, look, the more she plays the suppliant and tries to gain entrance into his heart, the more he holds himself aloof: he's an absentee! How I relish this!

DIRECTOR. We want to get going—on the second act, don't we?

STEPDAUGHTER. I won't say another word. But to play it all in the garden, as you want to, won't be possible.

DIRECTOR. Why won't it be possible?

STEPDAUGHTER. Because he (*the Son*) stays shut up in his room, on his own. Then again we need the house for the part about this poor bewildered little boy, as I told you.

DIRECTOR. Quite right. But on the other hand, we can't change the scenery in view of the audience three or four times in one act, nor can we stick up signs—

LEADING MAN. They used to at one time . . .

DIRECTOR. Yes, when the audiences were about as mature as that little girl.

LEADING LADY. They got the illusion more easily.

FATHER, *suddenly, rising.* The illusion, please don't say illusion! Don't use that word! It's especially cruel to us.

DIRECTOR, *astonished.* And why, if I may ask?

FATHER. Oh yes, cruel, cruel! You should understand that.

DIRECTOR. What word would you have us use anyway? The illusion of creating here for our spectators—

LEADING MAN. —By our performance—

DIRECTOR. —the illusion of a reality

FATHER. I understand, sir, but perhaps you do not understand us. Because, you see, for you and for your actors all this—quite rightly—is a game—

LEADING LADY, *indignantly interrupting.* Game! We are not children, sir. We act in earnest.

FATHER. I don't deny it. I just mean the game of your art which, as this gentleman rightly says, must provide a perfect illusion of reality.

DIRECTOR. Yes, exactly.

FATHER. But consider this. We (*he quickly indicates himself and the other five Characters*), we have no reality outside this illusion.

DIRECTOR, *astonished, looking at his Actors who remain bewildered and lost.* And that means?

FATHER, *after observing them briefly, with a pale smile.* Just that, ladies and gentlemen. How should we have any other reality? What for you is an illusion, to be created, is for us our unique reality. (*Short pause. He takes several short steps toward the Director, and adds:*) But not for us alone, of course. Think a moment. (*He looks into his eyes.*) Can you tell me who you are? (*And he stands there pointing his first finger at him.*)

DIRECTOR, *upset, with a half smile.* How do you mean, who I am? I am I.

FATHER. And if I told you that wasn't true because you are me?

DIRECTOR. I would reply that you are out of your mind. (*The Actors laugh.*)

FATHER. You are right to laugh: because this is a game. (*To the Director.*) And you can object that it's only in a game that that gentleman there (*Leading Man*), who is himself, must be me, who am *my*self. I've caught you in a trap, do you see that?

Actors start laughing again.

DIRECTOR, *annoyed.* You said all this before. Why repeat it?

FATHER. I won't—I didn't intend to say that. I'm inviting you to emerge from this game. (*He looks at the Leading Lady as if to forestall what she might say.*) This game of art which you are accustomed to play here with your actors. Let me again ask quite seriously: Who are you?

DIRECTOR, *turning to the Actors, amazed and at the same time irritated.* The gall of this fellow! Calls himself a character and comes here to ask me who I am!

FATHER, *dignified, but not haughty.* A character, sir, can always ask a man who he is. Because a character really has his own life, marked with his own characteristics, by virtue of which he is always someone. Whereas, a man—I'm not speaking of you now—*a man* can be no one.

DIRECTOR. Oh sure. But you are asking me! And I am the manager, understand?

FATHER, *quite softly with mellifluous modesty.* Only in order to know, sir, if you as you now are see yourself . . . for example, at a distance in time. Do you see the man you once were, with all the illusions you had then, with everything, inside you and outside, as it seemed then—as it was then for you!—Well sir, thinking back to those illusions which you don't have anymore, to all those things which no longer seem to be what at one time they were for you, don't you feel, not just the boards of this stage, but the very earth beneath slipping away from you? For will not all that you feel yourself to be now, your whole reality of today, as it is now, inevitably seem an illusion tomorrow?

DIRECTOR, *who has not followed exactly, but has been staggered by the plausibilities of the argument.* Well, well, what do you want to prove?

FATHER. Oh nothing sir. I just wanted to make you see that if *we* (*pointing again at himself and the other Characters*) have no reality outside of illusion, it would be well if you should distrust your reality because, though you breathe it and touch it today, it is destined like that of yesterday to stand revealed to you tomorrow as illusion.

DIRECTOR, *deciding to mock him.* Oh splendid! And you'll be telling me next that you and this play that you have come to perform for me are truer and more real than I am.

FATHER, *quite seriously.* There can be no doubt of that, sir.

DIRECTOR. Really?

FATHER. I thought you had understood that from the start.

DIRECTOR. More real than me?

FATHER. If your reality can change overnight . . .

DIRECTOR. Of course it can, it changes all the time, like everyone else's.

FATHER, *with a cry.* But ours does not, sir. You see, that is the difference. It does not change, it cannot ever change or be otherwise because it is already fixed, it is what is, just that, forever—a terrible thing, sir!—an immutable reality. You should shudder to come near us.

DIRECTOR, *suddenly struck by a new idea, he steps in front of the Father.* I should like to know, however, when anyone ever saw a character get out of his part and set about expounding and explicating it, delivering lectures on it. Can you tell me? I have never seen anything like that.

FATHER. You have never seen it, sir, because authors generally hide the travail of their creations. When characters are alive and turn up, living, before their author, all that author does is follow the words and gestures which they propose to him. He has to want them to be as they themselves want to be. Woe betide him if he doesn't! When a character is born, he at once acquires such an independence, even of his own author, that the whole world can imagine him in innumerable situations other than those the author thought to place him in. At times he acquires a meaning that the author never dreamt of giving him.

DIRECTOR. Certainly, I know that.

FATHER. Then why all this astonishment at us? Imagine what a misfortune it is for a character such as I described to you—given life in the imagination of an author who then wished to deny him life—and tell me frankly: isn't such a character, given life and left without life, isn't he right to set about doing just what we are doing now as we stand here before you, after having done just the same—for a very long time, believe me—before *him*, trying to persuade him, trying to push him . . . I would appear before him sometimes, sometimes she (*looks at Stepdaughter*) would go to him, sometimes that poor mother . . .

STEPDAUGHTER, *coming forward as if in a trance.* It's true. I too went there, sir, to tempt him, many times, in the melancholy of that study of his, at the twilight hour, when he would sit stretched out in his armchair, unable to make up his mind to switch the light on, and letting the evening shadows invade the room, knowing that these shadows were alive with us and that we were coming to tempt him . . . (*As if she saw herself still in that study and felt only annoyance at the presence of all of these Actors.*) Oh, if only you would all go away! Leave us alone! My mother there with her son—I with this little girl—the boy there always alone—then I with him (*the Father*)—then I by myself, I by myself . . . in those shadows. (*Suddenly she jumps up as if she wished to take hold of herself in the vision she has of herself lighting up the shadows and alive.*) Ah my life! What scenes, what scenes we went there to propose to him; I, I tempted him more than the others.

FATHER. Right, but perhaps that was the trouble: you insisted too much. You thought you could seduce him.

STEPDAUGHTER. Nonsense. He wanted me that way. (*She comes up to the Director to tell him as in confidence.*) If you ask me, sir, it was because he was so depressed, or because he despised the theater the public knows and wants . . .

DIRECTOR. Let's continue. Let's continue, for heaven's sake. Enough theories, I'd like some facts. Give me some facts.

STEPDAUGHTER. It seems to me that we have already given you more facts than you can handle—with our entry into his (*the Father's*) house! You said you couldn't change the scene every five minutes or start hanging signs.

DIRECTOR. Nor can we, of course not, we have to combine the scenes and group them in one simultaneous close-knit action. Not your idea at all. You'd like to see your brother come home from school and wander through the house like a ghost, hiding behind the doors, and brooding on a plan which—how did you put it—?

STEPDAUGHTER. —shrivels him up, sir, completely shrivels him up, sir.

DIRECTOR. Shrivels! What a word! All right then: his growth was stunted except for his eyes. Is that what you said?

STEPDAUGHTER. Yes, sir. Just look at him. (*She points him out next to the Mother.*)

DIRECTOR. Good girl. And then at the same time you want this little girl to be playing in the garden, dead to the world. Now, the boy in the house, the girl in the garden, is that possible?

STEPDAUGHTER. Happy in the sunshine! Yes, that is my only reward, her pleasure, her joy in that garden! After the misery, the squalor of a horrible room where we slept, all four of us, she with me: just think, of the horror of my contaminated body next to hers! She held me tight, oh so tight with her loving innocent little arms! In the garden she would run and take my hand as soon as she saw me. She did not see the big flowers, she ran around looking for the teeny ones and wanted to show them to me, oh the joy of it!

Saying this and tortured by the memory she breaks into prolonged desperate sobbing, dropping her head onto her arms which are spread out on the work table. Everyone is overcome by her emotion. The Director goes to her almost paternally and says to comfort her:

DIRECTOR. We'll do the garden. We'll do the garden, don't worry, and you'll be very happy about it. We'll bring all the scenes together in the garden. (*Calling a stagehand by name.*) Hey, drop me a couple of trees, will you, two small cypress trees, here in front of the fountain.

Two small cypress trees are seen descending from the flies. A Stagehand runs on to secure them with nails and a couple of braces.

DIRECTOR, *to the Stepdaughter.* Something to go on with anyway. Gives us an idea. (*Again calling the Stagehand by name.*) Hey, give me a bit of sky.

STAGEHAND, *from above.* What?

DIRECTOR. Bit of sky, a backdrop, to go behind that fountain. (*A white backdrop is seen descending from the flies.*) Not white, I said sky. It doesn't matter, leave it, I'll take care of it. (*Shouting.*) Hey, Electrician, put these lights out. Let's have a bit of atmosphere, lunar atmosphere, blue background, and give me a blue spot on that backdrop. That's right. That's enough. (*At his command a mysterious lunar scene is created which induces the Actors to talk and move as they would on an evening in the garden beneath the moon.*) (*To Stepdaughter.*) You see? And now instead of hiding behind doors in the house the boy could move around here in the garden and hide behind trees. But it will be difficult, you know, to find a little girl to play the scene where she shows you the flowers. (*Turning to the Boy.*) Come down this way a bit. Let's see how this can be worked out. (*And when the Boy doesn't move.*) Come on, come on. (*Then dragging him forward he tries to make him hold his head up but it falls down again every time.*) Oh dear, another problem, this boy . . . What *is* it? . . . My God, he'll have to say something . . . (*He goes up to him, puts a hand on his shoulder and leads him behind one of the tree drops.*) Come on. Come on. Let me see. You can hide a bit here . . . Like this . . . You can stick your head out a bit to look . . . (*He goes to one side to see the effect. The Boy has scarcely run through the actions when the Actors are deeply affected; and they remain quite overwhelmed.*) Ah! Fine! Splendid! (*He turns again to the Stepdaughter.*) If the little girl surprises him looking out and runs over to him, don't you think she might drag a few words out of him too?

STEPDAUGHTER, *jumping to her feet.* Don't expect him to speak while he's here. (*She points to the Son.*) You have to send *him* away first.

SON, *going resolutely toward one of the two stairways.* Suits me. Glad to go. Nothing I want more.

DIRECTOR, *immediately calling him.* No. Where are you going? Wait.

The Mother rises, deeply moved, in anguish at the thought that he is really going. She instinctively raises her arms as if to halt him, yet without moving away from her position.

SON, *arriving at the footlights, where the Director stops him.* I have absolutely nothing to do here. So let me go please. Just let me go.

DIRECTOR. How do you mean, you have nothing to do?

STEPDAUGHTER, *placidly, with irony.* Don't hold him! He won't go.

FATHER. He has to play the terrible scene in the garden with his mother.

SON, *unhesitating, resolute, proud.* I play nothing. I said so from the start. (*To the Director.*) Let me go.

STEPDAUGHTER, *running to the Director to get him to lower his arms so that he is no longer holding the Son back.* Let him go. (*Then turning to the Son as soon as the Director has let him go.*) Very well, go. (*The Son is all set to move toward the stairs but, as if held by some occult power, he cannot go down the steps. While the Actors are both astounded and deeply troubled, he moves slowly across the footlights straight to the other stairway. But having arrived there he remains poised for the descent but unable to descend. The Stepdaughter, who has followed him with her eyes in an attitude of defiance, bursts out laughing.*) He can't, you see. He can't. He has to stay here, has to. Bound by a chain, indissolubly. But if I who do take flight, sir, when that happens which has to happen, and precisely because of the hatred I feel for him, precisely so as not to see him again—very well, if *I* am still here and can bear the sight of him and his company—you can imagine whether *he* can go away. He who really must, must remain here with that fine father of his and that mother there who no longer has any other children. (*Turning again to the Mother.*) Come on, Mother, come on. (*Turning again to the Director and pointing to the Mother.*) Look, she got up to hold him back. (*To the Mother, as if exerting a magical power over her.*) Come. Come . . . (*Then to the Director.*) You can imagine how little she wants to display her love in front of your actors. But so great is her desire to get at him that—look, you see—she is even prepared to live her scene.

In fact the Mother has approached and no sooner has the Stepdaughter spoken her last words than she spreads her arms to signify consent.

SON, *without pause.* But *I* am not, *I* am not. If I cannot go I will stay here, but I repeat: I will play nothing.

FATHER, *to the Director, enraged.* You can force him, sir.

SON. No one can force me.

FATHER. I will force you.

STEPDAUGHTER. Wait, wait. First the little girl must be at the fountain. (*She runs to take the Little Girl, drops on her knees in front of her, takes her little face in her hands.*) My poor little darling, you look bewildered with those lovely big eyes of yours. Who knows where you think you are? We are on a stage my dear. What is a stage? It is a place where you play at being serious, a place for playacting, where we will now playact. But seriously! For real! You too . . . (*She embraces her, presses her to her bosom and rocks her a little.*) Oh, little darling, little darling, what an ugly play you will enact! What a horrible thing has been planned for you, the garden, the fountain . . . All pretense, of course, that's the trouble, my sweet, everything is make-believe here, but perhaps for you, my child, a make-believe fountain is nicer than a real one for playing in, hmm? It will be a game for the others, but not for you, alas, because you are real, my darling, and are actually playing in a fountain that is real, beautiful, big, green with many bamboo plants reflected in it and giving it shade. Many, many ducklings can swim in it, breaking the shade to bits. You want to take hold of one of these ducklings . . . (*With a shout that fills everyone with dismay.*) No! No, my Rosetta! Your mother is not looking after you because of that beast of a son. A thousand devils are loose in my head . . . and *he* . . . (*She leaves the Little Girl and turns with her usual hostility to the Boy.*) And what are you doing here, always looking like a beggar child? It will be your fault too if this little girl drowns—with all your standing around like that. As if I hadn't paid for everybody when I got you all into this house. (*Grabbing one of his arms to force him to take a hand out of his pocket.*) What have you got there? What are you hiding? Let's see this hand. (*Tears his hand out of his pocket, and to the horror of everyone discovers that it holds a small revolver. She looks at it for a moment as if satisfied and then says:*) Ah! Where did you get that and how? (*And as the Boy in his confusion, with his eyes staring and vacant all the time, does not answer her.*) Idiot, if I were you I wouldn't have killed myself, I would have killed one of those two—or both of them—the father and the son! (*She hides him behind the small cypress tree from which he had been looking out, and she takes the Little Girl and hides her in *the fountain, having her lie down in it in such a way as to be quite hidden. Finally, the Stepdaughter goes down on her knees with her face in her hands, which are resting on the rim of the fountain.)*

DIRECTOR. Splendid! (*Turning to the Son.*) And at the same time . . .

SON, *with contempt.* And at the same time, nothing. It is not true, sir. There was never any scene between me and her. (*He points to the Mother.*) Let her tell you herself how it was.

Meanwhile the Second Actress and the Juvenile Lead have detached themselves from the group of Actors. The former has started to observe the Mother, who is opposite her, very closely. And the other has started to observe the Son. Both are planning how they will re-create the roles.

MOTHER. Yes, it is true, sir. I had gone to his room.

SON. My room, did you hear that? Not the garden.

DIRECTOR. That is of no importance. We have to rearrange the action, I told you that.

SON, *noticing that the Juvenile Lead is observing him.* What do *you* want?

JUVENILE LEAD. Nothing. I am observing you.

SON, *turning to the other side where the Second Actress is.* Ah, and here we have you to re-create the role, eh? (*He points to the Mother.*)

DIRECTOR. Exactly, exactly. You should be grateful, it seems to me, for the attention they are giving you.

SON. Oh yes, thank you. But you still haven't understood that you cannot do this drama. We are not inside you, not in the least, and your actors are looking at us from the outside. Do you think it's possible for us to live before a mirror which, not content to freeze us in the fixed image it provides of our expression, also throws back at us an unrecognizable grimace purporting to be ourselves?

FATHER. That is true. That is true. You must see that.

DIRECTOR, *to the Juvenile Lead and the Second Actress.* Very well, get away from here.

SON. No good. I won't cooperate.

DIRECTOR. Just be quiet a minute and let me hear your mother. (*To the Mother.*) Well? You went into his room?

MOTHER. Yes sir, into his room. I was at the end of my tether. I wanted to pour out all of the anguish which was oppressing me. But as soon as he saw me come in—

SON. —There was no scene. I went away. I went away so there would be no scene. Because I have never made scenes, never, understand?

MOTHER. That's true. That's how it was. Yes.

DIRECTOR. But now there's got to be a scene between you and him. It is indispensable.

MOTHER. As for me, sir, I am ready. If only you could find some way to have me speak to him for one moment, to have me say what is in my heart.

FATHER, *going right up to the Son, very violent.* You will do it! For your mother! For your mother!

SON, *more decisively than ever.* I will do nothing!

FATHER, *grabbing him by the chest and shaking him.* By God, you will obey! Can't you hear how she is talking to you? Aren't you her son?

SON, *grabbing his Father.* No! No! Once and for all let's have done with it!

General agitation. The Mother, terrified, tries to get between them to separate them.

MOTHER, *as before.* Please, please!

FATHER, *without letting go of the Son.* You must obey, you must obey!

SON, *wrestling with his Father and in the end throwing him to the ground beside the little stairway, to the horror of everyone.* What's this frenzy that's taken hold of you? To show your shame and ours to everyone? Have you no restraint? I won't cooperate, I won't cooperate! And that is how I interpret the wishes of the man who did not choose to put us on stage.

DIRECTOR. But you came here.

SON, *pointing to his Father.* He came here—not me!

DIRECTOR. But aren't you here too?

SON. It was he who wanted to come, dragging the rest of us with him, and then getting together with you to plot not only what really happened, but also—as if that did not suffice—*what did not happen.*

DIRECTOR. Then tell me. Tell me what did happen. Just tell me. You came out of your room without saying a thing?

SON, *after a moment of hesitation.* Without saying a thing. In order not to make a scene.

DIRECTOR, *driving him on.* Very well, and then, what did you do then?

SON, *while everyone looks on in anguished attention, he moves a few steps on the front part of the stage.* Nothing . . . crossing the garden . . . *(He stops, gloomy, withdrawn.)*

DIRECTOR, *always driving him on to speak, impressed by his reticence.* Very well, crossing the garden?

SON, *desperate, hiding his face with one arm.* Why do you want to make me say it, sir? It is horrible.

The Mother trembles all over, and stifles groans, looking toward the fountain.

DIRECTOR, *softly, noticing this look of hers, turning to the Son, with growing apprehension.* The little girl?

SON, *looking out into the auditorium.* Over there—in the fountain . . .

FATHER, *on the ground, pointing compassionately toward the Mother.* And she followed him, sir.

DIRECTOR, *to the Son, anxiously.* And then you . . .

SON, *slowly, looking straight ahead all the time.* I ran out. I started to fish her out . . . but all of a sudden I stopped. Behind those trees I saw something that froze me: the boy, the boy was standing there, quite still. There was madness in the eyes. He was looking at his drowned sister in the fountain. (*The Stepdaughter, who has been bent over the fountain, hiding the Little Girl, is sobbing desperately, like an echo from the bottom. Pause.*) I started to approach and then . . .

From behind the trees where the Boy has been hiding, a revolver shot rings out.

MOTHER, *running up with a tormented shout, accompanied by the Son and all the Actors in a general tumult.* Son! My son! (*And then amid the hubbub and the disconnected shouts of the others.*) Help! Help!

DIRECTOR, *amid the shouting, trying to clear a space while the Boy is lifted by his head and feet and carried away behind the backdrop.* Is he wounded, is he wounded, really?

Everyone except the Director and the Father, who has remained on the ground beside the steps, has disappeared behind the backdrop which has served for a sky, where they can still be heard for a while whispering anxiously. Then from one side and the other of this curtain, the Actors come back on stage.

LEADING LADY, *reentering from the right, very much upset.* He's dead! Poor boy! He's dead! What a terrible thing!

LEADING MAN, *reentering from the left, laughing.* How do you mean, dead? Fiction, fiction, one doesn't believe such things.

OTHER ACTORS, *on the right.* Fiction? Reality! Reality! He is dead!

OTHER ACTORS, *on the left.* No! Fiction! Fiction!

FATHER, *rising, and crying out to them.* Fiction indeed! Reality, reality, gentlemen, reality! (*Desperate, he too disappears at the back.*)

DIRECTOR, *at the end of his rope.* Fiction! Reality! To hell with all of you! Lights, lights, lights! (*At a single stroke the whole stage and auditorium is flooded with very bright light. The Director breathes again, as if freed from an incubus, and they all look each other in the eyes, bewildered and lost.*) Things like this don't happen to me, they've made me lose a whole day. (*He looks at his watch.*) Go, you can all go. What could we do now anyway? It is too late to pick up the rehearsal where we left off. See you this evening. (*As soon as the Actors have gone he talks to the Electrician by name.*) Hey, Electrician, lights out. (*He has hardly said the word when the theater is plunged for a moment into complete darkness.*) Hey, for God's sake, leave me at least one light! I like to see where I am going!

Immediately, from behind the backdrop, as if the wrong switch had been pulled, a green light comes on which projects the silhouettes, clear-cut and large, of the Characters, minus the Boy and the Little Girl. Seeing the silhouettes, the Director, terrified, rushes from the stage. At the same time the light behind the backdrop goes out and the stage is again lit in nocturnal blue as before.

Slowly, from the right side of the curtain, the Son comes forward first, followed by the Mother with her arms stretched out toward him; then from the left side, the Father. They stop in the middle of the stage and stay there as if in a trance. Last of all from the right, the Stepdaughter comes out and runs toward the two stairways. She stops on the first step, to look for a moment at the other three, and then breaks into a harsh laugh before throwing herself down the steps; she runs down the aisle between the rows of seats; she stops one more time and again laughs, looking at the three who are still on stage; she disappears from the auditorium, and from the lobby her laughter is still heard. Shortly thereafter the curtain falls.

QUESTIONS

1. Why does the play present us with characters looking for an author?
2. According to the play, what are characters?
3. What is the "inner significance of the play" to which the stage directions refer? (172)
4. Why does Pirandello tell us the "fundamental sentiment" of the main characters (the Father's remorse, the Stepdaughter's revenge, the Son's disdain, the Mother's grief)? (172)
5. Why do all the characters but one, Madame Pace, go unnamed?
6. What does the Father mean when he says the characters are "less real, perhaps, but more true" than "those that breathe and wear clothes"? (175)
7. What does the Father mean when he says, "I always had these confounded aspirations toward a certain solidity, toward what is morally sound"? (184)
8. What does the Father mean by saying that while every person thinks of himself as one, "each of us is many"? (189)
9. Why does the Son say that he is "a character that, dramatically speaking, remains unrealized"? (190)
10. Why does the Director become interested in the characters' story?
11. Why does the Director say, "This is the theater! Our motto is: truth up to a certain point"? (211)
12. Why does the Father say that the word *illusion* is "especially cruel" to the six characters? (216)
13. Why should the "immutable reality" of the characters make the Director shudder to be near them? (218)
14. Why can't the Son leave the stage when the Director stops holding him back and the Stepdaughter tells the Son to go?
15. Why does the play end with the Stepdaughter's laughter echoing through the auditorium?

FOR FURTHER REFLECTION

1. How do characters in a play differ from characters in a prose narrative?
2. Can we distinguish between characters and actors in the world outside the stage?
3. Do you agree with the Father when he insists that unlike selves, characters are fixed and unified entities?
4. What are the most important "facts" that are debated in this play? Is it possible to arrive at some reasonable idea of what the facts are in the family drama depicted?

STEPHEN CRANE

Although he died at the age of just twenty-eight, Stephen Crane (1871–1900) led a remarkably full and productive life. Born in Newark, New Jersey, the youngest of fourteen children, Crane was raised in a religious home. His mother was involved in the temperance movement; his father was a Methodist minister. His ancestors included military men as well as a large number of Methodist clergymen.

After attending a Methodist boarding school for three years, Crane transferred to Claverack College, a military boarding school. Two years later he spent a semester at Lafayette College, where he flunked out, followed by a semester at Syracuse University. There he excelled as a baseball player and in his English literature class. He never earned a degree, but he began writing for the *New York Tribune,* which would lead to a career in freelance journalism that provided him with a meager income. After moving in with one of his brothers in New Jersey, he spent much of his time becoming acquainted with New York City and its artistic community, and continued to write for newspapers.

During this time, Crane also completed his first novel, *Maggie: A Girl of the Streets,* about the impoverished, brutal life of the Bowery. Publishers, afraid that it would shock readers, rejected it, so Crane sold shares of inherited stock to his brother and published the book at his own expense under a pseudonym in 1893. Despite poor sales, the book received favorable reviews from two influential writers, Hamlin Garland and William Dean Howells, the former editor of the *Atlantic Monthly*; both men became Crane's friends. It was Crane's second novel, *The Red Badge of Courage*, published in a shortened form as a syndicated newspaper serial in 1894 and as a book the following year, that led to lasting literary fame. The novel was a bestseller in the United States and widely acclaimed in England. Written in a highly original, impressionistic style, it contains startlingly realistic depictions of war, despite the fact that Crane had yet to witness combat firsthand. After *Red Badge* was published, Crane began to win assignments as a war correspondent.

In 1897, Crane was on his way to cover the Cuban revolution when his boat, which was carrying arms for rebels, sank off the coast of Florida. After more than a day, the dinghy carrying Crane and his comrades made it back to shore, and the experience became the basis for "The Open Boat," perhaps Crane's greatest work of fiction. While he recuperated in Jacksonville, Florida, he met Cora Taylor, the proprietor of a hotel that also served as a brothel. She sold her establishment and, hired by the *New York Journal* as a war correspondent, accompanied Crane to Greece later that year to cover the Greco-Turkish War. The couple settled in England in 1897; no evidence exists indicating they were ever legally married.

While in England, Crane wrote some of his best stories, including "The Bride Comes to Yellow Sky" and "The Blue Hotel." He also enjoyed the friendship and esteem of writers such as Joseph Conrad, Ford Madox Ford, and Henry James. But despite his literary reputation, Crane was constantly in financial straits, which forced him to maintain a grueling work schedule. Ill with tuberculosis and deep in debt, he was taken by Taylor to a spa in Badenweiler, Germany, where he died on June 5, 1900.

"The Open Boat," published in 1898, tells the simple story of four characters trying to reach the shore in a dinghy after their steamship has sunk. It is the elemental quality of the story, however, that allows Crane to infuse it with complex, timeless questions about our relationship to the natural world and the way in which we attempt to discover life's meaning.

STEPHEN CRANE

The Open Boat

1

None of them knew the color of the sky. Their eyes glanced level, and were fastened upon the waves that swept toward them. These waves were of the hue of slate, save for the tops, which were of foaming white, and all of the men knew the colors of the sea. The horizon narrowed and widened, and dipped and rose, and at all times its edge was jagged with waves that seemed thrust up in points like rocks.

Many a man ought to have a bathtub larger than the boat which here rode upon the sea. These waves were most wrongfully and barbarously abrupt and tall, and each froth-top was a problem in small-boat navigation.

The cook squatted in the bottom, and looked with both eyes at the six inches of gunwale which separated him from the ocean. His sleeves were rolled over his fat forearms, and the two flaps of his unbuttoned vest dangled as he bent to bail out the boat. Often he said, "Gawd! That was a narrow clip." As he remarked it he invariably gazed eastward over the broken sea.

The oiler, steering with one of the two oars in the boat, sometimes raised himself suddenly to keep clear of water that swirled in over the stern. It was a thin little oar, and it seemed often ready to snap.

The correspondent, pulling at the other oar, watched the waves and wondered why he was there.

The injured captain, lying in the bow, was at this time buried in that profound dejection and indifference which comes, temporarily at least, to even the bravest and most enduring when, willy-nilly, the firm fails, the army loses, the ship goes down. The mind of the master of a vessel is rooted deep in the timbers of her, though he command for a day or a decade, and this captain had on him the stern impression of a scene in the grays of dawn of seven turned faces, and later a stump of a topmast with a white ball on it, that slashed to and fro at the waves, went low and lower, and down. Thereafter there was something strange in his voice. Although steady, it was deep with mourning, and of a quality beyond oration or tears.

"Keep 'er a little more south, Billie," said he.

"A little more south, sir," said the oiler in the stern.

A seat in this boat was not unlike a seat upon a bucking bronco, and by the same token a bronco is not much smaller. The craft pranced and reared and plunged like an animal. As each wave came, and she rose for it, she seemed like a horse making at a fence outrageously high. The manner of her scramble over these walls of water is a mystic thing, and, moreover, at the top of them were ordinarily these problems in white water, the foam racing down from the summit of each wave requiring a new leap, and a leap from the air. Then, after scornfully bumping a crest, she would slide and race and splash down a long incline, and arrive bobbing and nodding in front of the next menace.

A singular disadvantage of the sea lies in the fact that after successfully surmounting one wave you discover that there is another behind it just as important and just as nervously anxious to do something effective in the way of swamping boats. In a ten-foot dinghy one can get an idea of the resources of the sea in the line of waves that is not probable to the average experience which is never at sea in a dinghy. As each slaty wall of water approached, it shut all else from the view of the men in the boat, and it was not difficult to imagine that this particular wave was the final outburst of the ocean, the last effort of the grim water. There was a terrible grace in the move of the waves, and they came in silence, save for the snarling of the crests.

In the wan light the faces of the men must have been gray. Their eyes must have glinted in strange ways as they gazed steadily astern. Viewed from a balcony, the whole thing would doubtless have been weirdly picturesque. But the men in the boat had no time to see it, and if they had had leisure, there were other things to occupy their minds. The sun swung steadily up the sky, and they knew it was broad day because the color of the sea changed from slate to emerald green streaked with amber lights, and the foam was like tumbling snow. The process of the breaking day was unknown to them. They were aware only of this effect upon the color of the waves that rolled toward them.

In disjointed sentences the cook and the correspondent argued as to the difference between a lifesaving station and a house of refuge. The cook had said: "There's a house of refuge just north of the Mosquito Inlet Light, and as soon as they see us they'll come off in their boat and pick us up."

"As soon as who see us?" said the correspondent.

"The crew," said the cook.

"Houses of refuge don't have crews," said the correspondent. "As I understand them, they are only places where clothes and grub are stored for the benefit of shipwrecked people. They don't carry crews."

"Oh, yes, they do," said the cook.

"No, they don't," said the correspondent.

"Well, we're not there yet, anyhow," said the oiler, in the stern.

"Well," said the cook, "perhaps it's not a house of refuge that I'm thinking of as being near Mosquito Inlet Light; perhaps it's a life-saving station."

"We're not there yet," said the oiler in the stern.

2

As the boat bounced from the top of each wave, the wind tore through the hair of the hatless men, and as the craft plopped her stern down again the spray slashed past them. The crest of each of these waves was a hill, from the top of which the men surveyed for a moment a broad tumultuous expanse, shining and wind-riven. It was probably splendid, it was probably glorious, this play of the free sea, wild with lights of emerald and white and amber.

"Bully good thing it's an onshore wind," said the cook. "If not, where would we be? Wouldn't have a show."

"That's right," said the correspondent.

The busy oiler nodded his assent.

Then the captain, in the bow, chuckled in a way that expressed humor, contempt, tragedy, all in one. "Do you think we've got much of a show now, boys?" said he.

Whereupon the three were silent, save for a trifle of hemming and hawing. To express any particular optimism at this time they felt to be childish and stupid, but they all doubtless possessed this sense of the situation in their minds. A young man thinks doggedly at such times. On the other hand, the ethics of their condition was decidedly against any open suggestion of hopelessness. So they were silent.

"Oh, well," said the captain, soothing his children, "we'll get ashore all right."

But there was that in his tone which made them think, so the oiler quoth, "Yes! If this wind holds."

The cook was bailing. "Yes! If we don't catch hell in the surf."

Canton-flannel gulls flew near and far. Sometimes they sat down on the sea, near patches of brown seaweed that rolled over the waves with a movement like carpets on a line in a gale. The birds sat comfortably in groups, and they were envied by some in the dinghy, for the wrath of the sea was no more to them than it was to a covey of prairie chickens a thousand miles inland. Often they came very close and stared at the men with black beadlike eyes. At these times they were uncanny and sinister in their unblinking scrutiny, and the men hooted angrily at them, telling them to be gone. One came, and evidently decided to alight on the top of the captain's head. The bird flew parallel to the boat and did not circle, but made short sidelong jumps in the air in chicken fashion. His black eyes were wistfully fixed upon the captain's head. "Ugly brute," said the oiler to the bird. "You look as if you were made with a jackknife." The cook and the correspondent swore darkly at the creature. The captain naturally wished to knock it away with the end of the heavy painter, but he did not dare do it, because anything resembling an emphatic gesture would have capsized this freighted boat, and so, with his open hand, the captain gently and carefully waved the gull away. After it had been discouraged from the pursuit the captain breathed easier on account of his hair, and others breathed easier because the bird struck their minds at this time as being somehow gruesome and ominous.

In the meantime the oiler and the correspondent rowed. And also they rowed. They sat together in the same seat, and each rowed an oar. Then the oiler took both oars; then the correspondent took both oars; then the oiler; then the correspondent. They rowed and they rowed. The very ticklish part of the business was when the time came for the reclining one in the stern to take his turn at the oars. By the very last star of truth, it is easier to steal eggs from under a hen than it was to change seats in the dinghy. First the man in the stern slid his hand along the thwart and moved with care, as if he were of Sèvres. Then the man in the rowing seat slid his hand along the other thwart. It was all done with the most extraordinary care. As the two sidled past each other, the whole party kept watchful eyes on the coming wave, and the captain cried: "Lookout, now! Steady, there!"

The brown mats of seaweed that appeared from time to time were like islands, bits of earth. They were traveling, apparently, neither one way nor the other. They were, to all intents, stationary. They informed the men in the boat that it was making progress slowly toward the land.

The captain, rearing cautiously in the bow after the dinghy soared on a great swell, said that he had seen the lighthouse at Mosquito Inlet. Presently the cook remarked that he had seen it. The correspondent was at the oars then, and for some reason he too wished to look at the lighthouse, but his back was toward the far shore, and the waves were important, and for some time he could not seize an opportunity to turn his head. But at last there came a wave more gentle than the others, and when at the crest of it he swiftly scoured the western horizon.

"See it?" said the captain.

"No," said the correspondent, slowly, "I didn't see anything."

"Look again," said the captain. He pointed. "It's exactly in that direction."

At the top of another wave the correspondent did as he was bid, and this time his eyes chanced on a small, still thing on the edge of the swaying horizon. It was precisely like the point of a pin. It took an anxious eye to find a lighthouse so tiny.

"Think we'll make it, Captain?"

"If this wind holds and the boat don't swamp, we can't do much else," said the captain.

The little boat, lifted by each towering sea and splashed viciously by the crests, made progress that in the absence of seaweed was not apparent to those in her. She seemed just a wee thing wallowing, miraculously top up, at the mercy of five oceans. Occasionally a great spread of water, like white flames, swarmed into her.

"Bail her, cook," said the captain, serenely.

"All right, Captain," said the cheerful cook.

3

It would be difficult to describe the subtle brotherhood of men that was here established on the seas. No one said that it was so. No one mentioned it. But it dwelt in the boat, and each man felt it warm him. They were a captain, an oiler, a cook, and a correspondent, and they were friends—friends in a more curiously iron-bound degree than may be common. The hurt captain, lying against the water jar in the bow, spoke always in a low voice and calmly, but he could never command a more ready and swiftly obedient crew than the motley three of the dinghy. It was more than a mere recognition of what was best for the common safety. There was surely in it a quality that was personal and heartfelt. And after this devotion to the commander of the boat, there was this comradeship, that the correspondent, for instance, who had been taught to be cynical of men, knew even at the time was the best experience of his life. But no one said that it was so. No one mentioned it.

"I wish we had a sail," remarked the captain. "We might try my overcoat on the end of an oar, and give you two boys a chance to rest." So the cook and the correspondent held the mast and spread wide the overcoat, the oiler steered, and the little boat made good way with her new rig.

Sometimes the oiler had to scull sharply to keep a sea from breaking into the boat, but otherwise sailing was a success.

Meanwhile the lighthouse had been growing slowly larger. It had now almost assumed color, and appeared like a little gray shadow on the sky. The man at the oars could not be prevented from turning his head rather often to try for a glimpse of this little gray shadow.

At last, from the top of each wave, the men in the tossing boat could see land. Even as the lighthouse was an upright shadow on the sky, this land seemed but a long black shadow on the sea. It certainly was thinner than paper. "We must be about opposite New Smyrna," said the cook, who had coasted this shore often in schooners. "Captain, by the way, I believe they abandoned that lifesaving station there about a year ago."

"Did they?" said the captain.

The wind slowly died away. The cook and the correspondent were not now obliged to slave in order to hold high the oar. But the waves continued their old impetuous swooping at the dinghy, and the little craft, no longer under way, struggled woundily over them. The oiler or the correspondent took the oars again.

Shipwrecks are apropos of nothing. If men could only train for them and have them occur when the men had reached pink condition, there would be less drowning at sea. Of the four in the dinghy none had slept any time worth mentioning for two days and two nights previous to embarking in the dinghy, and in the excitement of clambering about the deck of a foundering ship they had also forgotten to eat heartily.

For these reasons, and for others, neither the oiler nor the correspondent was fond of rowing at this time. The correspondent wondered ingenuously how in the name of all that was sane could there be people who thought it amusing to row a boat. It was not an amusement; it was a diabolical punishment, and even a genius of mental aberrations could never conclude that it was anything but a horror to the muscles and a crime against the back. He mentioned to the boat in general how the amusement of rowing struck him, and the weary-faced oiler smiled in full sympathy. Previously to the foundering, by the way, the oiler had worked double watch in the engine room of the ship.

"Take her easy now, boys," said the captain. "Don't spend yourselves. If we have to run a surf you'll need all your strength, because we'll sure have to swim for it. Take your time."

Slowly the land arose from the sea. From a black line it became a line of black and a line of white—trees and sand. Finally the captain said that he could make out a house on the shore. "That's the house of refuge, sure," said the cook. "They'll see us before long, and come out after us."

The distant lighthouse reared high. "The keeper ought to be able to make us out now, if he's looking through a glass," said the captain. "He'll notify the lifesaving people."

"None of those other boats could have got ashore to give word of the wreck," said the oiler, in a low voice, "else the lifeboat would be out hunting us."

Slowly and beautifully the land loomed out of the sea. The wind came again. It had veered from the northeast to the southeast. Finally a new sound struck the ears of the men in the boat. It was the low thunder of the surf on the shore. "We'll never be able to make the lighthouse now," said the captain. "Swing her head a little more north, Billie."

"A little more north, sir," said the oiler.

Whereupon the little boat turned her nose once more down the wind, and all but the oarsman watched the shore grow. Under the influence of this expansion doubt and direful apprehension were leaving the minds of the men. The management of the boat was still most absorbing, but it could not prevent a quiet cheerfulness. In an hour, perhaps, they would be ashore.

Their backbones had become thoroughly used to balancing in the boat, and they now rode this wild colt of a dinghy like circus men. The correspondent thought that he had been drenched to the skin, but happening to feel in the top pocket of his coat, he found therein eight cigars. Four of them were soaked with seawater; four were perfectly scatheless. After a search, somebody produced three dry matches, and thereupon the four waifs rode impudently in their little boat and, with an assurance of an impending rescue shining in their eyes, puffed at the big cigars, and judged well and ill of all men. Everybody took a drink of water.

4

"Cook," remarked the captain, "there don't seem to be any signs of life about your house of refuge."

"No," replied the cook. "Funny they don't see us!"

A broad stretch of lowly coast lay before the eyes of the men. It was of low dunes topped with dark vegetation. The roar of the surf was plain, and sometimes they could see the white lip of a wave as it spun up the beach. A tiny house was blocked out black upon the sky. Southward, the slim lighthouse lifted its little gray length.

Tide, wind, and waves were swinging the dinghy northward. "Funny they don't see us," said the men.

The surf's roar was here dulled, but its tone was nevertheless thunderous and mighty. As the boat swam over the great rollers the men sat listening to this roar. "We'll swamp sure," said everybody.

It is fair to say here that there was not a lifesaving station within twenty miles in either direction, but the men did not know this fact, and in consequence they made dark and opprobrious remarks concerning the eyesight of the nation's lifesavers. Four scowling men sat in the dinghy and surpassed records in the invention of epithets.

"Funny they don't see us."

The lightheartedness of a former time had completely faded. To their sharpened minds it was easy to conjure pictures of all kinds of incompetency and blindness and, indeed, cowardice. There was the shore of the populous land, and it was bitter and bitter to them that from it came no sign.

"Well," said the captain, ultimately, "I suppose we'll have to make a try for ourselves. If we stay out here too long, we'll none of us have strength left to swim after the boat swamps."

And so the oiler, who was at the oars, turned the boat straight for the shore. There was a sudden tightening of muscles. There was some thinking.

"If we don't all get ashore," said the captain—"if we don't all get ashore, I suppose you fellows know where to send news of my finish?"

They then briefly exchanged some addresses and admonitions. As for the reflections of the men, there was a great deal of rage in them. Perchance they might be formulated thus: "If I am going to be drowned—if I am going to be drowned—if I am going to be drowned, why, in the name of the seven mad gods who rule the sea, was I allowed to come thus far and contemplate sand and trees? Was I brought here merely to have my nose dragged away as I was about to nibble the sacred cheese of life? It is preposterous. If this old ninny-woman, Fate, cannot do better than this, she should be deprived of the management of men's fortunes. She is an old hen who knows not her intention. If she has decided to drown me, why did she not do it in the beginning and save me all this trouble? The whole affair is absurd. . . . But no; she cannot mean to drown me. She dare not drown me. She cannot drown me. Not after all this work." Afterward the man might have had an impulse to shake his fist at the clouds. "Just you drown me, now, and then hear what I call you!"

The billows that came at this time were more formidable. They seemed always just about to break and roll over the little boat in a turmoil of foam. There was a preparatory and long growl in the speech of them. No mind unused to the sea would have concluded that the dinghy could ascend these sheer heights in time. The shore was still afar. The oiler was a wily surfman. "Boys," he said swiftly, "she won't live three minutes more, and we're too far out to swim. Shall I take her to sea again, Captain?"

"Yes; go ahead!" said the captain.

This oiler, by a series of quick miracles and fast and steady oarsmanship, turned the boat in the middle of the surf and took her safely to sea again.

There was a considerable silence as the boat bumped over the furrowed sea to deeper water. Then somebody in gloom spoke: "Well, anyhow, they must have seen us from the shore by now."

The gulls went in slanting flight up the wind toward the gray, desolate east. A squall, marked by dingy clouds and clouds brick red like smoke from a burning building, appeared from the southeast.

"What do you think of those lifesaving people? Ain't they peaches?"

"Funny they haven't seen us."

"Maybe they think we're out here for sport! Maybe they think we're fishin'. Maybe they think we're damned fools."

It was a long afternoon. A changed tide tried to force them southward, but wind and wave said northward. Far ahead, where coastline, sea, and sky formed their mighty angle, there were little dots which seemed to indicate a city on the shore.

"St. Augustine?"

The captain shook his head. "Too near Mosquito Inlet."

And the oiler rowed, and then the correspondent rowed; then the oiler rowed. It was a weary business. The human back can become the seat of more aches and pains than are registered in books for the composite anatomy of a regiment. It is a limited area, but it can become the theater of innumerable muscular conflicts, tangles, wrenches, knots, and other comforts.

"Did you ever like to row, Billie?" asked the correspondent.

"No," said the oiler; "hang it!"

When one exchanged the rowing seat for a place in the bottom of the boat, he suffered a bodily depression that caused him to be careless of everything save an obligation to wiggle one finger. There was cold seawater swashing to and fro in the boat, and he lay in it. His head, pillowed on a thwart, was within an inch of the swirl of a wave crest, and sometimes a particularly obstreperous sea came inboard and drenched him once more. But these matters did not annoy him. It is almost certain that if the boat had capsized he would have tumbled comfortably out upon the ocean as if he felt sure that it was a great soft mattress.

"Look! There's a man on the shore!"

"Where?"

"There! See 'im? See 'im?"

"Yes, sure! He's walking along."

"Now he's stopped. Look! He's facing us!"

"He's waving at us!"

"So he is! By thunder!"

"Ah, now we're all right! Now we're all right! There'll be a boat out here for us in half an hour."

"He's going on. He's running. He's going up to that house there."

The remote beach seemed lower than the sea, and it required a searching glance to discern the little black figure. The captain saw a floating stick, and they rowed to it. A bath towel was by some weird chance in the boat, and, tying this on the stick, the captain waved it. The oarsman did not dare turn his head, so he was obliged to ask questions.

"What's he doing now?"

"He's standing still again. He's looking, I think. . . . There he goes again—toward the house. . . . Now he's stopped again."

"Is he waving at us?"

"No, not now; he was, though."

"Look! There comes another man!"

"He's running."

"Look at him go, would you!"

"Why, he's on a bicycle. Now he's met the other man. They're both waving at us. Look!"

"There comes something up the beach."

"What the devil is that thing?"

"Why, it looks like a boat."

"Why, certainly, it's a boat."

"No; it's on wheels."

"Yes, so it is. Well, that must be the lifeboat. They drag them along shore on a wagon."

"That's the lifeboat, sure."

"No by God, it's—it's an omnibus."

"I tell you, it's a lifeboat."

"It is not! It's an omnibus. I can see it plain. See? One of these big hotel omnibuses."

"By thunder, you're right. It's an omnibus, sure as fate. What do you suppose they are doing with an omnibus? Maybe they are going around collecting the life crew, hey?"

"That's it, likely. Look! There's a fellow waving a little black flag. He's standing on the steps of the omnibus. There come those other two fellows. Now they're all talking together. Look at the fellow with the flag. Maybe he ain't waving it!"

"That ain't a flag, is it? That's his coat. Why, certainly, that's his coat."

"So it is; it's his coat. He's taken it off and is waving it around his head. But would you look at him swing it!"

"Oh, say, there isn't any lifesaving station there. That's just a winter-resort hotel omnibus that has brought over some of the boarders to see us drown."

"What's that idiot with the coat mean? What's he signaling, anyhow?"

"It looks as if he were trying to tell us to go north. There must be a lifesaving station up there."

"No; he thinks we're fishing. Just giving us a merry hand. See? Ah, there, Willie!"

"Well, I wish I could make something out of those signals. What do you suppose he means?"

"He don't mean anything; he's just playing."

"Well, if he'd just signal us to try the surf again, or to go to sea and wait, or go north, or go south, or go to hell, there would be some reason in it. But look at him! He just stands there and keeps his coat revolving like a wheel. The ass!"

"There come more people."

"Now there's quite a mob. Look! Isn't that a boat?"

"Where? Oh, I see where you mean. No, that's no boat."

"That fellow is still waving his coat."

"He must think we like to see him do that. Why don't he quit it? It don't mean anything."

"I don't know. I think he is trying to make us go north. It must be that there's a lifesaving station there somewhere."

"Say, he ain't tired yet. Look at 'im wave!"

"Wonder how long he can keep that up. He's been revolving his coat ever since he caught sight of us. He's an idiot. Why aren't they getting men to bring a boat out? A fishing boat—one of those big yawls—could come out here all right. Why don't he do something?"

"Oh, it's all right now."

"They'll have a boat out here for us in less than no time, now that they've seen us."

A faint yellow tone came into the sky over the low land. The shadows on the sea slowly deepened. The wind bore coldness with it, and the men began to shiver.

"Holy smoke!" said one, allowing his voice to express his impious mood, "if we keep on monkeying out here! If we've got to flounder out here all night!"

"Oh, we'll never have to stay here all night! Don't you worry. They've seen us now, and it won't be long before they'll come chasing out after us."

The shore grew dusky. The man waving a coat blended gradually into this gloom, and it swallowed in the same manner the omnibus and the group of people. The spray, when it dashed uproariously over the side, made the voyagers shrink and swear like men who were being branded.

"I'd like to catch the chump who waved the coat. I feel like socking him one, just for luck."

"Why? What did he do?"

"Oh, nothing, but then he seemed so damned cheerful."

In the meantime the oiler rowed, and then the correspondent rowed, and then the oiler rowed. Gray-faced and bowed forward, they mechanically, turn by turn, plied the leaden oars. The form of the lighthouse had vanished from the southern horizon, but finally a pale star appeared, just lifting from the sea. The streaked saffron in the west passed before the all-merging darkness, and the sea to the east was black. The land had vanished, and was expressed only by the low and drear thunder of the surf.

"If I am going to be drowned—if I am going to be drowned—if I am going to be drowned, why, in the name of the seven mad gods who rule the sea, was I allowed to come thus far and contemplate sand and trees? Was I brought here merely to have my nose dragged away as I was about to nibble the sacred cheese of life?"

The patient captain, drooped over the water jar, was sometimes obliged to speak to the oarsman.

"Keep her head up! Keep her head up!"

"Keep her head up, sir." The voices were weary and low.

This was surely a quiet evening. All save the oarsman lay heavily and listlessly in the boat's bottom. As for him, his eyes were just capable of noting the tall black waves that swept forward in a most sinister silence, save for an occasional subdued growl of a crest.

The cook's head was on a thwart, and he looked without interest at the water under his nose. He was deep in other scenes. Finally he spoke. "Billie," he murmured, dreamfully, "what kind of pie do you like best?"

5

"Pie!" said the oiler and the correspondent, agitatedly. "Don't talk about those things, blast you!"

"Well," said the cook, "I was just thinking about ham sandwiches, and——"

A night on the sea in an open boat is a long night. As darkness settled finally, the shine of the light, lifting from the sea in the south, changed to full gold. On the northern horizon a new light appeared, a small bluish gleam on the edge of the waters. These two lights were the furniture of the world. Otherwise there was nothing but waves.

Two men huddled in the stern, and distances were so magnificent in the dinghy that the rower was enabled to keep his feet partly warm by thrusting them under his companions. Their legs indeed extended far under the rowing seat until they touched the feet of the captain forward. Sometimes, despite the efforts of the tired oarsman, a wave came piling into the boat, an icy wave of the night, and the chilling water soaked them anew. They would twist their bodies for a moment and groan, and sleep the dead sleep once more, while the water in the boat gurgled about them as the craft rocked.

The plan of the oiler and the correspondent was for one to row until he lost the ability, and then arouse the other from his seawater couch in the bottom of the boat.

The oiler plied the oars until his head drooped forward and the overpowering sleep blinded him, and he rowed yet afterward. Then he touched a man in the bottom of the boat, and called his name. "Will you spell me for a little while?" he said meekly.

"Sure, Billie," said the correspondent, awaking and dragging himself to a sitting position. They exchanged places carefully, and the oiler, cuddling down in the seawater at the cook's side, seemed to go to sleep instantly.

The particular violence of the sea had ceased. The waves came without snarling. The obligation of the man at the oars was to keep the boat headed so that the tilt of the rollers would not capsize her, and to preserve her from filling when the crests rushed past. The black waves were silent and hard to be seen in the darkness. Often one was almost upon the boat before the oarsman was aware.

In a low voice the correspondent addressed the captain. He was not sure that the captain was awake, although this iron man seemed to be always awake. "Captain, shall I keep her making for that light north, sir?"

The same steady voice answered him. "Yes. Keep it about two points off the port bow."

The cook had tied a life belt around himself in order to get even the warmth which this clumsy cork contrivance could donate, and he seemed almost stovelike when a rower, whose teeth invariably chattered wildly as soon as he ceased his labor, dropped down to sleep.

The correspondent, as he rowed, looked down at the two men sleeping underfoot. The cook's arm was around the oiler's shoulders, and, with their fragmentary clothing and haggard faces, they were the babes of the sea—a grotesque rendering of the old babes in the wood.

Later he must have grown stupid at his work, for suddenly there was a growling of water, and a crest came with a roar and a swash into the boat, and it was a wonder that it did not set the cook afloat in his life belt. The cook continued to sleep, but the oiler sat up, blinking his eyes and shaking with the new cold.

"Oh, I'm awful sorry, Billie," said the correspondent, contritely.

"That's all right, old boy," said the oiler, and lay down again and was asleep.

Presently it seemed that even the captain dozed, and the correspondent thought that he was the one man afloat on all the oceans. The wind had a voice as it came over the waves, and it was sadder than the end.

There was a long, loud swishing astern of the boat, and a gleaming trail of phosphorescence, like blue flame, was furrowed on the black waters. It might have been made by a monstrous knife.

Then there came a stillness, while the correspondent breathed with open mouth and looked at the sea.

Suddenly there was another swish and another long flash of bluish light, and this time it was alongside the boat, and might almost have been reached with an oar. The correspondent saw an enormous fin speed like a shadow through the water, hurling the crystalline spray and leaving the long glowing trail.

The correspondent looked over his shoulder at the captain. His face was hidden, and he seemed to be asleep. He looked at the babes of the sea. They certainly were asleep. So, being bereft of sympathy, he leaned a little way to one side and swore softly into the sea.

But the thing did not then leave the vicinity of the boat. Ahead or astern, on one side or the other, at intervals long or short, fled the long sparkling streak, and there was to be heard the *whirroo* of the dark fin. The speed and power of the thing was greatly to be admired. It cut the water like a gigantic and keen projectile.

The presence of this biding thing did not affect the man with the same horror that it would if he had been a picnicker. He simply looked at the sea dully and swore in an undertone.

Nevertheless, it is true that he did not wish to be alone with the thing. He wished one of his companions to awake by chance and keep him company with it. But the captain hung motionless over the water jar, and the oiler and the cook in the bottom of the boat were plunged in slumber.

6

"If I am going to be drowned—if I am going to be drowned—if I am going to be drowned, why, in the name of the seven mad gods who rule the sea, was I allowed to come thus far and contemplate sand and trees?"

During this dismal night, it may be remarked that a man would conclude that it was really the intention of the seven mad gods to drown him, despite the abominable injustice of it. For it was certainly an abominable injustice to drown a man who had worked so hard, so hard. The man felt it would be a crime most unnatural. Other people had drowned at sea since galleys swarmed with painted sails, but still——

When it occurs to a man that Nature does not regard him as important, and that she feels she would not maim the universe by disposing of him, he at first wishes to throw bricks at the temple, and he hates deeply the fact that there are no bricks and no temples. Any visible expression of nature would surely be pelleted with his jeers.

Then, if there be no tangible thing to hoot, he feels, perhaps, the desire to confront a personification and indulge in pleas, bowed to one knee, and with hands supplicant, saying, "Yes, but I love myself."

A high cold star on a winter's night is the word he feels that she says to him. Thereafter he knows the pathos of his situation.

The men in the dinghy had not discussed these matters, but each had, no doubt, reflected upon them in silence and according to his mind. There was seldom any expression upon their faces save the general one of complete weariness. Speech was devoted to the business of the boat.

To chime the notes of his emotion, a verse mysteriously entered the correspondent's head. He had even forgotten that he had forgotten this verse, but it suddenly was in his mind.

> A soldier of the Legion lay dying in Algiers;
> There was lack of woman's nursing, there was dearth of woman's tears;
> But a comrade stood beside him, and he took that comrade's hand,
> And he said, "I never more shall see my own, my native land."

In his childhood the correspondent had been made acquainted with the fact that a soldier of the Legion lay dying in Algiers, but he had never regarded the fact as important. Myriads of his schoolfellows had informed him of the soldier's plight, but the dinning had naturally ended by making him perfectly indifferent. He had never considered it his affair that a soldier of the Legion lay dying in Algiers, nor had it appeared to him as a matter for sorrow. It was less to him than the breaking of a pencil's point.

Now, however, it quaintly came to him as a human, living thing. It was no longer merely a picture of a few throes in the breast of a poet, meanwhile drinking tea and warming his feet at the grate; it was an actuality—stern, mournful, and fine.

The correspondent plainly saw the soldier. He lay on the sand with his feet out straight and still. While his pale left hand was upon his chest in an attempt to thwart the going of his life, the blood came between his fingers. In the far Algerian distance, a city of low square forms was set against a sky that was faint with the last sunset hues. The correspondent, plying the oars and dreaming of the slow and slower movements of the lips of the soldier, was moved by a profound and perfectly impersonal comprehension. He was sorry for the soldier of the Legion who lay dying in Algiers.

The thing which had followed the boat and waited had evidently grown bored at the delay. There was no longer to be heard the slash of the cutwater, and there was no longer the flame of the long trail. The light in the north still glimmered, but it was apparently no nearer to the boat. Sometimes the boom of the surf rang in the correspondent's ears, and he turned the craft seaward then and rowed harder. Southward, someone had evidently built a watch fire on the beach. It was too low and too far to be seen, but it made a shimmering, roseate reflection upon the bluff in back of it, and this could be discerned from the boat. The wind came stronger, and sometimes a wave suddenly raged out like a mountain cat, and there was to be seen the sheen and sparkle of a broken crest.

The captain, in the bow, moved on his water jar and sat erect. "Pretty long night," he observed to the correspondent. He looked at the shore. "Those lifesaving people take their time."

"Did you see that shark playing around?"

"Yes, I saw him. He was a big fellow, all right."

"Wish I had known you were awake."

Later the correspondent spoke into the bottom of the boat. "Billie!" There was a slow and gradual disentanglement. "Billie, will you spell me?"

"Sure," said the oiler.

As soon as the correspondent touched the cold, comfortable seawater in the bottom of the boat and had huddled close to the cook's life belt he was deep in sleep, despite the fact that his teeth played all the popular airs. This sleep was so good to him that it was but a moment before he heard a voice call his name in a tone that demonstrated the last stages of exhaustion. "Will you spell me?"

"Sure, Billie."

The light in the north had mysteriously vanished, but the correspondent took his course from the wide-awake captain.

Later in the night they took the boat farther out to sea, and the captain directed the cook to take one oar at the stern and keep the boat facing the seas. He was to call out if he should hear the thunder of the surf. This plan enabled the oiler and the correspondent to get respite together. "We'll give those boys a chance to get into shape again," said the captain. They curled down and, after a few preliminary chatterings and trembles, slept once more the dead sleep. Neither knew they had bequeathed to the cook the company of another shark, or perhaps the same shark.

As the boat caroused on the waves, spray occasionally bumped over the side and gave them a fresh soaking, but this had no power to break their repose. The ominous slash of the wind and the water affected them as it would have affected mummies.

"Boys," said the cook, with the notes of every reluctance in his voice, "she's drifted in pretty close. I guess one of you had better take her to sea again." The correspondent, aroused, heard the crash of the toppled crests.

As he was rowing, the captain gave him some whisky and water and this steadied the chills out of him. "If I ever get ashore and anybody shows me even a photograph of an oar——"

At last there was a short conversation.

"Billie! . . . Billie, will you spell me?"

"Sure," said the oiler.

7

When the correspondent again opened his eyes, the sea and the sky were each of the gray hue of the dawning. Later, carmine and gold was painted upon the waters. The morning appeared finally, in its splendor, with a sky of pure blue, and the sunlight flamed on the tips of the waves.

On the distant dunes were set many little black cottages, and a tall white windmill reared above them. No man, nor dog, nor bicycle appeared on the beach. The cottages might have formed a deserted village.

The voyagers scanned the shore. A conference was held in the boat. "Well," said the captain, "if no help is coming, we might better try a run through the surf right away. If we stay out here much longer we will be too weak to do anything for ourselves at all." The others silently acquiesced in this reasoning. The boat was headed for the beach. The correspondent wondered if none ever ascended the tall wind tower, and if then they never looked seaward. This tower was a giant, standing with its back to the plight of the ants. It represented in a degree, to the correspondent, the serenity of Nature amid the struggles of the individual—Nature in the wind, and Nature in the vision of men. She did not seem cruel to him then, nor beneficent, nor treacherous, nor wise. But she was indifferent, flatly indifferent. It is, perhaps, plausible that a man in this situation, impressed with the unconcern of the universe, should see the innumerable flaws of his life, and have them taste wickedly in his mind, and wish for another chance. A distinction between right and wrong seems absurdly clear to him, then, in this new ignorance of the grave-edge, and he understands that if he were given another opportunity he would mend his conduct and his words, and be better and brighter during an introduction or at a tea.

"Now, boys," said the captain, "she is going to swamp sure. All we can do is to work her in as far as possible, and then when she swamps, pile out and scramble for the beach. Keep cool now, and don't jump until she swamps sure."

The oiler took the oars. Over his shoulders he scanned the surf. "Captain," he said, "I think I'd better bring her about and keep her head-on to the seas and back her in."

"All right, Billie," said the captain. "Back her in." The oiler swung the boat then, and, seated in the stern, the cook and the correspondent were obliged to look over their shoulders to contemplate the lonely and indifferent shore.

The monstrous inshore rollers heaved the boat high until the men were again enabled to see the white sheets of water scudding up the slanted beach. "We won't get in very close," said the captain. Each time a man could wrest his attention from the rollers, he turned his glance toward the shore, and in the expression of the eyes during this contemplation there was a singular quality. The correspondent, observing the others, knew that they were not afraid, but the full meaning of their glances was shrouded.

As for himself, he was too tired to grapple fundamentally with the fact. He tried to coerce his mind into thinking of it, but the mind was dominated at this time by the muscles, and the muscles said they did not care. It merely occurred to him that if he should drown it would be a shame.

There were no hurried words, no pallor, no plain agitation. The men simply looked at the shore. "Now, remember to get well clear of the boat when you jump," said the captain.

Seaward the crest of a roller suddenly fell with a thunderous crash, and the long white comber came roaring down upon the boat.

"Steady now," said the captain. The men were silent. They turned their eyes from the shore to the comber and waited. The boat slid up the incline, leaped at the furious top, bounced over it, and swung down the long back of the wave. Some water had been shipped, and the cook bailed it out.

But the next crest crashed also. The tumbling, boiling flood of white water caught the boat and whirled it almost perpendicular. Water swarmed in from all sides. The correspondent had his hands on the gunwale at this time, and when the water entered at that place he swiftly withdrew his fingers, as if he objected to wetting them.

The little boat, drunken with this weight of water, reeled and snuggled deeper into the sea.

"Bail her out, cook! Bail her out!" said the captain.

"All right, Captain," said the cook.

"Now, boys, the next one will do for us sure," said the oiler. "Mind to jump clear of the boat."

The third wave moved forward, huge, furious, implacable. It fairly swallowed the dinghy, and almost simultaneously the men tumbled into the sea. A piece of life belt had lain in the bottom of the boat, and as the correspondent went overboard he held this to his chest with his left hand.

The January water was icy, and he reflected immediately that it was colder than he had expected to find it off the coast of Florida. This appeared to his dazed mind as a fact important enough to be noted at the time. The coldness of the water was sad; it was tragic. This fact was somehow mixed and confused with his opinion of his own situation, so that it seemed almost a proper reason for tears. The water was cold.

When he came to the surface he was conscious of little but the noisy water. Afterward he saw his companions in the sea. The oiler was ahead in the race. He was swimming strongly and rapidly. Off to the correspondent's left, the cook's great white and corked back bulged out of the water, and in the rear the captain was hanging with his one good hand to the keel of the overturned dinghy.

There is a certain immovable quality to a shore, and the correspondent wondered at it amid the confusion of the sea.

It seemed also very attractive, but the correspondent knew that it was a long journey, and he paddled leisurely. The piece of life preserver lay under him, and sometimes he whirled down the incline of a wave as if he were on a hand sled.

But finally he arrived at a place in the sea where travel was beset with difficulty. He did not pause swimming to inquire what manner of current had caught him, but there his progress ceased. The shore was set before him like a bit of scenery on a stage, and he looked at it and understood with his eyes each detail of it.

As the cook passed, much farther to the left, the captain was calling to him, "Turn over on your back, cook! Turn over on your back and use the oar."

"All right, sir." The cook turned on his back, and, paddling with an oar, went ahead as if he were a canoe. Presently the boat also passed to the left of the correspondent, with the captain clinging with one hand to the keel. He would have appeared like a man raising himself to look over a board fence if it were not for the extraordinary gymnastics of the boat. The correspondent marveled that the captain could still hold to it.

They passed on nearer to shore—the oiler, the cook, the captain—and following them went the water jar, bouncing gaily over the seas. The correspondent remained in the grip of this strange new enemy—a current. The shore, with its white slope of sand and its green bluff topped with little silent cottages, was spread like a picture before him. It was very near to him then, but he was impressed as one who, in a gallery, looks at a scene from Brittany or Algiers.

He thought: "I am going to drown? Can it be possible? Can it be possible? Can it be possible?" Perhaps an individual must consider his own death to be the final phenomenon of nature.

But later a wave perhaps whirled him out of this small deadly current, for he found suddenly that he could again make progress toward the shore. Later still, he was aware that the captain, clinging with one hand to the keel of the dinghy, had his face turned away from the shore and toward him, and was calling his name. "Come to the boat! Come to the boat!"

In his struggle to reach the captain and the boat, he reflected that when one gets properly wearied, drowning must really be a comfortable arrangement—a cessation of hostilities accompanied by a large degree of relief, and he was glad of it, for the main thing in his mind for some moments had been horror of the temporary agony. He did not wish to be hurt.

Presently he saw a man running along the shore. He was undressing with most remarkable speed. Coat, trousers, shirt, everything flew magically off him.

"Come to the boat," called the captain.

"All right, Captain." As the correspondent paddled, he saw the captain let himself down to bottom and leave the boat. Then the correspondent performed his one little marvel of the voyage. A large wave caught him and flung him with ease and supreme speed completely over the boat and far beyond it. It struck him even then as an event in gymnastics and a true miracle of the sea. An overturned boat in the surf is not a plaything to a swimming man.

The correspondent arrived in water that reached only to his waist, but his condition did not enable him to stand for more than a moment. Each wave knocked him into a heap, and the undertow pulled at him.

Then he saw the man who had been running and undressing, and undressing and running, come bounding into the water. He dragged ashore the cook, and then waded toward the captain; but the captain waved him away and sent him to the correspondent. He was naked—naked as a tree in winter, but a halo was about his head, and he shone like a saint. He gave a strong pull, and a long drag, and a bully heave at the correspondent's hand. The correspondent, schooled in the minor formulae, said, "Thanks, old man." But suddenly the man cried, "What's that?" He pointed a swift finger. The correspondent said, "Go."

In the shallows, face downward, lay the oiler. His forehead touched sand that was periodically, between each wave, clear of the sea.

The correspondent did not know all that transpired afterward. When he achieved safe ground he fell, striking the sand with each particular part of his body. It was as if he had dropped from a roof, but the thud was grateful to him.

It seems that instantly the beach was populated with men with blankets, clothes, and flasks, and women with coffee pots and all the remedies sacred to their minds. The welcome of the land to the men from the sea was warm and generous, but a still and dripping shape was carried slowly up the beach, and the land's welcome for it could only be the different and sinister hospitality of the grave.

When it came night, the white waves paced to and fro in the moonlight, and the wind brought the sound of the great sea's voice to the men on the shore, and they felt that they could then be interpreters.

QUESTIONS

1. Why does the narrator refer to the characters by their occupations instead of by their names? Why is the oiler, Billie, the only character whose name we learn?

2. Why do none of the men in the boat ever mention the comradeship that develops among them?

3. Why does the correspondent, "who had been taught to be cynical of men," call the comradeship and friendship among the men the best experience of his life? (237)

4. Why does the narrator repeat three times that the men might be silently wondering why, if they are going to drown, they have been "allowed to come thus far and contemplate sand and trees"? (240, 244, 246)

5. Why are the men in the boat unable to interpret the signals of the man on the shore waving his coat?

6. Why does the cook ask the oiler if he likes pie? Why does the question upset the oiler?

7. According to the story, would it be "a crime most unnatural" if "a man who had worked so hard, so hard" were to drown at sea? (247)

8. When describing a man's reaction to the realization of nature's disregard for him, why does the narrator say that "he at first wishes to throw bricks at the temple, and he hates deeply the fact that there are no bricks and no temples"? (247)

9. Why does the narrator think it "plausible" that, "impressed with the unconcern of the universe," one would wish for another chance at life? (249)

10. When the men jump out of the boat, why does the coldness of the water seem to the correspondent "almost a proper reason for tears"? (251)

11. What does the narrator mean by saying, "Perhaps an individual must consider his own death to be the final phenomenon of nature"? (252)

12. Why is the oiler the only one of the men who dies?

13. Why, once they've reached the shore, do the men feel "that they could then be interpreters"? (253)

14. Does the story suggest that the characters' search for meaning is futile?

FOR FURTHER REFLECTION

1. What accounts for the human tendency to perceive malicious intent in the workings of the natural world?

2. Does being in mortal danger help us understand things more clearly, or is it more likely to blind us to reality?

3. Does the natural world have any significance other than that which we assign to it?

4. Why is it sometimes difficult to speak openly of a spirit of kinship with others or dependence on others?

5. To what degree does chance shape an individual's life?

SHERWOOD ANDERSON

Sherwood Anderson (1876–1941), born in Camden, Ohio, grew up in the nearby town of Clyde, one of seven children. His father was a Union Army veteran who worked odd jobs, including sign painting and house painting. Anderson's early education was interrupted by the need to help support his family, and by the time he moved to Chicago at the age of seventeen, he had worked at racetracks and on farms, painted houses, and sold newspapers. In Chicago he took business classes at night and worked in a warehouse by day. Anderson served in Cuba during the Spanish-American War when he was twenty-two years old, and he returned to Ohio for a year to attend Wittenberg Academy before going back to Chicago, where he worked as an advertising writer for the next six years.

In 1906, Anderson moved back to Ohio. He began a family and worked as a paint manufacturer; during this time he also started to write fiction. In a dramatic episode, he left his family and paint business in 1912 and returned to Chicago. There he resumed his advertising job and, with support from the likes of Theodore Dreiser, Ben Hecht, and Carl Sandburg, Anderson pursued his career as a writer. His literary friends helped him publish his first two novels, *Windy McPherson's Son* (1916), and *Marching Men* (1917). Anderson's reputation as an author was largely made by the publication of his collection of short stories, *Winesburg, Ohio*, in 1919. More novels followed, including *Many Marriages* (1923) and *Dark Laughter* (1925), but most critical assessments consider his short fiction as his greatest triumph, including the collection *Death in the Woods*, published in 1933. Just as mentors had helped him at the start of his writing career, he encouraged other young authors, including Ernest Hemingway and William Faulkner.

In his writing, Anderson used his native Midwest as a principal setting. The region no longer had the adventurous character of the frontier; however, Anderson found inspiration in its mundane culture, describing his characters' struggles with the limitations they felt it imposed on them. Anderson wrote in prose style deliberately similar to everyday speech, but that apparent simplicity can be deceiving in light of his characters' motivations and desires.

In his personal life as in his art, Anderson defied the conventions of the time. He married four times, traveled widely, and lived for periods in New Orleans, New York, and Virginia. He died in Panama.

SHERWOOD ANDERSON

Death in the Woods

She was an old woman and lived on a farm near the town in which I lived. All country and small-town people have seen such old women, but no one knows much about them. Such an old woman comes into town driving an old worn-out horse or she comes afoot carrying a basket. She may own a few hens and have eggs to sell. She brings them in a basket and takes them to a grocer. There she trades them in. She gets some salt pork and some beans. Then she gets a pound or two of sugar and some flour.

Afterward she goes to the butcher's and asks for some dog meat. She may spend ten or fifteen cents, but when she does she asks for something. Formerly the butchers gave liver to anyone who wanted to carry it away. In our family we were always having it. Once one of my brothers got a whole cow's liver at the slaughterhouse near the fairgrounds in our town. We had it until we were sick of it. It never cost a cent. I have hated the thought of it ever since.

The old farm woman got some liver and a soup bone. She never visited with anyone, and as soon as she got what she wanted she lit out for home. It made quite a load for such an old body. No one gave her a lift. People drive right down a road and never notice an old woman like that.

There was such an old woman who used to come into town past our house one summer and fall when I was a young boy and was sick with what was called inflammatory rheumatism. She went home later carrying a heavy pack on her back. Two or three large gaunt-looking dogs followed at her heels.

The old woman was nothing special. She was one of the nameless ones that hardly anyone knows, but she got into my thoughts. I have just suddenly now, after all these years, remembered her and what happened. It is a story. Her name was Grimes, and she lived with her husband and son in a small unpainted house on the bank of a small creek four miles from town.

The husband and son were a tough lot. Although the son was but twenty-one, he had already served a term in jail. It was whispered about that the woman's husband stole horses and ran them off to some other county. Now and then, when a horse turned up missing, the man had also disappeared. No one ever caught him. Once, when I was loafing at Tom Whitehead's livery barn, the man came there and sat on the bench in front. Two or three other men were there, but no one spoke to him. He sat for a few minutes and then got up and went away. When he was leaving he turned around and stared at the men. There was a look of defiance in his eyes. "Well, I have tried to be friendly. You don't want to talk to me. It has been so wherever I have gone in this town. If, some day, one of your fine horses turns up missing, well, then what?" He did not say anything actually. "I'd like to bust one of you on the jaw," was about what his eyes said. I remember how the look in his eyes made me shiver.

The old man belonged to a family that had had money once. His name was Jake Grimes. It all comes back clearly now. His father, John Grimes, had owned a sawmill when the country was new, and had made money. Then he got to drinking and running after women. When he died there wasn't much left.

Jake blew in the rest. Pretty soon there wasn't any more lumber to cut and his land was nearly all gone.

He got his wife off a German farmer, for whom he went to work one June day in the wheat harvest. She was a young thing then and scared to death. You see, the farmer was up to something with the girl—she was, I think, a bound girl and his wife had her suspicions. She took it out on the girl when the man wasn't around. Then, when the wife had to go off to town for supplies, the farmer got after her. She told young Jake that nothing really ever happened, but he didn't know whether to believe it or not.

He got her pretty easy himself, the first time he was out with her. He wouldn't have married her if the German farmer hadn't tried to tell him where to get off. He got her to go riding with him in his buggy one night when he was threshing on the place, and then he came for her the next Sunday night.

She managed to get out of the house without her employer's seeing, but when she was getting into the buggy he showed up. It was almost dark, and he just popped up suddenly at the horse's head. He grabbed the horse by the bridle and Jake got out his buggy whip.

They had it out all right! The German was a tough one. Maybe he didn't care whether his wife knew or not. Jake hit him over the face and shoulders with the buggy whip, but the horse got to acting up and he had to get out.

Then the two men went for it. The girl didn't see it. The horse started to run away and went nearly a mile down the road before the girl got him stopped. Then she managed to tie him to a tree beside the road. (I wonder how I know all this. It must have stuck in my mind from small-town tales when I was a boy.) Jake found her there after he got through with the German. She was huddled up in the buggy seat, crying, scared to death. She told Jake a lot of stuff, how the German had tried to get her, how he chased her once into the barn, how another time, when they happened to be alone in the house together, he tore her dress open clear down the front. The German, she said, might have got her that time if he hadn't heard his old woman drive in at the gate. She had been off to town for supplies. Well, she would be putting the horse in the barn. The German managed to sneak off to the fields without his wife seeing. He told the girl he would kill her if she told. What could she do? She told a lie about ripping her dress in the barn when she was feeding the stock. I remember now that she was a bound girl and did not know where her father and mother were. Maybe she did not have any father. You know what I mean.

Such bound children were often enough cruelly treated. They were children who had no parents, slaves really. There were very few orphan homes then. They were legally bound into some home. It was a matter of pure luck how it came out.

2

She married Jake and had a son and daughter, but the daughter died.

Then she settled down to feed stock. That was her job. At the German's place she had cooked the food for the German and his wife. The wife was a strong woman with big hips and worked most of the time in the fields with her husband. She fed them and fed the cows in the barn, fed the pigs, the horses, and the chickens. Every moment of every day, as a young girl, was spent feeding something.

Then she married Jake Grimes and he had to be fed. She was a slight thing, and when she had been married for three or four years, and after the two children were born, her slender shoulders became stooped.

Jake always had a lot of big dogs around the house, that stood near the unused sawmill near the creek. He was always trading horses when he wasn't stealing something and had a lot of poor bony ones about. Also he kept three or four pigs and a cow. They were all pastured in the few acres left of the Grimes place and Jake did little enough work.

He went into debt for a threshing outfit and ran it for several years, but it did not pay. People did not trust him. They were afraid he would steal the grain at night. He had to go a long way off to get work and it cost too much to get there. In the winter he hunted and cut a little firewood, to be sold in some nearby town. When the son grew up he was just like the father. They got drunk together. If there wasn't anything to eat in the house when they came home the old man gave his old woman a cut over the head. She had a few chickens of her own and had to kill one of them in a hurry. When they were all killed she wouldn't have any eggs to sell when she went to town, and then what would she do?

She had to scheme all her life about getting things fed, getting the pigs fed so they would grow fat and could be butchered in the fall. When they were butchered her husband took most of the meat off to town and sold it. If he did not do it first the boy did. They fought sometimes and when they fought the old woman stood aside trembling.

She had got the habit of silence anyway—that was fixed. Sometimes, when she began to look old—she wasn't forty yet—and when the husband and son were both off trading horses or drinking or hunting or stealing, she went around the house and the barnyard muttering to herself.

How was she going to get everything fed?—that was her problem. The dogs had to be fed. There wasn't enough hay in the barn for the horses and the cow. If she didn't feed the chickens how could they lay eggs? Without eggs to sell how could she get things in town, things she had to have to keep the life of the farm going? Thank heaven, she did not have to feed her husband—in a certain way. That hadn't lasted long after their marriage and after the babies came. Where he went on his long trips she did not know. Sometimes he was gone from home for weeks, and after the boy grew up they went off together.

They left everything at home for her to manage and she had no money. She knew no one. No one ever talked to her in town. When it was winter she had to gather sticks of wood for her fire, had to try to keep the stock fed with very little grain.

The stock in the barn cried to her hungrily, the dogs followed her about. In the winter the hens laid few enough eggs. They huddled in the corners of the barn and she kept watching them. If a hen lays an egg in the barn in the winter and you do not find it, it freezes and breaks.

One day in winter the old woman went off to town with a few eggs and the dogs followed her. She did not get started until nearly three o'clock and the snow was heavy. She hadn't been feeling very well for several days and so she went muttering along, scantily clad, her shoulders stooped. She had an old grain bag in which she carried her eggs, tucked away down in the bottom. There weren't many of them, but in winter the price of eggs is up. She would get a little meat in exchange for the eggs, some salt pork, a little sugar, and some coffee perhaps. It might be the butcher would give her a piece of liver.

When she had got to town and was trading in her eggs, the dogs lay by the door outside. She did pretty well, got the things she needed, more than she had hoped. Then she went to the butcher and he gave her some liver and some dog meat.

It was the first time anyone had spoken to her in a friendly way for a long time. The butcher was alone in his shop when she came in and was annoyed by the thought of such a sick-looking old woman out on such a day. It was bitter cold and the snow, that had let up during the afternoon, was falling again. The butcher said something about her husband and her son, swore at them, and the old woman stared at him, a look of mild surprise in her eyes as he talked. He said that if either the husband or the son were going to get any of the liver or the heavy bones with scraps of meat hanging to them that he had put into the grain big, he'd see him starve first.

Starve, eh? Well, things had to be fed. Men had to be fed, and the horses that weren't any good but maybe could be traded off, and the poor thin cow that hadn't given any milk for three months.

Horses, cows, pigs, dogs, men.

3

The old woman had to get back before darkness came if she could. The dogs followed at her heels, sniffing at the heavy grain bag she had fastened on her back. When she got to the edge of town she stopped by a fence and tied the bag on her back with a piece of rope she had carried in her dress pocket for just that purpose. That was an easier way to carry it. Her arms ached. It was hard when she had to crawl over fences and once she fell over and landed in the snow. The dogs went frisking about. She had to struggle to get to her feet again, but she made it. The point of climbing over the fences was that there was a shortcut over a hill and through a woods. She might have gone around by the road, but it was a mile farther that way. She was afraid she couldn't make it. And then, besides, the stock had to be fed. There was a little hay left and a little corn. Perhaps her husband and son would bring some home when they came. They had driven off in the only buggy the Grimes family had, a rickety thing, a rickety horse hitched to the buggy, two other rickety horses led by halters. They were going to trade horses, get a little money if they could. They might come home drunk. It would be well to have something in the house when they came back.

The son had an affair on with a woman at the county seat, fifteen miles away. She was a rough enough woman, a tough one. Once in the summer the son had brought her to the house. Both she and the son had been drinking. Jake Grimes was away and the son and his woman ordered the old woman about like a servant. She didn't mind much; she was used to it. Whatever happened she never said anything. That was her way of getting along. She had managed that way when she was a young girl at the German's and ever since she had married Jake. That time her son brought his woman to the house they stayed all night, sleeping together just as though they were married. It hadn't shocked the old woman, not much. She had got past being shocked early in life.

With the pack on her back she went painfully along across an open field, wading in the deep snow, and got into the woods.

There was a path, but it was hard to follow. Just beyond the top of the hill, where the woods was thickest, there was a small clearing. Had someone once thought of building a house there? The clearing was as large as a building lot in town, large enough for a house and a garden. The path ran along the side of the clearing, and when she got there the old woman sat down to rest at the foot of a tree.

It was a foolish thing to do. When she got herself placed, the pack against the tree's trunk, it was nice, but what about getting up again? She worried about that for a moment and then quietly closed her eyes.

She must have slept for a time. When you are about so cold you can't get any colder. The afternoon grew a little warmer and the snow came thicker than ever. Then after a time the weather cleared. The moon even came out.

There were four Grimes dogs that had followed Mrs. Grimes into town, all tall gaunt fellows. Such men as Jake Grimes and his son always keep just such dogs. They kick and abuse them, but they stay. The Grimes dogs, in order to keep from starving, had to do a lot of foraging for themselves, and they had been at it while the old woman slept with her back to the tree at the side of the clearing. They had been chasing rabbits in the woods and in adjoining fields and in their ranging had picked up three other farm dogs.

After a time all the dogs came back to the clearing. They were excited about something. Such nights, cold and clear and with a moon, do things to dogs. It may be that some old instinct, come down from the time when they were wolves and ranged the woods in packs on winter nights, comes back into them.

The dogs in the clearing, before the old woman, had caught two or three rabbits and their immediate hunger had been satisfied. They began to play, running in circles in the clearing. Round and round they ran, each dog's nose at the tail of the next dog. In the clearing, under the snow-laden trees and under the wintry moon, they made a strange picture, running thus silently, in a circle their running had beaten in the soft snow. The dogs made no sound. They ran around and around in the circle.

It may have been that the old woman saw them doing that before she died. She may have awakened once or twice and looked at the strange sight with dim old eyes.

She wouldn't be very cold now, just drowsy. Life hangs on a long time. Perhaps the old woman was out of her head. She may have dreamed of her girlhood, at the German's, and before that, when she was a child and before her mother lit out and left her.

Her dreams couldn't have been very pleasant. Not many pleasant things had happened to her. Now and then one of the Grimes dogs left the running circle and came to stand before her. The dog thrust his face close to her face. His red tongue was hanging out.

The running of the dogs may have been a kind of death ceremony. It may have been that the primitive instinct of the wolf, having been aroused in the dogs by the night and the running, made them somehow afraid.

"Now we are no longer wolves. We are dogs, the servants of men. Keep alive, man! When man dies we become wolves again."

When one of the dogs came to where the old woman sat with her back against the tree and thrust his nose close to her face, he seemed satisfied and went back to run with the pack. All the Grimes dogs did it at some time during the evening, before she died. I knew all about it afterward, when I grew to be a man, because once in a woods in Illinois, on another winter night, I saw a pack of dogs act just like that. The dogs were waiting for me to die as they had waited for the old woman that night when I was a child, but when it happened to me I was a young man and had no intention whatever of dying.

The old woman died softly and quietly. When she was dead and when one of the Grimes dogs had come to her and had found her dead, all the dogs stopped running.

They gathered about her.

Well, she was dead now. She had fed the Grimes dogs when she was alive, what about now?

There was the pack on her back, the grain bag containing the piece of salt pork, the liver the butcher had given her, the dog meat, the soup bones. The butcher in town, having been suddenly overcome with a feeling of pity, had loaded her grain bag heavily. It had been a big haul for the old woman.

It was a big haul for the dogs now.

4

One of the Grimes dogs sprang suddenly out from among the others and began worrying the pack on the old woman's back. Had the dogs really been wolves, that one would have been the leader of the pack. What he did, all the others did.

All of them sank their teeth into the grain bag the old woman had fastened with ropes to her back.

They dragged the old woman's body out into the open clearing. The worn-out dress was quickly torn from her shoulders. When she was found a day or two later, the dress had been torn from her body clear to the hips, but the dogs had not touched her body. They had got the meat out of the grain bag, that was all. Her body was frozen stiff when it was found, and the shoulders were so narrow and the body so slight that in death it looked like the body of some charming young girl.

Such things happened in towns of the Middle West, on farms near town, when I was a boy. A hunter out after rabbits found the old woman's body and did not touch it. Something, the beaten round path in the little snow-covered clearing, the silence of the place, the place where the dogs had worried the body trying to pull the grain bag away or tear it open—something startled the man and he hurried off to town.

I was in Main Street with one of my brothers who was town newsboy and who was taking the afternoon papers to the stores. It was almost night.

The hunter came into a grocery and told his story. Then he went to a hardware shop and into a drugstore. Men began to gather on the sidewalks. Then they started out along the road to the place in the woods.

My brother should have gone on about his business of distributing papers but he didn't. Everyone was going to the woods. The undertaker went and the town marshal. Several men got on a dray and rode out to where the path left the road and went into the woods, but the horses weren't very sharply shod and slid about on the slippery roads. They made no better time than those of us who walked.

The town marshal was a large man whose leg had been injured in the Civil War. He carried a heavy cane and limped rapidly along the road. My brother and I followed at his heels, and as we went other men and boys joined the crowd.

It had grown dark by the time we got to where the old woman had left the road but the moon had come out. The marshal was thinking there might have been a murder. He kept asking the hunter questions. The hunter went along with his gun across his shoulders, a dog following at his heels. It isn't often a rabbit hunter has a chance to be so conspicuous. He was taking full advantage of it, leading the procession with the town marshal. "I didn't see any wounds. She was a beautiful young girl. Her face was buried in the snow. No, I didn't know her." As a matter of fact, the hunter had not looked closely at the body. He had been frightened. She might have been murdered and someone might spring out from behind a tree and murder him. In a woods in the late afternoon, when the trees are all bare and there is white snow on the ground, when all is silent, something creepy steals over the mind and body. If something strange or uncanny has happened in the neighborhood all you think about is getting away from there as fast as you can.

The crowd of men and boys had got to where the old woman had crossed the field and went, following the marshal and the hunter, up the slight incline and into the woods.

My brother and I were silent. He had his bundle of papers in a bag slung across his shoulder. When he got back to town he would have to go on distributing his papers before he went home to supper. If I went along, as he had no doubt already determined I should, we would both be late. Either mother or our older sister would have to warm our supper.

Well, we would have something to tell. A boy did not get such a chance very often. It was lucky we just happened to go into the grocery when the hunter came in. The hunter was a country fellow. Neither of us had ever seen him before.

Now the crowd of men and boys had got to the clearing. Darkness comes quickly on such winter nights, but the full moon made everything clear. My brother and I stood near the tree beneath which the old woman had died.

She did not look old, lying there in that light, frozen and still. One of the men turned her over in the snow and I saw everything. My body trembled with some strange mystical feeling and so did my brother's. It might have been the cold.

Neither of us had ever seen a woman's body before. It may have been the snow, clinging to the frozen flesh, that made it look so white and lovely, so like marble. No woman had come with the party from town; but one of the men, he was the town blacksmith, took off his overcoat and spread it over her. Then he gathered her into his arms and started off to town, all the others following silently. At that time no one knew who she was.

5

I had seen everything, had seen the oval in the snow, like a miniature race track, where the dogs had run, had seen how the men were mystified, had seen the white bare young-looking shoulders, had heard the whispered comments of the men.

The men were simply mystified. They took the body to the undertaker's, and when the blacksmith, the hunter, the marshal, and several others had got inside they closed the door. If father had been there perhaps he could have got in, but we boys couldn't.

I went with my brother to distribute the rest of his papers and when we got home it was my brother who told the story.

I kept silent and went to bed early. It may have been I was not satisfied with the way he told it.

Later, in the town, I must have heard other fragments of the old woman's story. She was recognized the next day and there was an investigation.

The husband and son were found somewhere and brought to town and there was an attempt to connect them with the woman's death, but it did not work. They had perfect enough alibis.

However, the town was against them. They had to get out. Where they went I never heard.

I remember only the picture there in the forest, the men standing about, the naked girlish-looking figure face down in the snow, the tracks made by the running dogs, and the clear cold winter sky above. White fragments of clouds were drifting across the sky. They went racing across the little open space among the trees.

The scene in the forest had become for me, without my knowing it, the foundation for the real story I am now trying to tell. The fragments, you see, had to be picked up slowly, long afterward.

Things happened. When I was a young man I worked on the farm of a German. The hired girl was afraid of her employer. The farmer's wife hated her.

I saw things at that place. Once later, I had a half-uncanny, mystical adventure with dogs in an Illinois forest on a clear, moonlit winter night. When I was a schoolboy, and on a summer day, I went with a boy friend out along a creek some miles from town and came to the house where the old woman had lived. No one had lived in the house since her death. The doors were broken from the hinges; the window lights were all broken. As the boy and I stood in the road outside, two dogs, just roving farm dogs no doubt, came running around the corner of the house. The dogs were tall, gaunt fellows and came down to the fence and glared through at us, standing in the road.

The whole thing, the story of the old woman's death, was to me as I grew older like music heard from far off. The notes had to be picked up slowly, one at a time. Something had to be understood.

The woman who died was one destined to feed animal life. Anyway, that is all she ever did. She was feeding animal life before she was born, as a child, as a young woman working on the farm of the German, after she married, when she grew old, and when she died. She fed animal life in cows, in chickens, in pigs, in horses, in dogs, in men. Her daughter had died in childhood and with her one son she had no articulate relations. On the night when she died she was hurrying homeward, bearing on her body food for animal life.

She died in the clearing in the woods and even after her death continued feeding animal life.

You see it is likely that, when my brother told the story that night when we got home and my mother and sister sat listening, I did not think he got the point. He was too young and so was I. A thing so complete has its own beauty.

I shall not try to emphasize the point. I am only explaining why I was dissatisfied then and have been ever since. I speak of that only that you may understand why I have been impelled to try to tell the simple story over again.

QUESTIONS

1. Why does the narrator tell us that what he remembers of the woman "is a story"? (259)

2. Why does the narrator suggest that the "running of the dogs may have been a kind of death ceremony"? (265)

3. Why does the narrator describe the dogs as thinking, "When man dies we become wolves again"? (265)

4. When the narrator sees the dead woman, why does his body tremble "with some strange mystical feeling"? (267) Why does the narrator describe his experience with dogs in an Illinois forest as "mystical"? (268)

5. Why is the narrator unsatisfied with the story his brother tells of the old woman's death?

6. Why does the narrator call his story the "real story"? How is the scene in the forest the "foundation" for it? (268)

7. What does the narrator mean when he says that, as he grew older, the woman's story was "like music heard from far off"? (268)

8. The narrator says that "something had to be understood" of the old woman's "real story." (268) What does the narrator finally understand about the life and death of the old woman?

9. Why does the narrator say that the woman was "destined to feed animal life"? (268) Why does he emphasize this behavior throughout his narrative?

10. Why does the narrator say that he and his brother were too young to get the point of the woman's story?

11. Why does the narrator say, "A thing so complete has its own beauty"? (269) What beauty does he see in the story, and why does he consider it so complete?

12. What compels the narrator "to try to tell the simple story over again"? (269)

FOR FURTHER REFLECTION

1. How can we explain the narrator's frequent interruptions of himself to remind us that he is making up a story out of fragments and incomplete remembrances?

2. Why does Anderson choose to tell the story of the old woman's death using a narrator whose memories are incomplete, instead of a more conventional omniscient narrator?

3. Does the fact that the narrator creates the "real story" out of fragments affect the story's validity? Why does the narrator call the story "real" instead of "true"?

4. Do you agree with the narrator that the "real story" is probably not the one that his brother told?

JORGE LUIS BORGES

Jorge Luis Borges (1899–1986), one of the most influential short-story writers of the twentieth century, was born in Buenos Aires. His father was a lawyer and a professor of psychology, and his mother translated the works of classic American and British authors into Spanish. English and Spanish were so interchangeable in his home that during his early years, he did not realize they were separate languages. From a young age, he was immersed in literature, and he began writing at about six, inspired by writers such as Miguel de Cervantes as well as stories of Argentina's frontier days told by his English paternal grandmother.

In 1914, Borges's family moved to Geneva, Switzerland, so that he and his sister could attend school there. Five years later, the family relocated to Spain, where Borges fell in with a group of avant-garde writers who called themselves Ultraists. When his family moved back to Buenos Aires in 1921, Borges brought a new perspective to his native city. In his poems and essays, he celebrated its culture and history. He published his first book, a collection of poems entitled *Fervor de Buenos Aires*, in 1923. Several years later, Borges underwent the first of numerous unsuccessful eye operations; he gradually lost his sight over the next thirty years, eventually becoming completely blind.

In the 1930s, Borges began to concentrate on writing short stories. He published a series of sketches in 1933 and 1934 that made up *Historia universal de la infamia* (*A Universal History of Infamy*), in which Borges reinvented the lives of historical figures. He published "The Approach to al-Mu'tasim" in 1935, a review of an imaginary book by an imaginary author. This story became a sort of template for the style that eventually established his reputation—metaphysically inquisitive, dotted with odd details and obscure facts, and paradoxical.

Borges took a job at a Buenos Aires library in 1937. Needing only an hour or so to complete his work each day, he devoted the rest of his time to reading and writing. In 1938, Borges suffered a severe head wound that became infected, threatening his life. The years immediately following this trauma found Borges at the height of his creative powers, and in 1944 he published *Ficciones*, a collection of stories that is widely regarded as his best work.

When Juan Perón came to power in 1946, Borges, a vocal critic of the regime, was dismissed from his job at the library and named inspector of poultry and rabbits in the public markets. Since he had made a name for himself as a writer, he was able to resign and earn a living writing and lecturing on literature. Police informants were often in attendance when he spoke. After Perón's overthrow in 1955, Borges was appointed director of the national library and, the following year, he became a professor of literature at the University of Buenos Aires.

In 1961, Borges shared the Formentor Prize with Samuel Beckett. This enhanced Borges's international reputation, and he traveled and lectured extensively over the next two decades. He was sixty-eight when he married Elsa Astete Millán, an old friend. The marriage was not a happy one, and they divorced three years later. Weeks before he died, at the age of eighty-six, Borges married his forty-one-year-old secretary and traveling companion, Maria Kodama.

"The Garden of Forking Paths," included in *Ficciones*, is in many respects typical of Borges's greatest stories. It consists primarily of an incomplete manuscript presented as if it might explain a fact noted in an actual book about the history of World War I. The story is, among other things, a meditation on the nature of time and chance, a riff on the conventional mystery narrative, and an old-fashioned tale of espionage. Information is gradually revealed as the story progresses, altering our perception of what we have already read, so it is only after a second reading that many of the story's interpretive issues begin to emerge.

JORGE LUIS BORGES

The Garden of Forking Paths

For Victoria Ocampo

On page 242 of *The History of the World War*, Liddell Hart tells us that an Allied offensive against the Serre-Montauban line (to be mounted by thirteen British divisions backed by 1,400 artillery pieces) had been planned for July 24, 1916, but had to be put off until the morning of the 29th. Torrential rains (notes Captain Liddell Hart) were the cause of that delay—a delay that entailed no great consequences, as it turns out. The statement which follows—dictated, reread, and signed by Dr. Yu Tsun, former professor of English in the *Hochschule* at Tsingtao—throws unexpected light on the case. The two first pages of the statement are missing.

. . . and I hung up the receiver. Immediately afterward, I recognized the voice that had answered in German. It was that of Captain Richard Madden. Madden's presence in Viktor Runeberg's flat meant the end of our efforts and (though this seemed to me quite secondary, or *should have seemed*) our lives as well. It meant that Runeberg had been arrested, or murdered.[1] Before the sun set on that day, I would face the same fate. Madden was implacable—or rather, he was obliged to be implacable. An Irishman at the orders of the English, a man accused of a certain lack of zealousness, perhaps even treason, how could he fail to embrace and give thanks for this miraculous favor—the discovery, capture, perhaps death, of two agents of the German Empire? I went upstairs to my room; absurdly, I locked the door, and then I threw myself, on my back, onto my narrow iron bed. Outside the window were the usual rooftops and the overcast six o'clock sun. I found it incredible that this day, lacking all omens and premonitions, should be the day of my implacable death.

1. A bizarre and despicable supposition. The Prussian spy Hans Rabener, alias Viktor Runeberg, had turned an automatic pistol on his arresting officer, Captain Richard Madden, in self-defense, inflicted the wounds on Rabener that caused his subsequent death. (Editor's note.)

Despite my deceased father, despite my having been a child in a symmetrical garden in Hai Feng—was I, now, about to die? Then I reflected that all things happen to oneself, and happen precisely, precisely now. Century follows century, yet events occur only in the present; countless men in the air, on the land and sea, yet everything that truly happens, happens to me. . . . The almost unbearable memory of Madden's horsey face demolished those mental ramblings. In the midst of my hatred and my terror (now I don't mind talking about terror—now that I have foiled Richard Madden, now that my neck hungers for the rope), it occurred to me that that brawling and undoubtedly happy warrior did not suspect that I possessed the Secret—the name of the exact location of the new British artillery park on the Ancre. A bird furrowed the gray sky, and I blindly translated it into an airplane, and that airplane into many (in the French sky), annihilating the artillery park with vertical bombs. If only my throat, before a bullet crushed it, could cry out that name so that it might be heard in Germany. . . . But my human voice was so terribly inadequate. How was I to make it reach the Leader's ear—the ear of that sick and hateful man who knew nothing of Runeberg and me save that we were in Staffordshire, and who was vainly awaiting word from us in his and office in Berlin, poring infinitely through the newspapers? . . . *I must flee*, I said aloud. I sat up noiselessly, in needless but perfect silence, as though Madden were already just outside my door. Something—perhaps the mere show of proving that my resources were nonexistent—made me go through my pockets. I found what I knew I would find: the American watch, the nickel-plated chain and quadrangular coin, the key ring with the compromising and useless keys to Runeberg's flat, the notebook, a letter I resolved to destroy at once (and never did), the false passport, one crown, two shillings, and a few odd pence, the red and blue pencil, the handkerchief, the revolver with its single bullet. Absurdly, I picked it up and hefted it, to give myself courage. I vaguely reflected that a pistol shot can be heard at a considerable distance. In ten minutes, my plan was ripe. The telephone book gave me the name of the only person able to communicate the information: he lived in a suburb of Fenton, less than a half-hour away by train.

I am a coward. I can say that, now that I have carried out a plan whose dangerousness and daring no man will deny. I know that it was a terrible thing to do. I did not do it for Germany. What do I care for a barbaric country that has forced me into the ignominy of spying? Furthermore, I know of a man of England—a modest man—who in my view is no less a genius that Goethe. I spoke with him for no more than an hour, but for one hour he was Goethe. . . . No—I did it because I sensed that the Leader looked down on the people of my race—the countless ancestors whose blood flows through my veins. I wanted to prove to him that a yellow man could save his armies. And I had to escape from Madden. His hands, his voice, could beat upon my door at any moment. I silently dressed, said goodbye to myself in the mirror, made my way downstairs, looked up and down the quiet street, and set off. The train station was not far from my flat, but I thought it better to take a cab. I argued that I ran less chance of being recognized that way; the fact is, I felt I was visible and vulnerable—infinitely vulnerable—in the deserted street. I recall that I told the driver to stop a little ways from the main entrance to the station. I got down from the cab with willed and almost painful slowness. I would be going to the village of Ashgrove, but I bought a ticket for a station farther down the line. The train was to leave at 8:50, scant minutes away. I had to hurry; the next train would not be until 9:30. There was almost no one on the platform. I walked through the cars; I recall a few workmen, a woman dressed in mourning weeds, a young man fervently reading Tacitus's *Annals*, and a cheerful-looking wounded soldier. The train pulled out at last. A man I recognized ran, vainly, out to the end of the platform; it was Captain Richard Madden. Shattered, trembling, I huddled on the other end of the seat, far from the feared window.

From that shattered state I passed into a state of almost abject cheerfulness. I told myself that my duel had begun, and that in dodging my adversary's thrust—even by forty minutes, even thanks to the slightest smile from fate—the first round had gone to me. I argued that this small win prefigured total victory. I argued that the win was not really even so small, since without the precious hour that the trains had given me, I'd be in jail or dead. I argued (no less sophistically) that my cowardly cheerfulness proved that I was a man capable of following this adventure through to its successful end. From that weakness I drew strength that was never to abandon me. I foresee that mankind will resign itself more and more fully every day to more and more horrendous undertakings; soon there will be nothing but warriors and brigands. I give them this piece of advice: *He who is to perform a horrendous act should imagine to himself that it is already done, should impose upon himself a future as irrevocable as the past.* That is what I did, while my eyes—the eyes of a man already dead—registered the flow of that day perhaps to be my last, and the spreading of the night. The train ran sweetly, gently, through woods of ash trees. It stopped virtually in the middle of the countryside. No one called out the name of the station. "Ashgrove?" I asked some boys on the platform. "Ashgrove," they said, nodding. I got off the train.

A lamp illuminated the platform, but the boys' faces remained within the area of shadow. "Are you going to Dr. Stephen Albert's house?" one queried. Without waiting for an answer, another of them said: "The house is a far way, but you'll not get lost if you follow that road there to the left, and turn left at every crossing." I tossed them a coin (my last), went down some stone steps, and started down the solitary road. It ran ever so slightly downhill and was of elemental dirt. Branches tangled overhead, and the low round moon seemed to walk along beside me.

For one instant, I feared that Richard Madden had somehow seen through my desperate plan, but I soon realized that that was impossible. The boy's advice to turn always to the left reminded me that that was the common way of discovering the central lawn of a certain type of maze. I am something of a connoisseur of mazes: not for nothing am I the great-grandson of that Ts'ui Pen who was governor of Yunnan province and who renounced all temporal power in order to write a novel containing more characters than the *Hung Lu Meng* and construct a labyrinth in which all men would lose their way. Ts'ui Pen devoted thirteen years to those disparate labors, but the hand of a foreigner murdered him and his novel made no sense and no one ever found the labyrinth. It was under English trees that I meditated on that lost labyrinth: I pictured it perfect and inviolate on the secret summit of a mountain; I pictured its outlines blurred by rice paddies, or underwater; I pictured it as infinite—a labyrinth not of octagonal pavilions and paths that turn back upon themselves, but of rivers and provinces and kingdoms. . . . I imagined a labyrinth of labyrinths, a maze of mazes, a twisting, turning, ever-widening labyrinth that contained both past and future and somehow implied the stars. Absorbed in those illusory imaginings, I forgot that I was a pursued man; I felt myself, for an indefinite while, the abstract perceiver of the world. The vague, living countryside, the moon, the remains of the day did their work in me; so did the gently downward road, which forestalled all possibility of weariness. The evening was near, yet infinite.

The road dropped and forked as it cut through the now-formless meadows. A keen and vaguely syllabic song, blurred by leaves and distance, came and went on the gentle gusts of breeze. I was struck by the thought that a man may be the enemy of other men, the enemy of other men's other moments, yet not be the enemy of a country—of fireflies, words, gardens, watercourses, zephyrs. It was amid such thoughts that I came to a high rusty gate. Through the iron bars I made out a drive lined with poplars, and a gazebo of some kind. Suddenly, I realized two things—the first trivial, the second almost incredible: the music I had heard was coming from that gazebo, or pavilion, and the music was Chinese. That was why unconsciously I had fully given myself over to it. I do not recall whether there was a bell or whether I had to clap my hands to make my arrival known.

The sputtering of the music continued, but from the rear of the intimate house, a lantern was making its way toward me—a lantern crosshatched and sometimes blotted out altogether by the trees, a paper lantern the shape of a drum and the color of the moon. It was carried by a tall man. I could not see his face because the light blinded me. He opened the gate and slowly spoke to me in my own language.

"I see that the compassionate Hsi P'eng has undertaken to remedy my solitude. You will no doubt wish to see the garden?"

I recognized the name of one of our consuls, but I could only disconcertedly repeat, "The garden?"

"The garden of forking paths."

Something stirred in my memory, and I spoke with incomprehensible assurance.

"The garden of my ancestor Ts'ui Pen."

"Your ancestor? Your illustrious ancestor? Please—come in."

The dew-drenched path meandered like the paths of my childhood. We came to a library of Western and Oriental books. I recognized, bound in yellow silk, several handwritten volumes of the Lost Encyclopedia compiled by the third emperor of the Luminous Dynasty but never printed. The disk on the gramophone revolved near a bronze phoenix. I also recall a vase of *famille rose* and another, earlier by several hundred years, of that blue color our artificers copied from the potters of ancient Persia. . . .

Stephen Albert, with a smile, regarded me. He was, as I have said, quite tall, with sharp features, gray eyes, and a gray beard. There was something priestlike about him, somehow, but something sailorlike as well; later he told me he had been a missionary in Tientsin "before aspiring to be a Sinologist."

We sat down, I on a long low divan, he with his back to the window and a tall circular clock. I figured that my pursuer, Richard Madden, could not possibly arrive for at least an hour. My irrevocable decision could wait.

"An amazing life, Ts'ui Pen's," Stephen Albert said. "Governor of the province in which he had been born, a man learned in astronomy, astrology, and the unwearying interpretation of canonical books, a chess player, a renowned poet and calligrapher—he abandoned it all in order to compose a book and a labyrinth. He renounced the pleasures of oppression, justice, the populous marriage bed, banquets, and even erudition in order to sequester himself for thirteen years in the Pavilion of Limpid Solitude. Upon his death, his heirs found nothing but chaotic manuscripts. The family, as you perhaps are aware, was about to deliver them to the fire, but his counselor—a Taoist or Buddhist monk—insisted upon publishing them."

"To this day," I replied, "we who are descended from Ts'ui Pen execrate that monk. It was senseless to publish those manuscripts. The book is a contradictory jumble of irresolute drafts. I once examined it myself; in the third chapter the hero dies, yet in the fourth he is alive again. As for Ts'ui Pen's other labor, his Labyrinth . . ."

"Here is the Labyrinth," Albert said, gesturing toward a tall lacquered writing cabinet.

"An ivory labyrinth!" I exclaimed. "A very small sort of labyrinth . . ."

"A labyrinth of symbols," he corrected me. "An invisible labyrinth of time. I, an English barbarian, have somehow been chosen to unveil the diaphanous mystery. Now, more than a hundred years after the fact, the precise details are irrecoverable, but it is not difficult to surmise what happened. Ts'ui Pen must at one point have remarked, 'I shall retire to write a book,' and at another point, 'I shall retire to construct a labyrinth.' Everyone pictured two projects; it occurred to no one that book and labyrinth were one and the same. The Pavilion of Limpid Solitude was erected in the center of a garden that was, perhaps, most intricately laid out; that fact might well have suggested a physical labyrinth. Ts'ui Pen died; no one in all the wide lands that had been his could find the labyrinth. The novel's confusion—confusedness, I mean, of course—suggested to me that it was that labyrinth. Two circumstances lent me the final solution of the problem—one, the curious legend that Ts'ui Pen had intended to construct a labyrinth which was truly infinite, and two, a fragment of a letter I discovered."

Albert stood. His back was turned to me for several moments; he opened a drawer in the black and gold writing cabinet. He turned back with a paper that had once been crimson but was now pink and delicate and rectangular. It was written in Ts'ui Pen's renowned calligraphy. Eagerly yet uncomprehendingly I read the words that a man of my own lineage had written with painstaking brushstrokes: *I leave to several futures (not to all) my garden of forking paths.* I wordlessly handed the paper back to Albert. He continued:

"Before unearthing this letter, I had wondered how a book could be infinite. The only way I could surmise was that it be a cyclical, or circular, volume, a volume whose last page would be identical to the first, so that one might go on indefinitely. I also recalled that night at the center of *The Thousand and One Nights*, when the queen Scheherazade (through some magical distractedness on the part of the copyist) begins to retell, verbatim, the story of *The Thousand and One Nights*, with the risk of returning once again to the night on which she is telling it—and so on, ad infinitum. I also pictured to myself a platonic, hereditary sort of work, passed down from father to son, in which each new individual would add a chapter or with reverent care correct his elders' pages. These imaginings amused and distracted me, but none of them seemed to correspond even remotely to Ts'ui Pen's contradictory chapters. As I was floundering about in the mire of these perplexities, I was sent from Oxford the document you have just examined. I paused, as you may well imagine, at the sentence *I leave to several futures (not to all) my garden of forking paths.* Almost instantly, I saw it—the garden of forking paths was the chaotic novel; the phrase *several futures (not all)* suggested to me the image of a forking in time, rather than in space. A full rereading of the book confirmed my theory. In all fictions, each time a man meets diverse alternatives, he chooses one and eliminates the others; in the work of the virtually impossible-to-disentangle Ts'ui Pen, the character chooses—simultaneously—all of them. *He creates*, thereby, several futures, several times, which themselves proliferate and fork. That is the explanation for the novel's contradictions. Fang, let us say, has a secret; a stranger knocks at his door; Fang decides to kill him. Naturally, there are various possible outcomes—Fang can kill the intruder, the intruder can kill Fang, they can both live, they can both be killed, and so on. In Ts'ui Pen's novel, all the outcomes in fact occur; each is the starting point for further bifurcations. Once in a while, the paths of that labyrinth converge: for example, you come to this house, but in one of the possible pasts you are my enemy, in another my friend. If you can bear my incorrigible pronunciation, we shall read a few pages."

His face, in the vivid circle of the lamp, was undoubtedly that of an old man, though with something indomitable and even immortal about it. He read with slow precision two versions of a single epic chapter. In the first, an army marches off to battle through a mountain wilderness; the horror of the rocks and darkness inspires in them a disdain for life, and they go on to an easy victory. In the second, the same army passes through a palace in which a ball is being held; the brilliant battle seems to them a continuation of the fete, and they win it easily.

I listened with honorable veneration to those ancient fictions, which were themselves perhaps not as remarkable as the fact that a man of my blood had invented them and a man of a distant empire was restoring them to me on an island in the West in the course of a desperate mission. I recall the final words, repeated in each version like some secret commandment: "Thus the heroes fought, their admirable hearts calm, their swords violent, they themselves resigned to killing and to dying."

From that moment on, I felt all about me and within my obscure body an invisible, intangible pullulation—not that of the divergent, parallel, and finally coalescing armies, but an agitation more inaccessible, more inward than that, yet one those armies somehow prefigured. Albert went on:

"I do not believe that your venerable ancestor played at idle variations. I cannot think it probable that he would sacrifice thirteen years to the infinite performance of a rhetorical exercise. In your country, the novel is a subordinate genre; at that time it was a genre beneath contempt. Ts'ui Pen was a novelist of genius, but he was also a man of letters, and surely would not have considered himself a mere novelist. The testimony of his contemporaries proclaims his metaphysical, mystical leanings—and his life is their fullest confirmation. Philosophical debate consumes a good part of his novel. I know that of all problems, none disturbed him, none gnawed at him like the unfathomable problem of time. How strange, then, that that problem should be the *only* one that does not figure in the pages of his *Garden*. He never even uses the word. How do you explain that willful omission?"

I proposed several solutions—all unsatisfactory. We discussed them; finally, Stephen Albert said:

"In a riddle whose answer is chess, what is the only word that must not be used?"

I thought for a moment.

"The word *chess*," I replied.

"Exactly," Albert said. "*The Garden of Forking Paths* is a huge riddle, or parable, whose subject is time; that secret purpose forbids Ts'ui Pen the merest mention of its name. To *always* omit one word, to employ awkward metaphors and obvious circumlocutions, is perhaps the most emphatic way of calling attention to that word. It is, at any rate, the tortuous path chosen by the devious Ts'ui Pen at each and every one of the turnings of his inexhaustible novel. I have compared hundreds of manuscripts, I have corrected the errors introduced through the negligence of copyists, I have reached a hypothesis for the plan of that chaos, I have reestablished, or believe I've reestablished, its fundamental order—I have translated the entire work; and I know that not once does the word *time* appear. The explanation is obvious: *The Garden of Forking Paths* is an incomplete, but not false, image of the universe as conceived by Ts'ui Pen. Unlike Newton and Schopenhauer, your ancestor did not believe in a uniform and absolute time; he believed in an infinite series of times, a growing, dizzying web of divergent, convergent, and parallel times. That fabric of times that approach one another, fork, are snipped off, or are simply unknown for centuries, contains *all* possibilities. In most of those times, we do not exist; in some, you exist but I do not; in others, I do and you do not; in others still, we both do. In this one, which the favoring hand of chance has dealt me, you have come to my home; in another, when you come through my garden you find me dead; in another, I say these same words, but I am an error, a ghost."

"In all," I said, not without a tremble, "I am grateful for, and I venerate, your re-creation of the garden of Ts'ui Pen."

"Not in all," he whispered with a smile. "Time forks, perpetually, into countless futures. In one of them, I am your enemy."

I felt again that pullulation I have mentioned. I sensed that the dew-drenched garden that surrounded the house was saturated, infinitely, with invisible persons. Those persons were Albert and myself—secret, busily at work, multiform—in other dimensions of time. I raised my eyes and the gossamer nightmare faded. In the yellow and black garden there was but a single man—but that man was as mighty as a statue, and that man was coming down the path, and he was Captain Richard Madden.

"The future is with us," I replied, "but I am your friend. May I look at the letter again?"

Albert rose once again. He stood tall as he opened the drawer of the tall writing cabinet; he turned his back to me for a moment. I had cocked the revolver. With utmost care, I fired. Albert fell without a groan, without a sound, on the instant. I swear that he died instantly—one clap of thunder.

The rest is unreal, insignificant. Madden burst into the room and arrested me. I have been sentenced to hang. I have most abhorrently triumphed: I have communicated to Berlin the secret name of the city to be attacked. Yesterday it was bombed—I read about it in the same newspapers that posed to all of England the enigma of the murder of the eminent Sinologist Stephen Albert by a stranger, Yu Tsun. The Leader solved the riddle. He knew that my problem was how to report (over the deafening noise of the war) the name of the city named Albert, and that the only way I could find was murdering a person of that name. He does not know (no one can know) my endless contrition, and my weariness.

QUESTIONS

1. What difference does it make to the story that the first two pages of Yu Tsun's statement are missing?

2. What "unexpected light" does Yu Tsun's statement shed on the anecdote about the Allied offensive planned for July 24, 1916? (275)

3. What does Yu Tsun mean when he reflects that "all things happen to oneself, and happen precisely, precisely now"? (276)

4. Why does Yu Tsun call himself a coward?

5. How does Yu Tsun's advice to the "warriors and brigands" of the future—"*He who is to perform a horrendous act should imagine to himself that it is already done, should impose upon himself a future as irrevocable as the past*"—affect our perception of him and his killing of Stephen Albert? (277)

6. Why does his meditation on the lost labyrinth of his great-grandfather make Yu Tsun forget that he is being pursued and cause him to feel himself to be, "for an indefinite while, the abstract perceiver of the world"? (278)

7. What does Yu Tsun mean when he says that "a man may be the enemy of other men, the enemy of other men's other moments, yet not be the enemy of a country"? (278)

8. Why is it that Yu Tsun comes to understand the mystery of Ts'ui Pen's labyrinth through meeting Stephen Albert, a self-described "English barbarian" whom Yu Tsun is about to kill? (280)

9. Why does Yu Tsun wait until Madden is about to arrive before killing Stephen Albert?

10. Is there a relationship between Ts'ui Pen's book and Yu Tsun's statement?

11. Is it "the favoring hand of chance," in Stephen Albert's words, that brings Yu Tsun to Stephen Albert's home? (282)

12. Why does Yu Tsun say, "I am your friend" before shooting Stephen Albert? (283)

13. After shooting Stephen Albert, why does Yu Tsun say that the rest of what happened is "unreal, insignificant"? (283)

14. What is the cause of the weariness that Yu Tsun says he feels at the end of his statement?

15. What purpose does Yu Tsun have in writing his statement?

FOR FURTHER REFLECTION

1. How does the knowledge that a manuscript is incomplete affect our response to it?

2. Is the course of history determined more by chance or by free will?

3. Is it comforting or disturbing to think that there might be other realities besides the one we experience?

4. Do you agree with Yu Tsun's characterization of himself as a coward?

SIMONE DE BEAUVOIR

The twentieth century's preeminent feminist writer and a leading figure of French existentialist thought, Simone de Beauvoir (1908–1986) was born and raised in Paris. Her father, a lawyer, was an agnostic and political conservative with a passion for literature and amateur theater; her mother, who came from a prosperous family, tried to instill in Simone and her sister traditional Catholic piety. By the age of fifteen, Beauvoir had rejected her mother's faith, declared her atheism, and determined to study and teach philosophy.

Beauvoir's academic abilities and love of books, nurtured by her father, were already apparent during her early education at a private Catholic school for girls. While there, Beauvoir formed a close friendship with a girl she called Zaza Mabille, and Zaza's experiences profoundly influenced Beauvoir's thinking about a woman's place in the world. According to the doctors, Zaza died in 1929 of meningitis. But Beauvoir believed her friend's death had to do with her family's attempts to limit her career choices and prohibit her marriage to a fellow student. Also in 1929, Beauvoir met Jean-Paul Sartre at the Sorbonne and began her lifelong partnership with him. And she completed her thesis on Gottfried Wilhelm Leibniz, becoming the youngest student in France ever to pass the notoriously difficult philosophy exam known as the *agrégation*, at the École Normale Supérieure. Sartre placed first (it was his second try), and Beauvoir was a close second.

From 1931 to 1943, Beauvoir taught philosophy in Marseille, Rouen, and Paris. In 1943, she published the novel *L'Invitée* (*She Came to Stay*), the first of her more than twenty books. Written between 1935 and 1937, the novel offers a fictionalized account of a love triangle based on herself, Sartre, and her student Olga Kosakievicz. In 1945, Beauvoir published a novel of the French Resistance, *Le sang de autres* (*The Blood of Others*), and with Sartre founded the influential monthly *Les Temps Modernes*.

In 1947, Beauvoir published *Pour une morale de l'ambiguïté* (*The Ethics of Ambiguity*), a lucid account of existentialist philosophy in which she strongly challenges Dostoevsky's famous assertion that if God does not exist, everything is permitted. She argues that in fact "far from God's absence authorizing all license, the contrary is the case, because man . . . bears the responsibility for a world which is not the work of a strange power, but of himself."

It was in her next major work, however, that Beauvoir stopped talking about humanity in the abstract and focused on issues of gender. *Le deuxième sexe* (*The Second Sex*), published in France in 1949 and in English translation in 1953, secured Beauvoir's reputation as a writer. The book shook up Western philosophy and effectively set the stage for the feminist revolution that would begin in the late 1960s. At the same time, the book demonstrated the influence of Beauvoir's ongoing engagement with psychoanalytic and Marxist thinking and came loaded with brilliant and memorable aphorisms. "One is not born, but becomes a woman," remains her most famous dictum.

Beauvoir continued to write fiction, as well. Her novel *Les Mandarins* (1954) received the Prix Goncourt; it includes a character believed to be based on Nelson Algren, who had become her lover during her visit to Chicago in 1947. One of the fascinations of Beauvoir's life is her lifelong companionship with Sartre, which endured despite both partners' independent ways. Long cast as the writer working in Sartre's shadow, Beauvoir is now seen as an independent thinker in her own right, although the influence of each can be glimpsed in the work of the other.

In the final phase of her career, Beauvoir explored the meaning of aging. *Le Vieillesse* (*The Coming of Age*), published in 1970, details the process of growing old as well as Western society's devaluation of the elderly. A year after Sartre's death in 1980, Beauvoir chronicled the details of his final illness: *Le cérémonie des adieux* (*Adieux: A Farewell to Sartre*). She lies buried beside him in Paris.

SIMONE DE BEAUVOIR

Introduction to *The Second Sex*

For a long time I have hesitated to write a book on woman. The subject is irritating, especially to women; and it is not new. Enough ink has been spilled in the quarreling over feminism, now practically over, and perhaps we should say no more about it. It is still talked about, however, for the voluminous nonsense uttered during the last century seems to have done little to illuminate the problem. After all, is there a problem? And if so, what is it? Are there women, really? Most assuredly the theory of the eternal feminine still has its adherents who will whisper in your ear: "Even in Russia women still are *women*"; and other erudite persons—sometimes the very same—say with a sigh: "Woman is losing her way, woman is lost." One wonders if women still exist, if they will always exist, whether or not it is desirable that they should, what place they occupy in this world, what their place should be. "What has become of women?" was asked recently in an ephemeral magazine.[1]

But first we must ask: what is a woman? "*Tota mulier in utero*," says one, "woman is a womb." But in speaking of certain women, connoisseurs declare that they are not women, although they are equipped with a uterus like the rest. All agree in recognizing the fact that females exist in the human species; today as always they make up about one half of humanity. And yet we are told that femininity is in danger; we are exhorted to be women, remain woman, become women. It would appear, then, that every female human being is not necessarily a woman; to be so considered she must share in that mysterious and threatened reality known as femininity. Is this attribute something secreted by the ovaries? Or is it a Platonic essence, a product of the philosophic imagination? Is a rustling petticoat enough to bring it down to earth? Although some women try zealously to incarnate this essence, it is hardly patentable. It is frequently described in vague and dazzling terms that seem to have been borrowed from the vocabulary of the seers, and indeed in the times of St. Thomas it was

1. *Franchise*, dead today.

considered an essence as certainly defined as the somniferous virtue of the poppy.

But conceptualism has lost ground. The biological and social sciences no longer admit the existence of unchangeably fixed entities that determine given characteristics, such as those ascribed to woman, the Jew, or the Negro. Science regards any characteristic as a reaction dependent in part upon a *situation*. If today femininity no longer exists, then it never existed. But does the word *woman*, then, have no specific content? This is stoutly affirmed by those who hold to the philosophy of the enlightenment, of rationalism, of nominalism; women, to them, are merely the human beings arbitrarily designated by the word *woman*. Many American women particularly are prepared to think that there is no longer any place for woman as such; if a backward individual still takes herself for a woman, her friends advise her to be psychoanalyzed and thus get rid of this obsession. In regard to a work, *Modern Woman: The Lost Sex*, which in other respects has its irritating features, Dorothy Parker has written: "I cannot be just to books which treat of woman as woman. . . . My idea is that all of us, men as well as women, should be regarded as human beings." But nominalism is a rather inadequate doctrine, and the antifemininists have had no trouble in showing that women simply *are not* men. Surely woman is, like man, a human being; but such a declaration is abstract. The fact is that every concrete human being is always a singular, separate individual. To decline to accept such notions as the eternal feminine, the black soul, the Jewish character, is not to deny that Jews, Negroes, women exist today—this denial does not represent a liberation for those concerned, but rather a flight from reality. Some years ago a well-known woman writer refused to permit her portrait to appear in a series of photographs especially devoted to women writers; she wished to be counted among the men. But in order to gain this privilege she made use of her husband's influence! Women who assert that they are men lay claim nonetheless to masculine consideration and respect. I recall also a young Trotskyite standing on a platform at a boisterous meeting and getting ready to use her fists, in spite of her evident fragility. She was denying her feminine weakness; but it was for love of a militant male whose equal she wished to be. The attitude of defiance of many American women proves that they are haunted by a sense of their femininity. In truth, to go for a walk with one's eyes open is enough to demonstrate that humanity is divided into two classes of individuals whose clothes, faces, bodies, smiles, gaits, interests, and occupations are manifestly different. Perhaps these differences are superficial, perhaps they are destined to disappear. What is certain is that right now they do most obviously exist.

If her functioning as a female is not enough to define woman, if we decline also to explain her through "the eternal feminine," and if nevertheless we admit, provisionally, that women do exist, then we must face the question: what is a woman?

To state the question is, to me, to suggest, at once, a preliminary answer. The fact that I ask it is in itself significant. A man would never get the notion of writing a book on the peculiar situation of the human male.[2] But if I wish to define myself, I must first of all say: "I am a woman"; on this truth must be based all further discussion. A man never begins by presenting himself as an individual of a certain sex; it goes without saying that he is a man. The terms *masculine* and *feminine* are used symmetrically only as a matter of form, as on legal papers. In actuality the relation of the two sexes is not quite like that of two electrical poles, for man represents both the positive and the neutral, as is indicated by the common use of *man* to designate human beings in general; whereas woman represents only the negative, defined by limiting criteria, without reciprocity. In the midst of an abstract discussion it is vexing to hear a man say: "You think thus and so because you are a woman"; but I know that my only defense is to reply: "I think thus and so because it is true," thereby removing my subjective self from the argument. It would be out of the question to reply: "And you think the contrary because you are a man," for it is understood that the fact of being a man is no peculiarity. A man is in the right in being a man; it is the woman who is in the wrong. It amounts to this: just as for the ancients there was an absolute vertical with reference to which the oblique was defined, so there is an absolute human type, the masculine. Woman has ovaries, a uterus; these peculiarities imprison her in her subjectivity, circumscribe her within the limits of her own nature. It is often said that she thinks with her glands. Man superbly ignores the fact that his anatomy also includes glands, such as the testicles, and that they secrete hormones. He thinks of his body as a direct and normal connection with the world, which he believes he apprehends objectively, whereas he regards the body of woman as a hindrance, a prison, weighed down by everything peculiar to it. "The female is a female by virtue of a certain *lack* of qualities," said Aristotle; "we should regard the female nature as afflicted with a natural defectiveness." And St. Thomas for his part pronounced woman to be an "imperfect man," an "incidental" being. This is symbolized in Genesis where Eve is depicted as made from what Bossuet called "a supernumerary bone" of Adam.

Thus humanity is male and man defines woman not in herself but as relative to him; she is not regarded as an autonomous being. Michelet writes: "Woman, the relative being. . . ." And Benda is most positive in his *Rapport d'Uriel*: "The body of man makes sense in itself quite apart

2. The Kinsey Report is no exception, for it is limited to describing the sexual characteristics of American men, which is quite a different matter.

from that of woman, whereas the latter seems wanting in significance by itself. . . . Man can think of himself without woman. She cannot think of herself without man." And she is simply what man decrees; thus she is called "the sex," by which is meant that she appears essentially to the male as a sexual being. For him she is sex—absolute sex, no less. She is defined and differentiated with reference to man and not he with reference to her; she is the incidental, the inessential as opposed to the essential. He is the Subject, he is the Absolute—she is the Other.[3]

The category of the *Other* is as primordial as consciousness itself. In the most primitive societies, in the most ancient mythologies, one finds the expression of a duality—that of the Self and the Other. This duality was not originally attached to the division of the sexes; it was not dependent upon any empirical facts. It is revealed in such works as that of Granet on Chinese thought and those of Dumézil on the East Indies and Rome. The feminine element was at first no more involved in such pairs as Varuna-Mitra, Uranus-Zeus, Sun-Moon, and Day-Night than it was in the contrasts between Good and Evil, lucky and unlucky auspices, right and left, God and Lucifer. Otherness is a fundamental category of human thought.

Thus it is that no group ever sets itself up as the One without at once setting up the Other over against itself. If three travelers chance to occupy the same compartment, that is enough to make vaguely hostile "others" out of all the rest of the passengers on the train. In small-town eyes all persons not belonging to the village are "strangers" and suspect; to the native of a country all who inhabit other countries are "foreigners"; Jews are "different" for the anti-Semite, Negroes are "inferior" for American racists, aborigines are "natives" for colonists, proletarians are the "lower class" for the privileged.

Lévi-Strauss, at the end of a profound work on the various forms of primitive societies, reaches the following conclusion: "Passage from the state of Nature to the state of Culture is marked by man's ability to view biological relations as a series of contrasts; duality, alternation, opposition, and symmetry, whether under definite or vague forms, constitute

3. E. Lévinas expresses this idea most explicitly in his essay *Temps et l'Autre*. "Is there not a case in which otherness, alterity, unquestionably marks the nature of a being, as its essence, an instance of otherness not consisting purely and simply in the opposition of two species of the same genus? I think that the feminine represents the contrary in its absolute sense, this contrariness being in no wise affected by any relation between it and its correlative and thus remaining absolutely other. Sex is not a certain specific difference . . . no more is the sexual difference a mere contradiction. . . . Nor does this difference lie in the duality of two complementary terms, for two complementary terms imply a pre-existing whole. . . . Otherness reaches its full flowering in the feminine, a term of the same rank as consciousness but of opposite meaning."

I suppose that Lévinas does not forget that woman, too, is aware of her own consciousness, or ego. But it is striking that he deliberately takes a man's point of view, disregarding the reciprocity of subject and object. When he writes that woman is mystery, he implies that she is mystery for man. Thus his description, which is intended to be objective, is in fact an assertion of masculine privilege.

not so much phenomena to be explained as fundamental and immediately given data of social reality."[4] These phenomena would be incomprehensible if in fact human society were simply a *Mitsein* or fellowship based on solidarity and friendliness. Things become clear, on the contrary, if, following Hegel, we find in consciousness itself a fundamental hostility toward every other consciousness; the subject can be posed only in being opposed—he sets himself up as the essential, as opposed to the other, the inessential, the object.

But the other consciousness, the other ego, sets up a reciprocal claim. The native traveling abroad is shocked to find himself in turn regarded as a "stranger" by the natives of neighboring countries. As a matter of fact, wars, festivals, trading, treaties, and contests among tribes, nations, and classes tend to deprive the concept *Other* of its absolute sense and to make manifest its relativity; willy-nilly, individuals and groups are forced to realize the reciprocity of their relations. How is it, then, that this reciprocity has not been recognized between the sexes, that one of the contrasting terms is set up as the sole essential, denying any relativity in regard to its correlative and defining the latter as pure otherness? Why is it that women do not dispute male sovereignty? No subject will readily volunteer to become the object, the inessential; it is not the Other who, in defining himself as the Other, establishes the One. The Other is posed as such by the One in defining himself as the One. But if the Other is not to regain the status of being the One, he must be submissive enough to accept this alien point of view. Whence comes this submission in the case of woman?

There are, to be sure, other cases in which a certain category has been able to dominate another completely for a time. Very often this privilege depends upon inequality of numbers—the majority imposes its rule upon the minority or persecutes it. But women are not a minority, like the American Negroes or the Jews; there are as many women as men on earth. Again, the two groups concerned have often been originally independent; they may have been formerly unaware of each other's existence, or perhaps they recognized each other's autonomy. But a historical event has resulted in the subjugation of the weaker by the stronger. The scattering of the Jews, the introduction of slavery into America, the conquests of imperialism are examples in point. In these cases the oppressed retained at least the memory of former days; they possessed in common a past, a tradition, sometimes a religion or a culture.

The parallel drawn by Bebel between women and the proletariat is valid in that neither ever formed a minority or a separate collective unit of mankind. And instead of a single historical event it is in both cases a

4. See C. Lévi-Strauss: *Les structures élémentaires de la parenté*. My thanks are due to C. Lévi-Strauss for his kindness in furnishing me with the proofs of his work, which, among others, I have used liberally in Part II.

historical development that explains their status as a class and accounts for the membership of *particular individuals* in that class. But proletarians have not always existed, whereas there have always been women. They are women in virtue of their anatomy and physiology. Throughout history they have always been subordinated to men, and hence their dependency is not the result of a historical event or a social change—it was not something that *occurred*. The reason why otherness in this case seems to be an absolute is in part that it lacks the contingent or incidental nature of historical facts. A condition brought about at a certain time can be abolished at some other time, as the Negroes of Haiti and others have proved; but it might seem that a natural condition is beyond the possibility of change. In truth, however, the nature of things is no more immutably given, once for all, than is historical reality. If woman seems to be the inessential which never becomes the essential, it is because she herself fails to bring about this change. Proletarians say "we"; Negroes also. Regarding themselves as subjects, they transform the bourgeois, the whites, into "others." But women do not say "we," except at some congress of feminists or similar formal demonstration; men say "women," and women use the same word in referring to themselves. They do not authentically assume a subjective attitude. The proletarians have accomplished the revolution in Russia, the Negroes in Haiti, the Indo-Chinese are battling for it in Indo-China; but the women's effort has never been anything more than a symbolic agitation. They have gained only what men have been willing to grant; they have taken nothing, they have only received.[5]

The reason for this is that women lack concrete means for organizing themselves into a unit which can stand face to face with the correlative unit. They have no past, no history, no religion of their own; and they have no such solidarity of work and interest as that of the proletariat. They are not even promiscuously herded together in the way that creates community feeling among the American Negroes, the ghetto Jews, the workers of Saint-Denis, or the factory hands of Renault. They live dispersed among the males, attached through residence, housework, economic condition, and social standing to certain men—fathers or husbands—more firmly than they are to other women. If they belong to the bourgeoisie, they feel solidarity with men of that class, not with proletarian women; if they are white, their allegiance is to white men, not to Negro women. The proletariat can propose to massacre the ruling class, and a sufficiently fanatical Jew or Negro might dream of getting sole possession of the atomic bomb and making humanity wholly Jewish or black; but woman cannot even dream of exterminating the males. The bond that unites her to her oppressors is not comparable to any other. The division of the sexes

5. See Part II, chap. viii.

is a biological fact, not an event in human history. Male and female stand opposed within a primordial *Mitsein*, and woman has not broken it. The couple is a fundamental unity with its two halves riveted together, and the cleavage of society along the line of sex is impossible. Here is to be found the basic trait of woman: she is the Other in a totality of which the two components are necessary to one another.

One could suppose that this reciprocity might have facilitated the liberation of woman. When Hercules sat at the feet of Omphale and helped with her spinning, his desire for her held him captive; but why did she fail to gain a lasting power? To revenge herself on Jason, Medea killed their children; and this grim legend would seem to suggest that she might have obtained a formidable influence over him through his love for his offspring. In *Lysistrata* Aristophanes gaily depicts a band of women who joined forces to gain social ends through the sexual needs of their men; but this is only a play. In the legend of the Sabine women, the latter soon abandoned their plan of remaining sterile to punish their ravishers. In truth woman has not been socially emancipated through man's need—sexual desire and the desire for offspring—which makes the male dependent for satisfaction upon the female.

Master and slave, also, are united by a reciprocal need, in this case economic, which does not liberate the slave. In the relation of master to slave the master does not make a point of the need that he has for the other; he has in his grasp the power of satisfying this need through his own action; whereas the slave, in his dependent condition, his hope and fear, is quite conscious of the need he has for his master. Even if the need is at bottom equally urgent for both, it always works in favor of the oppressor and against the oppressed. That is why the liberation of the working class, for example, has been slow.

Now, woman has always been man's dependent, if not his slave; the two sexes have never shared the world in equality. And even today woman is heavily handicapped, though her situation is beginning to change. Almost nowhere is her legal status the same as man's, and frequently it is much to her disadvantage. Even when her rights are legally recognized in the abstract, long-standing custom prevents their full expression in the mores. In the economic sphere men and women can almost be said to make up two castes; other things being equal, the former hold the better jobs, get higher wages, and have more opportunity for success than their new competitors. In industry and politics men have a great many more positions and they monopolize the most important posts. In addition to all this, they enjoy a traditional prestige that the education of children tends in every way to support, for the present enshrines the past—and in the past all history has been made by men. At the present time, when women are beginning to take part in the affairs of the world, it is still a world that belongs to men—they have no doubt of it at all and women have scarcely any. To decline to be the Other, to refuse to be a party to the deal—this would be for women to renounce all the advantages conferred upon them by their alliance with the superior caste. Man-the-sovereign will provide woman-the-liege with material protection and will undertake the moral justification of her existence; thus she can evade at once both economic risk and the metaphysical risk of a liberty in which ends and aims must be contrived without assistance. Indeed, along with the ethical urge of each individual to affirm his subjective existence, there is also the temptation to forgo liberty and become a thing. This is an inauspicious road, for he who takes it—passive, lost, ruined—becomes henceforth the creature of another's will, frustrated in his transcendence and deprived of every value. But it is an easy road—on it one avoids the strain involved in undertaking an authentic existence. When man makes of woman the *Other*, he may, then, expect her to manifest deep-seated tendencies toward complicity. Thus, woman may fail to lay claim to the status of subject because she lacks definite resources, because she feels the necessary bond that ties her to man regardless of reciprocity, and because she is often very well pleased with her role as the *Other*.

But it will be asked at once: how did all this begin? It is easy to see that the duality of the sexes, like any duality, gives rise to conflict. And doubtless the winner will assume the status of absolute. But why should man have won from the start? It seems possible that women could have won the victory; or that the outcome of the conflict might never have been decided. How is it that this world has always belonged to the men and that things have begun to change only recently? Is this change a good thing? Will it bring about an equal sharing of the world between men and women?

These questions are not new, and they have often been answered. But the very fact that woman is the *Other* tends to cast suspicion upon all the justifications that men have ever been able to provide for it. These have all too evidently been dictated by men's interest. A little-known feminist of the seventeenth century, Poulain de la Barre, put it this way: "All that has been written about women by men should be suspect, for the men are at once judge and party to the lawsuit." Everywhere, at all times, the males have displayed their satisfaction in feeling that they are the lords of creation. "Blessed be God . . . that he did not make me a woman," say the Jews in their morning prayers, while their wives pray on a note of resignation: "Blessed be the Lord, who created me according to his will." The first among the blessings for which Plato thanked the gods was that be had been created free, not enslaved; the second, a man, not a woman. But the males could not enjoy this privilege fully unless they believed it to be founded on the absolute and the eternal; they sought to make the fact of their supremacy into a right. "Being men, those who have made and compiled the laws have favored their own sex, and jurists have elevated these laws into principles," to quote Poulain de la Barre once more.

Legislators, priests, philosophers, writers, and scientists have striven to show that the subordinate position of woman is willed in heaven and advantageous on earth. The religions invented by men reflect this wish for domination. In the legends of Eve and Pandora men have taken up arms against women. They have made use of philosophy and theology, as the quotations from Aristotle and St. Thomas have shown. Since ancient times satirists and moralists have delighted in showing up the weaknesses of women. We are familiar with the savage indictments hurled against women throughout French literature. Montherlant, for example, follows the tradition of Jean de Meung, though with less gusto. This hostility may at times be well founded, often it is gratuitous; but in truth it more or less successfully conceals a desire for self-justification. As Montaigne says, "It is easier to accuse one sex than to excuse the other." Sometimes what is going on is clear enough. For instance, the Roman law limiting the rights of woman cited "the imbecility, the instability of the sex" just when the weakening of family ties seemed to threaten the interests of male heirs. And in the effort to keep the married woman under guardianship, appeal was made in the sixteenth century to the authority of St. Augustine, who declared that "woman is a creature neither decisive nor constant," at a time when the single woman was thought capable of managing her property. Montaigne understood clearly how arbitrary and unjust was woman's appointed lot: "Women are not in the wrong when they decline to accept the rules laid down for them, since the men make these rules without consulting them. No wonder intrigue and strife abound." But he did not go so far as to champion their cause.

It was only later, in the eighteenth century, that genuinely democratic men began to view the matter objectively. Diderot, among others, strove to show that woman is, like man, a human being. Later John Stuart Mill came fervently to her defense. But these philosophers displayed unusual impartiality. In the nineteenth century the feminist quarrel became again a quarrel of partisans. One of the consequences of the industrial revolution was the entrance of women into productive labor, and it was just here that the claims of the feminists emerged from the realm of theory and acquired an economic basis, while their opponents became the more aggressive. Although landed property lost power to some extent, the bourgeoisie clung to the old morality that found the guarantee of private property in the solidity of the family. Woman was ordered back into the home the more harshly as her emancipation became a real menace. Even within the working class the men endeavored to restrain woman's liberation, because they began to see the women as dangerous competitors—the more so because they were accustomed to work for lower wages.[6]

In proving woman's inferiority, the antifeminists then began to draw not only upon religion, philosophy, and theology, as before, but also upon science—biology, experimental psychology, etc. At most they were willing to grant "equality in difference" to the *other* sex. That profitable formula is most significant; it is precisely like the "equal but separate" formula of the Jim Crow laws aimed at the North American Negroes. As is well known, this so-called equalitarian segregation has resulted only in the most extreme discrimination. The similarity just noted is in no way due to chance, for whether it is a race, a caste, a class, or a sex that is reduced to a position of inferiority, the methods of justification are the same. "The eternal feminine" corresponds to "the black soul" and to "the Jewish character." True, the Jewish problem is on the whole very different from the other two—to the anti-Semite the Jew is not so much an inferior as he is an enemy for whom there is to be granted no place on earth, for whom annihilation is the fate desired. But there are deep similarities between the situation of woman and that of the Negro. Both are being emancipated today from a like paternalism, and the former master class wishes to "keep them in their place"—that is, the place chosen for them. In both cases the former masters lavish more or less sincere eulogies, either on the virtues of "the good Negro" with his dormant, childish, merry soul—the submissive Negro—or on the merits of the woman who is "truly feminine"—that is, frivolous, infantile, irresponsible—the submissive woman. In both cases the dominant class bases its argument on a state of affairs that it has itself created. As George Bernard Shaw puts it, in substance, "The American white relegates its black to the rank of shoeshine boy; and he concludes from this that the black is good for nothing but shining shoes." This vicious circle is met with in all analogous circumstances; when an individual (or a group of individuals) is kept in a situation of inferiority, the fact is that he *is* inferior. But the significance of the verb *to be* must be rightly understood here; it is in bad faith to give it a static value when it really has the dynamic Hegelian sense of "to have become." Yes, women on the whole today *are* inferior to men; that is, their situation affords them fewer possibilities. The question is: should that state of affairs continue?

Many men hope that it will continue; not all have given up the battle. The conservative bourgeoisie still see in the emancipation of women a menace to their morality and their interests. Some men dread feminine competition. Recently a male student wrote in the *Hebdo-Latin*: "Every woman student who goes into medicine or law robs us of a job." He never

6. See Part II, pp. 115–17.

questioned his rights in this world. And economic interests are not the only ones concerned. One of the benefits that oppression confers upon the oppressors is that the most humble among them is made to *feel* superior; thus, a "poor white" in the South can console himself with the thought that he is not a "dirty nigger"—and the more prosperous whites cleverly exploit this pride.

Similarly, the most mediocre of males feels himself a demigod as compared with women. It was much easier for M. de Montherlant to think himself a hero when he faced women (and women chosen for his purpose) than when he was obliged to act the man among men—something many women have done better than he, for that matter. And in September 1948, in one of his articles in the *Figaro littéraire*, Claude Mauriac—whose great originality is admired by all—could[7] write regarding woman: "*We* listen on a tone [*sic!*] of polite indifference . . . to the most brilliant among them, well knowing that her wit reflects more or less luminously ideas that come from *us*." Evidently the speaker referred to is not reflecting the ideas of Mauriac himself, for no one knows of his having any. It may be that she reflects ideas originating with men, but then, even among men there are those who have been known to appropriate ideas not their own; and one can well ask whether Claude Mauriac might not find more interesting a conversation reflecting Descartes, Marx, or Gide rather than himself. What is really remarkable is that by using the questionable *we* he identifies himself with St. Paul, Hegel, Lenin, and Nietzsche, and from the lofty eminence of their grandeur looks down disdainfully upon the bevy of women who make bold to converse with him on a footing of equality. In truth, I know of more than one woman who would refuse to suffer with patience Mauriac's "tone of polite indifference."

I have lingered on this example because the masculine attitude is here displayed with disarming ingenuousness. But men profit in many more subtle ways from the otherness, the alterity of woman. Here is miraculous balm for those afflicted with an inferiority complex, and indeed no one is more arrogant toward women, more aggressive or scornful, than the man who is anxious about his virility. Those who are not fear-ridden in the presence of their fellow men are much more disposed to recognize a fellow creature in woman; but even to these the myth of Woman, the Other, is precious for many reasons.[8] They cannot be blamed for not cheerfully

7. Or at least he thought he could.
8. A significant article on this theme by Michel Carrouges appeared in No. 292 of the *Cahiers du Sud*. He writes indignantly: "Would that there were no woman-myth at all but only a cohort of cooks, matrons, prostitutes, and bluestockings serving functions of pleasure or usefulness!" That is to say, in his view woman has no existence in and for herself; he thinks only of her *function* in the male world. Her reason for existence lies in man. But then, in fact, her poetic "function" as a myth might be more valued than any other. The real problem is precisely to find out why woman should be defined with relation to man.

relinquishing all the benefits they derive from the myth, for they realize what they would lose in relinquishing woman as they fancy her to be, while they fail to realize what they have to gain from the woman of tomorrow. Refusal to pose oneself as the Subject, unique and absolute, requires great self-denial. Furthermore, the vast majority of men make no such claim explicitly. They do not *postulate* woman as inferior, for today they are too thoroughly imbued with the ideal of democracy not to recognize all human beings as equals.

In the bosom of the family, woman seems in the eyes of childhood and youth to be clothed in the same social dignity as the adult males. Later on, the young man, desiring and loving, experiences the resistance, the independence of the woman desired and loved; in marriage, he respects woman as wife and mother, and in the concrete events of conjugal life she stands there before him as a free being. He can therefore feel that social subordination as between the sexes no longer exists and that on the whole, in spite of differences, woman is an equal. As, however, he observes some points of inferiority—the most important being unfitness for the professions—he attributes these to natural causes. When he is in a cooperative and benevolent relation with woman, his theme is the principle of abstract equality, and he does not base his attitude upon such inequality as may exist. But when he is in conflict with her, the situation is reversed: his theme will be the existing inequality, and he will even take it as justification for denying abstract equality.[9]

So it is that many men will affirm as if in good faith that women *are* the equals of man and that they have nothing to clamor for, while *at the same time* they will say that women can never be the equals of man and that their demands are in vain. It is, in point of fact, a difficult matter for man to realize the extreme importance of social discriminations which seem outwardly insignificant but which produce in woman moral and intellectual effects so profound that they appear to spring from her original nature.[10] The most sympathetic of men never fully comprehend woman's concrete situation. And there is no reason to put much trust in the men when they rush to the defense of privileges whose full extent they can hardly measure. We shall not, then, permit ourselves to be intimidated by the number and violence of the attacks launched against women, nor to be entrapped by the self-seeking eulogies bestowed on the "true woman," nor to profit by the enthusiasm for woman's destiny manifested by men who would not for the world have any part of it.

9. For example, a man will say that he considers his wife in no wise degraded because she has no gainful occupation. The profession of housewife is just as lofty, and so on. But when the first quarrel comes, he will exclaim: "Why, you couldn't make your living without me!"
10. The specific purpose of Book Two of this study is to describe this process.

We should consider the arguments of the feminists with no less suspicion, however, for very often their controversial aim deprives them of all real value. If the "woman question" seems trivial, it is because masculine arrogance has made of it a "quarrel"; and when quarreling one no longer reasons well. People have tirelessly sought to prove that woman is superior, inferior, or equal to man. Some say that, having been created after Adam, she is evidently a secondary being; others say on the contrary that Adam was only a rough draft and that God succeeded in producing the human being in perfection when he created Eve. Woman's brain is smaller; yes, but it is relatively larger. Christ was made a man; yes, but perhaps for his greater humility. Each argument at once suggests its opposite, and both are often fallacious. If we are to gain understanding, we must get out of these ruts; we must discard the vague notions of superiority, inferiority, equality which have hitherto corrupted every discussion of the subject and start afresh.

Very well, but just how shall we pose the question? And, to begin with, who are we to propound it at all? Man is at once judge and party to the case; but so is woman. What we need is an angel—neither man nor woman—but where shall we find one? Still, the angel would be poorly qualified to speak, for an angel is ignorant of all the basic facts involved in the problem. With a hermaphrodite we should be no better off, for here the situation is most peculiar; the hermaphrodite is not really the combination of a whole man and a whole woman, but consists of parts of each and thus is neither. It looks to me as if there are, after all, certain women who are best qualified to elucidate the situation of woman. Let us not be misled by the sophism that because Epimenides was a Cretan he was necessarily a liar; it is not a mysterious essence that compels men and women to act in good or in bad faith, it is their situation that inclines them more or less toward the search for truth. Many of today's women, fortunate in the restoration of all the privileges pertaining to the estate of the human being, can afford the luxury of impartiality—we even recognize its necessity. We are no longer like our partisan elders; by and large we have won the game. In recent debates on the status of women the United Nations has persistently maintained that the equality of the sexes is now becoming a reality, and already some of us have never had to sense in our femininity an inconvenience or an obstacle. Many problems appear to us to be more pressing than those which concern us in particular, and this detachment even allows us to hope that our attitude will be objective. Still, we know the feminine world more intimately than do the men because we have our roots in it, we grasp more immediately than do men what it means to a human being to be feminine; and we are more concerned with such knowledge. I have said that there are more pressing problems, but this does not prevent us from seeing some importance in asking how the fact of being women will affect our lives. What opportunities precisely have been given us and what withheld? What fate awaits our younger sisters, and what directions should they take? It is significant that books by women on women are in general animated in our day less by a wish to demand our rights than by an effort toward clarity and understanding. As we emerge from an era of excessive controversy, this book is offered as one attempt among others to confirm that statement.

But it is doubtless impossible to approach any human problem with a mind free from bias. The way in which questions are put, the points of view assumed, presuppose a relativity of interest; all characteristics imply values, and every objective description, so called, implies an ethical background. Rather than attempt to conceal principles more or less definitely implied, it is better to state them openly at the beginning. This will make it unnecessary to specify on every page in just what sense one uses such words as *superior*, *inferior*, *better*, *worse*, *progress*, *reaction*, and the like. If we survey some of the works on woman, we note that one of the points of view most frequently adopted is that of the public good, the general interest; and one always means by this the benefit of society as one wishes it to be maintained or established. For our part, we hold that the only public good is that which assures the private good of the citizens; we shall pass judgment on institutions according to their effectiveness in giving concrete opportunities to individuals. But we do not confuse the idea of private interest with that of happiness, although that is another common point of view. Are not women of the harem more happy than women voters? Is not the housekeeper happier than the workingwoman? It is not too clear just what the word *happy* really means and still less what true values it may mask. There is no possibility of measuring the happiness of others, and it is always easy to describe as happy the situation in which one wishes to place them.

In particular those who are condemned to stagnation are often pronounced happy on the pretext that happiness consists in being at rest. This notion we reject, for our perspective is that of existentialist ethics. Every subject plays his part as such specifically through exploits or projects that serve as a mode of transcendence; he achieves liberty only through a continual reaching out toward other liberties. There is no justification for present existence other than its expansion into an indefinitely open future. Every time transcendence falls back into immanence, stagnation, there is a degradation of existence into the *en-soi*—the brutish life of subjection to given conditions—and of liberty into constraint and contingence. This downfall represents a moral fault if the subject consents to it; if it is inflicted upon him, it spells frustration and oppression. In both cases it is an absolute evil. Every individual concerned to justify his existence feels that his existence involves an undefined need to transcend himself, to engage in freely chosen projects.

Now, what peculiarly signalizes the situation of woman is that she—a free and autonomous being like all human creatures—nevertheless finds herself living in a world where men compel her to assume the status of the Other. They propose to stabilize her as object and to doom her to immanence since her transcendence is to be overshadowed and forever transcended by another ego (conscience) which is essential and sovereign. The drama of woman lies in this conflict between the fundamental aspirations of every subject (ego)—who always regards the self as the essential—and the compulsions of a situation in which she is the inessential. How can a human being in woman's situation attain fulfillment? What roads are open to her? Which are blocked? How can independence be recovered in a state of dependency? What circumstances limit woman's liberty and how can they be overcome? These are the fundamental questions on which I would fain throw some light. This means that I am interested in the fortunes of the individual as defined not in terms of happiness but in terms of liberty.

Quite evidently this problem would be without significance if we were to believe that woman's destiny is inevitably determined by physiological, psychological, or economic forces. Hence I shall discuss first of all the light in which woman is viewed by biology, psychoanalysis, and historical materialism. Next I shall try to show exactly how the concept of the "truly feminine" has been fashioned—why woman has been defined as the Other—and what have been the consequences from man's point of view. Then from woman's point of view I shall describe the world in which women must live, and thus we shall be able to envisage the difficulties in their way as, endeavoring to make their escape from the sphere hitherto assigned them, they aspire to full membership in the human race.

The women of today are in a fair way to dethrone the myth of femininity; they are beginning to affirm their independence in concrete ways; but they do not easily succeed in living completely the life of a human being. Reared by women within a feminine world, their normal destiny is marriage, which still means practically subordination to man; for masculine prestige is far from extinction, resting still upon solid economic and social foundations. We must therefore study the traditional destiny of woman with some care. In Book Two I shall seek to describe how woman undergoes her apprenticeship, how she experiences her situation, in what kind of universe she is confined, what modes of escape are vouchsafed her.

Then only—with so much understood—shall we be able to comprehend the problems of women, the heirs of a burdensome past, who are striving to build a new future. When I use the words *woman* or *feminine* I evidently refer to no archetype, no changeless essence whatever; the reader must understand the phrase "in the present state of education and custom" after most of my statements. It is not our concern here to proclaim eternal verities, but rather to describe the common basis that underlies every individual feminine existence.

QUESTIONS

1. What answer does Beauvoir suggest to her question, "What is a woman?" (289, 291)

2. Why does Beauvoir say that "if today femininity no longer exists, then it never existed"? (290)

3. What does Beauvoir mean when she says that American women are "haunted by a sense of their femininity"? (290)

4. According to Beauvoir, why don't women dispute "male sovereignty"? (293)

5. Why does Beauvoir say that women have gained "only what men have been willing to grant"? (294)

6. How does Beauvoir explain why women "have no past, no history, no religion of their own"? (294)

7. Does Beauvoir suggest that the inferior status of women is a consequence of the male "inferiority complex"? (299)

8. Why does Beauvoir say that "the real problem is precisely to find out why woman should be defined with relation to man"? (299, footnote 8)

9. Why does Beauvoir say that men claim women are their equals while, at the same time, they say "that women can never be the equals of man"? (300)

10. Why does Beauvoir say that "we should consider the arguments of the feminists" with "suspicion"? (301)

11. What does Beauvoir mean when she writes, "If we are to gain understanding, . . . we must discard the vague notions of superiority, inferiority, equality"? (301)

12. What distinction does Beauvoir draw between happiness and liberty?

13. What does Beauvoir mean when she says, "The drama of woman lies in [the] conflict between the fundamental aspirations of every subject (ego) . . . and the compulsions of a situation in which she is the inessential"? (303)

FOR FURTHER REFLECTION

1. Does Beauvoir suggest that women must behave more like men in order to succeed?
2. Does Beauvoir believe that one day women will cease to be considered as "the Other"?
3. If we perfectly embrace the ideal of democracy, does the notion of "the Other" disappear?
4. Does Beauvoir believe that men are capable of understanding a "woman's concrete situation"?
5. What hints does Beauvoir provide as to how a human being in a woman's situation can begin to attain fulfillment?

GRACE PALEY

Grace Paley (1922–) was born to Russian immigrant parents in the Bronx, New York. She grew up in a neighborhood "so dense with Jews I thought we were the great imposing majority." Countless stories told by her father and aunts colored her childhood and provided material for her later writing. She grew up hearing Russian, Yiddish, and English—no doubt contributing to her unique writing voice. Paley briefly attended Hunter College, then studied poetry with W. H. Auden at the New School for Social Research. She married at the age of nineteen and had two children, but soon separated from her husband.

Writing only poetry into her thirties, Paley published her first book of stories, *The Little Disturbances of Man*, in 1959. In its focus on the details of women's everyday lives, the book now seems a forerunner to the feminism that would take hold during the 1960s. Paley had also become an antinuclear activist in the 1950s, and her devotion to political causes has continued throughout her life. One of the founders of the Greenwich Village Peace Center, Paley was jailed for her participation in protests against the Vietnam War. She has visited Hanoi and Moscow as a member of peace delegations, and she remains a vibrant voice denouncing war and advocating human rights, considering herself a "somewhat combative pacifist and cooperative anarchist." In a 1998 *Salon* interview she said, "Whatever your calling is, whether it's as a plumber or an artist, you have to make sure there's a little more justice in the world when you leave it than when you found it."

Paley's reputation as a masterful short-story writer grew with the publication of *Enormous Changes at the Last Minute* (1974) and *Later the Same Day* (1985). *The Collected Stories* (1994) won the National Book Award. Paley is also the author of *Just As I Thought* (1998), a collection of essays, and *Begin Again: Collected Poems* (2000). She has received awards and grants from the Guggenheim Foundation, the National Endowment for the Arts, and the National

Institute of Arts and Letters. She has taught at the City College of New York, Columbia University, Sarah Lawrence College, and Syracuse University.

Paley has said that she is interested in "a history of everyday life," implying that this history is separate from what passes for history in textbooks. She asks us to examine our assumptions about the roles we play in various contexts and the nature of the forces that shape our experience. In "An Interest in Life," Paley is especially concerned with relationships between women and men, the dynamics of family, and the inscrutable aspects of desire.

GRACE PALEY

An Interest in Life

My husband gave me a broom one Christmas. This wasn't right. No one can tell me it was meant kindly.

"I don't want you not to have anything for Christmas while I'm away in the Army," he said. "Virginia, please look at it. It comes with this fancy dustpan. It hangs off a stick. Look at it, will you? Are you blind or cross-eyed?"

"Thanks, chum," I said. I had always wanted a dustpan hooked up that way. It was a good one. My husband doesn't shop in bargain basements or January sales.

Still and all, in spite of the quality, it was a mean present to give a woman you planned on never seeing again, a person you had children with and got onto all the time, drunk or sober, even when everybody had to get up early in the morning.

I asked him if he could wait and join the Army in a half hour, as I had to get the groceries. I don't like to leave kids alone in a three-room apartment full of gas and electricity. Fire may break out from a nasty remark. Or the oldest decides to get even with the youngest.

"Just this once," he said. "But you better figure out how to get along without me."

"You're a handicapped person mentally," I said. "You should've been institutionalized years ago." I slammed the door. I didn't want to see him pack his underwear and ironed shirts.

I never got further than the front stoop, though, because there was Mrs. Raftery, wringing her hands, tears in her eyes as though she had a monopoly on all the good news.

"Mrs. Raftery!" I said, putting my arm around her. "Don't cry." She leaned on me because I am such a horsy build. "Don't cry, Mrs. Raftery, please!" I said.

"That's like you, Virginia. Always looking at the ugly side of things. 'Take in the wash. It's rainin'!' That's you. You're the first one knows it when the dumbwaiter breaks."

"Oh, come on now, that's not so. It just isn't so," I said. "I'm the exact opposite."

"Did you see Mrs. Cullen yet?" she asked, paying no attention.

"Where?"

"Virginia!" she said, shocked. "She's passed away. The whole house knows it. They've got her in white like a bride and you never saw a beautiful creature like that. She must be eighty. Her husband's proud."

"She was never more than an acquaintance; she didn't have any children," I said.

"Well, I don't care about that. Now, Virginia, you do what I say now, you go downstairs and you say like this—listen to me—say, 'I hear, Mr. Cullen, your wife's passed away. I'm sorry.' Then ask him how he is. Then you ought to go around the corner and see her. She's in Witson & Wayde. Then you ought to go over to the church when they carry her over."

"It's not my church," I said.

"That's no reason, Virginia. You go up like this," she said, parting from me to do a prancy dance. "Up the big front steps, into the church you go. It's beautiful in there. You can't help kneeling only for a minute. Then round to the right. Then up the other stairway. Then you come to a great oak door that's arched above you, then," she said, seizing a deep, deep breath, for all the good it would do her, "and then turn the knob slo-owly and open the door and see for yourself: Our Blessed Mother is in charge. Beautiful. Beautiful. Beautiful."

I sighed in and I groaned out, so as to melt a certain pain around my heart. A steel ring like arthritis, at my age.

"You are a groaner," Mrs. Raftery said, gawking into my mouth.

"I am not," I said. I got a whiff of her, a terrible cheap wine lush.

My husband threw a penny at the door from the inside to take my notice from Mrs. Raftery. He rattled the glass door to make sure I looked at him. He had a fat duffel bag on each shoulder. Where did be acquire so much worldly possession? What was in them? My grandma's goose feathers from across the ocean? Or all the diaper-service diapers? To this day the truth is shrouded in mystery.

"What the hell are you doing, Virginia?" he said, dumping them at my feet. "Standing out here on your hind legs telling everybody your business? The Army gives you a certain time, for God's sakes, they're not kidding." Then he said, "I beg your pardon," to Mrs. Raftery. He took hold of me with his two arms as though in love and pressed his body hard against mine so that I could feel him for the last time and suffer my loss. Then he kissed me in a mean way to nearly split my lip. Then he winked and said, "That's all for now," and skipped off into the future, duffel bags full of rags.

He left me in an embarrassing situation, nearly fainting, in front of that old widow, who can't even remember the half of it. "He's a crock," said Mrs. Raftery. "Is he leaving for good or just temporarily, Virginia?"

"Oh, he's probably deserting me," I said, and sat down on the stoop, pulling my big knees up to my chin.

"If that's the case, tell the Welfare right away," she said. "He's a bum, leaving you just before Christmas. Tell the cops," she said. "They'll provide the toys for the little kids gladly. And don't forget to let the grocer in on it. He won't be so hard on you expecting payment."

She saw that sadness was stretched worldwide across my face. Mrs. Raftery isn't the worst person. She said, "Look around for comfort, dear." With a nervous finger she pointed to the truckers eating lunch on their haunches across the street, leaning on the loading platforms. She waved her hand to include in all the men marching up and down in search of a decent luncheonette. She didn't leave out the six longshoremen loafing under the fish-market marquee. "If their lungs and stomachs ain't crushed by overwork, they disappear somewhere in the world. Don't be disappointed, Virginia. I don't know a man living'd last you a lifetime."

Ten days later Girard asked, "Where's Daddy?"

"Ask me no questions, I'll tell you no lies." I didn't want the children to know the facts. Present or past, a child should have a father.

"Where *is* Daddy?" Girard asked the week after that.

"He joined the Army," I said.

"He made my bunk bed," said Phillip.

"The truth shall make ye free," I said.

Then I sat down with pencil and pad to get in control of my resources. The facts, when I added and subtracted them, were that my husband had left me with fourteen dollars, and the rent unpaid, in an emergency state. He'd claimed he was sorry to do this, but my opinion is, out of sight, out of mind. "The city won't let you starve," he'd said. "After all, you're half the population. You're keeping up the good work. Without you the race would die out. Who'd pay the taxes? Who'd keep the streets clean? There wouldn't be no Army. A man like me wouldn't have no place to go."

I sent Girard right down to Mrs. Raftery with a request about the whereabouts of Welfare. She responded RSVP with an extra comment in left-handed script: "Poor Girard . . . he's never the boy my John was!"

Who asked her?

I called on Welfare right after the New Year. In no time I discovered that they're rigged up to deal with liars, and if you're truthful it's disappointing to them. They may even refuse to handle your case if you're too truthful.

They asked sensible questions at first. They asked where my husband had enlisted. I didn't know. They put some letter writers and agents after him. "He's not in the United States Army," they said. "Try the Brazilian Army," I suggested.

They have no sense of kidding around. They're not the least bit light-hearted and they tried. "Oh no," they said. "That was incorrect. He is not in the Brazilian Army."

"No?" I said. "How strange! He must be in the Mexican Navy."

By law, they had to hound his brothers. They wrote to his brother who has a first-class card in the Teamsters and owns an apartment house in California. They asked his two brothers in Jersey to help me. They have large families. Rightfully they laughed. Then they wrote to Thomas, the oldest, the smart one (the one they all worked so hard for years to keep him in college until his brains could pay off). He was the one who sent ten dollars immediately, saying, "What a bastard! I'll send something time to time, Ginny, but whatever you do, don't tell the authorities." Of course I never did. Soon they began to guess they were better people than me, that I was in trouble because I deserved it, and then they liked me better.

But they never fixed my refrigerator. Every time I called I said patiently, "The milk is sour . . ." I said, "Corn beef went bad." Sitting in that beer-stinking phone booth in Felan's for the sixth time (sixty cents) with the baby on my lap and Barbie tapping at the glass door with an American flag, I cried into the secretary's hardhearted ear, "I bought real butter for the holiday, and it's rancid . . ." They said, "You'll have to get a better bid on the repair job."

While I waited indoors for a man to bid, Girard took to swinging back and forth on top of the bathroom door, just to soothe himself, giving me the laugh, dreamy, nibbling calcimine off the ceiling. On first sight Mrs. Raftery said, "Whack the monkey, he'd be better off on arsenic."

But Girard is my son and I'm the judge. It means a terrible thing for the future, though I don't know what to call it.

It was from constantly thinking of my foreknowledge on this and other subjects, it was from observing when I put my lipstick on daily, how my face was just curling up to die, that John Raftery came from Jersey to rescue me.

On Thursdays, anyway, John Raftery took the tubes in to visit his mother. The whole house knew it. She was cheerful even before breakfast. She sang out loud in a girlish brogue that only came to tongue for grand occasions. Hanging out the wash, she blushed to recall what a remarkable boy her John had been. "Ask the sisters around the corner," she said to the open kitchen windows. "They'll never forget John."

That particular night after supper Mrs. Raftery said to her son, "John, how come you don't say hello to your old friend Virginia? She's had hard luck and she's gloomy."

"Is that so, Mother?" he said, and immediately climbed two flights to knock at my door.

"Oh, John," I said at the sight of him, hat in hand in a white shirt and blue-striped tie, spick-and-span, a Sunday-school man. "Hello!"

"Welcome, John!" I said. "Sit down. Come right in. How are you? You look awfully good. You do. Tell me, how've you been all this time, John?"

"How've I been?" he asked thoughtfully. To answer within reason, he described his life with Margaret, marriage, work, and children up to the present day.

I had nothing good to report. Now that he had put the subject around before my very eyes, every burnt-up day of my life smoked in shame, and I couldn't even get a clear view of the good half hours.

"Of course," he said, "you do have lovely children. Noticeable-looking, Virginia. Good looks is always something to be thankful for."

"Thankful?" I said. "I don't have to thank anything but my own foolishness for four children when I'm twenty-six years old, deserted, and poverty-struck, regardless of looks. A man can't help it, but I could have behaved better."

"Don't be so cruel on yourself, Ginny," he said. "Children come from God."

"You're still great on holy subjects, aren't you? You know damn well where children come from."

He did know. His red face reddened further. John Raftery has had that color coming out on him boy and man from keeping his rages so inward.

Still he made more sense in his conversation after that, and I poured fresh tea to tell him how my husband used to like me because I was a passionate person. That was until he took a look around and saw how in the long run this life only meant more of the same thing. He tried to turn away from me once he came to this understanding, and make me hate him. His face changed. He gave up his brand of cigarettes, which we had in common. He threw out the two pairs of socks I knitted by hand. "If there's anything I hate in this world, it's navy blue," he said. Oh, I could have dyed them. I would have done anything for him, if he were only not too sorry to ask me.

"You were a nice kid in those days" said John, referring to certain Saturday nights. "A wild, nice kid."

"Aaah," I said, disgusted. Whatever I was then, was on the way to where I am now. "I was fresh. If I had a kid like me, I'd slap her cross-eyed."

The very next Thursday John gave me a beautiful radio with a record player. "Enjoy yourself," he said. That really made Welfare speechless. We didn't own any records, but the investigator saw my burden was lightened and he scribbled a dozen pages about it in his notebook.

On the third Thursday he brought a walking doll (twenty-four inches) for Linda and Barbie with a card inscribed, "A baby doll for a couple of dolls." He had also had a couple of drinks at his mother's, and this made him want to dance. "La-la-la," he sang, a ramrod swaying in my kitchen chair. "La-la-la, let yourself go . . ."

"You gotta give a little," he sang, "live a little . . ." He said, "Virginia, may I have this dance?"

"Sssh, we finally got them asleep. Please, turn the radio down. Quiet. Deathly silence, John Raftery."

"Let me do your dishes, Virginia."

"Don't be silly, you're a guest in my house," I said. "I still regard you as a guest."

"I want to do something for you, Virginia."

"Tell me I'm the most gorgeous thing," I said, dipping my arm to the funny bone in dish soup.

He didn't answer. "I'm having a lot of trouble at work," was all he said. Then I heard him push the chair back. He came up behind me, put his arms around my waistline, and kissed my cheek. He whirled me around and took my hands. He said, "An old friend is better than rubies." He looked me in the eye. He held my attention by trying to be honest. And he kissed me a short sweet kiss on my mouth.

"Please sit down, Virginia," he said. He kneeled before me and put his head in my lap. I was stirred by so much activity. Then he looked up at me and, as though proposing marriage for life, he offered—because he was drunk—to place his immortal soul in peril to comfort me.

First I said, "Thank you." Then I said, "No."

I was sorry for him, but he's devout, a leader of the Fathers' Club at his church, active in all the lay groups for charities, orphans, etc. I knew that if he stayed late to love with me, he would not do it lightly but would in the end pay terrible penance and ruin his long life. The responsibility would be on me.

So I said no.

And Barbie is such a light sleeper. All she has to do, I thought, is wake up and wander in and see her mother and her new friend John with his pants around his knees, wrestling on the kitchen table. A vision like that could affect a kid for life.

I said no.

Everyone in this building is so goddamn nosy. That evening I had to say no.

But John came to visit, anyway, on the fourth Thursday. This time he brought the discarded dresses of Margaret's daughters, organdy party dresses and glazed cotton for every day. He gently admired Barbara and Linda, his blue eyes rolling to back up a couple of dozen oohs and ahs.

Even Phillip, who thinks God gave him just a certain number of hellos and he better save them for the final judgment, Phillip leaned on John and said, "Why don't you bring your boy to play with me? I don't have nobody who to play with." (Phillip's a liar. There must be at least seventy-one children in this house, pale pink to medium brown, English-talking and gibbering in Spanish, rough-and-tough boys, the Lone Ranger's bloody pals, or the exact picture of Supermouse. If a boy wanted a friend, he could pick the very one out of his neighbors.)

Also, Girard is a cold fish. He was in a lonesome despair. Sometimes he looked in the mirror and said, "How come I have such an ugly face? My nose is funny. Mostly people don't like me." He was a liar too. Girard has a face like his father's. His eyes are the color of those little blue plums in August. He looks like an advertisement in a magazine. He could be a child model and make a lot of money. He is my first child, and if he thinks he is ugly, I think I am ugly.

John said, "I can't stand to see a boy mope like that . . . What do the sisters say in school?"

"He doesn't pay attention is all they say. You can't get much out of them."

"My middle boy was like that," said John. "Couldn't take an interest. Aaah, I wish I didn't have all that headache on the job. I'd grab Girard by the collar and make him take notice of the world. I wish I could ask him out to Jersey to play in all that space."

"Why not?" I said.

"Why, Virginia, I'm surprised you don't know why not. You know I can't take your children out to meet my children."

I felt a lot of strong arthritis in my ribs.

"My mother's the funny one, Virginia." He felt he had to continue with the subject matter. "I don't know. I guess she likes the idea of bugging Margaret. She says, 'You goin' up, John?' 'Yes, Mother,' I say. 'Behave yourself, John,' she says. 'That husband might come home and hacksaw you into hell. You're a Catholic man, John,' she says. But I figured it out. She likes to know I'm in the building. I swear, Virginia, she wishes me the best of luck."

"I do too, John," I said. We drank a last glass of beer to make sure of a peaceful sleep. "Good night, Virginia," he said, looping his muffler neatly under his chin. "Don't worry. I'll be thinking of what to do about Girard."

I got into the big bed that I share with the girls in the little room. For once I had no trouble falling asleep. I only had to worry about Linda and

Barbara and Phillip. It was a great relief to me that John had taken over the thinking about Girard.

John was sincere. That's true. He paid a lot of attention to Girard, smoking out all his sneaky sorrows. He registered him into a wild pack of Cub Scouts that went up to the Bronx once a week to let off steam. He gave him a Junior Erector Set. And sometimes when his family wasn't listening he prayed at great length for him.

One Sunday, Sister Veronica said in her sweet voice from another life, "He's not worse. He might even be a little better. How are *you*, Virginia?" putting her hand on mine. Everybody around here acts like they know everything.

"Just fine," I said.

"We ought to start on Phillip," John said, "if it's true Girard's improving."

"You should've been a social worker, John."

"A lot of people have noticed that about me," said John.

"Your mother was always acting so crazy about you, how come she didn't knock herself out a little to see you in college? Like we did for Thomas?"

"Now, Virginia, be fair. She's a poor old woman. My father was a weak earner. She had to have my wages, and I'll tell you, Virginia, I'm not sorry. Look at Thomas. He's still in school. Drop him in this jungle and he'd be devoured. He hasn't had a touch of real life. And here I am with a good chunk of a family, a home of my own, a name in the building trades. One thing I have to tell you, the poor old woman is sorry. I said one day (oh, in passing—years ago) that I might marry you. She stuck a knife in herself. It's a fact. Not more than an eighth of an inch. You never saw such a gory Sunday. One thing—you would have been a better daughter-in-law to her than Margaret."

"Marry me?" I said.

"Well, yes. . . . Aaah—I always liked you, then . . . Why do you think I'd sit in the shade of this kitchen every Thursday night? For God's sakes, the only warm thing around here is this teacup. Yes, sir, I did want to marry you, Virginia."

"No kidding, John? Really?" It was nice to know. Better late than never, to learn you were desired in youth.

I didn't tell John, but the truth is, I would never have married him. Once I met my husband with his winking looks, he was my only interest. Wild as I had been with John and others, I turned all my wildness over to him and then there was no question in my mind.

Still, face facts, if my husband didn't budge on in life, it was my fault. On me, as they say, be it. I greeted the morn with a song. I had a hello for everyone but the landlord. Ask the people on the block, come or go—even the Spanish ones, with their sad dark faces—they have to smile when they see me.

But for his own comfort, he should have done better lifewise and moneywise. I was happy, but I am now in possession of knowledge that this is wrong. Happiness isn't so bad for a woman. She gets fatter, she gets older, she could lie down, nuzzling a regiment of men and little kids, she could just die of the pleasure. But men are different, they have to own money, or they have to be famous, or everybody on the block has to look up to them from the cellar stairs.

A woman counts her children and acts snotty, like she invented life, but men *must* do well in the world. I know that men are not fooled by being happy.

"A funny guy," said John, guessing where my thoughts had gone. "What stopped him up? He was nobody's fool. He had a funny thing about him, Virginia, if you don't mind my saying so. He wasn't much distance up, but he was all set and ready to be looking down on us all."

"He was very smart, John. You don't realize that. His hobby was crossword puzzles, and I said to him real often, as did others around here, that he ought to go out on *The $64 Question*. Why not? But he laughed. You know what he said? He said, 'That proves how dumb you are if you think I'm smart.'"

"A funny guy," said John. "Get it all off your chest," he said. "Talk it out, Virginia; it's the only way to kill the pain."

By and large, I was happy to oblige. Still I could not carry through about certain cruel remarks. It was like trying to move back into the dry mouth of a nightmare to remember that the last day I was happy was the middle of a week in March, when I told my husband I was going to have Linda. Barbara was five months old to the hour. The boys were three and four. I had to tell him. It was the last day with anything happy about it.

Later on he said, "Oh, you make me so sick, you're so goddamn big and fat, you look like a goddamn brownstone, the way you're squared off in front."

"Well, where are you going tonight?" I asked.

"How should I know?" he said. "Your big ass takes up the whole goddamn bed," he said. "There's no room for me." He bought a sleeping bag and slept on the floor.

I couldn't believe it. I would start every morning fresh. I couldn't believe that he would turn against me so, while I was still young and even his friends still liked me.

But he did, he turned absolutely against me and became no friend of mine. "All you ever think about is making babies. This place stinks like the men's room in the BMT. It's a fucking pissoir." He was strong on truth all through the year. "That kid eats more than the five of us put together," he said. "Stop stuffing your face, you fat dumbbell," he said to Phillip.

Then he worked on the neighbors. "Get that nosy old bag out of here," he said. "If she comes on once more with 'my son in the building trades' I'll squash her for the cat."

Then he turned on Spielvogel, the checker, his oldest friend, who only visited on holidays and never spoke to me (shy, the way some bachelors are). "That sonofabitch, don't hand me that friendship crap, all he's after is your ass. That's what I need—a little shitmaker of his using up the air in this flat."

And then there was no one else to dispose of. We were left alone fair and square, facing each other.

"Now, Virginia," he said, "I come to the end of my rope. I see a black wall ahead of me. What the hell am I supposed to do? I only got one life. Should I lie down and die? I don't know what to do anymore. I'll give it to you straight, Virginia, if I stick around, you can't help it, you'll hate me . . ."

"I hate you right now," I said. "So do whatever you like."

"This place drives me nuts," he mumbled. "I don't know what to do around here. I want to get you a present. Something."

"I told you, do whatever you like. Buy me a rattrap for rats."

That's when he went down to the House Appliance Store, and he brought back a new broom and a classy dustpan.

"A new broom sweeps clean," he said. "I got to get out of here," he said. "I'm going nuts." Then he began to stuff the duffel bags, and I went to the grocery store but was stopped by Mrs. Raftery, who had to tell me what she considered so beautiful—death—then he kissed and went to join some army somewhere.

I didn't tell John any of this, because I think it makes a woman look too bad to tell on how another man has treated her. He begins to see her through the other man's eyes, a sitting duck, a skinful of flaws. After all, I had come to depend on John. All my husband's friends were strangers now, though I had always said to them, "Feel welcome."

And the family men in the building looked too cunning, as though they had all personally deserted me. If they met me on the stairs, they carried the heaviest groceries up and helped bring Linda's stroller down, but they never asked me a question worth answering at all.

Besides that, Girard and Phillip taught the girls the days of the week: Monday, Tuesday, Wednesday, Johnday, Friday. They waited for him once a week, under the hallway lamp, half-asleep like bugs in the sun, sitting in their little chairs with their names on in gold, a birth present from my mother-in-law. At fifteen after eight he punctually came, to read a story, pass out some kisses, and tuck them into bed.

But one night, after a long Johnday of them squealing my eardrum split, after a rainy afternoon with brother constantly raising up his hand against brother, with the girls near ready to go to court over the proper ownership of Melinda Lee, the twenty-four-inch walking doll, the doorbell rang three times. Not any of those times did John's face greet me.

I was too ashamed to call down to Mrs. Raftery, and she was too mean to knock on my door and explain.

He didn't come the following Thursday either. Girard said sadly, "He must've run away, John."

I had to give him up after two weeks' absence and no word. I didn't know how to tell the children: something about right and wrong, goodness and meanness, men and women. I had it all at my fingertips, ready to hand over. But I didn't think I ought to take mistakes and truth away from them. Who knows? They might make a truer friend in this world somewhere than I have ever made. So I just put them to bed and sat in the kitchen and cried.

In the middle of my third beer, searching in my mind for the next step, I found the decision to go on *Strike It Rich.* I scrounged some paper and pencil from the toy box and I listed all my troubles, which must be done in order to qualify. The list when complete could have brought tears to the eye of God if he had a minute. At the sight of it my bitterness began to improve. All that is really necessary for survival of the fittest, it seems, is an interest in life, good, bad, or peculiar.

As always happens in these cases where you have begun to help yourself with plans, news comes from an opposite direction. The doorbell rang, two short and two long—meaning John.

My first thought was to wake the children and make them happy. "No! No!" he said. "Please don't put yourself to that trouble. Virginia, I'm dog-tired," he said. "Dog-tired. My job is a damn headache. It's too much. It's all day and it scuttles my mind at night, and in the end who does the credit go to?

"Virginia," he said, "I don't know if I can come anymore. I've been wanting to tell you. I just don't know. What's it all about? Could you answer me if I asked you? I can't figure this whole thing out at all."

I started the tea steeping because his fingers when I touched them were cold. I didn't speak. I tried looking at it from his man point of view, and I thought he had to take a bus, the tubes, and a subway to see me; and then the subway, the tubes, and a bus to go back home at 1 a.m. It wouldn't be any trouble at all for him to part with us forever. I thought about my life, and I gave strongest consideration to my children. If given the choice, I decided to choose not to live without him.

"What's that?" he asked, pointing to my careful list of troubles. "Writing a letter?"

"Oh no," I said, "it's for *Strike It Rich.* I hope to go on the program."

"Virginia, for goodness' sakes," he said, giving it a glance, "you don't have a ghost. They'd laugh you out of the studio. Those people really suffer."

"Are you sure, John?" I asked.

"No question in my mind at all," said John. "Have you ever seen that program? I mean, in addition to all of this—the little disturbances of man"—he waved a scornful hand at my list—"they *suffer.* They live in the forefront of tornadoes, their lives are washed off by floods—catastrophes of God. Oh, Virginia."

"Are you sure, John?"

"For goodness' sake . . ."

Sadly I put my list away. Still, if things got worse, I could always make use of it.

Once that was settled, I acted on an earlier decision. I pushed his cup of scalding tea aside. I wedged myself onto his lap between his hard belt buckle and the table. I put my arms around his neck and said, "How come you're so cold, John?" He has a kind face and he knew how to look astonished. He said, "Why, Virginia, I'm getting warmer." We laughed.

John became a lover to me that night.

Mrs. Raftery is sometimes silly and sick from her private source of cheap wine. She expects John often.

"Honor your mother, what's the matter with you, John?" she complains. "Honor. Honor."

"Virginia dear," she says. "You never would've taken John away to Jersey like Margaret. I wish he'd've married you."

"You didn't like me much in those days."

"That's a lie," she says. I know she's a hypocrite, but no more than the rest of the world.

What is remarkable to me is that it doesn't seem to conscience John as I thought it might. It is still hard to believe that a man who sends out the Ten Commandments every year for a Christmas card can be so easy buttoning and unbuttoning.

Of course we must be very careful not to wake the children or disturb the neighbors who will enjoy another person's excitement just so far, and then the pleasure enrages them. We must be very careful for ourselves too, for when my husband comes back, realizing the babies are in school and everything easier, he won't forgive me if I've started it all up again—noisy signs of life that are so much trouble to a man.

We haven't seen him in two and a half years. Although people have suggested it, I do not want the police or Intelligence or a private eye or anyone to go after him to bring him back. I know that if he expected to stay away forever he would have written and said so. As it is, I just don't know what evening, any time, he may appear. Sometimes, stumbling over a blockbuster of a dream at midnight, I wake up to vision his soft arrival.

He comes in the door with his old key. He gives me a strict look and says, "Well, you look older, Virginia." "So do you," I say, although he hasn't changed a bit.

He settles in the kitchen because the children are asleep all over the rest of the house. I unknot his tie and offer him a cold sandwich. He raps my backside, paying attention to the bounce. I walk around him as though he were a Maypole, kissing as I go.

"I didn't like the Army much," he says. "Next time I think I might go join the merchant marine."

"What army?" I say.

"It's pretty much the same everywhere," he says.

"I wouldn't be a bit surprised," I say.

"I lost my cuff link, goddamnit," he says, and drops to the floor to look for it. I go down too on my knees, but I know he never had a cuff link in his life. Still I would do a lot for him.

"Got you off your feet that time," he says, laughing. "Oh yes, I did." And before I can even make myself half comfortable on that polka-dotted linoleum, he got onto me right where we were, and the truth is, we were so happy, we forgot the precautions.

QUESTIONS

1. Why does Virginia think that being the judge of her children's behavior "means a terrible thing for the future"? (312)

2. What does Virginia mean when she says that John Raftery "came from Jersey to rescue me"? (312)

3. When Virginia describes her circumstances to John, saying, "A man can't help it, but I could have behaved better," what does this statement imply about the differences she sees between men and women? (313)

4. Why would Virginia "have done anything" that her husband asked even though he tried to make her hate him? (313)

5. Why does Virginia list all of her reasons for initially resisting John's advances?

6. What does Virginia mean when she says, "I was happy, but I am now in possession of knowledge that this is wrong"? (317)

7. What makes Virginia happy?

8. When Virginia decides not to mention anything about John's absence to her children, why does she say, "I didn't think I ought to take mistakes and truth away from them"? (319)

9. What does Virginia mean when she says, "All that is really necessary for survival of the fittest, it seems, is an interest in life, good, bad, or peculiar"? (319)

10. What makes Virginia decide to have a sexual relationship with John? Why does she say, "I decided to choose not to live without him"? (319)

11. Why does John declare that Virginia's "list of troubles" isn't true suffering? (319)

12. Does Virginia believe that John and her husband are essentially different from each other?

13. What makes Virginia think that her husband will come back? Why does she dream of having another baby with him?

FOR FURTHER REFLECTION

1. Can marriage satisfy men and women equally?
2. Do you agree with Virginia that "noisy signs of life . . . are so much trouble to a man"?
3. Is it possible to live completely free of hypocrisy?
4. What part of love is happiness?

WISLAWA SZYMBORSKA

Wislawa Szymborska (1923–) has said that "in the language of poetry, where every word is weighed, nothing is usual or normal." Among Szymborska's great gifts is the ability not only to present the world in a way that we've never seen it before, but also to elicit a sense of amazement at what might seem unremarkable outside of a poem. "The End and the Beginning," "Hatred," and "Reality Demands" are each a meditation on war—its causes, its aftermath, and its status as a phenomenon tightly woven into the fabric of history. As is typical in Szymborska's poems, her attention to one subject casts countless others in a new light.

Szymborska was born in Bnin (now part of Kórnik), Poland, in 1923. When she was eight, her family moved to Kraków, where she later studied Polish literature and sociology at Jagiellonian University. Szymborska published her first poem in a Kraków newspaper in 1945. Her first volume of poetry appeared in 1952 and her second in 1954, but she later disowned them because of their adherence to socialist realism, the style sanctioned by Poland's communist regime. In 1953, Szymborska became a poetry editor and columnist for *Zycie Literackie* (Literary Life), a weekly magazine, where she worked until 1981. In addition to translating French poetry, she continued to publish her own poems and essays, and her reputation grew steadily. *Wolanie do Yeti* (Calling Out to Yeti), published in 1957, was the first collection of poetry in which she adopted the style and voice that has since characterized her work—a quiet, personal, often ironic voice using a simple language to consider the most elemental questions posed by human experience.

In 1996, Szymborska was awarded the Nobel Prize in Literature. *Poems New and Collected 1957–1997*, an English translation by Stanislaw Baranczak and Clare Cavanagh, was published in 1998; *Nonrequired Reading: Prose Pieces* (2002) is a collection of her book reviews. In 2005, she published *Monologue of a Dog*, a collection of poems.

WISLAWA SZYMBORSKA

Selected Poems

The End and the Beginning

After every war
someone has to tidy up.
Things won't pick
themselves up, after all.

Someone has to shove
the rubble to the roadsides
so the carts loaded with corpses
can get by.

Someone has to trudge
through sludge and ashes,
through the sofa springs,
the shards of glass,
the bloody rags.

Someone has to lug the post
to prop the wall,
someone has to glaze the window,
set the door in its frame.

No sound bites, no photo opportunities,
and it takes years.
All the cameras have gone
to other wars.

The bridges need to be rebuilt,
the railroad stations, too.
Shirtsleeves will be rolled
to shreds.

Someone, broom in hand,
still remembers how it was.
Someone else listens, nodding
his unshattered head.
But others are bound to be bustling nearby
who'll find all that
a little boring.

From time to time someone still must
dig up a rusted argument
from underneath a bush
and haul it off to the dump.

Those who knew
what this was all about
must make way for those
who know little.
And less than that.
And at last nothing less than nothing.

Someone has to lie there
in the grass that covers up
the causes and effects
with a cornstalk in his teeth,
gawking at clouds.

Hatred

See how efficient it still is,
how it keeps itself in shape—
our century's hatred.
How easily it vaults the tallest obstacles.
How rapidly it pounces, tracks us down.

It's not like other feelings.
At once both older and younger.
It gives birth itself to the reasons
that give it life.
When it sleeps, it's never eternal rest.
And sleeplessness won't sap its strength; it feeds it.

One religion or another—
whatever gets it ready, in position.
One fatherland or another—
whatever helps it get a running start.
Justice also works well at the outset
until hate gets its own momentum going.
Hatred. Hatred.
Its face twisted in a grimace
of erotic ecstasy.

Oh these other feelings,
listless weaklings.
Since when does brotherhood
draw crowds?
Has compassion
ever finished first?
Does doubt ever really rouse the rabble?
Only hatred has just what it takes.

Gifted, diligent, hardworking.
Need we mention all the songs it has composed?
All the pages it has added to our history books?
All the human carpets it has spread
over countless city squares and football fields?

Let's face it:
it knows how to make beauty.
The splendid fire-glow in midnight skies.
Magnificent bursting bombs in rosy dawns.
You can't deny the inspiring pathos of ruins
and a certain bawdy humor to be found
in the sturdy column jutting from their midst.

Hatred is a master of contrast—
between explosions and dead quiet,
red blood and white snow.
Above all, it never tires
of its leitmotif—the impeccable executioner
towering over its soiled victim.

It's always ready for new challenges.
If it has to wait awhile, it will.
They say it's blind. Blind?
It has a sniper's keen sight
and gazes unflinchingly at the future
as only it can.

Reality Demands

Reality demands
that we also mention this:
Life goes on.
It continues at Cannae and Borodino,
at Kosovo Polje and Guernica.

There's a gas station
on a little square in Jericho,
and wet paint
on park benches in Bila Hora.
Letters fly back and forth
between Pearl Harbor and Hastings,
a moving van passes
beneath the eye of the lion at Chaeronea,
and the blooming orchards near Verdun
cannot escape
the approaching atmospheric front.

There is so much Everything
that Nothing is hidden quite nicely.
Music pours
from the yachts moored at Actium
and couples dance on their sunlit decks.

So much is always going on,
that it must be going on all over.
Where not a stone still stands,
you see the Ice Cream Man
besieged by children.
Where Hiroshima had been
Hiroshima is again,
producing many products
for everyday use.

This terrifying world is not devoid of charms,
of the mornings
that make waking up worthwhile.

The grass is green
on Maciejowice's fields,
and it is studded with dew,
as is normal with grass.

Perhaps all fields are battlefields,
those we remember
and those that are forgotten:
the birch forests and the cedar forests,
the snow and the sand, the iridescent swamps
and the canyons of black defeat,
where now, when the need strikes, you don't cower
under a bush but squat behind it.

What moral flows from this? Probably none.
Only the blood flows, drying quickly,
and, as always, a few rivers, a few clouds.

On tragic mountain passes
the wind rips hats from unwitting heads
and we can't help
laughing at that.

QUESTIONS

"THE END AND THE BEGINNING"

1. Are the first two lines of the poem—"After every war / someone has to tidy up"—meant as a statement of fact, a reminder, or a directive? (327)

2. Why does the speaker seem to focus primarily on the destruction wrought by war on inanimate objects, as opposed to the human casualties?

3. Why does the speaker suggest that some people will find listening to memories of life before the war "a little boring"? (328)

4. Why does the speaker refer to an argument as a "rusted" thing that someone must dig up "from underneath a bush" and haul "off to the dump"? (328)

5. What is the speaker's attitude toward the person who, in the last stanza, lies "in the grass that covers up / the causes and effects / with a cornstalk in his teeth, / gawking at clouds"? (328)

"HATRED"

1. What is implied about hatred by the image of "Its face twisted in a grimace / of erotic ecstasy"? (329)

2. What is the tone of the speaker's description of "these other feelings"—brotherhood, compassion, and doubt? (329)

3. Why does the poem describe hatred using words with positive connotations, such as "gifted, diligent, hardworking"? (329)

4. Why does the speaker ask us to admit that hatred "knows how to make beauty"? (330)

5. According to the poem, is hatred natural? Is it inevitable?

"REALITY DEMANDS"

1. What does the speaker mean by saying that "There is so much Everything / that Nothing is hidden quite nicely"? (331)
2. In what sense could "all fields" be battlefields? (332)
3. Are we meant to be troubled or comforted when the speaker asks, "What moral flows from this?" and answers, "Probably none"? (332)
4. According to the poem, are we better off remembering or forgetting what took place at the sites of terrible battles?
5. Why does the poem end with an image that, according to the speaker, "we can't help / laughing at"? (332)

FOR FURTHER REFLECTION

1. Does human nature evolve or essentially remain unchanged?
2. Does thinking about war as an inevitable feature of human life compromise the effort to prevent it?
3. Is the concept of war crimes morally logical?
4. Is there any feeling we experience that could be called inhuman?

MICHEL FOUCAULT

Sometimes read as a philosopher, other times as a historian or a literary critic, Michel Foucault (1926–1984) cannot really be confined to any single discipline; for many readers, he is one of the most prominent figures in a field of study known simply as theory. As a leading French intellectual after World War II—and sometimes viewed as a generational successor to Jean-Paul Sartre—Foucault raised fundamental questions about the way that knowledge and power coincide and are transmitted through institutional means. Most important, he disputed the conventional Enlightenment notion that knowledge is the result of objective, disinterested investigation. Instead, he famously proposed that "we are subjected to the production of truth through power and we cannot exercise power except through the production of truth." This goes considerably further than the older Baconian concept of "knowledge is power," in which knowledge and power are still perceived as entities basically independent of each other.

Foucault grew up in the town of Poitiers, the second of three children. His father wanted his son to follow in his own professional footsteps as a surgeon, but the young man was more interested in history, literature, and philosophy. Foucault studied at the Lycée Henri-IV with the philosopher Jean Hyppolite, a schoolmate and contemporary of Sartre, and in 1946 Foucault was one of only thirty-eight students to pass the entrance exam at the École Normale Supérieure in Paris.

In his studies, Foucault read Martin Heidegger and Karl Marx under the direction of the philosopher Louis Althusser. Foucault also read Sartre, then the world's most famous living philosopher and proponent of existentialism, as well as French avant-garde writers such as Georges Bataille. During this time, Foucault came to recognize his homosexual orientation and suffered through major bouts of depression. With the encouragement of Althusser, he joined the Communist Party in 1950, only to leave it three years later, dismayed in part by the party's condemnation of homosexuality.

After holding several academic and diplomatic posts abroad in Sweden, Germany, and Poland during the 1950s, Foucault returned to France in 1960 to finish his doctorate in psychology. That same year, he met Daniel Defert, who would become his lifelong partner. Foucault's dissertation, published in English under the title *Madness and Civilization* (1965), marked the beginning of his international fame, and the numerous books he published throughout the rest of his career include *The Order of Things* (1970), *The Archaeology of Knowledge* (1972), and the multivolume *History of Sexuality* (1978–1986).

Foucault's reputation grew not simply because of his scholarly output but also because of his controversial public profile; his outspokenness on a variety of political causes earned him both celebrity and vilification. He openly supported the cause of the Brazilian left after the 1964 military coup in that country; flirted with the Maoist movement in France in the late 1960s; and traveled to Iran in 1978, which led to a series of optimistic assessments of the Islamic revolution that had overthrown the Shah. When he died of AIDS in 1984, he was a public intellectual with a wide international following. His writings continue to stir controversy. *Discipline and Punish: The Birth of the Prison* (1977) is among Foucault's best-known works; in this famous opening chapter, the author begins his description of the relationship between knowledge and social control.

MICHEL FOUCAULT

The Body of the Condemned

On March 2, 1757, Damiens the regicide was condemned "to make the *amende honorable* before the main door of the Church of Paris," where he was to be "taken and conveyed in a cart, wearing nothing but a shirt, holding a torch of burning wax weighing two pounds"; then, "in the said cart, to the place de Grève, where, on a scaffold that will be erected there, the flesh will be torn from his breasts, arms, thighs, and calves with red-hot pincers, his right hand, holding the knife with which he committed the said parricide, burnt with sulfur, and, on those places where the flesh will be torn away, poured molten lead, boiling oil, burning resin, wax, and sulfur melted together and then his body drawn and quartered by four horses and his limbs and body consumed by fire, reduced to ashes and his ashes thrown to the winds."[1]

"Finally, he was quartered," recounts the *Gazette d'Amsterdam* of April 1, 1757. "This last operation was very long, because the horses used were not accustomed to drawing; consequently, instead of four, six were needed; and when that did not suffice, they were forced, in order to cut off the wretch's thighs, to sever the sinews and hack at the joints. . . .

"It is said that, though he was always a great swearer, no blasphemy escaped his lips; but the excessive pain made him utter horrible cries, and he often repeated: 'My God, have pity on me! Jesus, help me!' The spectators were all edified by the solicitude of the parish priest of St. Paul's who despite his great age did not spare himself in offering consolation to the patient."

Bouton, an officer of the watch, left us his account: "The sulfur was lit, but the flame was so poor that only the top skin of the hand was burnt, and that only slightly. Then the executioner, his sleeves rolled up, took the steel pincers, which had been especially made for the occasion, and which were about a foot and a half long, and pulled first at the calf of the right leg, then at the thigh, and from there at the two fleshy parts of the right arm; then at the breasts. Though a strong, sturdy fellow, this executioner found it so difficult to tear away the pieces of flesh that he set about the same spot two or three times, twisting the pincers as he did so, and what he took away formed at each part a wound about the size of a six-pound crown piece.

"After these tearings with the pincers, Damiens, who cried out profusely, though without swearing, raised his head and looked at himself; the same executioner dipped an iron spoon in the pot containing the boiling potion, which he poured liberally over each wound. Then the ropes that were to be harnessed to the horses were attached with cords to the patient's body; the horses were then harnessed and placed alongside the arms and legs, one at each limb.

"Monsieur Le Breton, the clerk of the court, went up to the patient several times and asked him if he had anything to say. He said he had not; at each torment, he cried out, as the damned in hell are supposed to cry out, 'Pardon, my God! Pardon, Lord.' Despite all this pain, he raised his head from time to time and looked at himself boldly. The cords had been tied so tightly by the men who pulled the ends that they caused him indescribable pain. Monsieur Le Breton went up to him again and asked him if he had anything to say; he said no. Several confessors went up to him and spoke to him at length; he willingly kissed the crucifix that was held out to him; he opened his lips and repeated: 'Pardon, Lord.'

"The horses tugged hard, each pulling straight on a limb, each horse held by an executioner. After a quarter of an hour, the same ceremony was repeated and finally, after several attempts, the direction of the horses had to be changed, thus: those at the arms were made to pull towards the head, those at the thighs towards the arms, which broke the arms at the joints. This was repeated several times without success. He raised his head and looked at himself. Two more horses had to be added to those harnessed to the thighs, which made six horses in all. Without success.

"Finally, the executioner, Samson, said to Monsieur Le Breton that there was no way or hope of succeeding, and told him to ask their Lordships if they wished him to have the prisoner cut into pieces. Monsieur Le Breton, who had come down from the town, ordered that renewed efforts be made, and this was done; but the horses gave up and one of those harnessed to the thighs fell to the ground. The confessors returned and spoke to him again. He said to them (I heard him): 'Kiss me, gentlemen.' The parish priest of St. Paul's did not dare to, so Monsieur de Marsilly slipped under the rope holding the left arm and kissed him on the forehead. The executioners gathered round and Damiens told them not to swear, to carry out their task and that he did not think ill of them; he begged them to pray to God for him, and asked the parish priest of St. Paul's to pray for him at the first mass.

"After two or three attempts, the executioner Samson and he who had used the pincers each drew out a knife from his pocket and cut the body at the thighs instead of severing the legs at the joints; the four horses gave a tug and carried off the two thighs after them, namely, that of the right side first, the other following; then the same was done to the arms, the shoulders, the armpits and the four limbs; the flesh had to be cut almost to the bone, the horses pulling hard carried off the right arm first and the other afterward.

"When the four limbs had been pulled away, the confessors came to speak to him; but his executioner told them that he was dead, though the truth was that I saw the man move, his lower jaw moving from side to side as if he were talking. One of the executioners even said shortly afterward that when they had lifted the trunk to throw it on the stake, he was still alive. The four limbs were untied from the ropes and thrown on the stake set up in the enclosure in line with the scaffold, then the trunk and the rest were covered with logs and faggots, and fire was put to the straw mixed with this wood.

". . . In accordance with the decree, the whole was reduced to ashes. The last piece to be found in the embers was still burning at half-past ten in the evening. The pieces of flesh and the trunk had taken about four hours to burn. The officers, of whom I was one, as also was my son, and a detachment of archers remained in the square until nearly eleven o'clock.

"There were those who made something of the fact that a dog had lain the day before on the grass where the fire had been, had been chased away several times, and had always returned. But it is not difficult to understand that an animal found this place warmer than elsewhere."[2]

Eighty years later, Léon Faucher drew up his rules "for the House of young prisoners in Paris":

> Art. 17. The prisoners' day will begin at six in the morning in winter and at five in summer. They will work for nine hours a day throughout the year. Two hours a day will be devoted to instruction. Work and the day will end at nine o'clock in winter and at eight in summer.
>
> Art. 18. *Rising.* At the first drumroll, the prisoners must rise and dress in silence, as the supervisor opens the cell doors. At the second drumroll, they must be dressed and make their beds. At the third, they must line up and proceed to the chapel for morning prayer. There is a five-minute interval between each drumroll.
>
> Art. 19. The prayers are conducted by the chaplain and followed by a moral or religious reading. This exercise must not last more than half an hour.

Art. 20. *Work.* At a quarter to six in the summer, a quarter to seven in winter, the prisoners go down into the courtyard where they must wash their hands and faces, and receive their first ration of bread. Immediately afterward, they form into work teams and go off to work, which must begin at six in summer and seven in winter.

Art. 21. *Meal.* At ten o'clock the prisoners leave their work and go to the refectory; they wash their hands in their courtyards and assemble in divisions. After the dinner, there is recreation until twenty minutes to eleven.

Art. 22. *School.* At twenty minutes to eleven, at the drumroll, the prisoners form into ranks, and proceed in divisions to the school. The class lasts two hours and consists alternately of reading, writing, drawing, and arithmetic.

Art. 23. At twenty minutes to one, the prisoners leave the school, in divisions, and return to their courtyards for recreation. At five minutes to one, at the drumroll, they form into work teams.

Art. 24. At one o'clock they must be back in the workshops; they work until four o'clock.

Art. 25. At four o'clock the prisoners leave their workshops and go into the courtyards where they wash their hands and form into divisions for the refectory.

Art. 26. Supper and the recreation that follows it last until five o'clock; the prisoners then return to the workshops.

Art. 27. At seven o'clock in the summer, at eight in winter, work stops; bread is distributed for the last time in the workshops. For a quarter of an hour one of the prisoners or supervisors reads a passage from some instructive or uplifting work. This is followed by evening prayer.

Art. 28. At half-past seven in summer, half-past eight in winter, the prisoners must be back in their cells after the washing of hands and the inspection of clothes in the courtyard; at the first drumroll, they must undress, and at the second get into bed. The cell doors are closed and the supervisors go the rounds in the corridors, to ensure order and silence.[3]

We have, then, a public execution and a timetable. They do not punish the same crimes or the same type of delinquent. But they each define a certain penal style. Less than a century separates them. It was a time when, in Europe and in the United States, the entire economy of punishment was redistributed. It was a time of great "scandals" for traditional justice, a time of innumerable projects for reform. It saw a new theory of law and crime, a new moral or political justification of the right to punish; old laws were abolished, old customs died out. "Modern" codes were planned or drawn up: Russia, 1769; Prussia, 1780; Pennsylvania and Tuscany, 1786; Austria, 1788; France, 1791, year IV, 1808, and 1810. It was a new age for penal justice.

Among so many changes, I shall consider one: the disappearance of torture as a public spectacle. Today we are rather inclined to ignore it; perhaps, in its time, it gave rise to too much inflated rhetoric; perhaps it has been attributed too readily and too emphatically to a process of "humanization," thus dispensing with the need for further analysis. And, in any case, how important is such a change, when compared with the great institutional transformations, the formulation of explicit, general codes and unified rules of procedure; with the almost universal adoption of the jury system, the definition of the essentially corrective character of the penalty and the tendency, which has become increasingly marked since the nineteenth century, to adapt punishment to the individual offender? Punishment of a less immediately physical kind, a certain discretion in the art of inflicting pain, a combination of more subtle, more subdued sufferings, deprived of their visible display, should not all this be treated as a special case, an incidental effect of deeper changes? And yet the fact remains that a few decades saw the disappearance of the tortured, dismembered, amputated body, symbolically branded on face or shoulder, exposed alive or dead to public view. The body as the major target of penal repression disappeared.

By the end of the eighteenth and the beginning of the nineteenth century, the gloomy festival of punishment was dying out, though here and there it flickered momentarily into life. In this transformation, two processes were at work. They did not have quite the same chronology or the same raison d'être. The first was the disappearance of punishment as a spectacle. The ceremonial of punishment tended to decline; it survived only as a new legal or administrative practice. The *amende honorable* was first abolished in France in 1791, then again in 1830 after a brief revival; the pillory was abolished in France in 1789 and in England in 1837. The use of prisoners in public works, cleaning city streets or repairing the highways, was practiced in Austria, Switzerland, and certain of the United States, such as Pennsylvania. These convicts, distinguished by their "infamous dress" and shaven heads, "were brought before the public. The sport of the idle and the vicious, they often become incensed, and naturally took violent revenge upon the aggressors. To prevent them from returning injuries which might be inflicted on them, they were encumbered with iron collars and chains to which bombshells were attached, to be dragged along while they performed their degrading service, under the eyes of keepers armed with swords, blunderbusses, and other weapons of destruction."[4] This practice was abolished practically everywhere at the end of the eighteenth or the beginning of the nineteenth century. The public exhibition of prisoners was maintained in France in 1831, despite violent criticism—"a disgusting scene," said Réal;[5] it was finally abolished in April 1848. While the chain gang, which had dragged convicts across the whole of France, as far as Brest and Toulon, was replaced in 1837 by inconspicuous black-painted cell carts. Punishment had gradually ceased to be a spectacle. And whatever theatrical elements it still retained were now downgraded, as if the functions of the penal ceremony were gradually ceasing to be understood, as if this rite that "concluded the crime" was suspected of being in some undesirable way linked with it. It was as if the punishment was thought to equal, if not to exceed, in savagery the crime itself, to accustom the spectators to a ferocity from which one wished to divert them, to show them the frequency of crime, to make the executioner resemble a criminal, judges murderers, to reverse roles at the last moment, to make the tortured criminal an object of pity or admiration. As early as 1764, Beccaria remarked: "The murder that is depicted as a horrible crime is repeated in cold blood, remorselessly."[6] The public execution is now seen as a hearth in which violence bursts again into flame.

Punishment, then, will tend to become the most hidden part of the penal process. This has several consequences: it leaves the domain of more or less everyday perception and enters that of abstract consciousness; its effectiveness is seen as resulting from its inevitability, not from its visible intensity; it is the certainty of being punished and not the horrifying spectacle of public punishment that must discourage crime; the exemplary mechanics of punishment changes its mechanisms. As a result, justice no longer takes public responsibility for the violence that is bound up with its practice. If it too strikes, if it too kills, it is not as a glorification of its strength, but as an element of itself that it is obliged to tolerate, that it finds difficult to account for. The apportioning of blame is redistributed: in punishment-as-spectacle, a confused horror spread from the scaffold; it enveloped both executioner and condemned; and, although it was always ready to invert the shame inflicted on the victim into pity or glory, it often turned the legal violence of the executioner into shame. Now the scandal and the light are to be distributed differently; it is the conviction itself that marks the offender with the unequivocally negative sign: the publicity has shifted to the trial, and to the sentence; the execution itself is like an additional shame that justice is ashamed to impose on the condemned man; so it keeps its distance from the act, tending always to entrust it to others, under the seal of secrecy. It is ugly to be punishable, but there is no glory in punishing. Hence that double system of protection that justice has set up between itself and the punishment it imposes. Those who carry out the penalty tend to become an autonomous sector; justice is relieved of responsibility for it by a bureaucratic concealment of the penalty itself. It is typical that in France the administration of the prisons should for so long have been the responsibility of the Ministry of the Interior, while responsibility for the *bagnes*, for penal servitude in the convict ships and penal settlements, lay with the Ministry of the Navy or the Ministry of the Colonies. And beyond this distribution of roles operates a theoretical disavowal: do not imagine that the sentences that we judges pass are activated by a desire to punish; they are intended to correct, reclaim, "cure"; a technique of improvement represses, in the penalty, the strict expiation of evildoing, and relieves the magistrates of the demeaning task of punishing. In modern justice and on the part of those who dispense it, there is a shame in punishing, which does not always preclude zeal. This sense of shame is constantly growing: the psychologists and the minor civil servants of moral orthopaedics proliferate on the wound it leaves.

The disappearance of public executions marks therefore the decline of the spectacle; but it also marks a slackening of the hold on the body. In 1787, in an address to the Society for Promoting Political Inquiries, Benjamin Rush remarked: "I can only hope that the time is not far away when gallows, pillory, scaffold, flogging, and wheel will, in the history of punishment, be regarded as the marks of the barbarity of centuries and of countries and as proofs of the feeble influence of reason and religion over the human mind."[7] Indeed, sixty years later, Van Meenen, opening the second penitentiary congress, in Brussels, recalled the time of his childhood as of a past age: "I have seen the ground strewn with wheels, gibbets, gallows, pillories; I have seen hideously stretched skeletons on wheels."[8] Branding had been abolished in England (1834) and in France (1832); in 1820, England no longer dared to apply the full punishment reserved for traitors (Thistlewood was not quartered). Only flogging still remained in a number of penal systems (Russia, England, Prussia). But, generally speaking, punitive practices had become more reticent. One no longer touched the body, or at least as little as possible, and then only to reach something other than the body itself. It might be objected that imprisonment, confinement, forced labor, penal servitude, prohibition from entering certain areas, deportation—which have occupied so important a place in modern penal systems—are "physical" penalties: unlike fines, for example, they directly affect the body. But the punishment-body relation is not the same as it was in the torture during public executions. The body now serves as an instrument or intermediary: if one intervenes upon it to imprison it, or to make it work, it is in order to deprive the individual of a liberty that is regarded both as a right and as property. The body, according to this penality, is caught up in a system of constraints and privations, obligations and prohibitions. Physical pain, the pain of the body itself, is no longer the constituent element of the penalty. From being an art of unbearable sensations punishment has become an economy of suspended rights. If it is still necessary for the law to reach and manipulate the body of the convict, it will be at a distance, in the proper way, according to strict rules, and with a much "higher" aim. As a result of this new restraint, a whole army of technicians took over from the executioner, the immediate anatomist of pain: warders, doctors, chaplains, psychiatrists, psychologists, educationalists; by their very presence near the prisoner, they sing the praises that the law needs: they reassure it that the body and pain are not the ultimate objects of its punitive action. Today a doctor must watch over those condemned to death, right up to the last moment—thus juxtaposing himself as the agent of welfare, as the alleviator of pain, with the official whose task it is to end life. This is worth thinking about. When the moment of execution approaches, the patients are injected with tranquilizers. A utopia of judicial reticence: take away life, but prevent the patient from feeling it; deprive the prisoner of all rights, but do not inflict pain; impose penalties free of all pain. Recourse to psychopharmacology and to various physiological "disconnectors," even if it is temporary, is a logical consequence of this "noncorporal" penality.

The modern rituals of execution attest to this double process: the disappearance of the spectacle and the elimination of pain. The same movement has affected the various European legal systems, each at its own rate: the same death for all—the execution no longer bears the specific mark of the crime or the social status of the criminal; a death that lasts only a moment—no torture must be added to it in advance, no further actions performed upon the corpse; an execution that affects life rather than the body. There are no longer any of those long processes in which death was both retarded by calculated interruptions and multiplied by a series of successive attacks. There are no longer any of those combinations of tortures that were organized for the killing of regicides, or of the kind advocated, at the beginning of the eighteenth century, by the anonymous author of *Hanging Not Punishment Enough* (1701), by which the condemned man would be broken on the wheel, then flogged until he fainted, then hung up with chains, then finally left to die slowly of hunger. There are no longer any of those executions in which the condemned man was dragged along on a hurdle (to prevent his head smashing against the cobblestones), in which his belly was opened up, his entrails quickly ripped out, so that he had time to see them, with his own eyes, being thrown on the fire; in which he was finally decapitated and his body quartered.[9] The reduction of these "thousand deaths" to strict capital punishment defines a whole new morality concerning the act of punishing.

As early as 1760, a hanging machine had been tried out in England (for the execution of Lord Ferrer). It made use of a support, which opened under the feet of the condemned man, thus avoiding slow deaths and the altercations that occurred between victim and executioner. It was improved and finally adopted in 1783, the same year in which the traditional procession from Newgate to Tyburn was abolished, and in which the opportunity offered by the rebuilding of the prison, after the Gordon Riots, was used to set up the scaffolds in Newgate itself.[10] The celebrated article 3 of the French Code of 1791—"Every man condemned to death will have his head cut off"—bears this triple signification: an equal death for all ("Crimes of the same kind will be punished by the same kind of punishment, whatever the rank and state of the guilty man may be," in the words of the motion proposed by Guillotin and passed on December 1, 1789); one death per condemned man, obtained by a single blow, without recourse to those "long and consequently cruel" methods of execution, such as the gallows, denounced by Le Peletier; lastly, punishment for the condemned man alone, since decapitation, the capital punishment of the nobility, was the least shaming for the criminal's family.[11] The guillotine, first used in March 1792, was the perfect vehicle for these principles. Death was reduced to a visible, but instantaneous event. Contact between the law, or those who carry it out, and the body of the criminal, is reduced to a split second. There is no physical confrontation; the executioner need be no more than a meticulous watchmaker. "Experience and reason demonstrate that the method used in the past to cut off the head of a criminal exposed him to a torture more frightful than the loss of life alone, which is the express intention of the law; the execution should therefore be carried out in a single moment and with a single blow; examples show how difficult it is to achieve this. For the method to work perfectly, it must necessarily depend on invariable mechanical means whose force and effect may also be determined. . . . It is an easy enough matter to have such an unfailing machine built; decapitation will be performed in a moment according to the intention of the new law. If this apparatus seems necessary, it will cause no sensation and will be scarcely noticed."[12] The guillotine takes life almost without touching the body, just as prison deprives of liberty or a fine reduces wealth. It is intended to apply the law not so much to a real body capable of feeling pain as to a juridical subject, the possessor, among other rights, of the right to exist. It had to have the abstraction of the law itself.

No doubt something of the old public execution was, for a time, superimposed in France on the sobriety of the new method. Parricides—and the regicides who were regarded as such—were led to the scaffold wearing a black veil; there, until 1832, one of their hands was cut off. Thereafter, nothing remained but the ornamental crêpe. Thus it was in the case of Fieschi, the would-be assassin of Louis-Philippe, in November 1836: "He will be taken to the place of execution wearing a shirt, barefoot, his head covered with a black veil; he will be exhibited upon a scaffold while an usher reads the sentence to the people, and he will be immediately executed." We should remember Damiens—and note that the last addition to penal death was a mourning veil. The condemned man was no longer to be seen. Only the reading of the sentence on the scaffold announced the crime—and that crime must be faceless. (The more monstrous a criminal was, the more he must be deprived of light: he must not see, or be seen. This was a common enough notion at the time. For the parricide one should "construct an iron cage or dig an impenetrable dungeon that would serve him as an eternal retreat."[13]) The last vestige of the great public execution was its annulment: a drapery to hide a body. Benoît, triply infamous (his mother's murderer, a homosexual, an assassin), was the first of the parricides not to have a hand cut off. "As the sentence was being read, he stood on the scaffold supported by the executioners. It was a horrible sight; wrapped in a large white shroud, his face covered with black crêpe, the parricide escaped the gaze of the silent crowd, and beneath these mysterious and gloomy clothes, life was manifested only by frightful cries, which soon expired under the knife."[14]

At the beginning of the nineteenth century, then, the great spectacle of physical punishment disappeared; the tortured body was avoided; the theatrical representation of pain was excluded from punishment. The age of sobriety in punishment had begun. By 1830–1848, public executions, preceded by torture, had almost entirely disappeared. Of course, this generalization requires some qualification. To begin with, the changes did not come about at once or as part of a single process. There were delays. Paradoxically, England was one of the countries most loath to see the disappearance of the public execution: perhaps because of the role of model that the institution of the jury, public hearings, and respect of habeas corpus had given to her criminal law; above all, no doubt, because she did not wish to diminish the rigor of her penal laws during the great social disturbances of the years 1780–1820. For a long time, Romilly, Mackintosh, and Fowell Buxton failed in their attempts to attenuate the multiplicity and severity of the penalties laid down by English law—that "horrible butchery," as Rossi described it. Its severity (in fact, the juries regarded the penalties laid down as excessive and were consequently more lenient in their application) had even increased: in 1760, Blackstone had listed 160 capital crimes in English legislation, while by 1819 there were 223. One should also take into account the advances and retreats that the process as a whole underwent between 1760 and 1840; the rapidity of reform in certain countries such as Austria, Russia, the United States, France under the Constituent Assembly, then the retreat at the time of the counterrevolutions in Europe and the great social fear of the years 1820–1848; more or less temporary changes introduced by emergency courts or laws; the gap between the laws and the real practice of the courts (which was by no means a faithful reflection of the state of legislation). All these factors account for the irregularity of the transformation that occurred at the turn of the century.

It should be added that, although most of the changes had been achieved by 1840, although the mechanisms of punishment had by then assumed their new way of functioning, the process was far from complete. The reduction in the use of torture was a tendency that was rooted in the great transformation of the years 1760–1840, but it did not end there; it can be said that the practice of the public execution haunted our penal system for a long time and still haunts it today. In France, the guillotine, that machine for the production of rapid and discreet deaths, represented a new ethic of legal death. But the Revolution had immediately endowed it with a great theatrical ritual. For years it provided a spectacle. It had to be removed to the Barrière Saint-Jacques; the open cart was replaced by a closed carriage; the condemned man was hustled from the vehicle straight to the scaffold; hasty executions were organized at unexpected times. In the end, the guillotine had to be placed inside prison walls and made inaccessible to the public (after the execution of Weidmann in 1939), by blocking the streets leading to the prison in which the scaffold was hidden, and in which the execution would take place in secret (the execution of Buffet and Bontemps at the Santé in 1972). Witnesses who described the scene could even be prosecuted, thereby ensuring that the execution should cease to be a spectacle and remain a strange secret between the law and those it condemns. One has only to point out so many precautions to realize that capital punishment remains fundamentally, even today, a spectacle that must actually be forbidden.

Similarly, the hold on the body did not entirely disappear in the mid-nineteenth century. Punishment had no doubt ceased to be centered on torture as a technique of pain; it assumed as its principal object loss of wealth or rights. But a punishment like forced labor or even imprisonment—mere loss of liberty—has never functioned without a certain additional element of punishment that certainly concerns the body itself: rationing of food, sexual deprivation, corporal punishment, solitary confinement. Are these the unintentional, but inevitable, consequence of imprisonment? In fact, in its most explicit practices, imprisonment has always involved a certain degree of physical pain. The criticism that was often levelled at the penitentiary system in the early nineteenth century (imprisonment is not a sufficient punishment: prisoners are less hungry, less cold, less deprived in general than many poor people or even workers) suggests a postulate that was never explicitly denied: it is just that a condemned man should suffer physically more than other men. It is difficult to dissociate punishment from additional physical pain. What would a noncorporal punishment be?

There remains, therefore, a trace of "torture" in the modern mechanisms of criminal justice—a trace that has not been entirely overcome, but which is enveloped, increasingly, by the noncorporal nature of the penal system.

The reduction in penal severity in the last two hundred years is a phenomenon with which legal historians are well acquainted. But, for a long time, it has been regarded in an overall way as a quantitative phenomenon: less cruelty, less pain, more kindness, more respect, more "humanity." In fact, these changes are accompanied by a displacement in the very object of the punitive operation. Is there a diminution of intensity? Perhaps. There is certainly a change of objective.

If the penality in its most severe forms no longer addresses itself to the body, on what does it lay hold? The answer of the theoreticians—those who, about 1760, opened up a new period that is not yet at an end—is simple, almost obvious. It seems to be contained in the question itself: since it is no longer the body, it must be the soul. The expiation that once rained down upon the body must be replaced by a punishment that acts in depth on the heart, the thoughts, the will, the inclinations. Mably formulated the principle once and for all: "Punishment, if I may so put it, should strike the soul rather than the body."[15]

It was an important moment. The old partners of the spectacle of punishment, the body and the blood, gave way. A new character came on the scene, masked. It was the end of a certain kind of tragedy; comedy began, with shadow play, faceless voices, impalpable entities. The apparatus of punitive justice must now bite into this bodiless reality.

Is this any more than a mere theoretical assertion, contradicted by penal practice? Such a conclusion would be overhasty. It is true that, today, to punish is not simply a matter of converting a soul; but Mably's principle has not remained a pious wish. Its effects can be felt throughout modern penality.

To begin with, there is a substitution of objects. By this I do not mean that one has suddenly set about punishing other crimes. No doubt the definition of offenses, the hierarchy of their seriousness, the margins of indulgence, what was tolerated in fact and what was legally permitted—all this has considerably changed over the last two hundred years; many crimes have ceased to be so because they were bound up with a certain exercise of religious authority or a particular type of economic activity; blasphemy has lost its status as a crime; smuggling and domestic larceny some of their seriousness. But these displacements are perhaps not the most important fact: the division between the permitted and the forbidden has preserved a certain constancy from one century to another. On the other hand, "crime," the object with which penal practice is concerned, has profoundly altered: the quality, the nature, in a sense the substance of which the punishable element is made, rather than its formal definition. Under cover of the relative stability of the law, a mass of subtle and rapid changes has occurred. Certainly the "crimes" and "offenses" on which judgment is passed are juridical objects defined by the code, but judgment is also passed on the passions, instincts, anomalies, infirmities, maladjustments, effects of environment or heredity; acts of aggression are punished—so also, through them, is aggressivity; rape, but at the same time perversions; murders, but also drives and desires. But, it will be objected, judgment is not actually being passed on them; if they are referred to at all, it is to explain the actions in question, and to determine to what extent the subject's will was involved in the crime. This is no answer. For it *is* these shadows lurking behind the case itself that are judged and punished. They are judged indirectly as "attenuating circumstances" that introduce into the verdict not only "circumstantial" evidence, but something quite different, which is not juridically codifiable: the knowledge of the criminal; one's estimation of him; what is known about the relations between him, his past, and his crime; and what might be expected of him in the future. They are also judged by the interplay of all those notions that have circulated between medicine and jurisprudence since the nineteenth century (the "monsters" of Georget's times, Chaumié's "psychical anomalies," the "perverts" and "maladjusted" of our own experts) and which, behind the pretext of explaining an action, are ways of defining an individual. They are punished by means of a punishment that has the function of making the offender "not only desirous, but also capable, of living within the law and of providing for his own needs"; they are punished by the internal economy of a penalty which, while intended to punish the crime, may be altered (shortened or, in certain cases, extended) according to changes in the prisoner's behavior; and they are punished by the "security measures" that accompany the penalty (prohibition of entering certain areas, probation, obligatory medical treatment), and which are intended not to punish the offense, but to supervise the individual, to neutralize his dangerous state of mind, to alter his criminal tendencies, and to continue even when this change has been achieved. The criminal's soul is not referred to in the trial merely to explain his crime and as a factor in the juridical apportioning of responsibility; if it is brought before the court, with such pomp and circumstance, such concern to understand and such "scientific" application, it is because it too, as well as the crime itself, is to be judged and to share in the punishment. Throughout the penal ritual, from the preliminary investigation to the sentence and the final effects of the penalty, a domain has been penetrated by objects that not only duplicate, but also dissociate the juridically defined and coded objects. Psychiatric expertise, but also in a more general way criminal anthropology and the repetitive discourse of criminology, find one of their precise functions here: by solemnly inscribing offenses in the field of objects susceptible of scientific knowledge, they provide the mechanisms of legal punishment with a justifiable hold not only on offenses, but on individuals; not only on what they do, but also on what they are, will be, may be. The additional factor of the offender's soul, which the legal system has laid hold of, is only apparently explanatory and limitative, and is in fact expansionist. During the one hundred and fifty or two hundred years that Europe has been setting up its new penal systems, the judges have gradually, by means of a process that goes back very far indeed, taken to judging something other than crimes, namely, the "soul" of the criminal.

And, by that very fact, they have begun to do something other than pass judgment. Or, to be more precise, within the very judicial modality of judgment, other types of assessment have slipped in, profoundly altering its rules of elaboration. Ever since the Middle Ages slowly and painfully built up the great procedure of investigation, to judge was to establish the truth of a crime, it was to determine its author and to apply a legal punishment. Knowledge of the offense, knowledge of the offender, knowledge of the law: these three conditions made it possible to ground a judgment in truth. But now a quite different question of truth is inscribed in the course of the penal judgment. The question is no longer simply, has the act been established and is it punishable? But also: What *is* this act, what *is* this act of violence or this murder? To what level or to what field of reality does it belong? Is it a fantasy, a psychotic reaction, a delusional episode, a perverse action? It is no longer simply, who committed it? But: How can we assign the causal process that produced it? Where did it originate in the author himself? Instinct, unconscious, environment, heredity? It is no longer simply, what law punishes this offense? But: What would be the most appropriate measures to take? How do we see the future development of the offender? What would be the best way of rehabilitating him? A whole set of assessing, diagnostic, prognostic, normative judgments concerning the criminal have become lodged in the framework of penal judgment. Another truth has penetrated the truth that was required by the legal machinery; a truth which, entangled with the first, has turned the assertion of guilt into a strange scientifico-juridical complex. A significant fact is the way in which the question of madness has evolved in penal practice. According to the 1810 code, madness was dealt with only in terms of article 64. Now, this article states that there is neither crime nor offense if the offender was of unsound mind at the time of the act. The possibility of ascertaining madness was, therefore, a quite separate matter from the definition of an act as a crime; the gravity of the act was not altered by the fact that its author was insane, nor the punishment reduced as a consequence; the crime itself disappeared. It was impossible, therefore, to declare that someone was both guilty and mad; once the diagnosis of madness had been accepted, it could not be included in the judgment; it interrupted the procedure and loosened the hold of the law on the author of the act. Not only the examination of the criminal suspected of insanity, but the very effects of this examination had to be external and anterior to the sentence. But, very soon, the courts of the nineteenth century began to misunderstand the meaning of article 64. Despite several decisions of the supreme court of appeal confirming that insanity could not result either in a light penalty, or even in an acquittal, but required that the case be dismissed, the ordinary courts continued to bring the question of insanity to bear on their verdicts. They accepted that one could be both guilty and mad; less guilty the madder one was; guilty certainly, but someone to be put away and treated rather than punished; not only a guilty man, but also dangerous, since quite obviously sick, etc. From the point of view of the penal code, the result was a mass of juridical absurdities. But this was the starting point of an evolution that jurisprudence and legislation itself was to precipitate in the course of the next one hundred and fifty years: already the reform of 1832, introducing attenuating circumstances, made it possible to modify the sentence according to the supposed degrees of an illness or the forms of a semi-insanity. And the practice of calling on psychiatric expertise, which is widespread in the assize courts and sometimes extended to courts of summary jurisdiction, means that the sentence, even if it is always formulated in terms of legal punishment, implies, more or less obscurely, judgments of normality, attributions of causality, assessments of possible changes, anticipations as to the offender's future. It would be wrong to say that all these operations give substance to a judgment from the outside; they are directly integrated in the process of forming the sentence. Instead of insanity eliminating the crime according to the original meaning of article 64, every crime and even every offense now carries within it, as a legitimate suspicion, but also as a right that may be claimed, the hypothesis of insanity, in any case of anomaly. And the sentence that condemns or acquits is not simply a judgment of guilt, a legal decision that lays down punishment; it bears within it an assessment of normality and a technical prescription for a possible normalization. Today the judge—magistrate or juror—certainly does more than "judge."

And he is not alone in judging. Throughout the penal procedure and the implementation of the sentence there swarms a whole series of subsidiary authorities. Small-scale legal systems and parallel judges have multiplied around the principal judgment: psychiatric or psychological experts, magistrates concerned with the implementation of sentences, educationalists, members of the prison service, all fragment the legal power to punish; it might be objected that none of them really shares the right to judge; that some, after sentence is passed, have no other right than to implement the punishment laid down by the court and, above all, that others—the experts—intervene before the sentence not to pass judgment, but to assist the judges in their decision. But as soon as the penalties and the security measures defined by the court are not absolutely determined, from the moment they may be modified along the way, from the moment one leaves to others than the judges of the offense the task of deciding whether the condemned man "deserves" to be placed in semiliberty or conditional liberty, whether they may bring his penal tutelage to an end, one is handing over to them mechanisms of legal punishment to be used at their discretion: subsidiary judges they may be, but they are judges all the same. The whole machinery that has been developing for years around the implementation of sentences, and their adjustment to individuals, creates a proliferation of the authorities of judicial decision-making and extends its powers of decision well beyond the sentence. The psychiatric experts, for their part, may well refrain from judging. Let us examine the three questions to which, since the 1958 ruling, they have to address themselves: Does the convicted person represent a danger to society? Is he susceptible to penal punishment? Is he curable or readjustable? These questions have nothing to do with article 64, nor with the possible insanity of the convicted person at the moment of the act. They do not concern "responsibility." They concern nothing but the administration of the penalty, its necessity, its usefulness, its possible effectiveness; they make it possible to show, in an almost transparent vocabulary, whether the mental hospital would be a more suitable place of confinement than the prison, whether this confinement should be short or long, whether medical treatment or security measures are called for. What, then, is the role of the psychiatrist in penal matters? He is not an expert in responsibility, but an adviser on punishment; it is up to him to say whether the subject is "dangerous," in what way one should be protected from him, how one should intervene to alter him, whether it would be better to try to force him into submission or to treat him. At the very beginning of its history, psychiatric expertise was called upon to formulate "true" propositions as to the part that the liberty of the offender had played in the act he had committed; it is now called upon to suggest a prescription for what might be called his "medico-judicial treatment."

To sum up, ever since the new penal system—that defined by the great codes of the eighteenth and nineteenth centuries—has been in operation, a general process has led judges to judge something other than crimes; they have been led in their sentences to do something other than judge; and the power of judging has been transferred, in part, to other authorities than the judges of the offense. The whole penal operation has taken on extrajuridical elements and personnel. It will be said that there is nothing extraordinary in this, that it is part of th law to absorb little by little elements that are alien to it. B about modern criminal justice is that, although it has taken on extrajuridical elements, it has done so not in order to be able to defi them juridically and gradually to integrate them into the actual power to punish; on the contrary, it has done so in order to make them function within the penal operation as nonjuridical elements; in order to stop this operation being simply a legal punishment; in order to exculpate the judge from being purely and simply he who punishes. Of course, we pass sentence, but this sentence is not in direct relation to the crime. It is quite clear that for us it functions as a way of treating a criminal. We punish, but this is a way of saying that we wish to obtain a cure. Today, criminal justice functions and justifies itself only by this perpetual reference to something other than itself, by this unceasing reinscription in nonjuridical systems. Its fate is to be redefined by knowledge.

Beneath the increasing leniency of punishment, then, one may map a displacement of its point of application; and through this displacement, a whole field of recent objects, a whole new system of truth and a mass of roles hitherto unknown in the exercise of criminal justice. A corpus of knowledge, techniques, "scientific" discourses is formed and becomes entangled with the practice of the power to punish.

This book is intended as a correlative history of the modern soul and of a new power to judge; a genealogy of the present scientifico-legal complex from which the power to punish derives its bases, justifications, and rules, from which it extends its effects and by which it masks its exorbitant singularity.

But from what point can such a history of the modern soul on trial be written? If one confined oneself to the evolution of legislation or of penal procedures, one would run the risk of allowing a change in the collective sensibility, an increase in humanization, or the development of the human sciences to emerge as a massive, external, inert, and primary fact. By studying only the general social forms, as Durkheim did,[16] one runs the risk of positing as the principle of greater leniency in punishment processes of individualization that are rather one of the effects of the new tactics of power, among which are to be included the new penal mechanisms. This study obeys four general rules:

1. Do not concentrate the study of the punitive mechanisms on their "repressive" effects alone, on their "punishment" aspects alone, but situate them in a whole series of their possible positive effects, even if these seem marginal at first sight. As a consequence, regard punishment as a complex social function.

2. Analyze punitive methods not simply as consequences of legislation or as indicators of social structures, but as techniques possessing

their own specificity in the more general field of other ways of exercising power. Regard punishment as a political tactic.

3. Instead of treating the history of penal law and the history of the human sciences as two separate series whose overlapping appears to have had on one or the other, or perhaps on both, a disturbing or useful effect, according to one's point of view, see whether there is not some common matrix or whether they do not both derive from a single process of "epistemologico-juridical" formation; in short, make the technology of power the very principle both of the humanization of the penal system and of the knowledge of man.

4. Try to discover whether this entry of the soul onto the scene of penal justice, and with it the insertion in legal practice of a whole corpus of "scientific" knowledge, is not the effect of a transformation of the way in which the body itself is invested by power relations.

In short, try to study the metamorphosis of punitive methods on the basis of a political technology of the body in which might be read a common history of power relations and object relations. Thus, by an analysis of penal leniency as a technique of power, one might understand both how man, the soul, the normal or abnormal individual have come to duplicate crime as objects of penal intervention; and in what way a specific mode of subjection was able to give birth to man as an object of knowledge for a discourse with a "scientific" status.

But I am not claiming to be the first to have worked in this direction.[17]

Rusche and Kirchheimer's great work, *Punishment and Social Structures*, provides a number of essential reference points. We must first rid ourselves of the illusion that penality is above all (if not exclusively) a means of reducing crime and that, in this role, according to the social forms, the political systems or beliefs, it may be severe or lenient, tend toward expiation of obtaining redress, toward the pursuit of individuals or the attribution of collective responsibility. We must analyze rather the "concrete systems of punishment," study them as social phenomena that cannot be accounted for by the juridical structure of society alone, nor by its fundamental ethical choices; we must situate them in their field of operation, in which the punishment of crime is not the sole element; we must show that punitive measures are not simply "negative" mechanisms that make it possible to repress, to prevent, to exclude, to eliminate; but that they are linked to a whole series of positive and useful effects which it is their task to support (and, in this sense, although legal punishment is carried out in order to punish offenses, one might say that the definition of offenses and their prosecution are carried out in turn in order to maintain the punitive mechanisms and their functions). From this point of view, Rusche and Kirchheimer relate the different systems of punishment with the systems of production within which they operate: thus, in a slave economy, punitive mechanisms serve to provide an additional labor force—and to constitute a body of "civil" slaves in addition to those provided by war or trading; with feudalism, at a time when money and production were still at an early stage of development, we find a sudden increase in corporal punishments—the body being in most cases the only property accessible; the penitentiary (the Hôpital Général, the Spinhuis, or the Rasphuis), forced labor and the prison factory appear with the development of the mercantile economy. But the industrial system requires a free market in labor and, in the nineteenth century, the role of forced labor in the mechanisms of punishment diminishes accordingly and "corrective" detention takes its place. There are no doubt a number of observations to be made about such a strict correlation.

But we can surely accept the general proposition that, in our societies, the systems of punishment are to be situated in a certain "political economy" of the body: even if they do not make use of violent or bloody punishment, even when they use "lenient" methods involving confinement or correction, it is always the body that is at issue—the body and its forces, their utility and their docility, their distribution and their submission. It is certainly legitimate to write a history of punishment against the background of moral ideas or legal structures. But can one write such a history against the background of a history of bodies, when such systems of punishment claim to have only the secret souls of criminals as their objective?

Historians long ago began to write the history of the body. They have studied the body in the field of historical demography or pathology; they have considered it as the seat of needs and appetites, as the locus of physiological processes and metabolisms, as a target for the attacks of germs or viruses; they have shown to what extent historical processes were involved in what might seem to be the purely biological base of existence; and what place should be given in the history of society to biological "events" such as the circulation of bacilli, or the extension of the life span.[18] But the body is also directly involved in a political field; power relations have an immediate hold upon it; they invest it, mark it, train it, torture it, force it to carry out tasks, to perform ceremonies, to emit signs. This political investment of the body is bound up, in accordance with complex reciprocal relations, with its economic use; it is largely as a force of production that the body is invested with relations of power and domination; but, on the other hand, its constitution as labor power is possible only if it is caught up in a system of subjection (in which need is also a political instrument meticulously prepared, calculated, and used); the body becomes a useful force only if it is both a productive body and a subjected body. This subjection is not only obtained by the instruments of violence or ideology; it can also be direct, physical, pitting force against force, bearing on material elements, and yet without involving violence; it may be calculated, organized, technically thought out; it may be subtle, make use neither of weapons nor of terror, and yet remain of a physical order. That is to say, there may be a "knowledge" of the body that is not exactly the science of its functioning, and a mastery of its forces that is more than the ability to conquer them: this knowledge and this mastery constitute what might be called the political technology of the body. Of course, this technology is diffuse, rarely formulated in continuous, systematic discourse; it is often made up of bits and pieces; it implements a disparate set of tools or methods. In spite of the coherence of its results, it is generally no more than a multiform instrumentation. Moreover, it cannot be localized in a particular type of institution or state apparatus. For they have recourse to it; they use, select, or impose certain of its methods. But, in its mechanisms and its effects, it is situated at a quite different level. What the apparatus and institutions operate is, in a sense, a microphysics of power, whose field of validity is situated in a sense between these great functionings and the bodies themselves with their materiality and their forces.

Now, the study of this microphysics presupposes that the power exercised on the body is conceived not as a property, but as a strategy, that its effects of domination are attributed not to "appropriation," but to dispositions, maneuvers, tactics, techniques, functionings; that one should decipher in it a network of relations, constantly in tension, in activity, rather than a privilege that one might possess; that one should take as its model a perpetual battle rather than a contract regulating a transaction or the conquest of a territory. In short, this power is exercised rather than possessed; it is not the "privilege," acquired or preserved, of the dominant class, but the overall effect of its strategic positions—an effect that is manifested and sometimes extended by the position of those who are dominated. Furthermore, this power is not exercised simply as an obligation or a prohibition on those who "do not have it"; it invests them, is transmitted by them and through them; it exerts pressure upon them, just as they themselves, in their struggle against it, resist the grip it has on them. This means that these relations go right down into the depths of society, that they are not localized in the relations between the state and its citizens or on the frontier between classes and that they do not merely reproduce, at the level of individuals, bodies, gestures, and behavior, the general form of the law or government; that, although there is continuity (they are indeed articulated on this form through a whole series of complex mechanisms), there is neither analogy nor homology, but a specificity of mechanism and modality. Lastly, they are not univocal; they define innumerable points of confrontation, focuses of instability, each of which has its own risks of conflict, of struggles, and of an at least temporary inversion of the power relations. The overthrow of these "micropowers" does not, then, obey the law of all or nothing; it is not acquired once and for all by a new control of the apparatus nor by a new functioning or a destruction of the institutions; on the other hand, none of its localized episodes may be inscribed in history except by the effects that it induces on the entire network in which it is caught up.

Perhaps, too, we should abandon a whole tradition that allows us to imagine that knowledge can exist only where the power relations are suspended and that knowledge can develop only outside its injunctions, its demands, and its interests. Perhaps we should abandon the belief that power makes mad and that, by the same token, the renunciation of power is one of the conditions of knowledge. We should admit rather that power produces knowledge (and not simply by encouraging it because it serves power or by applying it because it is useful); that power and knowledge directly imply one another; that there is no power relation without the correlative constitution of a field of knowledge, nor any knowledge that does not presuppose and constitute at the same time power relations. These "power-knowledge relations" are to be analyzed, therefore, not on the basis of a subject of knowledge who is or is not free in relation to the power system, but, on the contrary, the subject who knows, the objects to be known, and the modalities of knowledge must be regarded as so many effects of these fundamental implications of power-knowledge and their historical transformations. In short, it is not the activity of the subject of knowledge that produces a corpus of knowledge, useful or resistant to power, but power-knowledge, the processes and struggles that traverse it and of which it is made up, that determines the forms and possible domains of knowledge.

To analyze the political investment of the body and the microphysics of power presupposes, therefore, that one abandons—where power is concerned—the violence-ideology opposition, the metaphor of property, the model of the contract or of conquest; that—where knowledge is concerned—one abandons the opposition between what is "interested" and what is "disinterested," the model of knowledge and the primacy of the subject. Borrowing a word from Petty and his contemporaries, but giving it a different meaning from the one current in the seventeenth century, one might imagine a political "anatomy." This would not be the study of a state in terms of a "body" (with its elements, its resources, and its forces), nor would it be the study of the body and its surroundings in terms of a small state. One would be concerned with the "body politic," as a set of material elements and techniques that serve as weapons, relays, communication routes, and supports for the power and knowledge relations that invest human bodies and subjugate them by turning them into objects of knowledge.

It is a question of situating the techniques of punishment—whether they seize the body in the ritual of public torture and execution or whether they are addressed to the soul—in the history of this body politic; of considering penal practices less as a consequence of legal theories than as a chapter of political anatomy.

Kantorowitz gives a remarkable analysis of "The King's Body": a double body according to the juridical theology of the Middle Ages, since it involves not only the transitory element that is born and dies, but another that remains unchanged by time and is maintained as the physical yet intangible support of the kingdom; around this duality, which was originally close to the Christological model, are organized an iconography, a political theory of monarchy, legal mechanisms that distinguish between as well as link the person of the king and the demands of the Crown, and a whole ritual that reaches its height in the coronation, the funeral, and the ceremonies of submission. At the opposite pole, one might imagine placing the body of the condemned man; he, too, has his legal status; he gives rise to his own ceremonial and he calls forth a whole theoretical discourse, not in order to ground the "surplus power" possessed by the person of the sovereign, but in order to code the "lack of power" with which those subjected to punishment are marked. In the darkest region of the political field, the condemned man represents the symmetrical, inverted figure of the king. We should analyze what might be called, in homage to Kantorowitz, "the least body of the condemned man."

If the surplus power possessed by the king gives rise to the duplication of his body, has not the surplus power exercised on the subjected body of the condemned man given rise to another type of duplication? That of a "noncorporal," a "soul," as Mably called it. The history of this "microphysics" of the punitive power would then be a genealogy or an element in a genealogy of the modern "soul." Rather than seeing this soul as the reactivated remnants of an ideology, one would see it as the present correlative of a certain technology of power over the body. It would be wrong to say that the soul is an illusion, or an ideological effect. On the contrary, it exists, it has a reality, it is produced permanently around, on, within the body by the functioning of a power that is exercised on those punished—and, in a more general way, on those one supervises, trains, and corrects, over madmen, children at home and at school, the colonized, over those who are stuck at a machine and supervised for the rest of their lives. This is the historical reality of this soul, which, unlike the soul represented by Christian theology, is not born in sin and subject to punishment, but is born rather out of methods of punishment, supervision, and constraint. This real, noncorporal soul is not a substance; it is the element in which are articulated the effects of a certain type of power and the reference of a certain type of knowledge, the machinery by which the power relations give rise to a possible corpus of knowledge, and knowledge extends and reinforces the effects of this power. On this reality-reference, various concepts have been constructed and domains of analysis carved out: psyche, subjectivity, personality, consciousness, etc.; on it have been built scientific techniques and discourses, and the moral claims of humanism. But let there be no misunderstanding: it is not that a real man, the object of knowledge, philosophical reflection, or technical intervention, has been substituted for the soul, the illusion of the theologians. The man described for us, whom we are invited to free, is already in himself the effect of a subjection much more profound than himself. A "soul" inhabits him and brings him to existence, which is itself a factor in the mastery that power exercises over the body. The soul is the effect and instrument of a political anatomy; the soul is the prison of the body.

That punishment in general and the prison in particular belong to a political technology of the body is a lesson that I have learned not so much from history as from the present. In recent years, prison revolts have occurred throughout the world. There was certainly something paradoxical about their aims, their slogans, and the way they took place. They were revolts against an entire state of physical misery that is over a century old: against cold, suffocation, and overcrowding, against decrepit walls, hunger, physical maltreatment. But they were also revolts against model prisons, tranquillizers, isolation, the medical or educational services. Were they revolts whose aims were merely material? Or contradictory revolts: against the obsolete, but also against comfort; against the warders, but also against the psychiatrists? In fact, all these movements—and the innumerable discourses that the prison has given rise to since the early nineteenth century—have been about the body and material things. What has sustained these discourses, these memories and invectives, are indeed those minute material details. One may, if one is so disposed, see them as no more than blind demands or suspect the existence behind them of alien strategies. In fact, they were revolts, at the level of the body, against the very body of the prison. What was at issue was not whether the prison environment was too harsh or too aseptic, too primitive or too efficient, but its very materiality as an instrument and vector of power; it is this whole technology of power over the body that the technology of the "soul"—that of the educationalists, psychologists, and psychiatrists—fails either to conceal or to compensate, for the simple reason that it is one of its tools. I would like to write the history of this prison, with all the political investments of the body that it gathers together in its closed architecture. Why? Simply because I am interested in the past? No, if one means by that writing a history of the past in terms of the present. Yes, if one means writing the history of the present.[19]

Notes

1. *Pièces originales et procédures du process fait à Robert-François Damiens*, III, (1757), 372–374.
2. Quoted in A. L. Zevaes, *Damiens le regicide* (1937), 201–214.
3. L. Faucher, *De la réforme de prisons* (1838), 274–282.
4. Roberts Vaux, *Notices*, 21, quoted in N. K. Teeters, *They Were in Prison* (1937), 24.
5. Cf. A. Réal, *Arch. parl.*, 2e série, LXXII, December 1, 1831.
6. C. de Beccaria, *Traité des délits et des peines* (1764, ed. 1856), 101.
7. N. K. Teeters, *The Cradle of the Penitentiary* (1935), 30.
8. P. van Meenen, "Congrès pénitentiare de Bruxelles," *Annales de la Charité*, (1947): 529–530.
9. The public execution of traitors described by William Blackstone, *Commentaries on the Laws of England*, vol. 4 (1776): 9, 89. Since the French translation was intended to bring out the humaneness of English legislation, in contrast with the old ordinance of 1760, the French translator adds the following note: "In this form of execution, which is so terrifying to see, the guilty man does not suffer much pain, or for long."
10. See C. Hibbert, *The Roots of Evil* (1966), 85–86.
11. Le Peletier de Saint-Fargeau, *Arch. parl.*, XXVI (June 3, 1791), 720.
12. Saint-Edme (E. Bourg), *Dictionnaire de pénalité*, IV (1825), 161.
13. A. de Molene, *De l'humanité des lois criminelles*, (1830), 275–277.
14. *Gazette des tribunaux* (August 30, 1832).
15. G. de Mably, *De la législation, Oeuvres completes*, IX (1789), 326.
16. Cf. E. Durkheim, "Deux lois de l'évolution pénale," *Année sociologique* IV (1899–1900).
17. In any case, I could give no notion by references or quotations what this book owes to Gilles Deleuze and the work he is undertaking with Félix Guattari. I should also have quoted a number of pages from R. Castell's *Psychanalysme* and say how much I am indebted to Pierre Nora.
18. Cf. E. Le Roy-Lauderie, *Contrepoint* (1973) and "L'histore immbolie," *Annales* (May–June 1974).
19. I shall study the birth of the prison only in the French penal system. Differences in historical developments and institutions would make a detailed comparative examination too burdensome and any attempt to describe the phenomenon as a whole too schematic.

QUESTIONS

1. Why is Foucault concerned that punishment has become "the most hidden part of the penal process"? (342)
2. According to Foucault, why is there "a shame in punishing" in modern justice? (343)
3. Why does modern punishment try to reach the soul rather than the body of the condemned?
4. What does it mean that punishment has become "an economy of suspended rights"? (344)
5. Why does the law want to apply punishment to a "juridical subject" rather than to a "real body capable of feeling pain"? (345)
6. Why does Foucault say that "comedy began" with the shift in punishment away from the body, to the soul? (348)
7. Why is it important that crime, "the object with which penal practice is concerned, has profoundly altered . . . the substance of which the punishable element is made"? (348–349)
8. Why is Foucault concerned that legal punishment has come to acquire "a justifiable hold not only on offenses, but on individuals"? (350)
9. Does the author object to "the present scientifico-legal complex"? (353)
10. What does the author mean when he says that he will "try to study the metamorphosis of punitive methods on the basis of a political technology of the body in which might be read a common history of power relations and object relations"? (354)
11. What does it mean that the study of the microphysics of power "presupposes that the power exercised on the body is conceived not as a property, but as a strategy"? (356)
12. According to Foucault, how does the concept of power-knowledge affect one's view of punishment?

13. Why does Foucault assert that the surplus power exercised on the body of a condemned man gives rise to "another type of duplication"? (358)

14. What does it mean that rather than seeing the modern soul as "the reactivated remnants of an ideology, one would see it as the present correlative of a certain technology of power over the body"? (358)

15. What does Foucault mean when he says, "The soul is the effect and instrument of a political anatomy; the soul is the prison of the body"? (359)

FOR FURTHER REFLECTION

1. Why do we punish? Should we? If so, who or what should be the agent of punishment?

2. Are the effects of Mably's principle—"strike the soul rather than the body"—being felt throughout the modern penal system? If so, how?

3. Is Foucault correct in asserting that we must "rid ourselves of the illusion that penality is above all . . . a means of reducing crime"?

4. Do you think that the modern system of punishment illustrates Foucault's observation that "the body becomes a useful force only if it is both a productive body and a subjected body"?

JHUMPA LAHIRI

Jhumpa Lahiri (1967–) was born in London to Bengali immigrant parents; her father was a librarian and her mother a teacher. The family later relocated to South Kingstown, Rhode Island, where Lahiri spent her teenage years.

Lahiri began to write when she was in grade school, creating short "novels" with her friends during recess. From an early age, she accompanied her parents on periodic visits to India, where she experienced a sense of not belonging in the place her parents still called home. At the same time, she has said that she never felt quite at home in the United States either. Lahiri graduated from Barnard College and then attended Boston University, where she earned three master's degrees—in English, creative writing, and comparative studies in literature and the arts—as well as a PhD in Renaissance studies. She has taught creative writing at Boston University and the Rhode Island School of Design.

"Interpreter of Maladies" is the title story of Lahiri's first collection of short stories, published in 1999. The book won numerous awards, including the O. Henry Award, the PEN/Hemingway Award, the *Louisville Review*'s fiction prize, and the American Academy of Arts and Letters Metcalf Award. In 2000, Lahiri became the first Indian-American woman to be awarded the Pulitzer Prize for Fiction, and in 2002, she received a Guggenheim Fellowship. Lahiri published her first novel, *The Namesake*, in 2003.

To date, most of Lahiri's fiction explores what it means to belong and what it means to be estranged. Her characters, often first- and second-generation Indian immigrants, grapple with problems of identity, separation, and isolation, not only as part of the Indian diaspora, but also within their own communities and families. While most of her stories revolve around characters who struggle to maintain a footing in two worlds, the stories transcend the immigrant experience by acknowledging that one does not have to leave home to feel like an exile.

JHUMPA LAHIRI

Interpreter of Maladies

At the tea stall Mr. and Mrs. Das bickered about who should take Tina to the toilet. Eventually Mrs. Das relented when Mr. Das pointed out that he had given the girl her bath the night before. In the rearview mirror Mr. Kapasi watched as Mrs. Das emerged slowly from his bulky white Ambassador, dragging her shaved, largely bare legs across the back seat. She did not hold the little girl's hand as they walked to the restroom.

They were on their way to see the Sun Temple at Konarak. It was a dry, bright Saturday, the mid-July heat tempered by a steady ocean breeze, ideal weather for sightseeing. Ordinarily Mr. Kapasi would not have stopped so soon along the way, but less than five minutes after he'd picked up the family that morning in front of Hotel Sandy Villa, the little girl had complained. The first thing Mr. Kapasi had noticed when he saw Mr. and Mrs. Das, standing with their children under the portico of the hotel, was that they were very young, perhaps not even thirty. In addition to Tina they had two boys, Ronny and Bobby, who appeared very close in age and had teeth covered in a network of flashing silver wires. The family looked Indian but dressed as foreigners did, the children in stiff, brightly colored clothing and caps with translucent visors. Mr. Kapasi was accustomed to foreign tourists; he was assigned to them regularly because he could speak English. Yesterday he had driven an elderly couple from Scotland, both with spotted faces and fluffy white hair so thin it exposed their sunburnt scalps. In comparison, the tanned, youthful faces of Mr. and Mrs. Das were all the more striking. When he'd introduced himself, Mr. Kapasi had pressed his palms together in greeting, but Mr. Das squeezed hands like an American so that Mr. Kapasi felt it in his elbow. Mrs. Das, for her part, had flexed one side of her mouth, smiling dutifully at Mr. Kapasi, without displaying any interest in him.

As they waited at the tea stall, Ronny, who looked like the older of the two boys, clambered suddenly out of the back seat, intrigued by a goat tied to a stake in the ground.

"Don't touch it," Mr. Das said. He glanced up from his paperback tour book, which said "INDIA" in yellow letters and looked as if it had been published abroad. His voice, somehow tentative and a little shrill, sounded as though it had not yet settled into maturity

"I want to give it a piece of gum," the boy called back as he trotted ahead.

Mr. Das stepped out of the car and stretched his legs by squatting briefly to the ground. A clean-shaven man, he looked exactly like a magnified version of Ronny. He had a sapphire blue visor, and was dressed in shorts, sneakers, and a T-shirt. The camera slung around his neck, with an impressive telephoto lens and numerous buttons and markings, was the only complicated thing he wore. He frowned, watching as Ronny rushed toward the goat, but appeared to have no intention of intervening. "Bobby, make sure that your brother doesn't do anything stupid."

"I don't feel like it," Bobby said, not moving. He was sitting in the front seat beside Mr. Kapasi, studying a picture of the elephant god taped to the glove compartment.

"No need to worry," Mr. Kapasi said. "They are quite tame." Mr. Kapasi was forty-six years old, with receding hair that had gone completely silver, but his butterscotch complexion and his unlined brow, which he treated in spare moments to dabs of lotus-oil balm, made it easy to imagine what he must have looked like at an earlier age. He wore gray trousers and a matching jacket-style shirt, tapered at the waist, with short sleeves and a large pointed collar, made of a thin but durable synthetic material. He had specified both the cut and the fabric to his tailor—it was his preferred uniform for giving tours because it did not get crushed during his long hours behind the wheel. Through the windshield he watched as Ronny circled around the goat, touched it quickly on its side, then trotted back to the car.

"You left India as a child?" Mr. Kapasi asked when Mr. Das had settled once again into the passenger seat.

"Oh, Mina and I were both born in America," Mr. Das announced with an air of sudden confidence. "Born and raised. Our parents live here now, in Assansol. They retired. We visit them every couple years." He turned to watch as the little girl ran toward the car, the wide purple bows of her sundress flopping on her narrow brown shoulders. She was holding to her chest a doll with yellow hair that looked as if it had been chopped, as a punitive measure, with a pair of dull scissors. "This is Tina's first trip to India, isn't it, Tina?"

"I don't have to go to the bathroom anymore," Tina announced.

"Where's Mina?" Mr. Das asked.

Mr. Kapasi found it strange that Mr. Das should refer to his wife by her first name when speaking to the little girl. Tina pointed to where

Mrs. Das was purchasing something from one of the shirtless men who worked at the tea stall. Mr. Kapasi heard one of the shirtless men sing a phrase from a popular Hindi love song as Mrs. Das walked back to the car, but she did not appear to understand the words of the song, for she did not express irritation, or embarrassment, or react in any other way to the man's declarations.

He observed her. She wore a red-and-white-checkered skirt that stopped above her knees, slip-on shoes with a square wooden heel, and a close-fitting blouse styled like a man's undershirt. The blouse was decorated at chest-level with a calico appliqué in the shape of a strawberry. She was a short woman, with small hands like paws, her frosty pink fingernails painted to match her lips, and was slightly plump in her figure. Her hair, shorn only a little longer than her husband's, was parted far to one side. She was wearing large dark brown sunglasses with a pinkish tint to them, and carried a big straw bag, almost as big as her torso, shaped like a bowl, with a water bottle poking out of it. She walked slowly, carrying some puffed rice tossed with peanuts and chili peppers in a large packet made from newspapers. Mr. Kapasi turned to Mr. Das.

"Where in America do you live?"

"New Brunswick, New Jersey."

"Next to New York?"

"Exactly. I teach middle school there."

"What subject?"

"Science. In fact, every year I take my students on a trip to the Museum of Natural History in New York City. In a way we have a lot in common, you could say, you and I. How long have you been a tour guide, Mr. Kapasi?"

"Five years."

Mrs. Das reached the car. "How long's the trip?" she asked, shutting the door.

"About two and a half hours," Mr. Kapasi replied.

At this Mrs. Das gave an impatient sigh, as if she had been traveling her whole life without pause. She fanned herself with a folded Bombay film magazine written in English.

"I thought that the Sun Temple is only eighteen miles north of Puri," Mr. Das said, tapping on the tour book.

"The roads to Konarak are poor. Actually it is a distance of fifty-two miles," Mr. Kapasi explained.

Mr. Das nodded, readjusting the camera strap where it had begun to chafe the back of his neck.

Before starting the ignition, Mr. Kapasi reached back to make sure the cranklike locks on the inside of each of the back doors were secured. As soon as the car began to move the little girl began to play with the lock on her side, clicking it with some effort forward and backward, but Mrs. Das said nothing to stop her. She sat a bit slouched at one end of the back seat, not offering her puffed rice to anyone. Ronny and Tina sat on either side of her, both snapping bright green gum.

"Look," Bobby said as the car began to gather speed. He pointed with his finger to the tall trees that lined the road. "Look."

"Monkeys!" Ronny shrieked. "Wow!"

They were seated in groups along the branches, with shining black faces, silver bodies, horizontal eyebrows, and crested heads. Their long gray tails dangled like a series of ropes among the leaves. A few scratched themselves with black leathery hands, or swung their feet, staring as the car passed.

"We call them the hanuman," Mr. Kapasi said. "They are quite common in the area."

As soon as he spoke, one of the monkeys leaped into the middle of the road, causing Mr. Kapasi to brake suddenly. Another bounced onto the hood of the car, then sprang away. Mr. Kapasi beeped his horn. The children began to get excited, sucking in their breath and covering their faces partly with their hands. They had never seen monkeys outside of a zoo, Mr. Das explained. He asked Mr. Kapasi to stop the car so that he could take a picture.

While Mr. Das adjusted his telephoto lens, Mrs. Das reached into her straw bag and pulled out a bottle of colorless nail polish, which she proceeded to stroke on the tip of her index finger.

The little girl stuck out a hand. "Mine too. Mommy, do mine too."

"Leave me alone," Mrs. Das said, blowing on her nail and turning her body slightly "You're making me mess up."

The little girl occupied herself by buttoning and unbuttoning a pinafore on the doll's plastic body.

"All set," Mr. Das said, replacing the lens cap.

The car rattled considerably as it raced along the dusty road, causing them all to pop up from their seats every now and then, but Mrs. Das continued to polish her nails. Mr. Kapasi eased up on the accelerator, hoping to produce a smoother ride. When he reached for the gearshift the boy in front accommodated him by swinging his hairless knees out of the way. Mr. Kapasi noted that this boy was slightly paler than the other children. "Daddy, why is the driver sitting on the wrong side in this car, too?" the boy asked.

"They all do that here, dummy," Ronny said.

"Don't call your brother a dummy," Mr. Das said. He turned to Mr. Kapasi. "In America, you know . . . it confuses them."

"Oh yes, I am well aware," Mr. Kapasi said. As delicately as he could, he shifted gears again, accelerating as they approached a hill in the road. "I see it on *Dallas*, the steering wheels are on the left-hand side."

"What's *Dallas*?" Tina asked, banging her now naked doll on the seat behind Mr. Kapasi.

"It went off the air," Mr. Das explained. "It's a television show."

They were all like siblings, Mr. Kapasi thought as they passed a row of date trees. Mr. and Mrs. Das behaved like an older brother and sister, not parents. It seemed that they were in charge of the children only for the day; it was hard to believe they were regularly responsible for anything other than themselves. Mr. Das tapped on his lens cap, and his tour book, dragging his thumbnail occasionally across the pages so that they made a scraping sound. Mrs. Das continued to polish her nails. She had still not removed her sunglasses. Every now and then Tina renewed her plea that she wanted her nails done, too, and so at one point Mrs. Das flicked a drop of polish on the little girl's finger before depositing the bottle back inside her straw bag.

"Isn't this an air-conditioned car?" she asked, still blowing on her hand. The window on Tina's side was broken and could not be rolled down.

"Quit complaining," Mr. Das said. "it isn't so hot."

"I told you to get a car with air-conditioning," Mrs. Das continued. "Why do you do this, Raj, just to save a few stupid rupees. What are you saving us, fifty cents?"

Their accents sounded just like the ones Mr. Kapasi heard on American television programs, though not like the ones on *Dallas*.

"Doesn't it get tiresome, Mr. Kapasi, showing people the same thing every day?" Mr. Das asked, rolling down his own window all the way. "Hey, do you mind stopping the car. I just want to get a shot of this guy."

Mr. Kapasi pulled over to the side of the road as Mr. Das took a picture of a barefoot man, his head wrapped in a dirty turban, seated on top of a cart of grain sacks pulled by a pair of bullocks. Both the man and the bullocks were emaciated. In the back seat Mrs. Das gazed out another window, at the sky, where nearly transparent clouds passed quickly in front of one another.

"I look forward to it, actually," Mr. Kapasi said as they continued on their way. "The Sun Temple is one of my favorite places. In that way it is a reward for me. I give tours on Fridays and Saturdays only. I have another job during the week."

"Oh? Where?" Mr. Das asked.

"I work in a doctor's office."

"You're a doctor?"

"I am not a doctor. I work with one. As an interpreter."

"What does a doctor need an interpreter for?"

"He has a number of Gujarati patients. My father was Gujarati, but many people do not speak Gujarati in this area, including the doctor. And so the doctor asked me to work in his office, interpreting what the patients say."

"Interesting. I've never heard of anything like that," Mr. Das said.

Mr. Kapasi shrugged. "It is a job like any other."

"But so romantic," Mrs. Das said dreamily, breaking her extended silence. She lifted her pinkish brown sunglasses and arranged them on top of her head like a tiara. For the first time, her eyes met Mr. Kapasi's in the rearview mirror: pale, a bit small, their gaze fixed but drowsy.

Mr. Das craned to look at her. "What's so romantic about it?"

"I don't know. Something." She shrugged, knitting her brows together for an instant. "Would you like a piece of gum, Mr. Kapasi?" she asked brightly. She reached into her straw bag and handed him a small square wrapped in green-and-white-striped paper. As soon as Mr. Kapasi put the gum in his mouth a thick sweet liquid burst onto his tongue.

"Tell us more about your job, Mr. Kapasi," Mrs. Das said.

"What would you like to know, madame?"

"I don't know," she shrugged, munching on some puffed rice and licking the mustard oil from the corners of her mouth. "Tell us a typical situation." She settled back in her seat, her head tilted in a patch of sun, and closed her eyes. "I want to picture what happens."

"Very well. The other day a man came in with a pain in his throat."

"Did he smoke cigarettes?"

"No. It was very curious. He complained that he felt as if there were long pieces of straw stuck in his throat. When I told the doctor he was able to prescribe the proper medication."

"That's so neat."

"Yes," Mr. Kapasi agreed after some hesitation.

"So these patients are totally dependent on you," Mrs. Das said. She spoke slowly, as if she were thinking aloud. "In a way, more dependent on you than the doctor."

"How do you mean? How could it be?"

"Well, for example, you could tell the doctor that the pain felt like a burning, not straw. The patient would never know what you had told the doctor, and the doctor wouldn't know that you had told the wrong thing. It's a big responsibility."

"Yes, a big responsibility you have there, Mr. Kapasi," Mr. Das agreed.

Mr. Kapasi had never thought of his job in such complimentary terms. To him it was a thankless occupation. He found nothing noble in interpreting people's maladies, assiduously translating the symptoms of so many swollen bones, countless cramps of bellies and bowels, spots on people's palms that changed color, shape, or size. The doctor, nearly half his age, had an affinity for bell-bottom trousers and made humorless jokes about the Congress party. Together they worked in a stale little infirmary where Mr. Kapasi's smartly tailored clothes clung to him in the heat, in spite of the blackened blades of a ceiling fan churning over their heads.

The job was a sign of his failings. In his youth he'd been a devoted scholar of foreign languages, the owner of an impressive collection of dictionaries. He had dreamed of being an interpreter for diplomats and dignitaries, resolving conflicts between people and nations, settling disputes of which he alone could understand both sides. He was a self-educated man. In a series of notebooks, in the evenings before his parents settled his marriage, he had listed the common etymologies of words, and at one point in his life he was confident that he could converse, if given the opportunity, in English, French, Russian, Portuguese, and Italian, not to mention Hindi, Bengali, Orissi, and Gujarati. Now only a handful of European phrases remained in his memory, scattered words for things like saucers and chairs. English was the only non-Indian language he spoke fluently anymore. Mr. Kapasi knew it was not a remarkable talent. Sometimes he feared that his children knew better English than he did, just from watching television. Still, it came in handy for the tours.

He had taken the job as an interpreter after his first son, at the age of seven, contracted typhoid—that was how he had first made the acquaintance of the doctor. At the time Mr. Kapasi had been teaching English in a grammar school, and he bartered his skills as an interpreter to pay the increasingly exorbitant medical bills. In the end the boy had died one evening in his mother's arms, his limbs burning with fever, but then there was the funeral to pay for, and the other children who were born soon enough, and the newer, bigger house, and the good schools and tutors, and the fine shoes and the television, and the countless other ways he tried to console his wife and to keep her from crying in her sleep, and so when the doctor offered to pay him twice as much as he earned at the grammar school, he accepted. Mr. Kapasi knew that his wife had little regard for his career as an interpreter. He knew it reminded her of the son she'd lost, and that she resented the other lives he helped, in his own small way, to save. If ever she referred to his position, she used the phrase "doctor's assistant," as if the process of interpretation were equal to taking someone's temperature, or changing a bedpan. She never asked him about the patients who came to the doctor's office, or said that his job was a big responsibility.

For this reason it flattered Mr. Kapasi that Mrs. Das was so intrigued by his job. Unlike his wife, she had reminded him of its intellectual challenges. She had also used the word "romantic." She did not behave in a romantic way toward her husband, and yet she had used the word to describe him. He wondered if Mr. and Mrs. Das were a bad match, just as he and his wife were. Perhaps they, too, had little in common apart from three children and a decade of their lives. The signs he recognized from his own marriage were there—the bickering, the indifference, the protracted silences. Her sudden interest in him, an interest she did not express in either her husband or her children, was mildly intoxicating. When Mr. Kapasi thought once again about how she had said "romantic," the feeling of intoxication grew.

He began to check his reflection in the rearview mirror as he drove, feeling grateful that he had chosen the gray suit that morning and not the brown one, which tended to sag a little in the knees. From time to time he glanced through the mirror at Mrs. Das. In addition to glancing at her face he glanced at the strawberry between her breasts, and the golden brown hollow in her throat. He decided to tell Mrs. Das about another patient, and another: the young woman who had complained of a sensation of raindrops in her spine, the gentleman whose birthmark had begun to sprout hairs. Mrs. Das listened attentively, stroking her hair with a small plastic brush that resembled an oval bed of nails, asking more questions, for yet another example. The children were quiet, intent on spotting more monkeys in the trees, and Mr. Das was absorbed by his tour book, so it seemed like a private conversation between Mr. Kapasi and Mrs. Das. In this manner the next half hour passed, and when they stopped for lunch at a roadside restaurant that sold fritters and omelette sandwiches, usually something Mr. Kapasi looked forward to on his tours so that he could sit in peace and enjoy some hot tea, he was disappointed. As the Das family settled together under a magenta umbrella fringed with white and orange tassels, and placed their orders with one of the waiters who marched about in tricornered caps, Mr. Kapasi reluctantly headed toward a neighboring table.

"Mr. Kapasi, wait. There's room here," Mrs. Das called out. She gathered Tina onto her lap, insisting that he accompany them. And so, together, they had bottled mango juice and sandwiches and plates of onions and potatoes deep-fried in graham-flour batter. After finishing two omelette sandwiches Mr. Das took more pictures of the group as they ate.

"How much longer?" he asked Mr. Kapasi as he paused to load a new roll of film in the camera.

"About half an hour more."

By now the children had gotten up from the table to look at more monkeys perched in a nearby tree, so there was a considerable space between Mrs. Das and Mr. Kapasi. Mr. Das placed the camera to his face and squeezed one eye shut, his tongue exposed at one corner of his mouth. "This looks funny. Mina, you need to lean in closer to Mr. Kapasi."

She did. He could smell a scent on her skin, like a mixture of whiskey and rosewater. He worried suddenly that she could smell his perspiration, which he knew had collected beneath the synthetic material of his shirt. He polished off his mango juice in one gulp and smoothed his silver hair with his hands. A bit of the juice dripped onto his chin. He wondered if Mrs. Das had noticed.

She had not. "What's your address, Mr. Kapasi?" she inquired, fishing for something inside her straw bag.

"You would like my address?"

"So we can send you copies," she said. "Of the pictures." She handed him a scrap of paper which she had hastily ripped from a page of her film magazine. The blank portion was limited, for the narrow strip was crowded by lines of text and a tiny picture of a hero and heroine embracing under a eucalyptus tree.

The paper curled as Mr. Kapasi wrote his address in clear, careful letters. She would write to him, asking about his days interpreting at the doctor's office, and he would respond eloquently, choosing only the most entertaining anecdotes, ones that would make her laugh out loud as she read them in her house in New Jersey. In time she would reveal the disappointment of her marriage, and he his. In this way their friendship would grow, and flourish. He would possess a picture of the two of them, eating fried onions under a magenta umbrella, which he would keep, he decided, safely tucked between the pages of his Russian grammar. As his mind raced, Mr. Kapasi experienced a mild and pleasant shock. It was similar to a feeling he used to experience long ago when, after months of translating with the aid of a dictionary, he would finally read a passage from a French novel, or an Italian sonnet, and understand the words, one after another, unencumbered by his own efforts. In those moments Mr. Kapasi used to believe that all was right with the world, that all struggles were rewarded, that all of life's mistakes made sense in the end. The promise that he would hear from Mrs. Das now filled him with the same belief.

When he finished writing his address Mr. Kapasi handed her the paper, but as soon as he did so he worried that he had either misspelled his name, or accidentally reversed the numbers of his postal code. He dreaded the possibility of a lost letter, the photograph never reaching him, hovering somewhere in Orissa, close but ultimately unattainable. He thought of asking for the slip of paper again, just to make sure he had written his address accurately, but Mrs. Das had already dropped it into the jumble of her bag.

They reached Konarak at two-thirty. The temple, made of sandstone, was a massive pyramid-like structure in the shape of a chariot. It was dedicated to the great master of life, the sun, which struck three sides of the edifice as it made its journey each day across the sky. Twenty-four giant wheels were carved on the north and south sides of the plinth. The whole thing was drawn by a team of seven horses, speeding as if through the heavens. As they approached, Mr. Kapasi explained that the temple had been built between AD 1243 and 1255, with the efforts of twelve hundred artisans, by the great ruler of the Ganga dynasty, King Narasimhadeva the First, to commemorate his victory against the Muslim army.

"It says the temple occupies about a hundred and seventy acres of land," Mr. Das said, reading from his book.

"It's like a desert," Ronny said, his eyes wandering across the sand that stretched on all sides beyond the temple.

"The Chandrabhaga River once flowed one mile north of here. It is dry now," Mr. Kapasi said, turning off the engine.

They got out and walked toward the temple, posing first for pictures by the pair of lions that flanked the steps. Mr. Kapasi led them next to one of the wheels of the chariot, higher than any human being, nine feet in diameter.

"'The wheels are supposed to symbolize the wheel of life,'" Mr. Das read. "'They depict the cycle of creation, preservation, and achievement of realization.' Cool." He turned the page of his book. "'Each wheel is divided into eight thick and thin spokes, dividing the day into eight equal parts. The rims are carved with designs of birds and animals, whereas the medallions in the spokes are carved with women in luxurious poses, largely erotic in nature.'"

What he referred to were the countless friezes of entwined naked bodies, making love in various positions, women clinging to the necks of men, their knees wrapped eternally around their lovers' thighs. In addition to these were assorted scenes from daily life, of hunting and trading, of deer being killed with bows and arrows and marching warriors holding swords in their hands.

It was no longer possible to enter the temple, for it had filled with rubble years ago, but they admired the exterior, as did all the tourists Mr. Kapasi brought there, slowly strolling along each of its sides. Mr. Das trailed behind, taking pictures. The children ran ahead, pointing to figures of naked people, intrigued in particular by the Nagamithunas, the half-human, half-serpentine couples who were said, Mr. Kapasi told them, to live in the deepest waters of the sea. Mr. Kapasi was pleased that they liked the temple, pleased especially that it appealed to Mrs. Das. She stopped every three or four paces, staring silently at the carved lovers, and the processions of elephants, and the topless female musicians beating on two-sided drums.

Though Mr. Kapasi had been to the temple countless times, it occurred to him, as he, too, gazed at the topless women, that he had never seen his own wife fully naked. Even when they had made love she kept the panels of her blouse hooked together, the string of her petticoat knotted around her waist. He had never admired the backs of his wife's legs the way he now admired those of Mrs. Das, walking as if for his benefit alone. He had, of course, seen plenty of bare limbs before, belonging to the American and European ladies who took his tours. But Mrs. Das was different. Unlike the other women, who had an interest only in the temple, and kept their noses buried in a guidebook, or their eyes behind the lens of a camera, Mrs. Das had taken an interest in him.

Mr. Kapasi was anxious to be alone with her, to continue their private conversation, yet he felt nervous to walk at her side. She was lost behind her sunglasses, ignoring her husband's requests that she pose for another picture, walking past her children as if they were strangers. Worried that he might disturb her, Mr. Kapasi walked ahead, to admire, as he always did, the three life-sized bronze avatars of Surya, the sun god, each emerging from its own niche on the temple facade to greet the sun at dawn, noon, and evening. They wore elaborate headdresses, their languid, elongated eyes closed, their bare chests draped with carved chains and amulets. Hibiscus petals, offerings from previous visitors, were strewn at their gray-green feet. The last statue, on the northern wall of the temple, was Mr. Kapasi's favorite. This Surya had a tired expression, weary after a hard day of work, sitting astride a horse with folded legs. Even his horse's eyes were drowsy. Around his body were smaller sculptures of women in pairs, their hips thrust to one side.

"Who's that?" Mrs. Das asked. He was startled to see that she was standing beside him.

"He is the Astachala-Surya," Mr. Kapasi said. "The setting sun."

"So in a couple of hours the sun will set right here?" She slipped a foot out of one of her square-heeled shoes, rubbed her toes on the back of her other leg.

"That is correct."

She raised her sunglasses for a moment, then put them back on again. "Neat."

Mr. Kapasi was not certain exactly what the word suggested, but he had a feeling it was a favorable response. He hoped that Mrs. Das had understood Surya's beauty, his power. Perhaps they would discuss it further in their letters. He would explain things to her, things about India, and she would explain things to him about America. In its own way this correspondence would fulfill his dream, of serving as an interpreter between nations. He looked at her straw bag, delighted that his address lay nestled among its contents. When he pictured her so many thousands of miles away he plummeted, so much so that he had an overwhelming urge to wrap his arms around her, to freeze with her, even for an instant, in an embrace witnessed by his favorite Surya. But Mrs. Das had already started walking.

"When do you return to America?" he asked, trying to sound placid.

"In ten days."

He calculated: A week to settle in, a week to develop the pictures, a few days to compose her letter, two weeks to get to India by air. According to his schedule, allowing room for delays, he would hear from Mrs. Das in approximately six weeks' time.

The family was silent as Mr. Kapasi drove them back, a little past four-thirty, to Hotel Sandy Villa. The children had bought miniature granite versions of the chariot's wheels at a souvenir stand, and they turned them round in their hands. Mr. Das continued to read his book. Mrs. Das untangled Tina's hair with her brush and divided it into two little ponytails.

Mr. Kapasi was beginning to dread the thought of dropping them off. He was not prepared to begin his six-week wait to hear from Mrs. Das. As he stole glances at her in the rearview mirror, wrapping elastic bands around Tina's hair, he wondered how he might make the tour last a little longer. Ordinarily he sped back to Puri using a shortcut, eager to return home, scrub his feet and hands with sandalwood soap, and enjoy the evening newspaper and a cup of tea that his wife would serve him in silence. The thought of that silence, something to which he'd long been resigned, now oppressed him. It was then that he suggested visiting the hills at Udayagiri and Khandagiri, where a number of monastic dwellings were hewn out of the ground, facing one another across a defile. It was some miles away, but well worth seeing, Mr. Kapasi told them.

"Oh yeah, there's something mentioned about it in this book," Mr. Das said. "Built by a Jain king or something."

"Shall we go then?" Mr. Kapasi asked. He paused at a turn in the road. "It's to the left."

Mr. Das turned to look at Mrs. Das. Both of them shrugged.

"Left, left," the children chanted.

Mr. Kapasi turned the wheel, almost delirious with relief. He did not know what he would do or say to Mrs. Das once they arrived at the hills. Perhaps he would tell her what a pleasing smile she had. Perhaps he would compliment her strawberry shirt, which he found irresistibly becoming. Perhaps, when Mr. Das was busy taking a picture, he would take her hand.

He did not have to worry. When they got to the hills, divided by a steep path thick with trees, Mrs. Das refused to get out of the car. All along the path, dozens of monkeys were seated on stones, as well as on the branches of the trees. Their hind legs were stretched out in front and raised to shoulder level, their arms resting on their knees.

"My legs are tired," she said, sinking low in her seat. "I'll stay here."

"Why did you have to wear those stupid shoes?" Mr. Das said. "You won't be in the pictures."

"Pretend I'm there."

"But we could use one of these pictures for our Christmas card this year. We didn't get one of all five of us at the Sun Temple. Mr. Kapasi could take it."

"I'm not coming. Anyway, those monkeys give me the creeps."

"But they're harmless," Mr. Das said. He turned to Mr. Kapasi. "Aren't they?"

"They are more hungry than dangerous," Mr. Kapasi said. "Do not provoke them with food, and they will not bother you."

Mr. Das headed up the defile with the children, the boys at his side, the little girl on his shoulders. Mr. Kapasi watched as they crossed paths with a Japanese man and woman, the only other tourists there, who paused for a final photograph, then stepped into a nearby car and drove away. As the car disappeared out of view some of the monkeys called out, emitting soft whooping sounds, and then walked on their flat black hands and feet up the path. At one point a group of them formed a little ring around Mr. Das and the children. Tina screamed in delight. Ronny ran in circles around his father. Bobby bent down and picked up a fat stick on the ground.

When he extended it, one of the monkeys approached him and snatched it, then briefly beat the ground.

"I'll join them," Mr. Kapasi said, unlocking the door on his side. "There is much to explain about the caves."

"No. Stay a minute," Mrs. Das said. She got out of the back seat and slipped in beside Mr. Kapasi. "Raj has his dumb book anyway." Together, through the windshield, Mrs. Das and Mr. Kapasi watched as Bobby and the monkey passed the stick back and forth between them.

"A brave little boy," Mr. Kapasi commented.

"It's not so surprising," Mrs. Das said.

"No?"

"He's not his."

"I beg your pardon?"

"Raj's. He's not Raj's son."

Mr. Kapasi felt a prickle on his skin. He reached into his shirt pocket for the small tin of lotus-oil balm he carried with him at all times, and applied it to three spots on his forehead. He knew that Mrs. Das was watching him, but he did not turn to face her. Instead he watched as the figures of Mr. Das and the children grew smaller, climbing up the steep path, pausing every now and then for a picture, surrounded by a growing number of monkeys.

"Are you surprised?" The way she put it made him choose his words with care.

"It's not the type of thing one assumes," Mr. Kapasi replied slowly. He put the tin of lotus-oil balm back in his pocket.

"No, of course not. And no one knows, of course. No one at all. I've kept it a secret for eight whole years." She looked at Mr. Kapasi, tilting her chin as if to gain a fresh perspective. "But now I've told you."

Mr. Kapasi nodded. He felt suddenly parched, and his forehead was warm and slightly numb from the balm. He considered asking Mrs. Das for a sip of water, then decided against it.

"We met when we were very young," she said. She reached into her straw bag in search of something, then pulled out a packet of puffed rice. "Want some?"

"No, thank you."

She put a fistful in her mouth, sank into the seat a little, and looked away from Mr. Kapasi, out the window on her side of the car. "We married when we were still in college. We were in high school when he proposed. We went to the same college, of course. Back then we couldn't stand the thought of being separated, not for a day, not for a minute. Our parents were best friends who lived in the same town. My entire life I saw him every weekend, either at our house or theirs. We were sent upstairs to play together while our parents joked about our marriage. Imagine! They never caught us at anything, though in a way I think it was all more or less a setup. The things we did those Friday and Saturday nights, while our parents sat downstairs drinking tea . . . I could tell you stories, Mr. Kapasi."

As a result of spending all her time in college with Raj, she continued, she did not make many close friends. There was no one to confide in about him at the end of a difficult day, or to share a passing thought or a worry. Her parents now lived on the other side of the world, but she had never been very close to them, anyway. After marrying so young she was overwhelmed by it all, having a child so quickly, and nursing, and warming up bottles of milk and testing their temperature against her wrist while Raj was at work, dressed in sweaters and corduroy pants, teaching his students about rocks and dinosaurs. Raj never looked cross or harried, or plump as she had become after the first baby.

Always tired, she declined invitations from her one or two college girlfriends, to have lunch or shop in Manhattan. Eventually the friends stopped calling her, so that she was left at home all day with the baby, surrounded by toys that made her trip when she walked or wince when she sat, always cross and tired. Only occasionally did they go out after Ronny was born, and even more rarely did they entertain. Raj didn't mind; he looked forward to coming home from teaching and watching television and bouncing Ronny on his knee. She had been outraged when Raj told her that a Punjabi friend, someone whom she had once met but did not remember, would be staying with them for a week for some job interviews in the New Brunswick area.

Bobby was conceived in the afternoon, on a sofa littered with rubber teething toys, after the friend learned that a London pharmaceutical company had hired him, while Ronny cried to be freed from his playpen. She made no protest when the friend touched the small of her back as she was about to make a pot of coffee, then pulled her against his crisp navy suit. He made love to her swiftly, in silence, with an expertise she had never known, without the meaningful expressions and smiles Raj always insisted on afterward. The next day Raj drove the friend to JFK. He was married now, to a Punjabi girl, and they lived in London still, and every year they exchanged Christmas cards with Raj and Mina, each couple tucking photos of their families into the envelopes. He did not know that he was Bobby's father. He never would.

"I beg your pardon, Mrs. Das, but why have you told me this information?" Mr. Kapasi asked when she had finally finished speaking, and had turned to face him once again.

"For God's sake, stop calling me Mrs. Das. I'm twenty-eight. You probably have children my age."

"Not quite." It disturbed Mr. Kapasi to learn that she thought of him as a parent. The feeling he had had toward her, that had made him check his reflection in the rearview mirror as they drove, evaporated a little.

"I told you because of your talents." She put the packet of puffed rice back into her bag without folding over the top.

"I don't understand," Mr. Kapasi said.

"Don't you see? For eight years I haven't been able to express this to anybody, not to friends, certainly not to Raj. He doesn't even suspect it. He thinks I'm still in love with him. Well, don't you have anything to say?"

"About what?"

"About what I've just told you. About my secret, and about how terrible it makes me feel. I feel terrible looking at my children, and at Raj, always terrible. I have terrible urges, Mr. Kapasi, to throw things away. One day I had the urge to throw everything I own out the window, the television, the children, everything. Don't you think it's unhealthy?"

He was silent.

"Mr. Kapasi, don't you have anything to say? I thought that was your job."

"My job is to give tours, Mrs. Das."

"Not that. Your other job. As an interpreter."

"But we do not face a language barrier. What need is there for an interpreter?"

"That's not what I mean. I would never have told you otherwise. Don't you realize what it means for me to tell you?"

"What does it mean?"

"It means that I'm tired of feeling so terrible all the time. Eight years, Mr. Kapasi, I've been in pain eight years. I was hoping you could help me feet better, say the right thing. Suggest some kind of remedy."

He looked at her, in her red plaid skirt and strawberry T-shirt, a woman not yet thirty, who loved neither her husband nor her children, who had already fallen out of love with life. Her confession depressed him, depressed him all the more when he thought of Mr. Das at the top of the path, Tina clinging to his shoulders, taking pictures of ancient monastic cells cut into the hills to show his students in America, unsuspecting and unaware that one of his sons was not his own. Mr. Kapasi felt insulted that Mrs. Das should ask him to interpret her common, trivial little secret. She did not resemble the patients in the doctor's office, those who came glassy-eyed and desperate, unable to sleep or breathe or urinate with ease, unable, above all, to give words to their pains. Still, Mr. Kapasi believed it was his duty to assist Mrs. Das. Perhaps he ought to tell her to confess the truth to Mr. Das. He would explain that honesty was the best policy. Honesty, surely, would help her feel better, as she'd put it. Perhaps he would offer to preside over the discussion, as a mediator. He decided to begin with the most obvious question, to get to the heart of the matter, and so he asked, "Is it really pain you feel, Mrs. Das, or is it guilt?"

She turned to him and glared, mustard oil thick on her frosty pink lips. She opened her mouth to say something, but as she glared at Mr. Kapasi some certain knowledge seemed to pass before her eyes, and she stopped. It crushed him; he knew at that moment that he was not even important enough to be properly insulted. She opened the car door and began walking up the path, wobbling a little on her square wooden heels, reaching into her straw bag to eat handfuls of puffed rice. It fell through her fingers, leaving a zigzagging trail, causing a monkey to leap down from a tree and devour the little white grains. In search of more, the monkey began to follow Mrs. Das. Others joined him, so that she was soon being followed by about half a dozen of them, their velvety tails dragging behind.

Mr. Kapasi stepped out of the car. He wanted to holler, to alert her in some way, but he worried that if she knew they were behind her, she would grow nervous. Perhaps she would lose her balance. Perhaps they would pull at her bag or her hair. He began to jog up the path, taking a fallen branch in his hand to scare away the monkeys. Mrs. Das continued walking, oblivious, trailing grains of puffed rice. Near the top of the incline, before a group of cells fronted by a row of squat stone pillars, Mr. Das was kneeling on the ground, focusing the lens of his camera. The children stood under the arcade, now hiding, now emerging from view.

"Wait for me," Mrs. Das called out. "I'm coming."

Tina jumped up and down. "Here comes Mommy!"

"Great," Mr. Das said without looking up. "Just in time. We'll get Mr. Kapasi to take a picture of the five of us."

Mr. Kapasi quickened his pace, waving his branch so that the monkeys scampered away, distracted, in another direction.

"Where's Bobby?" Mrs. Das asked when she stopped.

Mr. Das looked up from the camera. "I don't know. Ronny, where's Bobby?"

Ronny shrugged. "I thought he was right here."

"Where is he?" Mrs. Das repeated sharply. "What's wrong with all of you?"

They began calling his name, wandering up and down the path a bit. Because they were calling, they did not initially hear the boy's screams. When they found him, a little farther down the path under a tree, he was surrounded by a group of monkeys, over a dozen of them, pulling at his T-shirt with their long black fingers. The puffed rice Mrs. Das had spilled was scattered at his feet, raked over by the monkeys' hands. The boy was silent, his body frozen, swift tears running down his startled face. His bare legs were dusty and red with welts from where one of the monkeys struck him repeatedly with the stick he had given to it earlier.

"Daddy, the monkey's hurting Bobby," Tina said.

Mr. Das wiped his palms on the front of his shorts. In his nervousness he accidentally pressed the shutter on his camera; the whirring noise of the advancing film excited the monkeys, and the one with the stick began to beat Bobby more intently. "What are we supposed to do? What if they start attacking?"

"Mr. Kapasi," Mrs. Das shrieked, noticing him standing to one side. "Do something, for God's sake, do something!"

Mr. Kapasi took his branch and shooed them away, hissing at the ones that remained, stomping his feet to scare them. The animals retreated slowly, with a measured gait, obedient but unintimidated. Mr. Kapasi gathered Bobby in his arms and brought him back to where his parents and siblings were standing. As he carried him he was tempted to whisper a secret into the boy's ear. But Bobby was stunned, and shivering with fright, his legs bleeding slightly where the stick had broken the skin. When Mr. Kapasi delivered him to his parents, Mr. Das brushed some dirt off the boy's T-shirt and put the visor on him the right way. Mrs. Das reached into her straw bag to find a bandage which she taped over the cut on his knee. Ronny offered his brother a fresh piece of gum. "He's fine. Just a little scared, right, Bobby?" Mr. Das said, patting the top of his head.

"God, let's get out of here," Mrs. Das said. She folded her arms across the strawberry on her chest. "This place gives me the creeps."

"Yeah. Back to the hotel, definitely," Mr. Das agreed.

"Poor Bobby," Mrs. Das said. "Come here a second. Let Mommy fix your hair." Again she reached into her straw bag, this time for her hairbrush, and began to run it around the edges of the translucent visor. When she whipped out the hairbrush, the slip of paper with Mr. Kapasi's address on it fluttered away in the wind. No one but Mr. Kapasi noticed. He watched as it rose, carried higher and higher by the breeze, into the trees where the monkeys now sat, solemnly observing the scene below. Mr. Kapasi observed it too, knowing that this was the picture of the Das family he would preserve forever in his mind.

QUESTIONS

1. Why does Mrs. Das refer to Mr. Kapasi's job of interpreter in a doctor's office as "romantic"? (370)

2. Why does Mr. Kapasi see his job as a "thankless occupation" and a "sign of his failings"? (370, 371)

3. Why does Mr. Kapasi fantasize about corresponding with Mrs. Das and imagine both of them revealing the disappointments of their marriages?

4. Why does the promise that he would hear from Mrs. Das again fill Mr. Kapasi with the belief that "all was right with the world, that all struggles were rewarded, that all of life's mistakes made sense in the end"? (373)

5. Why does Mrs. Das show more interest in Mr. Kapasi's work at the doctor's office than she does in the tour?

6. Why does Mr. Kapasi think that correspondence between him and Mrs. Das would fulfill his dream of serving as "an interpreter between nations"? (375)

7. After keeping her secret for eight years, why does Mrs. Das confide in Mr. Kapasi?

8. Why does Mrs. Das object to Mr. Kapasi addressing her by her married name?

9. What does Mrs. Das mean when she says she has "terrible urges . . . to throw things away"? Why does she think that Mr. Kapasi can "suggest some kind of remedy"? (379, 380)

10. Why does Mr. Kapasi regard Mrs. Das's confidence as a "common, trivial little secret?" (380)

11. If Mr. Kapasi feels insulted that Mrs. Das should ask him to interpret her secret, why does he feel it is his duty to assist her?

12. When Mr. Kapasi asks, "Is it really pain you feel, Mrs. Das, or is it guilt?" why does she glare at him and get out of the car? (380) Why does her reaction crush him?

13. When carrying Bobby back to his parents after the monkey attack, why is Mr. Kapasi tempted to whisper a secret in Bobby's ear?
14. How do Mrs. Das's perceptions of herself affect her relationships with her husband and children?
15. Why is the scene at the end of the story "the picture of the Das family [that Mr. Kapasi] would preserve forever in his mind"? (382)

FOR FURTHER REFLECTION

1. How can a visit to one's family's country of origin affirm identity and how can it confound identity?
2. Why are some people willing to tell a stranger something they would not tell their best friend?
3. Does culture mostly help or hinder us in understanding ourselves and others?
4. How can misperceptions about others sometimes sustain a relationship but at other times undermine it?

DISCUSSION GUIDES FOR

The Prince
by Niccolò Machiavelli

Jane Eyre
by Charlotte Brontë

NICCOLÒ MACHIAVELLI

What we know of the personal character of Niccolò Machiavelli (1469–1527) is at odds with the treachery implied in the adjective derived from his name. Evidence suggests that Machiavelli was an upright man, a good father, and a husband who lived in affectionate harmony with his wife, Marietta Corsini, with whom he had six children.

Throughout his life, Machiavelli was a zealous republican. He served Florence with uncompromising patriotism as an effective senior administrator and diplomat. But his single-minded service to the republic of Florence ended when the army of the Holy League of Pope Julius II returned the Medici family to power as benevolent despots of the city. In the resulting political purge, Machiavelli not only lost his position in the city government but, when a conspiracy against the Medicis was uncovered in early 1513, he also was accused of complicity simply because his name was on a list taken from the conspirators. Thrown into prison and subjected to the kind of torture that forced blameless men to confess their guilt, Machiavelli nevertheless maintained his innocence and was eventually released.

Reduced to poverty, and with restrictions placed on his movements around the city, Machiavelli sought refuge in the little property, outside Florence, that he had inherited from his father. There he produced not only *The Prince,* which he completed between the spring and autumn of 1513, but also a variety of political commentaries and histories and a number of well-received literary works. After the death of Pope Julius II in 1513, the son of Lorenzo de' Medici (called the Magnificent) became Pope Leo X—one of three popes the Medici family produced. It was Machiavelli's hope that by dedicating *The Prince* to Lorenzo de' Medici, son of the most famous of all the Medicis, he would obtain an office that would return him to public life. That hope was in vain. Machiavelli died at the age of fifty-eight, still exiled from Florence.

ABOUT *THE PRINCE*

Readers have differed sharply in their assessments of *The Prince*, as well as the character of its author, Niccolò Machiavelli, since the book's publication in 1532. In his own time, Machiavelli was known as the author of histories, poems, and plays (including a widely produced popular comedy). Highly respected as a statesman, he represented Florence on foreign missions and wrote reports admired for their style and substance. But the Catholic Church censured Machiavelli for his criticism of Christianity and for the tone and content of the political counsel he offered, especially in *The Prince*. By the seventeenth century, the name Machiavelli was synonymous with diabolical cunning, a meaning that it still carries today. Modern readers exhibit the same ambivalence about Machiavelli, alternately recognizing him as a precursor of the discipline of political science and recoiling from the ruthless principles he frequently articulates. Both views of Machiavelli, as innovative modernist and cynical politician, have their origins in *The Prince*.

Machiavelli wrote *The Prince* in 1513, just after he was forced to leave Florence as a political exile. Dedicated to Lorenzo de' Medici, the book is Machiavelli's advice to the current ruler of Florence on how to stay in power. It was also his effort, though unsuccessful, to gain an advisory post in the Medici government. *The Prince* was not published until five years after Machiavelli's death. Leaders as diverse as Oliver Cromwell, Frederick the Great, Louis XIV, Napoleon I, Otto von Bismarck, and John F. Kennedy have read, contemplated, and debated Machiavelli's ideas.

Machiavelli's book makes a clear break from the Western tradition of political philosophy that preceded him. Beginning with Plato and Aristotle, the thinkers of this tradition were concerned with issues of justice and human happiness, and with the constitution of the ideal state. Except for its final chapter, *The Prince* is a sometimes shockingly direct how-to manual for rulers who aim either to establish and retain control of a new state or to seize and control an existing one. Rather than basing his advice on ethical or philosophical principles, Machiavelli founds his political program on real-life examples. When explaining what a prince should or should not do in pursuit of his ambitions, Machiavelli cites the actions of well-known historical and contemporary leaders, both successful and unsuccessful. Throughout *The Prince,* Machiavelli explicitly aims to give an unsentimental analysis of actual human behavior and the uses of power. "I have thought it proper," Machiavelli writes of a prince's conduct toward his subjects, "to represent things as they are in a real truth, rather than as they are imagined." (50)

The accuracy of Machiavelli's view of human nature and the social world is debatable. Is Machiavelli simply being clear-sighted and objective, or is he providing spurious justifications for the worst impulses of those who seek power? In *The Prince,* the results of actions are what matter. Murder, the incitement of quarrels among citizens, the purchase of temporary loyalties, and betrayal—all are permissible and, indeed, recommended if they advance the prince's goal of attaining and securing power. In Machiavelli's view, the preservation of the state warrants such actions, since the state is necessary to ensure security, peace, and order for the people. He sets the ambitions of the prince and the need of the people for order side by side, seeing the two as complementary. Perhaps they are, or perhaps this equation is merely a self-serving way for those who crave power to defend injustices. To what extent the means that Machiavelli promotes in *The Prince* are justified by the ends, and whether the means actually bring about the ends, remain open questions.

Machiavelli's view of the Italy of his day—"leaderless, lawless, crushed, despoiled, torn, overrun" (82)—underwrites the advice he gives in *The Prince.* It also leads him to end his treatise with an "Exhortation to liberate Italy from the barbarians." Machiavelli calls for "a new prince . . . to introduce a new order" (82) that would bring unity and stability to the often warring city-states of the Italian peninsula. In this portion of *The Prince* and in some of his other writings, Machiavelli appears more idealistic and friendly toward a form of government that would give citizens a say. In his *Discourses,* Machiavelli portrays the ideal government as a republic that allows groups with differing opinions to speak openly.

Machiavelli thus sets the stage for an enduring discussion among his readers. Is he best understood as a seeker of unity and peace, concerned to make his advice practical and effective? Is he an opportunist offering aid and comfort to would-be tyrants? Do the moral and political goals he outlines in the final chapter of *The Prince* justify the actions he advocates in the preceding chapters? These questions seem destined to remain with us as long as Machiavelli's book continues to occupy a central place in modern political thought.

Note: All page references are from the Penguin edition of *The Prince* (2003).

QUESTIONS

1. Why does Machiavelli support his arguments by citing examples of real historical and contemporary rulers? Why does he emphasize his "long acquaintance with contemporary affairs and a continuous study of the ancient world"? (3)

2. Does *The Prince* present justice as nothing more than the interest of the stronger?

3. What constraints on a prince's freedom of action does Machiavelli recognize?

4. Does Machiavelli believe that ethical considerations have a role to play in the conduct of a prince?

5. According to Machiavelli, what roles do fate and fortune play in human life?

6. Does Machiavelli believe that political entities are created by human effort, or do they exist naturally?

7. In securing the state, to what extent should a prince be motivated by the happiness of the people?

8. Why does Machiavelli believe that a prince must be willing to use force to achieve his ends?

9. According to Machiavelli, do moral ends justify immoral means?

10. How does Machiavelli define virtue?

11. Why does Machiavelli end his work with a plea for the House of Medici to liberate Italy?

FOR FURTHER REFLECTION

1. Under what circumstances is someone charged with upholding the law justified in breaking it?
2. Must political power always be a corrupting influence on those who possess it?

CHARLOTTE BRONTË

Marked by grief, obscurity, and determination, the life of Charlotte Brontë (1816–1855) closely resembles that of her most famous heroine. Left motherless at an early age, Charlotte, her brother, and her four sisters were raised in the Yorkshire village of Haworth, where their father was curate. Charlotte's two older sisters died of illnesses contracted at the Cowan Bridge boarding school, which Charlotte used as the basis for Lowood in *Jane Eyre*. At nine, she became the eldest of the four surviving siblings.

Charlotte, Emily, and Anne, along with their brother, Branwell, read voraciously and created an elaborate fantasy world. The four wrote prolifically, which served as an apprenticeship for the later literary efforts of the three sisters. Charlotte attended school, worked for a time as a teacher, and had a brief career as a governess. In 1842, she and Emily went to Brussels to study languages. Charlotte's teacher there was the charismatic M. Heger, a married man with whom she fell in love. Her emotionally fraught, though celibate, relationship with him served as the basis for her first novel, *The Professor*. Written in 1846, it was not published until after her death.

In 1845, Charlotte, Emily, and Anne published *Poems by Currer, Ellis, and Acton Bell*. Though it sold virtually no copies, the sisters continued to write, and, in 1847, Charlotte published *Jane Eyre,* which was a resounding popular success. Both Branwell and Emily died in 1848, with Anne following the next year. Charlotte went on to publish *Shirley* (1849) and *Vilette* (1853). In 1854, she married Arthur Bell Nicholls, her father's curate, but died during pregnancy the next year.

ABOUT *JANE EYRE*

Even people who have never read *Jane Eyre* usually know its general outline. Like *Frankenstein* and *Dracula,* it is a Victorian novel that has passed into common consciousness and proved remarkably adaptable, generating several film and stage versions. That *Jane Eyre* shares this fate with the two greatest horror novels of the nineteenth century is instructive. Like them, it speaks to deep, timeless human urges and fears, using the conventions of Gothic literature to chart the mind's recesses.

The detailed exploration of a strong female character's consciousness has made *Jane Eyre* an influential feminist text. The novel works both as the absorbing story of an individual woman's quest and as a narrative of the universal dilemmas that confront women. Its mythic quality is enhanced by the fact that at the time of its writing its author was, like her heroine, unmarried and unremarked, and considered unattractive. In *Jane Eyre,* Charlotte Brontë created a fully imagined character defined by her strength of will. Though Jane is nothing more than an impoverished governess, she can retort to her haughty employer Rochester: "Do you think, because I am poor, obscure, plain, and little, I am soulless and heartless?—You think wrong!" (284) Jane's willfulness scandalized many contemporary critics, who called her (and the novel) "coarse" and "unfeminine." Such criticisms were powerless against the novel's popularity, and Jane's indomitable voice continues to enthrall readers more than 150 years after the novel's original publication.

In its first-person narration and autobiographical structure, which follows the title character from childhood to adulthood, *Jane Eyre* has much in common with another durable Victorian novel, *David Copperfield.* Like Dickens's novel, some of the scenes readers are most likely to remember are those in which the child narrator is nearly overwhelmed by cruelty. *Jane Eyre* famously opens with orphaned, ten-year-old Jane's forcible eviction from her window-seat refuge by her vicious and pampered cousin, John Reed. When Mrs. Reed promptly takes John's side and locks Jane in the red room, the pattern of Jane's oppression by authority figures is set. At Lowood School Jane is singled out for abuse by the tyrannical and self-righteous headmaster, Mr. Brocklehurst. Though her outward status defines powerlessness—since she is young, female, virtually without family, and poor—she defies the humiliations Brocklehurst imposes on her.

Jane presents the soft-spoken, forgiving Helen Burns as an example of moral perfection, but Jane's outraged resistance threatens to be more appealing.

Through the adult Jane, Brontë explores the romantic prospects of a young woman lacking the social advantages of family, money, and beauty, and therefore especially vulnerable to the allure of admiration and security. By creating two suitors who exemplify opposing threats to Jane's selfhood, Brontë is able to dramatize Jane's internal struggles against competing temptations. Because we have access to Jane's innermost thoughts and feelings, her efforts to resist both the ascetic St. John Rivers and the sybaritic Rochester provide the most powerful drama in the book. In Jane, Brontë gives us a character able to withstand St. John's missionary call to self-immolation in a marriage to serve humanity and Rochester's attempts to persuade her to indulge her sexual and romantic desires at the expense of violating her own moral code.

Central to the novel as Jane's conflicted relationship to Rochester is, her connection with his mad, despised first wife Bertha Mason Rochester is at least as intriguing, though the two women hardly meet and never converse. The revelation of Bertha's existence, which Rochester has concealed from Jane, saves her from the bigamous marriage that Rochester has planned. Though Brontë's characterization of the animalistic, insane Bertha, locked away on a top floor, plays into many nineteenth-century stereotypes of the "native" or "primitive" woman, it also suggests a close kinship between Bertha and Jane. Both women are attracted to Rochester; both live in his house; and both are mistreated by him. Critics and readers have sharply differed about how best to understand this connection. To what extent is Bertha a double for Jane, acting on her behalf? To what extent is she a figure for the fate—inarticulate, imprisoned, hopeless—that awaits Jane if she surrenders to the corrupt Rochester?

A similar ambiguity pervades the novel's ending. While Jane's "Reader, I married him" (498) carries a note of relief and triumph, the path to this ending is so convoluted and disturbing as to raise questions about how we are to understand it. If Jane and Rochester's marriage as equals requires not only Rochester's moral regeneration, blinding, and partial crippling, but also Jane's inheriting a small fortune, what is the novel saying about the real-life prospects of a woman like Jane enjoying such a union? Throughout the novel, Brontë asks how a woman in her society can have passion and integrity, love and independence. *Jane Eyre* does not so much suggest definitive answers as pose the questions with an urgency and a depth of imagination that challenge readers to think them through for themselves.

Note: All page references are from the Penguin edition of *Jane Eyre* (2003).

QUESTIONS

1. Why does Brontë juxtapose Jane's musings about women's social restraints with the mysterious laugh that Jane attributes to Grace Pool?
2. Rochester tells Jane, "if you are cast in a different mould to the majority, it is no merit of yours: Nature did it." (153–154) Are we intended to agree or disagree with this statement?
3. After Mason's visit to Thornfield, Jane asks herself, "What crime was this, that lived incarnate in this sequestered mansion, and could neither be expelled nor subdued by the owner?" (237) What crime does Bertha represent? Why does Rochester keep her at Thornfield?
4. Does Rochester ever actually intend to marry Blanche? If so, when does he change his mind? If not, why does he go to such lengths to make Jane believe he does?
5. Rochester's disastrous marriage to Bertha is based on passion, while St. John refuses to marry Rosamund because of his passion for her. What is Brontë saying about the role passion should play in marriage?
6. What does St. John feel for Jane? Why does Jane end her story with his prayer?
7. Jane asserts her equality to the Reed children, Rochester, and St. John. What does Jane mean by equality, and why is it so important to her?
8. When Jane first appears at Moor House, Hannah assumes she is a prostitute, but St. John and his sisters do not. What distinguishes the characters who misjudge Jane from those who recognize her true nature?
9. When Jane hears Rochester's voice calling while he is miles away, she says the phenomenon "is the work of nature." (467) What does she mean by this? What are we intended to conclude about the meaning of this experience?

10. Brontë populates the novel with many female characters roughly the same age as Jane—Georgiana and Eliza Reed, Helen Burns, Blanche Ingram, Mary and Diana Rivers, and Rosamund Oliver. How do comparisons with these characters shape the reader's understanding of Jane's character?

11. What is the balance of power between Jane and Rochester when they marry? Does this balance change from the beginning of the marriage to the time ten years later that Jane describes at the end of the novel?

FOR FURTHER REFLECTION

1. In a romantic relationship, does one partner inevitably dominate the other?

2. Should an individual who holds a position of authority be granted the respect of others, regardless of his or her character?

CONNECTING THEMES

This anthology can be read sequentially or thematically; there are any number of general topics or themes, and it is likely that perceptive readers will see some of these interconnections between the fifteen different readings as well as the two longer works for which there are discussion guides. In some instances, the authors represented in *Great Conversations 3* were familiar with the works of the others—both as predecessors and contemporaries—and their writings seem to respond to one another directly, sometimes echoing another writer's ideas, sometimes reacting to a similar subject in a slightly different way or disagreeing entirely.

Here are some different possibilities for considering these readings in clusters organized by topic and theme. In certain instances, teachers or group leaders may want to consider a pair of readings on a particular theme; the lists that follow, neither exhaustive nor definitive, can be plundered selectively to good effect. What is important is that readers of *Great Conversations 3* enter into the dialogue with these authors, as contemporary participants.

I. Art and Artists

Shelley

Balzac

Pirandello

Borges

II. Domestic Life

Kipling

Crane

Anderson

Beauvoir

Paley

Lahiri

Brontë

III. Exercising Power

Shelley

Tolstoy

Kipling

Beauvoir

Paley

Foucault

Machiavelli

Brontë

IV. History Lessons

Tolstoy

Kipling

Beauvoir

Foucault

Szymborska

Machiavelli

V. Love and Marriage

Beauvoir

Anderson

Paley

Lahiri

Brontë

VI. Social Critique

Chaucer

Tolstoy

Kipling

Beauvoir

Szymborska

Foucault

VII. Subjectivity

Hume

Crane

Anderson

Borges

Pirandello

Brontë

VIII. Violence

Chaucer

Kipling

Anderson

Borges

Szymborska

Foucault

Brontë

ACKNOWLEDGMENTS

All possible care has been taken to trace ownership and secure permission for each selection in this anthology. The Great Books Foundation wishes to thank the following authors, publishers, and representatives for permission to reprint copyrighted material:

The Pardoners Tale, from THE CANTERBURY TALES, by Geoffrey Chaucer, as translated into modern verse by David Wright. Copyright © 1985 by the Estate of David Wright. Reprinted by permission of PFD (www.pfd.co.uk) on behalf of the Estate of David Wright.

A Defence of Poetry, from SHELLEY'S POETRY AND PROSE, 2nd edition, by Percy Bysshe Shelley, edited by Donald H. Reiman and Neil Fraistat. Copyright © 2002 by Donald H. Reiman, Neil Fraistat, and Rebecca Thompson. Copyright © 1977 by Donald H. Reiman and Sharon B. Powers. Reprinted by permission of W. W. Norton & Company, Inc.

The Unknown Masterpiece, from HONORÉ DE BALZAC: SELECTED STORIES/CONTES CHOISIS: A DUAL LANGUAGE BOOK, by Honoré de Balzac, edited and translated by Stanley Appelbaum. Copyright © 2000 by Dover Publications, Inc. Courtesy of Dover Publications, Inc.

Second Epilogue, from WAR AND PEACE, by Leo Tolstoy, translated by Aylmer Maude and edited by George Gibian. Copyright © 1966, 1996 by W. W. Norton & Company. Reprinted by permission of W. W. Norton & Company, Inc.

Six Characters in Search of an Author, from PIRANDELLO: PLAYS, by Luigi Pirandello, translated by Eric Bentley. Copyright © 1970 by Eric Bentley. Reprinted by permission of Northwestern University Press.

Death in the Woods, from THE EGG AND OTHER STORIES, by Sherwood Anderson, edited with an introduction by Charles E. Modlin. Copyright © 1926 by Sherwood Anderson; © renewed 1953 by Eleanor Copenhaver Anderson. Reprinted by permission of Harold Ober Associates.

The Garden of Forking Paths, from COLLECTED FICTIONS, by Jorge Luis Borges, translated by Andrew Hurley. Copyright © 1998 by Maria Kodama. Translation copyright © 1998 by Penguin Putnam Inc. Reprinted by permission of Viking Penguin, a division of Penguin Group (USA) Inc.

Introduction, from THE SECOND SEX, by Simone de Beauvior, translated by H. M. Parshley. Copyright © 1952; © renewed 1980 by Alfred A. Knopf. Reprinted by permission of Alfred A. Knopf, a division of Random House, Inc.

An Interest in Life, from THE LITTLE DISTURBANCES OF MAN, by Grace Paley. Copyright © 1956, 1957, 1958, 1959 by Grace Paley. Reprinted by permission of Penguin Books, a division of Penguin Group (USA) Inc.

The End and the Beginning, *Hatred*, and *Reality Demands*, from POEMS NEW AND COLLECTED: 1957–1997, by Wislawa Szymborska. Copyright © 1998 by Harcourt, Inc. Reprinted by permission of Harcourt, Inc.

The Body of the Condemned, from DISCIPLINE AND PUNISH, by Michel Foucault, translated from the French by Alan Sheridan. Translation copyright © 1977 by Alan Sheridan (New York: Pantheon). Originally published in French as *Surveiller et Punir*, copyright © 1975 by Editions Gallimard. Reprinted by permission of Georges Borchardt, Inc., for Editions Gallimard.

Interpreter of Maladies, from INTERPRETER OF MALADIES, by Jhumpa Lahiri. Copyright © 1999 by Jhumpa Lahiri. Reprinted by permission of Houghton Mifflin Company. All rights reserved.